N INDOLOGY

MOTILAL BANARSIDASS PUBLISHERS
DELHI

2003

NARSIDASS

SHERS

THE LITERATURE OF THE PERSONALISTS OF EARLY BUDDHISM

BUDDHIST TRADITION SERIES

VOLUME 39

Edited by
ALEX WAYMAN

The Literature of the Personalists of Early Buddhism

BHIKSHU THÍCH THIÊN CHÂU

English translation by

SARA BOIN-WEBB

MOTILAL BANARSIDASS PUBLISHERS
PRIVATE LIMITED • DELHI

First Edition: Vietnam, 1996
First Indian Edition: Delhi, 1999

This work originally appeared under the title of *Les Sectes personnalistes (Pudgalavādin) du bouddhisme ancien* - Thèse pour le Doctorat d'État ès-Lettres et Sciences humaines, Université de la Sorbonne Nouvelle (Paris III), 1977.

ISBN: 81-208-1622-6

Also available at:

MOTILAL BANARSIDASS

41 U.A. Bungalow Road, Jawahar Nagar, Delhi 110 007
8 Mahalaxmi Chamber, Warden Road, Mumbai 400 026
120 Royapettah High Road, Mylapore, Chennai 600 004
Sanas Plaza, 1302, Baji Rao Road, Pune 411 002
16 St. Mark's Road, Bangalore 560 001
8 Camac Street, Calcutta 700 017
Ashok Rajpath, Patna 800 004
Chowk, Varanasi 221 001

PRINTED IN INDIA
BY JAINENDRA PRAKASH JAIN AT SHRI JAINENDRA PRESS,
A-45 NARAINA, PHASE I, NEW DELHI 110 028
AND PUBLISHED BY NARENDRA PRAKASH JAIN FOR
MOTILAL BANARSIDASS PUBLISHERS PRIVATE LIMITED,
BUNGALOW ROAD, DELHI 110 007

EDITOR'S FOREWORD

This is indeed a remarkable book. It has the best treatment of the schools called Vātsiputrīya and four other minor ones (p.5) that espoused the theory that a *pudgala* (a sort of person) supported the five personal aggregates (*skandha*) and made possible the Intermediate State (*antarābhava*) between death and rebirth. The author, Bhikshu Thích Thiên Châu, points out that this school of the Personalists (Pudgalavādin) once had its own version of three classes of scriptures (*āgama*) but they are now lost. The remaining schools of Buddhism condemned these personalists. And the author mentions that there are only four surviving texts of this sect, which are in the Chinese language (listed, p. 19). The author, obviously skilled in that period in the development of the Chinese language, devotes the major part of this book, originally written in French, to presenting the contents of those four treatises.

Sara Boin-Webb deserves credit for translating his book from French into English (including a number of long, technical footnotes). The technical terms—however translated—do not alter the superb coverage of this work on the 'Personalists'.

Alex Wayman
New York, Nov. 1998

FOREWORD

Comme le prouvent des témoignages nombreux, divers et sérieux, les sectes ou écoles 'personnalistes' (*pudgalavādin*) du bouddhisme indien ancien comptèrent parmi les plus importantes de celui-ci et formèrent un groupe bien défini qui subsista une dizaine de siècles. Les docteurs theravādin et sarvāstivādin consacrèrent de nombreux et parfois fort longs passages de leurs oeuvres à exposer et critiquer les thèses personnalistes; un certain nombre d'inscriptions attestent l'existence de leurs différentes écoles en divers points du territoire indien au début de notre ère; enfin les grands pèlerins chinois Hiuan-tsang et I-tsing signalent avec précision leur implantation et leur importance numérique considérable, au VIIe siècle, en plusieurs régions de l'Inde et aussi de l'Asie du Sud-Est. Si l'on en croit certaines traditions, les Vātsiputrīyas se seraient détachés les premiers du groupe des Sthaviravādin peu avant le règne d'Aśoka en soutenant l'existence du *pudgala*, sorte de substitut du principe personnel, *ātman* ou *jīva*, que niait l'enseignement attribué au Bouddha. Plus tard seraient apparues d'autres écoles personnalistes, dont celles des Sāmmitīya, qui devint bientôt la principale d'entre elles, puis celles des Dharmottarīya, des Bhadrayānīya et des Ṣaṇṇāgārika ou Ṣaṇḍagiriya.

Malheureusement, toute leur littérature, qui a dû être volumineuse comme celle des autres sectes antiques, a disparu depuis bien longtemps, à la seule exception de deux traités assez courts, conservés seulement dans leur traduction chinoise. Pour comble de malchance, ces deux témoignages, que leur rareté rend d'autant plus précieux pour notre con- naissance de ces écoles personnalistes, sont très difficiles à utiliser à cause de la grande médiocrité de ces traductions, qui manquent beaucoup de clarté et de précision. Contrairement à ce qui est généralement le cas avec les très nombreuses versions chinoises classiques d'anciens ouvrages bouddhiques dont le texte indien a disparu, il est souvent impossible de retrouver dans ces deux traités les termes techniques du vocabulaire bouddhique sanskrit avec un degré satisfaisant de probabilité et, à plus forte raison, de donner de ces deux ouvrages une traduction complète en une langue occidentale.

Cela est d'autant plus décevant que la discussion des thèses proprement personnalistes semble bien avoir été à l'origine de la métaphysique bouddhiste, qui allait bientôt atteindre un tel développement et donner naissance, plus tard, aux subtiles conceptions des grands maîtres du Mahāyāna. Cela est aussi décevant parce que les écoles pudgalavādin prirent une part fort active aux controverses qui opposèrent les docteurs du bouddhisme indien sur des problèmes doctrinaux très divers, comme le prouvent les commentaires critiques transmis jusqu'à nous par leurs adversaires theravādin et sarvāstivādin, qui nous renseignent ainsi, mais trop succinctement, sur les positions adoptées par les écoles personnalistes dans ces discussions.

On doit donc remercier le Vénérable Thich Thien Chau d'avoir pu, grâce à sa grande érudition, tirer le maximum d'informations de ces deux petits traités et d'apporter ainsi une contribution de haute valeur à notre connaissance des doctrines du bouddhisme ancien dans l'ouvrage ici présenté.

La carrière et les titres de l'auteur de ce dernier l'avaient bien préparé à accomplir une telle tâche. Après avoir passé cinq ans à étudier à l'Université bouddhique de Nālandā, au Bihar, alors récemment créée, et y avoir obtenu les diplômes de B.A. et de M.A., attestent sa sérieuse connaissance du sanskrit et du pāli, le Vénérable séjourna pendant deux années à la School of Oriental and African Studies de l'Université de Londres pour s'initier aux méthodes de la recherche, puis il vint à Paris pour suivre l'étude du bouddhisme. Il y prépara et soutint d'abord une thèse de doctorat d'Université portant sur l'un des deux traités pudgalavādin, puis une thèse de doctorat d'Etat dont le texte est reproduit ci-après.

André Bareau

PREFACE

Personalism (*pudgalavāda*) was a remarkable and durable aspect of an important part of early Buddhism. For more than ten centuries it was taught and defended by several schools and had numerous followers but was strongly criticised by other Buddhist schools.

The literature of the Buddhist Personalist schools is practically entirely lost, so much so that we know their doctrine mainly through the attacks of their adversaries.

Of importance to us is that four authentic works pertaining to the Vātsīputrīyas and Sāṃmitīyas have been preserved. The four works are:

1) The *San fa tu lun* 三法度論 (Tridharmakaśāstra), Taishō XXV, No.1506.
2) The *Ssŭ a-han-mu ch'ao chieh* 四阿鋡暮抄解 Taishō XXV, No.1505.
3) The *San-mi-ti pu lun* 三彌底部論 (Sāṃmitīyanikāyaśāstra) Taishō XXXII, No.1649.
4) The *Lü êrh-shih-êrh ming-liao lun* 律二十二明了論 (Vinayadvāviṃśatividyāśāstra), Taishō XXIV, No.1461.

This thesis, entitled *The Literature of the Personalists (Pudgalavādins) of Early Buddhism*, attempts to present an historical overview of the Personalist schools and studies on the formation and content of the doctrine (*dharma*) and monastic discipline (*vinaya*) of the Pudgalavādins, in accordance with the documentation available.

With respect to the doctrinal problem, the literary evidence which exists has revealed to us the main thesis of the Pudgalavādins, the *pudgala*, and fifteen other secondary theses. The *pudgala*, the ineffable, being neither identical to nor different from the aggregates (*skandha*), entails three designations:

a) the *pudgala*-designated-by-the-support (*āśrayaprajñaptapudgala*),
b) the *pudgala*-designated-by-transmigration (*saṃkramaprajñaptapudgala*),
c) the *pudgala*-designated-by-cessation (*nirodhaprajñaptapudgala*).

The creation of the theory of the *pudgala* represents a reaction to the depersonalisation of the dogmatic Abhi- dharma masters. The Personalists (*pudgalavādin*), however, were determined to preserve the essence of the doctrine of insubstantiality (*anātmavāda*). They insisted on the fact that adherence to the *pudgala* did not prevent the attainment of the knowledges (*jñāna*) and fruits (*phala*). The position of the *pudgala* was misinterpreted by its adversaries. Nonetheless, the theory of the *pudgala* offered much of interest in the doctrinal domain for Buddhist theoreticians.

It is most agreeable for us to be able to express here our profound gratitude to Professor André Bareau, of the Collège de France, who was kind enough to direct our research in this field. We would also like to thank Michel Soymié, Director of Studies at the École Pratique des Hautes Etudes, who took the trouble to give us valuable advice. We also offer our profound gratitude to Professor Paul Demiéville, Membre de l'Institut, Honorary Professor at the Collège de France, who has done us the honour of rereading the manuscript with patience and compassion, and correcting its essentials.

Our deepest thanks also go to the Centre Nationale de la Recherche Scientifique which supported us in our research by giving us working contracts for several years; it is due to its financial assistance that this research could be brought to a successful conclusion.

Bhikshu Thích Thiện Châu
Paris 1977

PREFACE TO THE ENGLISH EDITION

We would like to express our profound gratitude to Sara Boin-Webb for undertaking this English translation, to Ven. Dr Dhammaratna for his careful perusal of the proofs, and to Most Ven. Dr. Thich Minh Chau, President of the Institute for Buddhist Studies of Vienam in Ho Chi Minh City, for publishing this work.

Bhikshu Thích Thiện Châu
Paris 1996

ABBREVIATIONS

L'Absolu	*L'Absolu en philosophie bouddhique*, by A. Bareau, Paris 1951
L'Aide-mémoire	*L'Aide-mémoire de la Vraie Loi (Saddharmasmṛtyupasthāna-sūtra)*, by Lin Li-kouang, Paris 1949
AN	Aṅguttara Nikāya (PTS)
BCE	Before the Common Era
BEFEO	*Bulletin de l'Ecole française d'Extrême- Orient*
Bud. Sects	*Buddhist Sects in India*, by N. Dutt, Calcutta 1970, repr. Delhi 1978
Canon bouddh.	*Le Canon bouddhique en Chine*, by P.C. Bagchi, Paris 1927-38
CE	Common Era
Ch'u	*Chu san-tsang chi chi* (T LV, 2145)
Compendium	*Le Compendium de la super-doctrine (philosophie) (Abhidharmasamuccaya) d'Asaṅga*, tr. W. Rahula, Paris 1971
DĀ	Dīrghāgama (T I, 1)
Dhp	Dhammapada (PTS)
DN	Dīgha Nikāya (PTS)
EA	*Etudes Asiatiques*
EĀ	Ekottarāgama (T II, 125)
EFEO	Ecole Française d'Extrême-Orient
EP	Era of the Parinirvāṇa and (= EN: Era of the Nirvāṇa)
EI	*Epigraphia Indica*
History	*History of Buddhism in India*, by É. Lamotte, English translation by Sara Boin-Webb, (PIOL 36), Louvain-la-Neuve 1988
Hōbōgirin	*Dictionnaire encyclopédique du Boud- dhisme d'après les sources chinoises et japonaises*, Tokyo and Paris 1927 —
Hōbōgirin, Rép.	*Répertoire di Canon bouddhique sino-japonais* (Édition du Taishō), Fascicule annexe du *Hōbōgirin*, rev. ed., Paris and Tokyo 1978.
Iptllsc	*I pu tsung lun lun shu-chi*, by K'uei-chi, *Annales du Musée Guimet* LX, Paris 1955
JAOS	*Journal of the American Oriental Society*
Jā	Jātaka (PTS)
Kao	*Kao-sêng ch'uan* (T L, 2059).
Kośa	*L'Abhidharmakośa de Vasubandhu*, translated by L. de La Vallée Poussin, Paris, 1923-31, repr. Brussels 1971 — English version by Leo M. Pruden, *Abhidharmakośabhāṣyam*, Berkeley 1988
Lü ming-liao lun	*Lü êrh-shih-êrh ming-liao lun* (Vinayadvā- viṃśatividyāśāstra, T XXIV, 1461)
MĀ	Madhyamāgama (T I, 26)
MN	Majjhima Nikāya (PTS)
MN-A	Majjhima Nikāya aṭṭhakathā (PTS)

'L'origine'	'L'origine des sectes bouddhiques d'après Paramārtha' by P. Demiéville, Brussels 1931-2
Nanjio	Bunyū Nanjio, *Catalogue of the Chinese Translation of the Buddhist Tripiṭaka*, Oxford 1883, repr. Delhi 1989.
PTS	Pali Text Society, London and Oxford
Pug	Puggalapaññatti (PTS)
Pug-A	Puggalapaññatti aṭṭhakathā (PTS)
Record	I-ching, *A Record of the Buddhist Religions as Practised in India and the Malay Archipelago* tr. J. Takakusu, Oxford 1896.
Religions	*Les Religions de l'Inde (Bouddhisme)*, by A. Bareau, Paris 1951
SĀ	Saṃyuktāgama (T II, 99)
Samayabhed.	Samayabhedoparacanacakra of Vasumitra (*I pu tsung lun lun* - T XLIX, 2031)
Sectes	*Les sectes bouddhiques du Petit Véhicule*, by A. Bareau, Saigon 1955
SN	Saṃyutta Nikāya (PTS)
Sn	Suttanipāta (PTS)
Sns	Sāṃmitīyanikāyaśāstra (*San-mi-ti pu lun* — T XXXII, 1649)
Ssŭ	*Ssŭ a-han-mu ch'ao-chieh* (T XXV, 1505)
T	*Taishō shinshū daizōkyō* (Sino-Japanese Buddhist Canon), Tokyo 1924-35
Tds	Tridharmakaśāstra (*San fa tu lun* — T XXV, 1506)
Traité	*Le Traité de la grande vertu de sagesse de Nāgārjuna (Mahāprajñāpāramitāśāstra [upadeśa])*, by E. Lamotte, 5 vols, Louvain and Louvain-la-Neuve 1944-80 [English version in the press]
Ud-a	Udāna aṭṭhakathā (PTS)
Vin.	(Pāli) Vinaya (PTS)
Vism	Visuddhimagga (PTS)

TABLE OF CONTENTS

FOREWORD by Alex Wayman V

FOREWORD by André Bareau VII

PREFACE by the Author IX

ABBREVIATIONS XI

CHAPTER ONE: HISTORICAL SURVEY
- A. Early Buddhism 1
  - I. The Sthavira School 3
  - II. The Mahāsāṃghika School 4
- B. The Personalist Schools (*Pudgalavādins*) 4
  - I. The Vātsīputrīyas 5
  - II. The Vātsīputrīya Sub-schools 10
    - 1 — The Sāṃmitīyas 11
    - 2 -- The Dharmottarīyas, Bhadrayānīyas and Ṣaṇṇāgārikas 15

CHAPTER TWO: THE LITERATURE AND DOCTRINE OF THE PUDGALAVĀDINS
- A. Generalities: 19
  - I. The Pudgalavādin Tripiṭaka 18
    - 1 — The Pudgalavādin Sūtrapiṭaka 20
    - 2 — The Pudgalavādin Abhidharmapiṭaka 25
    - 3 — The Pudgalavādin Vinayapiṭaka 27
  - II. Languages used by the Pudgalavādins 31
- B. The Pudgalavādin Treatises 32
  - I. The *San fa tu lun* 33
  - II. The *Ssŭ a-han-mu ch'ao chieh* 85
  - III. The *San-mi-ti pu lun* 99
  - IV. The *Lü êrh-shih-êrh ming-liao lun* 117

CHAPTER THREE: THE THESES OF THE PUDGALAVĀDINS
- A. The Original Teaching of the Buddha 123
  - I. Essential Doctrines 123
  - II. Application of these Doctrines 125
  - III. Characteristics and efficacity of these Doctrines 127
- B. The Theses of the Pudgalavādins: 136
  - I. The Main Thesis: The *Pudgala* 130
    - 1 — Definitions of *Pudgala* 130
    - 2 — *Pudgala* according to the extant Pudgalavādin works 135
      - a) *Pudgala*-designated-by-the-supports (*āśrayaprajñaptapudgala*) 143

b) *Pudgala*-designated-by transmigration (*saṅkramaprajñaptapudgala* ?) 162
c) *Pudgala*-designated-by-cessation (*nirodhaprajñaptapudgala*) 175
II. Secondary Theses of the Pudgalavādins 188
1 — The Existence of an imperishable thing (*avipraṇāśa* ?) 188
2 — The twelve Knowledges in the Path of Vision (*darśanamārga*) 189
3 — The Adjoining Concentration consists of four Stages: Patience (*kṣānti*), the Name (*nāma*), the Notion (*saṃjñā*) and the Supreme Worldly Dharma (*laukikāgradharma*) 193
4 — Clear Comprehension (*abhisamaya*) is progressive (*anupūrva*) 195
5 — The five Superknowledges (*abhijñā*) can be acquired by Worldlings (*pṛthagjana*) or Heretics (*tīrthika*) 196
6 — Morality (*śīla*) designates (actions) of Body (*kāyakarman*) and Speech (*vacīkarman*) 197
7 — Merit (*puṇya*) accumulates continually even during Sleep 198
8 — It is impossible to say whether the Characteristic of Dharmas (*dharmalakṣaṇa*) is permanent or impermanent 199
9 — There is an Intermediate Absorption (*dhyānātara*) between the first and second Absorption 200
10 — Only one Absolute Truth exists: Nirvāṇa 201
11 — There are five, six or seven Destinies (*gati*) 203
12 — Knowledge (*jñāna*) is also called the Path (*mārga*) 204
13 — The Arhat is susceptible to Regression 205
14 — There is an Intermediate Existence (*antarābhava*) in the World of Desire (*kāmadhātu*) and the World of Form (*rūpadhātu*) 207
15 — There are seventeen Categories of Heavenly Beings in the World of Form (*rūpadhātu*) 209
C. The Pudgalavādin Lists of Śrāvakas: 212
I. The Vātsīputrīya List in the Tds 212
II. The Sāṃmitīya List in the Sns 220

CONCLUSION 224

BIBLIOGRAPHY 226

INDEX 233

CHAPTER ONE

HISTORICAL SURVEY

A – *EARLY BUDDHISM*

Shortly after the Parinirvāṇa[1] of the Buddha (in about 420 BCE[2]), his teaching was interpreted in different ways by his disciples. The divisions due to interpretations of the Doctrine and Discipline led to successive schisms in the community of monks.

After the First Council, that of Vaiśālī (in about 100 years of the Era of the Parinirvāṇa of the Buddha, abbreviated to EP)[3], the teaching of the Buddha was interpreted in various ways. Consequently Buddhism, after the appearance of the schisms, was divided into several schools or sub-schools. Furthermore, it was then introduced and implanted outside India, such as in Sri Lanka, Central Asia, China, Tibet, etc. In the countries neighbouring on India, Buddhism had necessarily to adapt to foreign languages, mentalities and beliefs. At present it is difficult to rediscover the exact form of original Buddhism. The teachings of the Theravādin school, despite its antiquity, cannot be considered to be the original teaching of the Buddha[4]. That is why it is necessary, before tackling the school of the Personalists (*Pudgalavādins*), to distinguish, by using existing documents as a basis, the different forms of Buddhism under their doctrinal aspects:

1) Original Buddhism, the teachings of which have been preserved to a certain degree, in Pāli in the Nikāyas, in Sanskrit and Chinese in the Āgamas, as well as in

---

1 Of interest regarding the dating of the Parinirvāṇa is a symposium on 'The Date of the Historical Buddha and the Importance of its Determination for Indian Historiography and World History' which was held in Göttingen in April 1988, the results of which have been published in two volumes, *The Dating of the Historical Buddha*, Abhandlungen der Akademie der Wissenschaften, Göttingen 1991–2.

2 Abbreviation of Before the Common Era, more acceptable in non-Christian works than BC (hence for AD, read CE = Common Era).

3 On the date of the Council of Vaiśālī, see A. Bareau, *Les premiers conciles bouddhiques*, p.31, n.1.

4 The Theravādin school was introduced into Sri Lanka under the auspices of Aśoka in 242 BCE, i.e., after the first schisms in the community of monks. Furthermore, the literature of this school in which the Pāli language was much influenced by Sanskrit literature (É. Lamotte, *Histoire du Bouddhisme indien dès origines à l'ère Śaka* – the version referred to here being the English translation by Sara Boin-Webb entitled *History of Indian Buddhism* (abbreviated to *History*), pp.567–8), is no older than that of other schools, particularly that of the Sarvāstivādins (see, e.g. Edward Conze, 'Recent Progress in Buddhist Studies', repr. in *Thirty Years of Buddhist Studies*, Oxford 1967, p.3), and that of the Pudgalavādins (cf. 'Le Tridharmakaśāstra (Etude philologique et doctrinale)', Conclusion, my unpublished thesis). [Tr.] 'According to tradition, the editing of the Canon took place in Sri Lanka, shortly before the Common Era; the commentaries were compiled from the fifth century onwards by Buddhaghosa (of Magadha) and his followers; in contrast, the manuscripts are no earlier than the twelfth century (L. Renou, *Les Littératures de l'Inde*, p.62). Hence it is impossible to say that they preserve original Buddhism in its entirety without the intervention of opinions, interpretations, events, etc., subsequent to the Parinirvāna of the Buddha'.

the Vinaya collections[5].
2) Early Buddhism, the doctrine of which is recorded in the literature of various schools, with interpretations in the Nikāyas, Āgamas, Vinaya collections and, especially, in the Abhidhamma (Sanskrit, Abhidharma) syntheses and the Śāstras[6].
3) Mahāyāna Buddhism which consists of multiple texts which form a developed literature quite distinct from the two preceding forms of Buddhism[7].

It is in the second form, that is, in early Buddhism, that we situate the doctrine of the Personalist schools (*Pudgalavādins*). This early Buddhism included schools or sub-schools which developed in the second or third century EP and lasted for approximately fifteen centuries in India[8]. Its history is muddled and obscure, since the various sources are full of confusions and contradictions.

Nonetheless, several Orientalists have made efforts to reconstruct the historical facets of the development of the Buddhists schools during this period[9]. By basing ourselves on this research, we present here a short introduction on the development of these schools, before tackling in detail the history of the Personalist schools which is the main subject of this study.

According to Bareau, the Council of Vaiśālī and the dispute over the ten disciplinary usages[10] did not lead to a major scission, at least in the doctrinal domain

---

5 Among the three collections or 'baskets' of canonical texts (Tripiṭaka), only the two Vinaya and Sūtra (Āgama, Nikāya) collections in general preserve the original teaching of the Buddha.

6 The main characteristic of the literature of early Buddhism is the interpretation of or commentary on the Sūtrapiṭaka. In consequence, the Abhidhamma or Abhidharma books are exegetical works, based on the Nikāyas and Āgamas, of Buddhism as attested in the first phase.

On the literature of early Buddhism, see A. Bareau, *Les Religions de l'Inde (Bouddhisme)* (abridged to *Religions*), pp.93–106.

7 On the literature of Mahāyāna Buddhism, see Bareau, *Religions*, pp.150–68.

8 Cf. Lamotte, *History*, p.520.

9 Cf. P. Demiéville, 'L'origine des sectes bouddhiques d'après Paramārtha' (abbrev. 'L'origine'); Lamotte, *History*; A. Bareau, *Les sectes bouddhiques du Petit Véhicule* (abbrev. *Sectes*) and N. Dutt, *Buddhist Sects in India* (abbrev. *Bud. Sects*).

10 The ten wrong usages appear frequently in the accusations levelled by the Sthaviras at the monks of Vaiśālī, in the Pāli texts; I quote them according to the interpretation to be found in *Inde classique* II, § 2217:

1) Storing salt in a horn (*siṅgiloṇa kappa*),

2) Accepting food when midday has passed by two fingers' breadth on the sun-dial (or by taking it with two fingers) (*dvaṅgula kappa*),

3) Taking food on a journey to another village (*gāmantara kappa*),

4) Holding separate meetings (in different residences of the same monastery) (*āvāsa kappa*),

5) Taking decisions in an assembly without a quorum being reached (*anumati kappa*),

6) Behaving in all ways like one's preceptor (or blindly following usage, or persisting inconsiderately in occupations from before entry into the community (*ācinna kappa*),

7) Consuming unchurned milk (*amathita*),

8) Consuming new palm-wine (*jalogiṃ pātum*),

9) Using an unfringed mat (*adasakaṃ nisīdanaṃ*),

10) Accepting gold and silver (*jātarūparajataṃ*).

Cf. *History*, p.126 (note: read 'mats with*out* fringes'); N. Dutt, *Bud. Sects*, pp.16–22; and especially the detailed exposition with a comparison of different lists by Bareau in *Les premiers conciles bouddhiques*, p.67 sq.

of early Buddhism. However, it was the divergence of opinion over the five propositions of Mahādeva[11] in 137, 116 or 160 EP, after the Council of Vaiśālī, which provoked a serious doctrinal scission in the community of monks (*bhikṣusaṃgha*). The consequence of this scission was the separation of the Elders (Sthaviras, in Pāli: Theras) who contested the five propositions, and the majority (Mahāsāṃghikas) who approved them.

Since that schism, the division in the community of monks was irreparable, and eventually these two fundamental schools successively incurred series of schisms which resulted in the appearance of twenty different schools including the two parental ones: the Sthaviras and Mahāsāṃghikas[12].

I - *The Sthavira School.*

The first schism in the school of the Sthaviras was provoked by the Vātsīputrīyas, at about the end of the second century EP. Later, in the reign of the emperor Aśoka, another major schism was started by the Sarvāstivādins. After becoming detached from the Sthavira trunk, these two branches later gave rise to other sub-schools.

The Vātsīputrīyas caused the appearance of the following four sub-schools: the Dharmottarīyas, Bhadrayānīyas, Sāṃmitīyas and Ṣaṇṇāgārikas or Ṣaṇḍagiriyas. Among the other Sthaviras arose the following sub-schools: the Sarvāstivādins, Sautrāntikas and Kāśyapas. The orthodox Sthaviras were henceforth known as Vibhajyavādins in order to distinguish them from their adversaries. From them developed the Thera-

---

11 On Mahādeva, the author of the five theses, the *I pu tsung lun lun shu-chi* 異部宗輪論述記 (abbrev. Iptllsc) 15*b*1–4 says: Two hundred years after (the Buddha's Parinirvāṇa), there was an heretical monk who renounced the false way and returned to the right way; he also was called Mahādeva, left the world and received full ordination in the Mahāsāṃghika school. He was learned (*bahuśruta*) and vigorous (*vīryavat*), and resided in the Caityaśaila. With the community of monks of that school, he again explained the five theses. This provoked argumentative discussions and a division into three schools, Caityaśaila, Aparaśaila and Uttaraśaila. Cf. also *Shih pa pu lun* 十八部論 ,T XLIX, 2032, 18*a*17–20; *Pu chih i lun* 部執異論 , T XLIX, 2033, 20*b*2–4.

The five theses are:

1 – An Arhat may be subjected to demoniacal temptations (may have a nocturnal emission under the influence of one of Māra's goddesses);

2 – he is still subject to ignorance;

3 – to doubt;

4 – he may learn with the help of others;

5 – he may attain the Noble Path by means of words.

Cf. *Inde classique* II, § 2218. Cf. also Bareau, *Religions*, p.84; id., *Sectes*, pp.64–5; L. de La Vallée Poussin, 'The Five Points of Mahādeva and the Kathāvatthu', JRAS, 1910, pp.413, 423; Lamotte, *History*, pp.274–85, with full details of the five theses, their author and a comparison; Demiéville, 'L'origine', under the title 'Les thèses de Mahādeva et la scission doctrinale des écoles Sthavirīya et Mahāsaṅghika sous la règle d'Aśoka', pp.30–40.

These theses, the main point of which is that the Arhat may regress, were admitted by all sub-schools of the Mahāsāṃghika group and rejected by the whole Sthaviravādin group. Cf. Bareau, *Sectes*, p.261.

12 Only the main schools are listed here. In his *Sectes* (pp.15–35), Bareau deals with 36 schools or sects in all. There are several different lists of schools or sub-schools in related studies, a bibliography of which can be found in Lamotte, *History*, p.518, footnote. Cf. also 'The Buddhist Sects' in *ibid.*, pp.518–48.

vādins of Ceylon who considered themselves to be the oldest and most orthodox, the Mahīśāsakas and the Dharmaguptakas. Another small school, the Haimavatas, is considered as descending from the Sthaviras. Hence, in all, fourteen schools belong to the Sthavira tradition.

II - *The Mahāsāṃghika School.*

Like the Sthaviras, the Mahāsāṃghikas split into several sub-schools. The Ekavyāvahārikas (= Lokottaravādins) and the Gokulikas appeared very early on. From the latter came first the Bahuśrutīyas and the Prajñaptivādins, and then the Caitikas.

Although the dates of the appearance of the schools have not yet been established, a table is necessary to give us a general view of the entirety of the two schools and their sub-schools[13]:

Parinirvāṇa of the Buddha

- Sthaviras (2nd cent. EP)
  - Haimavatas
  - Vātsīputrīyas (towards the end of 2nd cent. EP)
    - Dharmottarīyas
    - Bhadrayānīyas
    - Sāṃmitīyas
    - Ṣaṇṇāgārikas
  - Sarvāstivādins (beginning of 3rd cent. EP)
    - Sautrāntikas
    - Kaśyapīyas
  - Vibhajyavādins (towards the end of 3rd cent. EP)
    - Theravādins
    - Mahīśāsakas
    - Dharmaguptakas
- Mahāsāṃghikas (2nd cent. EP)
  - Ekavyāvahārikas (= Lokottaravādins
  - Gokulikas
    - Bahusrutīyas
    - Prajñaptivāda
    - --------> Caitikas

B — *THE PERSONALIST SCHOOLS*

The Personalist schools (*Pudgalavādins*) were based on the main theme of the *pudgala* or *pudgalavāda*, which can be translated as personalism. Of course, the notion of personalism in Buddhism is something quite unusual. It has nothing to do with the notion of personalism used by ancient or modern philosophers, whether Eastern or Western. Obviously, the universe of the person is always the universe of mankind. In this sense, such as it is, Buddhist personalism is not a system of thought, but more a particular interpretation of the person within the framework of the Buddhist teaching. In other words, this interpretation is not very far from the teaching of the Buddha. Nonetheless, its central affirmation is the existence of the person as a

13 This simplified table of the appearance of the Buddhist schools is taken from Bareau, *Religions*, pp.81–93.

principle which would explain the doctrine of insubstantiality (*anātmavāda*) without falling into nihilism.

Hence the personalism of early Buddhism and other types of personalism, such as Christian and agnostic personalism, differ in their sources as well as in their philosophical structure. However, they emphasize a point in common: this is the fundamental affirmation of the existence of the person. It is also the reason for which the word person is used in Buddhism.

Generally speaking, early Buddhism comprised twenty main schools which can be divided into two groups. The first group includes the schools which, despite their various doctrinal interpretations, faithfully accepted the doctrine of insubstantiality (*anātmavāda*) in all its strictness. They affirmed the continuity of the five aggregates which lies at the heart of the problem of insubstantiality. However, this explanation did not satisfy everyone. The second group is represented by the schools which opposed radical depersonalisation and accepted the thesis of the *pudgala*. Being Personalists (*pudgalavādins*), they were condemned as 'inner heresies'[14]. Although they were attacked by many opposing schools, the numerical importance of their followers and the persistance of these schools prove that they constituted a very important branch of early Buddhism.

The Pudgalavādins consisted of the Vātsīputrīyas, Sāṃmitīyas, Dharmottarīyas, Bhadrayānīyas and Ṣaṇḍagarikas.

Obviously, sources concerning the history of the Personalist schools are extremely limited. Therefore research on this subject undertaken by scholars such as P. Demiéville, É. Lamotte, A. Bareau, and N. Dutt is much appreciated[15]. An historical reconstruction is necessary in order to approach further studies, namely, the literature. doctrine and theses of the Personalists.

I — *THE VĀTSĪPUTRĪYAS*

All the direct or indirect sources indicate that the Vātsīputrīya school is the mother school of the Pudgalavādin sub-schools derived from the Sthaviras. Although very little is known about the first schism of the Sthavirian branch, the majority of Orientalists agree in thinking that the schism occurred in about the year 200 EP, that is, at the beginning of the third century BCE. This date is also given by the Sāṃmitīya tradition and confirmed by works on Buddhist history in Tibetan such as Bu-ston, *History of Buddhism* (tr. E. Obermiller, Vol.II, p.96), *Tāranātha's History of Buddhism in India* (tr. L. Chimpa and A. Chattopadhyaya, pp.71-4). It was adopted by La Vallée Poussin in *The Encylopaedia of Religion and Ethics*, Vol.VI, p.193, by A. Bareau (*Le Bouddhisme indien*, p.84) and by É. Lamotte (*History*, p.281), etc.

This is an important passage on the development of the schools, according to a Sāṃmitīya tradition which is generally accepted:

---

14 Cf. *Kathāvatthu* (*Points of Controversy*), translated by S.Z. Aung and C.A.F. Rhys Davids, p.8 ff; *Abhidharmakośa de Vasubandhu* (abbrev. *Kośa*), translated and annotated by L. de La Vallée Poussin, Chapter IX, p.227, preliminary notes 2 (English translation by Leo M. Pruden, Berkeley 1990, p.1356).
15 Cf. above, n.9.

'One hundred and thirty-seven years after the Parinirvāṇa of the Buddha, under the kings Nanda and Mahāpadma, when a number of very conspicuous Elders — Mahākāśyapa, Mahāloma, Mahātyāga, Uttara, Revata, etc. — were assembled in Pāṭaliputra, Māra the Wicked assumed the form of a bhikṣu named Bhadra and manifested various wonders and, with the help of the five theses, caused a great debate in the Community [of monks].

Later, those five theses were adopted by the Sthaviras Nāga (Nāgasena) and Sāramati. From then on the Community split into two sects: the Sthaviras and the Mahāsāṃghikas.

In the year 63 after this scission was completed, that is in the year 200 after the Nirvāṇa, the doctrine was reviewed by the Sthavira Vātsīputra'[16].

As to the founder of the Vātsīputrīya school, we must suppose that a brahmin named Vātsīputra, converted by the Sthaviras, upheld the thesis of the *pudgala*. This Arhat Vātsīputra was the instigator of the Sthavirian scission. His theory convinced other monks who formed a separate school called Vātsīputrīya.

With regard to the name of this school, Vātsīputrīya, it means either 1) the disciples of the Arhat named 'son of the *Vatsa* country' (Vatsyaputra) the capital of which was Kauśāmbī[17] ; or 2) 'son of the woman Vatsa'[18], personal names composed in this way were common in ancient India, such as, e.g., Śāriputra, Videhīputra, etc.; or 3) 'son of the heifer' (Vātsīputra), linked with the following legend recorded by K'uei-chi:

> 'Vātsīputra (son of a heifer) is the by-name of a Vinaya master. In times long past, there was a sage living in a tranquil spot on the mountain. When sexual desire arose, he was unable to control himself. There was a female buffalo nearby. Because of that sexual congress she gave birth to a child. The family of that sage was then named Vātsīputra; it was a brahmin family'[19].

A treatise by Chi-tsang[20] gives some indications on the date of the schism and the

---

16 Quoted in Lamotte, *History*, p.281 and footnote.

17 This is the definition given by Paramārtha. Cf. K'uei-chi 窺基 , Iptllsc, 220*c*. According to Lamotte, *Vatsa*: Allahābād . . ., an important centre of communications, was in direct contact with Mathurā and Ujjayinī to the west and Pāṭaliputra to the east. Cf. *History*, p.322; N.N. Ghosh, *Early History of Kauśāmbi*, Allahabad 1935; B.C. Law, *Kauśāmbi in Ancient Literature*, Delhi 1939; J. Przyluski, *Le concile de Rājagṛha, Introduction à l'Histoire des canons et des sectes bouddhiques*, p.330.

18 According to the Tibetan, *gnas-ma-bu*, literally, son of *Vatsa*. Cf. *Tāranātha's History of Buddhism in India*, p.14.

19 K'uei-chi, Iptllsc, p.220a. On the biography of K'uei-chi. cf. *Sung kao sêng chuan* 宋高僧傳 (Biographies of Eminent Monks compiled in the Sung period, 988) IV, T L, 2061, 725–6. Translated and annotated by R. Shih, *Biographies des Moines Eminents (Kao seng tchouan) de Houei-Kiao*, Bibliothèque du Muséon 54, Louvain 1968.

20 Chi-tsang 吉藏 (549–623) was the son of a Parthian merchant married to a Chinese woman from Nanking. Despite his foreign origin, his education was Chinese. His father became a monk after his birth and Chi-tsang himself, in his childhood (aged seven or thirteen), joined the Community as a novice. He then became a disciple of Master Fa – lang was and became famous as a student of the San-lun School 三輪玄義 . He was honoured by the emperors of the Sui and T'ang dynasties. Besides commentaries concerning the School's doctrine, he wrote a commentary on a treatise on Vasumitra by Paramārtha. This work was translated and annotated by P. Demiéville in 'L'origine'.

name of the founder of the Vātsīputrīya school (let us leave aside the problem of the Abhidharma inheritance which we will speak of in the chapter on the literature of the Pudgalavādins).

> 'In the year 300', says Chi-tsang, 'from the Sarvāstivādin school there emerged a school called of the "disciples of the son of the Inhabitant" (*Vatsyaputrīya*); this is (what was called) formerly "school of the Heifer's Son" (*Vatsīputrīya*). As for the name of that school, there was a *ṛṣi* named *K'ê-chu* 可住 ("who can inhabit": *Vatsya? Vāsī?*); a woman of the race of that *ṛṣi* had an son who was an Arhat named "Son of the Inhabitant" (*Vatsyaputra*); since that school was formed of disciples of that Arhat, it was called Vatsyaputrīya[21]. Vatsyaputra, whose disciples formed that school, had Śāriputra as his *upādhyāya*. Śāriputra had explained the Buddha's teaching in nine parts; that is what is called the Abhidharma of the characteristics of the Dharma (*Dharmalakṣaṇa-Abhidharma*)[22]. Rāhula had propagated (transmitted) the Abhidharma of Śāriputra, Vatsyaputra the teachings of Rāhula. That school in turn propagated the teachings of Vatsyaputra'[23].

On this subject, A. Bareau has written in his *Sectes bouddhiques du Petit Véhicule*:

> 'According to the agreement of all the sources, the school of the Vātsīputrīyas is the first derivation from the Sthavirian trunk, possibly, however, after that of the Haimavatas. The schism that gave rise to it would have occurred exactly 200 years after the Nirvāṇa, that is, about 280 BCE, according to the Sāṃmitīya tradition which must be based on the Vātsīputrīya tradition

---

21 Note by P. Demiéville: [tr.] 'Root *vas*, basis of the future *vatsya*; *vāsī*, "inhabitant", etc; similar etymology in Bhavya (Rockhill, *Life of the Buddha*, p.184). Of the two inscriptions given by Paramārtha, Po-tz'ŭ 婆雌, archaic B'ua-ts'ie (< ts'ia) and P'o-ssŭ 跋私, archaic B'uat-si (cf. above and *Taishō*, 2033, p.220), the former seems to correspond to Vatsya and the latter to Vatsī. It is this latter form which is followed by Hsüan-tsang and K'uei-chi, who translate "school of the Heifer's Son" and explain that the founder was born in a brahmin clan descended from a *ṛṣi* and an heifer'. Demiéville, 'L'origine', p.57.

22 Note by P. Demiéville: [tr.] 'Cf. Mahāprajñāpāramitāśāstra, tr. Przyluski, *Concile*, p.73: When the Buddha was in this world, Śāriputra, in order to explain the Buddha's words, made the Abhidharma. Later, the Vatsīputrīya monks recited (that work). Until today, that is what is called the Śāriputra Abhidharma. The late T. Kimura showed, in his excellent Researches on the *Abhidharma* (Tokyo 1922), the close analogy which exists between the Chinese version of the Śāriputra Abhidharma (Nanjio 1268) and the Pāli Abhidhamma, in particular the Vibhaṅga and Puggalapaññatti. He even thinks the two treatises go back to the same source as the Śāriputra Abhidharma. From the doctrinal point of view, Kimura's investigation leads to the following conclusions: if we compare the Śāriputra Abhidharma to those which the Vibhāṣā and *Kośa* attribute to different schools, it is the school which in these two works is called Vibhajyavāda, and not the Vatsīputrīya, to which the Śāriputra Abhidharma is closest; as for the Pāli Abhidhamma, it is closest to the doctrines attributed in the same works to the Mahāsāṃghika school. We saw above that Pāramārtha links that (Bahuśrutika-) Vibhajyavāda school with the Mahāsaṅghika school. Cf. p.49, n.a. — For the expression *Dharmalakṣaṇa-abhidharma*, cf. the definition of *Abhidharma* given at the beginning of the Vibhāṣā (*Taishō*, 1545, p.4a): "It is called *Abhidharma* because it consists of making a clear and perfect analysis (*nirvedha*) of the characteristics of the Dharma (*dharmalakṣaṇa*)". A similar definition is attributed, in a later passage of the Vibhāṣā, to Venerable Vasumitra'. Demiéville, 'L'origine', pp.57–8.

23 Tr. after P. Demiéville, 'L'origine', pp.58–9.

itself, or at the beginning of the third century of the Era of the Nirvāṇa, that is, shortly after 280 BCE, according to the North-Western traditions. We would not go far wrong in placing that event in the reign of Bindusāra Maurya (289-264 BCE). The Vātsīputrīyas derive their name from the founder of their school, Vātsīputra. According to the Mañjuśrīparipṛcchāsūtra, the latter was a discipline master (*vinayadhara*). According to K'uei-chi, he was from the brahmin caste. Paramārtha makes him a disciple of Śāriputra'[24].

Tāranātha gives us some facets of his personality and career, as follows: 'There was then in Kashmir a monk called Vatsa born in a *brahmaṇa* family. He was cruel, wicked and, though vastly learned, was in favour of the doctrine of the (permanent) soul (*ātmaka-vāda*). He went around corrupting the common monks to the wrong view. This resulted in a minor controversy within the *saṃgha*'[25].

In this connection, some people claim that the Arhat Gopa was the precursor of the Pudgalavādins because he was a contemporary of Devaśarman who died about 100 years after the Nirvāṇa[26]. In the account of his travels, Hsüan-tsang[27] informs us that in Viśoka, the place where Devaśarman wrote his Vijñānakāyapādaśāstra, in which he denies the existence of the *pudgala* like that of the *ātman*, lived the Arhat Gopa who wrote a treatise in which he, in contrast, defended the existence of the *pudgala*. According to Hsüan-tsang, there was a lively controversy on these doctrinal points between the two masters[28].

Unfortunately, we cannot know Gopa's exact opinion on the *pudgala*, since his treatise does not exist, either in Chinese or Tibetan.

The author of the Vijñānakāyapādaśāstra presents the theory of the *pudgala*, with his interpretation and intention to criticise it. According to Devaśarman, the *pudgala* is susceptible to being perceived in reality, it is considered as an individual which transmigrates from one life to another, and which obtains the fruits of the Path. This *pudgala* is subject to the creation of actions (*karman*) and the reaping of

---

24 Tr. after A. Bareau, *Sectes*, p.19.

25 *Tāranātha's History of Buddhism in India*, pp.71–2.

26 Cf. J. Masuda, 'Origin and Doctrines of Early Buddhist Schools', p.53, n.4; *Kośa*, Introduction — Fragment of Kārikās — Index — Additions, p.XXXIII; Eng. tr., p.21.

27 Hsüan-tsang 玄奘 (602–664) was born into a good family of literati in Honan and entered a monastery in Lo-yang at the age of 13. In 618, he went to Ch'ang-an and received full ordination (*upasampadā*) as soon as he was 20. His Buddhist studies were mainly concentrated on the Abhidharma. At the age of 25 or 27 Hsüan-tsang set out, with imperial consent, for India (in 627 or 629) to deepen his knowledge. His outward journey lasted nearly two years. He then spent a dozen years in India and returned to Ch'ang-an with 657 works in 645. From the age of 43 until the end of his life, Hsüan-tsang devoted all his time (645–664) to translating 75 works. He was the greatest scholar and Chinese translator of Buddhism.

For a full biography, cf. *Hsü kao sêng chuan* 續高僧傳 (Supplement to the biographies of eminent monks), IV–V, T L, 2060, 446–59. Cf. also Samuel Beal, *Si-yu ki (Buddhist Records of the Western World)*, 2 vols, Boston 1962, repr. in 1 vol, Delhi 1981; T. Watters, *On Yuan Chwang's Travels in India*, 2 vols, London 1904–05; *L'Inde classique* II, §§ 2057–60.

On the list of the 75 works translated by Hsüan-tsang, cf. Thích Minh Chau, *Hsuan-tsang: The Pilgrim and Scholar*, Vietnamese Buddhist Institute, Nhatrang–Vietnam 1963, pp.85–89.

28 Cf. S. Beal, *Si-yu ki* 西域記 *(Buddhist Records of the Western World)* I, p.240.

pleasant or painful fruition. It is the centre of knowledge with respect to external phenomena[29].

A. Bareau does not share this opinion and considers that the story of Gopa, precursor of the *Pudgalavādins* or *Vātsīputrīyas*, is certainly legendary or, rather, that it occurred much later, since Buddhist works had not begun to be written down until just before the Common Era; until then they were only transmitted orally. The Vijñānakāyapādaśāstra, pertaining to the Sarvāstivādin Abhidharma[30], therefore post-dates the appearance of the latter and therefore even more so that of the Vātsīputrīyas. It dates at the earliest three hundred years after the Nirvāṇa.

According to J. Przyluski, the Vātsīputrīyas formed a distinct group around Kauśambi, the ancient Buddhist capital[31]. The inscription on an Aśokan pillar, from the Gupta period (fourth century CE), at Sārnāth (Vārānaṣī)[32], indicates that it existed in parallel with the Sāṃmitīyas. It existed as an independent school in the fifth century CE[33].

According to Tāranātha, the school still existed separately along with the other five schools, namely, the Kaurukullakas, the main Sāṃmitīya school, the Prajñaptivādins, Lokottaravādins, Tāmraśatīyas and Mūlasarvāstivādins, at the time of the Pāla kings (eighth century CE)[34]. However, the Vātsīputrīyas themselves have not left much trace of their residence in India or elsewhere. The certain outcome was that

---

29 Cf. *A-pi-ta-mo shih shên tsu lun* 阿毘達磨識身足論 Vijñānakāyapādaśāstra, T XXVI, 1539, 537a–543b; La Vallée Poussin, 'Le controverse du temps et du Pudgala dans le Vijñānakāya', EA, pp.358–76.

30 The Vijñānakāya of Devaśarman is one of the seven books of the Sarvāstivādin Abhidharma, entitled Ṣadpādābhidharma (Abhidharma with six feet):

1 — The Jñānaprasthāna of Kātyāyaṇiputra, T XXVI, 1543, is like a body, the six feet (*pāda*) or supplements of which are:

2 — the Prakaraṇapāda of Vasumitra, T XXVI, 1541 and 1542;

3 — the Vijñānakāya of Devaśarman, T XXVI, 1539;

4 — the Dharmaskandha of Śāriputra, T XXVI, 1537;

5 — the Prajñaptiśāstra of Maugalyāyana, T XXVI, 1538;

6 — the Dhātukāya of Pūrṇa, T XXVI, 1540;

7 — the Saṃgītiparyāya of Mahākauṣṭhila, T XXVI, 1536.

Of these seven texts, the first was translated by Gautama Saṅghadeva with the collaboration of Chu Fo-nien 竺佛念 in 383 CE. The other six books were translated by Hsüan-tsang between 651 and 660 CE. 2 has been edited by J. Imanishi, *Fragmente des Abhidharmaprakaraṇabhāṣyam*, Göttingen 1975; 4 by S. Dietz, *Fragmente des Dharmaskandha*, Göttingen 1984; and 7 ed. and tr. by K. Mittal and V. Stache-Rosen, *Das Saṅgītisūtra und sein Kommentar Saṅgītiparyāya*, Berlin 1968.

Cf. J. Takakusu, 'The Abhidharma Literature of the Sarvāstivādins', in *Journal of the Pali Text Society*, 1905, pp.67–146; N. Dutt, *Bud. Sects*, p.152; Bareau, *Sectes*, p.135; Lamotte, *History*, pp.184–5.

31 Cf. EI VII, p.172, No.1; list by Lüders, 923; Sukumar Dutt, *Buddhist Monks and Monasteries of India*, p.216.

32 Cf. Przyluski, *Le concile de Rājagṛha*, p.330.

33 The Abhidharmakośa of Vasubandhu (*A-p'i-ta-mo-chu-shê lun* 阿毘達磨俱舍論, T XXIX, 1558), the important treatise which appeared in the 5th cent. CE, devotes its ninth chapter to criticising the principle thesis of the *pudgala* of the Vātsīputrīyas as an independent school and not associated with the Sāṃmitīyas (cf. *Kośa*, Ch.IX, p.227 ff; Engl. tr, p.1313 ff). Hence the Vātsīputrīyas were the strongest adversaries of the Sarvāstivādins as well as the Sautrāntikas, particularly in the doctrinal sphere.

34 Cf. *Tāranātha's History of Indian Buddhism*, pp.341–2. Cf. also Bareau, *Religions*, p.92.

they were soon eclipsed by one of their sub-schools, the Sāṃmitīyas[35]. Notwithstanding, the Vātsīputrīya school was 'one of the most powerful and flourishing of early Buddhism'. The Vātsīputrīyas had no connection with the Vṛjiputaka (Pāli, Vajjiputtaka) monks who were condemned at the Council of Vaiśalī as practitioners of the ten usages against discipline[36].

II – *THE VĀTSĪPUTRĪYA SUB-SCHOOLS*

In that they were dissatisfied with the Abhidharma of the mother school (Śāriputrābhidharma in nine parts, or Dharmalakṣaṇābhidharma), the disciples of Vātsīputra 'attempted to complete its meaning by means of śāstras [Lamotte's 'sūtras' should correctly read 'śāstras'], and that enrichment of the doctrine caused the blossoming of four new schools: Dharmottarīyas, Bhadrayānīyas, Sāṃmitīyas and Channagirikas'[37].

Chi-tsang gives the following explanation of the development of these four sub-schools:

> 'Then, within three hundred years, from the Vātsyaputrīya school emerged a further four schools. . . Dissatisfied with the Śāriputrābhidharma, which they considered incomplete, they each compiled śāstras in order to complete the meaning of the sūtras. Since their opinions differed, they formed four schools bearing the following names: 1) school of the Elevation of the Dharma (Dharmottarīya), which was in antiquity called *T'an-wu-tê* 曇無德 ; 2) school of the Vehicle of the Sages (Bhadrayānīya); 3) school of the disciples of the "Correct Measure" (Saṃmitīya); that is, the disciples of the Arhat (named) Correct Measure (Saṁmita); 4) school of the Dense Forest (Ṣaṇḍagairika), which takes its name from its residence'[38].

According to North-western sources, the four sub-schools appeared during the third century EP. However, if the birth of those sub-schoools was caused by different interpretations of the Abhidharmapiṭaka, as is claimed by Paramārtha[39], their appearance must date to the first century BCE or CE, as the development of the Abhidharma could not have existed before then[40].

Before tackling the situation of the four sub-schools in detail, it is useful to summarise the ideas concerning the origin and development of the Vātsīputrīya school by means of the following table:

---

35 Bareau, *Sectes*, p.115. According to Vinitadeva, the Sāṃmitīyas were sub-divided into three sub-schools: Kaurukullakas, Avantakas and Vātsīputrīyas. Thus, at that time, these last were considered as a sub-school of the Sāṃmitīyas. *Tāranātha's History of Indian Buddhism*, p.340; Bu-ston, *History of Buddhism* II, tr. Obermiller, p.100.

36 Bareau, *Sectes*, pp.115–16; *Religions*, p.85. Cf. also *id.*, 'Une confusion entre Mahāsāṃghika et Vātsīputrīya', JA, 1953, pp.388–406.

37 Lamotte, *History*, p.531.

38 Tr. after Demiéville, L'origine' pp.58–9.

39 On the biography of Paramārtha, cf. below, 'The translator of the *Lü êrh-shih-êrh ming-liao lun*'.

40 Cf. Bareau, *Sectes*, pp.121, 127, 128, 130.

Parinirvāṇa of the Buddha
100 I
or I EP
110 I

Sthaviras	3rd C. EP		Mahāsāṃghikas
	—	Dharmottarīyas	
	1st C.	Bhadrayānīyas	
3rd C. E.P. — Vātsīputrīyas	BCE	Sāṃmitīyas	Avantakas
	or CE	Ṣaṇṇāgārikas	Kurukallakas

1. *THE SĀṂMITĪYAS*

Among the four sub-schools which emerged from the Vātsīputrīya school, that of the Sāṃmitīyas is most noteworthy. It was the most developed sub-school in India, perhaps in the seventh century CE, despite its possible appearance later than the other sub-schools[41]. Its founder, according to Bhavya, was the Arhat Saṁmita whose history is not known. According to Bareau, the meaning of this name is not established since there are various spellings of it:

1) Sammatīyas: those who live in accord, or those who should be respected.
2) Samitīyas (Pāli): those who are assembled or equal.
3) Sāṃmitīyas: those who have a correct measure, or the equal[42].

The school appeared between the second century BCE and the first century CE[43].

The main reason for the schism of the Sāṃmitīyas among the Vātsīputrīyas, according to Vasumitra, was because of the divergent explanations of those who, later, were to form the three sub-schools based on the following stanza:

'Being delivered, one regresses again.
The fall comes from covetousness; one can return.
The obtaining of security and joy, such is happiness.
Following the practices of happiness, one reaches happiness'[44].

The Sāṃmitīyas, according to K'uei-chi, explained that to 'the four fruits (*phala*)

41 According to the lists by the Sthaviras and Bhavya, the Sāṃmitīyas appeared after the Dharmottarīyas and Bhadrayānīyas; the lists of the Mahāsāṃghikas in the Śāriputraparipṛcchā and Manjuśrīparipṛcchā: after the Dharmottarīyas and Bhadrayānīyas and before the Ṣaṇṇāgārikas (the list in the Śāriputraparipṛcchā gives the date of the 3rd centry EP); the Pāli and Sāṃmitīya lists: they appeared last in relation to the other three sub-schools. Cf. *Tāranātha's History of Buddhism in India*, pp.339–40; Lamotte, *History*, pp.530–6.

42 Bareau, *Sectes*, p.121; Demiéville, 'L'origine', p.59.

43 Bareau, *Sectes*, p.121.

44 *Ibid.*, pp.122–3. The importance of the stanza obliges us to reproduce its Chinese translation:

己解脫更墮　墮由貪復還
獲安喜所樂　墮樂行至樂

Cf. K'uei-chi, Iptllsc, 230*b*, 1, 2.

correspond six kinds of person:
1) he who is delivered (*vimukta*); that is, the 'Stream-winner' (*srotaāpanna*) who has obtained deliverance (*vimukti*);
2) he who goes from family to family (*kukaṃkula*), that is, he who is aiming for the second fruit;
3) he who has obtained the fruit of a single rebirth (*sakṛdā- gāmin*);
4) he who has only a single interval (*ekavīcika*);
5) he who will not return again (*anāgāmin*)'
6) the Arhat.
The first line of the verse (*pāda*) indicates the one who is delivered but who can regress to delusion.
The second line indicates he who goes from family to family; the fourth person, who can regress due to craving (*kāma*), and the third person, who will return to this world.
The third indicates the fifth person (who will not return to this world), and the fourth line designates the Arhat'[45].

Basing ourselves on the Tridharmakaśāstra (abbrev. TDS, T XXV, 1506) and the Sāṃmitīyanikāyaśāstra (abbrev. SNS, T XXXII, 1649), we can ask ourselves a question: is it possible that one of the causes of the scission between the Sāṃmitīyas and the Vātsīputrīyas could have been the difference in the lists of the Śrāvaka fruits, the Vātsīputrīya list consisting of 29 categories[46] while that of the Sāṃmitīyas contains only ten or eleven categories[47]?

The presence of the school is proved by two inscriptions: one in Mathurā, from the Kuṣāna period (second century CE)[48], the other at Sārnāth, from the Gupta period (fourth century CE)[49]. The first attests the installation of a statue of a Bodhisattva dedicated to the Sāṃmitīya monks, at the Sirivihāra, made by a monk whose master was Dharmaka. The second bears witness to the presence of Sāṃmitīya masters otherwise known as Vātsīputrīyas (*ācāryānāmparigrahe Vātsīputridānām*).

It was around the third or fourth century CE that the Sāṃmitīyas became so influential and popular that they replaced the Sarvāstivādins in Sārnāth[50]. That school flourished most noticeably in the reign of King Harṣavardhana (606-647 CE)[51]. It is

45 Bareau, *Sectes*, pp.122–3.

46 Cf. Thich Thiện Châu, 'Le Tridharmakaśāstra', Ch.IV.

47 *Ibid.*, Ch.I; below, 'The Śrāvaka lists of the Pudgalavādins'.

48 Bareau, *Sectes*, p.121; N. Dutt, *Bud. Sects*, p.194; cf. EI VIII, p.172; Sahni, *Catalogue of the Museum at Sarnath*, p.30; H. Sastri, EI XIX, p.67.

49 Lüders, 923 of the Sāṃmitīyas at Sārnāth.

50 Bareau, *Sectes*, p.121; cf. Hultzch, EI III (Calcutta, 1905–6), p.172; Lüders, 923 of the Vātsīputrīyas and *id.*, 923 of the Sāṃmitīyas at Sārnāth.

51 Harṣavardhana (606–647 CE) succeeded his father, King Prabhākaravardhana, called Pratāpaśīla, of the kingdom of Thanesvar, founded by Puṣpabhūti. According to Hsüan-tsang, the frontiers of India in the reign of Harṣavardhana went no further than Uttar Pradesh, Bihar, Bengal and Orissa. This king is described by Hsüan-tsang as a king in accord with the Dharma. 'He was just in his administration and punctilious in the execution of his duties. In his devotion to good works, he forgot to eat or sleep. He banned the consumption of animals throughout the five Indias, and forbade killing under the most serious of punishments' (tr. after P. Lévi, 'Les pèlerins chinois en Inde', *Présence du Bouddhisme*, p.417.

said that the king's sister Rājyaśrī became a nun (*bhikṣuṇī*) in the Sāṃmitīya women's Order[52].

According to I-ching[53], the Sāṃmitīyas were represented in the regions of Lāta and Sindhu, that is, eastern India[54].

The importance of the school was very obvious, as Hsüan-tsang, the Chinese pilgrim, observed in the second quarter of the seventh century: more than 1,351 monasteries scattered thoughout nearly all the large regions, sheltering approximately 66,500 monks.

The table below, based on information supplied by Hsüan-tsang [and the chart in Lamotte, *History*, p.542], gives us an idea of the Sāṃmitīya communities' expansion:

Cf. T. Watters, *On Yuan Chwang's Travels in India* I, p.344).

Although Harṣavardhana belonged to the Vaiśya caste, he was a generous patron of philosophers, poets, sages and the religious of Hinduism as of Buddhism. He erected about a thousand stūpas on the banks of the Ganges, built monasteries in the Buddhist holy places and generously endowed the Mahāvihāra at Nālandā. Owing to his religious policy, Buddhism regained its former vigour. This is proved by the fact that in Kanauj (Kanyākubja), Harṣavardhana's capital, Hsüan-tsang counted more than an hundred monasteries and more than ten thousand Buddhist monks; whereas, two centuries earlier, Fa-hsien had only counted two monasteries. It was in particular during the reign of Harṣavardhana that the Sāṃmitīya school flourished the most.

Cf. N. Dutt, *Bud. Sects*, p.53; *L'Inde classique* II, § 230; Lamotte, *History*, p.338–9; L.M. Joshi, *Studies in the Buddhist Culture of India*, pp.32–3.

52 According to Bāṇa, in his Harṣacarita, Rājyaśrī (c. end of 6th cent. or beginning of 7th cent. CE) was the younger daughter of Emperor Prabhākaravardhana, called Pratāpaśīla, and Queen Yaśomatī. This king was a sun-worshipper and skilful warrior who vanquished the Hūṇas of the North-west, the Gurjara king of Rajputana and the lords of Sindhu, Gandhāra, Lāṭa and Mālava. Rājyaśrī was intelligent, cultured and actively interested in Buddhism. She married Grahavarman, the son of Avantivarman of the Maukhari family of Kanauj. Her husband was soon killed in a plot hatched by the Mālava king and Rājyaśrī was herself imprisoned in Kanauj, her feet in fetters. At the time when her brothers Rājyavardhana and Harṣavardhana were involved in military operations against the Hūṇas of the North, King Prabhākaravardhana died. Harṣavardhana, who had not joined the battle with his brother, returned to the capital. Rājyavardhana, on the way to attack the Mālava king, was killed by the Gauḍa king Śaśāṅka. Harṣavardhana was then able to mount the throne. His friend, Kumāragupta, the Mālava king's son, rescued his sister Rājyaśrī.

Once released from prison and informed that her husband Grahavarman had been killed, Rājyaśrī entered the Vindhya forest and decided to commit suicide. Harṣavardhana set out in search of his sister, found her in the forest before she could take her life and persuaded her to abandon her decision. Rājyaśrī then became a nun in the Bhikṣuṇī Saṃgha of the Sāṃmitīyas (after the article 'Harṣavardhana and Harṣacarita' by N. Dutt in his *Mahāyāna Buddhism*, London 1978, pp.48–50; cf. Harṣacarita, Ch.VIII, English tr. by Cowell and Thomas; cf. also L.M. Joshi, *Studies in the Buddhistic Culture of India*. pp.32–3).

53 I-ching (634–713; 635– says Takakusu) is the foremost of the great Chinese pilgrims in India. He was born in Chih-li 直隸, near Peking. When seven years old, he entered a monastery and, at the age of fifteen, resolved to go to India. He embarked on a Persian ship at Yang-chou 江州 and stayed ten years in India. Returning to Lo-yang in summer 695, he brought back 400 works composed of 500,000 *ślokas*. From 700 to 712 he translated 56 works consisting of 230 volumes. I-ching died in Lo-yang in 713 in his 79th year. (Cf. *Nan hai chi kuei nei fa chuan* 南海寄歸內法傳 T LIV, 2125, 204c–234a; the article 'Yi-tsing' by Paul Lévi, in 'Les pèlerins chinois en Inde', *Présence du Bouddhisme*, pp.432–6; *L'Inde classique* II, 2063, pp.407–8).

54 I-ching, *A Record of the Buddhist Religion as Practised in India and the Malay Archipelago* (A.D. 671–695) (abbrev. *Record*), translated by J. Takakusu, pp.XXIV, 14, 20.

REGIONS	NUMBER OF MONASTERIES	NUMBER OF RELIGIOUS
1. Ahicchatra	10 +	1,000 +
2. Kapitha (Sāmkāśya)	4	1,000 +
3. Ayumukha (in Oudh)	5	1,000 +
4. Viśoka (in Oudh)	20 +	3,000 +
5. Śrāvastī	some hundreds in ruins	very small number
6. Kapilavastu	1,000 in ruins	30
7. Vārāṇasī	30 +	3,000 +
8. Mṛgadāva	1	1,500
9. Vaiśālī	1	very small number
10. Īraṇaparvata (Monghyr)	10 +	4,000 +
11. Karṇasuvarṇa	10 +	2,000 +
12. Mālava	some hundreds	20,000 +
13. Valabhī (in Kāthiāwār)	100 +	6,000 +
14. Ānandapura	10 +	1,000 -
15. Sindh	some hundreds	10,000 +
16. Aviddhakarṇa (A-tien-p'o-ch'ih-lo Indus delta)	80 +	5,000 +
17. Badakshan (Pi-to-chih-lo delta area)	50 +	3,000 +
18. A-fan-t'u (Middle Sindh)	20 +	2,000 +
TOTAL	1,351 +	66,500 +

These numbers of monasteries and religious inhabitants are larger than those relating to other schools of the period pertaining to early Buddhism.

Sthaviras	401 monasteries	36,800 religious
Mahāsāṃghikas	24 "	1,100 "
Sarvāstivādins	158 "	23,700 "
Unspecified	145 "	6,700 "
	728 monasteries	68,300 religious

The important point in Hsüan-tsang's narrative is that there is no trace of the existence of the Vātsīputrīya school, which reinforces the likelihood that the Vātsīputrīyas were, to a certain degree, eclipsed by the Sāṃmitīyas. This is what is known as the Vātsīputrīya-Sāṃmitīya school[55]. On the other hand, being so widespread, the Sāṃmitīyas divided into two sub-schools: 1) the Avantakas, that is, the Sāṃmitīyas of Avanta or Avanti residing to north of the Narbada and east of the lower Indus; 2) the Kurukulas, that is, the Sāṃmitīyas of the Kuru family, residing in Kurukṣetra on the upper Ganges, around Sthāneśvara[56]. About half a century after Hsüan-tsang's departure from India, another Chinese pilgrim, I-ching, supplies some details on the presence of the Sāṃmitīyas. According to him, the Ārya-Sāṃmitīya school was, at that time, subdivided into four sub-schools which were above all represented in Lāṭa and Sindhu; they were also active in Magadha and, a little, in the south of India; they co-existed with other schools in eastern India[57]. I-ching notes that there were some Sāṃmitīyas in the Sunda Islands and a large group in Champa, where they predominated[58]. According to Tāranātha, the Avantaka sub-school had disappeared by the seventh century[59]. Only the Kurukula sub-school, which came under the influence of the Mahāyāna in the eighth century, continued until the time of the Pāla kings (ninth-tenth centuries CE)[60].

2. *THE DHARMOTTARĪYAS, BHADRAYĀNĪYAS AND ṢAṆṆĀGĀRIKAS*

We do not have much documentation concerning the Dharmottarīyas, Bhadrayānīyas or Ṣaṇṇāgārikas, which is why these three sub-schools will be dealt with together.

a) *The Dharmottarīyas*

The appearance of the Dharmottarīyas may date back to the middle of the third century EP. This school, according to Bhavya, took its title from the name of its founder, Dharmottara: the Dharma is superior, the superiority of the Dharma[61], the elevation of the Dharma[62]. Dharmottara was a Vinaya master[63]. The causes of the Dharmottarīya scission from the Vātsīputrīyas may have been:
1) discontent concerning the Abhidharma of the Vātsīputrīyas, according to Paramārtha;
2) divergent interpretations among the four sub-schools of the stanza common to the school, according to Vasumitra.

With regard to the stanza common to the Vātsīputrīyas, the Dharmottarīyas said,

---

55 *Kośa*, Ch.IX, p.232, n.2; Engl tr., p.1360, n.8.
56 Bareau, *Sectes*, p.122.
57 Cf. Lamotte, *History*, p.544–5.
58 Cf. Bareau, *Sectes*, p.121; Takakusu, *Record*, p.XXIV 8, sq.
59 Cf. Bareau, *Sectes*, p.126.
60 *Ibid.*
61 *Ibid.*, p.127; cf. K'uei-chi, Iptllsc, p.234a l.
62 Cf. Lamotte, *History*, p.520; Demiéville, 'L'origine', p.59.
63 Bareau, *Sectes*, p.127; cf. Mañjuśrīparipṛcchā, T XIV, 468, 501*b*.

according to K'uei-chi: 'The Arhat has dharmas of regression (*parihāṇi*), stability (*sthiti*) and progress; the first two lines of the verse concern regression, the third, stability, and the fourth, progress[64].

The presence of the sub-school is attested by some inscriptions:

1) on pillars 8 and 9 of the caitya at Kārle in the second century, marking the installation of the pillar with relics by the Thera Sātimita, the son of Nanda and disciple of a master from the Dharmottarīya Community in Śūrpāraka[65] ;

2) in a cave at Junnar, in mountains of the Bombay region, a dedication concerning a cave and a tank, by Patibadhaka Giribhuti Sakhuryani, son of Savagin Yaśa of the Apaguriyas. These establishments and a nunnery belonged to the Dharmottarīyas of the town[66].

The date of this sub-school's disappearance is unknown.

b) *The Bhadrayānīyas*

The Bhadrayānīyas seemingly appeared about the middle of the third century EP. According to Bhavya, the name Bhadrayānīya means: those whose way (*yāna*) is auspicious (*bhadra*)[67], or the vehicle of the sages[68]. While, according to K'uei-chi, Bhadrayānīya can be defined as meaning: disciples of the descendants of the Arhat Bhadra[69].

The causes of the sub-school's scission may have been similar to those of the Dharmottarīyas, namely:

1) dissatisfaction with the Vātsīputrīya Abhidharma;

2) divergent interpretations among the four sub-schools of the stanza common to the Vātsīputrīyas.

According to K'uei-chi, the Bhadrayānīyas explained the common stanza as follows: 'The first two lines of the verse apply to the Arhats, who can therefore regress; the third line concerns the Pratyekabuddhas, and the last line the Buddhas proper'[70].

The existence of this sub-school is also confirmed by several inscriptions:

An inscription in the cave at Kānheri, in the reign of Yajñaśrī Śātakarṇi (174-203 CE)[71], and two epigraphs in the cave at Nāsik which were engraved in the year 19 of the reign of Sātavāhana king Vāsiṣṭhīputra Pulomā (130-150 CE)[72] contain the name of Bhadrayānīya. One of the inscriptions at Nāsik (Lüders' list No.1123) ends by indicating the gift of a cave and village of the Pisājipadakas to the south-west of Mount Tiraṇhu (Triraśmi) (Bombay) by Queen Gotamī Balaśrī and Vāsiṣṭhīputra Pulomā, lord of

---

64 Bareau, *Sectes*, p.127; cf. K'uei-chi, Iptllsc, 230*b*, 1, 2; *Kośa*, IV, p.253 ff; Engl. tr., p.1001 sq.

65 Lüders, 1094–5.

66 *Ibid.*, 1152; cf. A.M. Shastri, *An Outline of Early Buddhism*, p.83.

67 Bareau, *Sectes*, p.128 and n.1.

68 Lamotte, *History*, p.520; Demiéville, 'L'origine', p.59.

69 *Ibid.*; cf. K'uei-chi, Iptllsc, 234*a* 1.

70 Bareau, *Sectes*, p.129 and n.1; cf. K'uei-chi, Iptllsc, pp.230, 1–2.

71 Lüders, 987.

72 *Ibid.*, 1123.

Dakṣiṇāpatha (Dakhināpathesaro), to the Bhadrayāniya Community.

In the second inscription, still in the cave at Nāsik (Lüders' list No.1124), Vāsiṣṭhīputra Pulomā orders his Sivikhandila officials from Govardhana[73] to give the village of Samalipada to the monks of the Bhadrayānīya school in exchange for the village of Sudasana (Sudarśana). These facts inform us that the Bhadrayānīyas had a residence at Nāsik and were supported by the Satavāhana royal family in the mid-second century CE. The sub-school flourished equally in Kānheri where a caitya (Lüders' list No.987) was constructed and a cave and a water tank (Lüders' list No.1018) donated to the Bhadrayānīyas.

c) *The Ṣaṇṇāgārikas*

The Ṣaṇṇāgārika or Ṣaṇḍagiriya sub-school is considered as the last to have emerged from the Vātsīputrīyas and appeared in the middle of the third century EP.

The name of the school has several meanings:
Ṣaṇṇāgārika means 'those with six (*ṣaḍ*) towns (*nagara*)',
Ṣaṇḍagiriya, 'those who dwell on the mountain (*giri*) of brushwood (*ṣaṇḍa*)'. K'uei-chi explains that the Ṣaṇḍagiriyas took their name from their master's dwelling, a dense forest situated near a mountain[74].

The causes of the scission of the Ṣaṇṇāgārikas or Ṣaṇḍagiriyas from the Vātsīputrīyas are:

1) discontent as to the Vātsīputrīya Abhidharma, according to Paramārtha;
2) divergent interpretations of the common stanza, according to Vasumitra.

The Ṣaṇṇāgārikas or Ṣaṇḍagiriyas, according to K'uei-chi, interpreted the stanza as follows: 'There are six kinds of wise people (*aśaikṣa*), that is, of Arhats, who are repectively characterised by regression (*parihāṇi*), cogitation (*cetanā*), protection (*anurakṣāṇā*), stability (*sthitā*), penetration (*prativedhanā*) and immovability (*akopya*); he who is already delivered is the second, he who can regress is the first, he who reverts to the passions because of his regression is the third, he who returns is the fourth, the third line of the verse concerns the fifth, and the last line the sixth'[75].

No geographical or epigraphical trace of this sub-school has yet been discovered. However, it is certain that its followers lived in western India, as did other sub-schools of the Vātsīputrīyas. The date of its disappearance is equally unknown.

---

73 According to A.M. Shastri, Govardhana is identical to the modern village of Govardhan. Gangapur is on the right bank of the River Godavarī, about six miles to the west of Nāsik. Formerly, it was the centre of a territorial division (*Bombay Gazetteer* XVI, p.541). Cf. A.M. Shastri, *An Outline of Early Buddhism*, p.84, n.4.

74 Bareau, *Sectes*, p.130 and nn.1, 2, Demiéville, 'L'origine', p.59; cf. K'uei-chi, Iptllsc, 234*a* 1.

75 Bareau, *Sectes*, p.130 and n.5; cf. K'uei-chi, Iptllsc, 230*b* 2.

CHAPTER TWO

THE LITERATURE AND DOCTRINE OF THE PUDGALAVĀDINS

A - *GENERALITIES*

I. *The Pudgaḷavādin Tripiṭaka*

The Buddha did not produce any literary works during his lifetime; he only expounded his teaching. His disciples listened to him, learnt his teaching by heart and verbally transmitted it to others. It is probable that little use of writing was made in India at that time. Furthermore, the oral transmission of knowledge was traditional in religious circles. Throughout most of his life, the Buddha carried out his ministry in the regions of the Ganges Delta. That is why it is thought that he generally spoke the dialects of Magadha, Kośala and others from neigbouring provinces. He was not attached to any particular language, as he said:

'I allow, monks, each of you to learn the Word of the Buddha in your tongue'[76].

According to tradition, immediately after the decease of the Buddha, his disciples assembled at a Council in Rājagṛha in order to recite and fix his teachings in two collections, namely, the Vinaya, and the Dharma or Sūtras.

After the formation of the schools, these two collections were established in canonical texts, parallel to the output of scholastic works: Abhidharma and Śāstra. Hence the schools separately elaborated their three collections of Canonical Texts or Tripiṭaka.

It is probable that the Pudgalavādins possessed a large collection of canonical and post-canonical texts in relation to the number of their sub-schools: Vātsīputrīyas, Sāṃmitīyas, Dharmottarīyas, Bhadrayānīyas and Ṣaṇṇāgārikas, which lasted for about fifteen centuries. They possessed large numbers of monasteries and monks in comparison to the seventh-century schools.

Since the Sāṃmitīya sub-school rapidly eclipsed the mother school, that of the Vātsīputrīyas, and the three other sub-schools which were too small and which left no trace of literature, it is difficult to distinguish the Sāṃmitīya literature from that of the other four schools.

In this sense, the Sāṃmitīya literature can, in general, be considered as that of the Pudgalavādinṣ.

According to I-ching, the Tripiṭaka of the Sāṃmitīyas contained 200,000 *ślokas* for a single Vinayapiṭaka[77]. Hsüan-tsang had brought back fifteen works of the Tripiṭaka of the Sāṃmitīya school from India, but he did not translate them[78].

The Pudgalavādins have left few traces of their literature. Once and for all, only the following four treatises remain:

---

76 Vin., Cullavagga V, 33, I, p.139: *Anujānāmi bhikkhave sakāya niruttiyā buddhavacanaṃ pariyāpunitum.*

77 J. Takakusu, *Record*, pp.XXIV and 8.

78 Watters, *On Yuan Chwang's Travels in India* I, pp.20–1.

1. The *San fa tu lun* 三法度論 Tridharmakaśāstra (abbrev. Tds) (T XXV, 1506); this is a treatise that systematises the basic doctrinal elements of the Pudgalavādins in general, and the Vātsīputrīyas in particular.

2. The *Ssŭ a-han-mu ch'ao chieh* 四阿鋡暮抄解 (abbrev. *Ssŭ*) (T XXV, 1505); it is probable that this treatise is another version of the Tds since its contents are similar to the latter; also, the same title *San fa tu* 三法度 (Tridharmaka) is indicated in the last line of the text (*Ssŭ*, 15*b* 25);

3. The *San-mi-ti pu lun* 三彌底部論 Sāṃmitīyanikāyaśāstra (abbrev. Sns) (T XXXII, 1649); this treatise elucidates in particular the Sāṃmitīya theses of the *pudgala* and intermediate existence (*antarābhava*), as is indicated by the title.

4. The *Lü êrh-shih-êrh ming-liao lun* 律二十二明了論 Vinayadvāviṃśatividyāśāstra (abbrev. *Lü ming-liao lun*) (T XXIV, 1461); this is a short Vinaya treatise pertaining to the Sāṃmitīyas.

Due to these works, together with the details they supply, we can confirm that the Pudgalavādins, like the Sarvāstivādins, Theravādins, etc., possessed three collections of canonical texts plus some treatises. Here are some justifications of this:

1. Regarding the existence of the Tripiṭaka and its significance, the Tds describes them under the heading of erudition (*bahuśrutatā*) as follows:

> 'Erudition (*bahuśrutatā*) is (comprehension) of Sūtra, Abhidharma and Vinaya . . . Of the three, Sūtras, Abhidharma and Vinaya, the Sūtras (contain the discourses) expounded and approved by the Omniscient One (*sarvajña*). The Sūtras explain the defilements and purities, illustrate the four Noble Truths (*āryasatya*) and the elimination of countless wrongs. The Abhidharma is the exhaustive analysis of the Sūtras. The Vinaya explains conduct and ceremonies leading to purification. These are the three elements of erudition. Of these three elements, the Vinaya especially curbs desire (*kāma*), and the Abhidharma especially curbs hatred (*dveṣa*). The Abhidharma explains the nature of actions (*karmabhava*), that is why it can dispel hatred, which is the cause (*hetu*) of infractions of the discipline (*duḥśīla*). Through such infractions, one falls into the hells. The Sūtras especially curb delusion (*moha*). They explain the twelve factors of dependent origination (*pratītyasamutpāda*)' (Tds, 17*a* 4-13).

2. Substantially the same as the Tds, the *Ssŭ* also mentions the existence of the Tripiṭaka in the definition of erudition (*bahuśrutatā*), the additional commentary to which reaffirms: 'This is the Tripiṭaka' (*Ssŭ*, 2*b* 28).

3. In the *Lü ming-liao lun*, the author notes the existence of the Pudgalavādin Tripiṭaka, saying: 'relying on the Tripiṭaka, the three studies (*śikṣa*) are established' (*Lü ming-liao lun*, 665*c* 14-15).

At all events, we can confirm that the Pudgalavādins had their own texts, as La Vallée Poussin mentions: 'While we are not willing to maximise the importance of the few scriptural texts which affirm the existence of a Self, under the name of *pudgala* (an individual, a person), these texts cannot be ignored altogether. They are old; they are no less authentic than the selflessness texts; they are the authoritative texts of the Sāṃmitīya sect, an important school'[79].

Having affirmed the existence of the Pudgalavādins' three collections of canonical texts, we will examine them in detail, according to the order given by the Tds or *Ssŭ.*

1. *Pudgalavādin Sūtrapiṭaka*

Each school, or group of schools, had its own Āgama or Nikāya, different from those of the other schools and compiled in the language particular to that school (Sanskrit, whether more or less hybrid, Gandhārī, Prākrit, Pāli . . .). At present, apart from the five Nikāyas in Pāli, we still have the four Āgamas in Chinese, and fragments of Āgamas in Sanskrit[80]. The four Āgamas in Chinese were translated between the final years of the fourth century and the middle of the fifth century CE. There are still no integral studies on the origin of the four Āgamas that we possess today in the Chinese translation, except for the Madhyamāgama (*Chung-a-han* 中阿含 , T I, 26 translated by Gautama Saṅghadeva between 397 and 398), which is presented as the work of the Sarvāstivādins[81]. According to Bareau, the Dīrghāgama (*Ch'ang-a-han* 長阿含, T I, 1, 30 sūtras, translated by Buddhayaśas between 412 and 413) pertained to the Dharmaguptakas; the Ekottarāgama (*Tsêng-i-a-han* 增一阿含 , T II, 125, translated by Gautama Saṅghadeva between 397 and 398) seems to belong to the Mahāsāṃghikas; the Samyuktāgama (*Tsa-a-han* 雜阿含 , T II, 99, 1,362 sūtras, translated by Guṇabhadra between 436 and 443) probably comes from a school connected with the Sthaviras, the Sarvāstivāda.

There is another partial Saṃyuktāgama (*Pieh-i tsa-a-han* 別譯雜阿含 , T II, 100, 364 sūtras), translated by an unknown hand in the year 400 and which pertained to the Kāśyapīya school, according to Lamotte[82].

Tao-an 道安 (312-385)[83], in his preface to the *Ssŭ*, confirms that the *Ssŭ* or the Tds is a summary of the four Āgamas or the twelve sections (*dvādaśāṅga*)[84] (Preface

---

79 La Vallée Poussin, *The Way to Nirvāṇa*, pp.133–4.

80 Cf. Minh Chau, *The Chinese Madhyama Āgama and the Pāli Majjhima Nikāya*, pp.19–20.

81 *Ibid.*, p.18.

82 É. Lamotte, *History*, p.154.

83 Tao–an 道安 (312–385), born into a family already famous for its studies of the classics, was drawn to Buddhism while still quite young. He studied the canonical texts at Lo–yang, where he also took instruction on Buddhism from the best intellectuals who were shortly to become the most respected teachers in the whole country, then subjected to the Northern Wei (北魏 386–416 CE). He invited to China many Indian scholars, then settled in Central Asia, to teach Buddhism and translate Buddhist texts. Tao–an himself was not a translator or direct collaborator but acted as general manager or adviser playing an extremely important part in the translating activities. He wrote several prefaces to translations of that time and Kumārajīva called him 'The Saint of the East'. Cf. *Kao* V, T L, 2059, 351c 4; E. Zürcher, *The Buddhist Conquest of China*, pp.187–204; Ui Hakuju 宇井伯壽 , *Shaku Dōan kenkyū* 釋道安研究 Tokyo 1956.

84 The twelve sections including those of the texts of the Small Vehicle (*dvādaśāṅga*) constitute a traditional classification of all the Sanskrit Buddhist texts, which is distinct from another classification of texts consisting of only nine sections. They are:

1. *Suttas*: discourses by the Buddha and others.
2. *Geyas*: discourses with verses.
3. *Vyākaraṇas*: solemn statements, announcements, predictions.

to the *Ssû a-han*, 1*a*). Furthermore, through the additonal commentary on the word *sūtra* in the same text, its translator Kumārabuddhi[85] writes:

'The Sūtras, that is, the four Āgamas which are the explanation of the twelve sections' (*Ssŭ*, 2*b* 27). However, we have no information enabling us to know which kind of Āgama is indicated by Tao-an and Kumārabuddhi since there are, in fact, many collections bearing the name Āgama. What did the Sūtrapiṭaka or the four Āgamas of the Pudgalavādins contain? Until now we have received no clarification and the question remains unanswered. Hence, although the four Āgamas which Kumārabuddhi indicates are not the four Āgamas which exist in Chinese translation, it cannot be denied that the Pudgalavādins certainly possessed their own Sūtrapiṭaka.

Moreover, several titles of discourses appear in the existing treatises, for example: *Shêng fa yin ching* 聖法印經, Āryadharmamudrāsūtra (Tds, 19*a* 19)[86]; *Shuo ch'u ching* 說處經, Deśanasthānaśāstra (Tds, 19*a* 23)[87] (the same two titles exist respectively in the *Ssŭ*, 4*b* 17; 4*c* 21); *Tsui-shang-nü-jên hsiu-to- lo* 最上女人修多羅 Uttamāstrīsūtra (Sns, 463*a* 25); *Pa-ch'a-yeh-na hsiu-to- lo* 跋蹉耶那修多羅 Vātsyāyanasūtra (Sns, 471a 12), etc.

---

4. *Gāthās*: stanzas.
5. *Nidānas*: introductions of circumstances.
6. *Udānas*: elevated utterances.
7. *Ityuktas*: 'Thus has it been said's.
8. *Jātakas*: stories of former births.
9. *Vaipulyas*: developed texts.
10. *Adbhūtadharmas*: stories of marvels.
11. *Avadānas*: various adventures.
12. *Upadeśas*: detailed explanations.

The nine sections of the Pāli Canon are found in MN I, 133; AN II, 103, 178; III, 86, 117:

1. *Suttas*, 2. *Geyyas*, 3. *Veyyākaranas*, 4. *Gāthās*, 5. *Udānas*, 6. *Itivuttakas*, 7. *Jātakas*, 8. *Abbhutadhammas*, 9. *Vedallas*.

On this subject, cf. Lamotte, *History*, pp.143–8; *L'Inde classique* II, §§ 1746–2003.

85 On the biography of Kumārabuddhi, see below, 'The translators of the *Ssŭ a-han-mu ch'ao chieh*'.

86 *Shêng fa yin ching* 聖法印經 or *Fo shuo shêng fa yin ching* 佛說聖法印經, T II, 103, 500*a–b*, translated by Shu Fa-hu 竺法護 (Dharmarakṣa) of Yüeh-chih origin, born in Tun-huang 敦煌 under the Western Chin (*Hsi Chin* 西晉) dynasty, deals with the following basic points:

1. Emptiness (*k'ung* 空 *śūnyatā*), 2. signlessness (*wu-hsiang* 無想, *asaṃjña = animitta*), 3. wishlessness (*wu-yü* 無欲 = *wu-yüan* 無願, *apraṇihita*), 4. consciousness is dependently originated, that is why it is impermanent and empty; consequently pride and immodesty have no basis.

There is another discourse, the title and contents of which are similar to the former: this is the *Fa yin ching* 法印經 or *Fo shuo fa yin ching* 佛說法印經, T II, 104, 500*b-c*, translated by Shih Hu 詩護 (Dānapāla ?). It deals with the following basic points: 1. the nature of emptiness (*k'ung hsing* 空性, *śūnyatatā*), 2. the three doors to deliverance: a) deliverance through the concentration on emptiness (*k'ung chieh t'uo mên* 空解脫門), b) deliverance through the concentration on signlessness (*wu hsiang chieh t'uo mên* 無想解脫門), c) deliverance through the concentration on non-action (*wu tso chieh t'uo mên* 無作解脫門).

87 According to Leon Hurvitz, *Shuo ch'u ching* 說處經 (Deśanasthānaśāstra) is the name of two treatises in the Madhyamāgama (26–86, T I, 26 562*a*–566*a*; 29–110 *ibid.*, 609). The first is similar to the Chachakkasutta of MN, No.148. However, in these three discourses there is no passage corresponding to that cited. Cf. L. Hurvitz, 'The Road to Buddhist Salvation as Described by Vasubhadra', JAOS 87, No.4, Oct.–Dec 1967, p.439, n.51.

On the other hand, owing to several passages from extant texts and also to other equivalent sources, in either Chinese or Pāli, we can infer the titles of these discourses. The idea of a good life-style without a family is expressed in the Tds, 17*b* 12:

'The peacock (*barhin*, *mayāra*) with majestic wings
and wondrously decorated green plumage
will nonetheless never catch up with
the wild goose (*haṃsa*) in flight.
Equally, the householder (*gṛhi*)
will never equal the monk (*pravrajita*)
who lives in serenity, far (from all care).
Leisurely, seated, he is absorbed in meditation (*dhyāna*)'[88].

Ssŭ, 3*a* 17-19:

'Just as the peacock with the lovely green neck
Does not equal the wild goose in flight,
So the layman is not like
a monk, a sage (*muni*) who meditates in solitude'[89].

These two passages with the same contents resemble the following passage which is found in Pāli in the Munisutta of Sn:

'Just as the peacock will never attain
the speed of a wild goose,
So the householder
can never resemble a monk,
a sage meditating in solitude in the forest'[90].

Another example is in Sns, 466*c* 2-3:

'As the *T'ien-shi hsiu-to-lo* 天使修多羅
(Devadūtasūtra: 'Discourse of the heavenly messenger') says:
"He speaks to King Yama: that person formerly

---

88 Tds, 17*b*–12: 如飾葉鳥青鵾妙色
終不能及鵝鷹飛行
在家如是不及比丘
牟尼遠離閑居坐禪

89 *Ssŭ*, 3*a* 17–19 如孔雀好青項鳥
飛行不如野鷹步
如是白衣不似比
立牟尼坐空野禪

90 Sn, 221: *Sikhī yathā nīlagīvo vihaṅgamo*
haṃsassa nopeti javaṃ kudācanaṃ
evaṃ gihī nanukarotti bhikkhuno
munino vivittassa vanamhi jhāyato ti.

In the *Traité* I, p.232, there is another verse expressing similar ideas, the origin of which is unknown:

'The peacock (*barhin*, *mayura*), despite its splendid body,
Cannot fly as far as the swan (*haṃsa*),
In the same way, the layman (*avadātavasana*), despite his fortune and nobility,
Cannot equal the monk (*pravrajita*) whose qualities are prominent'.

recognised neither his parents, nor his brothers, etc.;
he recognised neither merit, nor good, nor bad, etc.
I wish (Your Majesty) to teach him . . .'"[91].

This passage has its equivalent in following Pāli passage from the Devadūtasutta in AN:

'Then the guardians of hell hold him by both arms
and lead him to Yama, the king (of death), saying:
"This person, Your Majesty, has not respected either his mother,
or his father, or monks, or brahmins;
he has not revered the family elders.
I wish Your Majesty to punish him!"'[92].

The same context, but not word-for-word text, is found in the *T'ien-shih ching* 天使經 (Devadūtasūtra. 'Discourse of the Heavenly Messenger') in Chinese in MĀ (T I, 503*c* 25):

'The man of King Yama seizes and then leads (the hell-bound) to the king's residence and says: "This living being, when he was a man, had no filial piety towards his parents, nor respected monks or brahmins; did not practise in accordance with the truth, did not perform meritorious acts, did not fear (the result) of misdeeds in the future life. May Your Majesty condemn him according to his misdeeds"'[93].

Another example, in Sns, 463*b* 11:

'The Buddha said: "The burden is the five aggregates; the bearer is the person"'[94].

and Sns, 465*b* 10:

'Basing oneself on the burden, one says that (the bearer of the burden) exists'[95].

and Sns, 463*b* 9-12:

'Furthermore, some schools admit that the person is different from the five aggregates. Why? Answer — Because it is like a person bearing a burden'.

'The Buddha said: "The burden is the five aggregates; the bearer is the person". Hence, the person is separate from the five aggregates. That is why the

---

91 Sns, 446*c* 2–3: 如天使修多羅所說：上啓閻羅，此人先不知父母兄弟等
不知功德；不知善惡等，願教其如是

92 AN I, 138: *'Tam enaṃ bhikkhave niryapālā nānā bāhāsu gahetvā Yamassa rañño dassenti: Ayaṃ eva puriso ametteyo apetteyo asāmañño abrahmañño na kule jeṭṭhāpacāyī, imassa devo daṇḍaṃ paṇetū ti'*

There is another discourse also entitled Devadūtasutta, MN, No.130, but in the paragraph expressing similar ideas (MN III, 179) the word *apetteyo* (. . . or his father) is missing.

93 *T'ien-shih ching* 天使經：, T I, 26, 503*c*: 25–29: 閻王人收送詣王所白曰： 天王此眾生本為人時，不孝父母，不知尊敬沙門梵志，不行如實，不作福業，不畏後世罪，唯願天王處當其罪。

There are other discourses, the contents of which are similar to the passage mentioned, for example:

1. *T'ien ch'ang ni-li ching* 鐵 城 泥 犁 經 (T I, 42, 826*c*–828*b*).
2. *Yen-lo wang wu t'ien shih chê ching* 閻羅王五千使者經 (T I, 43, 826*b*–829b).
3. EĀ, T II, 125, 674*b*–676*b* (*T'ien-tsê ching*).

94 Sns, 463*b* 11: 重擔是五陰擔者是人，如是

95 Sns, 465*b* 10: 依擔故說有擔.

person is different from the aggregates'[96].

The three passages above are certainly found in a sūtra with a similar title to that of the Pāli: Bhāra(hāra)-sutta in SN III, 25, the following sentence of which is characteristic:

'The burden is really the five aggregates.
The bearer of the burden is the person'[97].

The contents of the Sns here are also similar to those of two Chinese translations of the *Chung-tan ching*, 重擔經, the original texts of which are different: one is in the SĀ (T II, 99, 19*a*), the other in the EĀ (T II, 125, 631*c*)[98].

Another example in Sns, 463*c* 4-5:

'The cycle of birth and death in which all
living beings turn is without beginning.
The origin of birth and death is inconceivable'[99]

This passage recalls the Pāli discourse in the Tiṇakaṭṭhasutta in SN (II, 178):

---

96 Sns, 463*b* 12: 又諸部説人異五陰，何以故。答如擔重擔人故，佛言重擔是五陰。擔者是人，如是，以是故人與因各，是故與陰異，如是。

97 SN III, 25: *Bhārāhave pañcakkhandhā,*
bhārahāro ca puggalo.

The Tds does not contain any trace of a discourse with a title and contents similar to the Bhārahārasutta. In the Sns there is proof of the use of this kind of discourse not only by the Pudgalavādins (Sns, 465*b* 9–10: 我等今説，依擔故説有擔(人)，我等 , here, indicates the Sāṃmitīyas or Pudgalavādins) but also by other schools which maintain that the person is different from the aggregates (Sns, 463*b* 9–10: 又諸部説人異五陰，何以故。 答如擔重擔人故，佛言重擔是五陰，擔者是人如是。

The *Kośa* IX, p.256; Eng. tr. p.1328, asserts that the Vātsīputrīyas made use of the arguments in this discourse to establish the thesis of the *pudgala* by registering the words of the Vātsīputrīyas as follows: 'If the *pudgala* is not the name given to the elements, it cannot be the bearer of the burden. Why? — Simply because it is unheard of'. Whereas the Vijñānakāyapādaśāstra of Devaśarman, by refuting the thesis of the *pudgala*, does not mention the status of the discourse as the basic text of the Pudgalavādin school. (Cf. *Kośa*, Introd. — Fragment of Kārikās — Index — Additions).

98 Here are the two different main paragraphs of these two discourses:

1) SĀ, T II, 99, 19*a* 22–24:

What does the bearer of the burden mean? It is the person with such and such a name, such and such a birth, such and such a family, such and such food, such and such pleasant or unpleasant feelings, such and such a longevity, such and such a stay, such and such a limited life (云何擔者？謂士夫是。士夫者，如是名，如是生，如是性族，如是食，如是 受苦樂，如是長壽，如是久住，如是壽命齊限)

2) SĀ, T II, 99, 631*c* ·18–23:

Why it is called the bearer of the burden? The bearer of the burden is the human body with such and such a first name, such and such a surname, such and such a birth: (it) eats such and such food, possesses such and such pleasant or unpleasant feelings; its life is long or short; that is what is called the bearer of the burden, that is the conditions of desire and attachment. It is not separate from craving and associated mental states. That is what is called the condition of the burden (彼云何名為持擔人，所謂持擔仁者，人生是也。字某名某，如是生，食如是食 ，受如是苦樂，壽命長短是謂名為持擔人，彼云何名為擔因緣。所謂擔因緣者 愛者因緣是與欲共俱心不違，是謂名為擔因緣。

99 Sns, 463*c* 4–5. 生死無本眾生輪轉，生死原本不可知如是

> 'Monks, the beginning of the cycle of rebirth of beings is inconceivable. It is impossible to discover the first point from which beings, veiled in ignorance, fettered by craving, wanders at random from birth to birth.'[100].

This is the same discourse in Chinese: *Wu-chih ching* 無始經 of SĀ (T II, 99, *69b-c*):

> 'The cycle of birth and death is beginningless; it is veiled in ignorance, fettered by the bonds of craving; in this very long round of rebirth, the origin of suffering cannot be known'[101].

The writings of the Pudgalavādins are virtually all lost. Consequently, it is difficult to ascertain out what characterised their collections of canonical texts. Nonetheless, while waiting for a full comparison of the Āgamas of the Dharmaguptakas, Mahāsāṃghikas, Sarvāstivādins, etc., we believe the majority of main points of the three doctrinal treatises, namely, the Tds, *Ssū* and Sns, are identical to those of the Pāli texts. It is probable that *both* schools started out from the same source for their canons. There are certainly divergencies between the two canonical collections of texts of the two schools — Pudgalavādin and Theravādin — over certain specific points, but not over general ideas; over the letter but not the spirit. There are doctrinal affinities between the two canons. As La Vallée Poussin wrote:

> 'The Pāli Canon contains the majority of documents which are relied on by the partisans — heretics in the eyes of the Pāli school — on the permanent principle and "docetism"'[102].

Hence, we can conclude that the Pudgalavādins not only composed orally but also fixed in writing their own Sūtrapiṭaka.

2. *The Pudgalavādin Abhidharmapiṭaka*

The Abhidharmapiṭaka played a very important role in the separation of the Buddhist schools. Whilst the Sūtrapiṭaka was the joint inheritance of the doctrine of all the schools and the Vinayapiṭaka the rules of the life of the community of monks, only the Abhidharmapiṭaka was the systematisation of the teachings contained in the sūtras according to the more or less free interpretation of individuals or groups. Generally, each school or sub-school had its Abhidharmapiṭaka in which its doctrinal interpretations were delineated and defended.

Consequently, except for a few schools such as the Sautrāntikas and Mahāsaṃghikas[103], nearly all the schools compiled their Abhidharma or their śāstras to illustrate their doctrinal point of view. Several schools possessed a very developed

---

100 SN II, 178 (Tiṇakaṭṭhasutta): *Anamataggāyaṃ bhikkhave saṃsāro pubbākoṭi na paññāyati avijjānīvarāṇanaṃ sattānaṃ taṇhāsaṃyojānaṃ sandhāvataṃ saṃsaratam.*

101 SĀ, T II, 99, 69*b* 5–6: 於無始生死，無明所蓋，愛結所繫， 長夜輪迴不知苦之本際。

and SĀ, T II, 99, 69*c* 3–5: 眾生於無始生死，無明所蓋，愛結所繫，長夜輪迴生死，不知苦際。

102 Tr. after La Vallée Poussin, *Nirvāṇa*, p.23, n.l.

103 Lamotte, *History*, p.181.

Abhidharmapiṭaka, such as the Theravādins[104] or Sarvāstivādins[105].

With regard to the Pudgalavādin Abhidharmapiṭaka, as things are at present, we have not yet found any of that type of text, except for treatises (*śāstra*) which we are still studying. However, it is from these treatises that we learn that the Pudgalavādins assuredly possessed Abhidharma texts.

We often find the word Abhidharma in them, such as in the second collection, in the Tds (17*a* 5 ff, 30*a* 7) and the Sns (2*b* 28; 15*b* 18); in the *Lü ming-liao lun* in particular, the word Abhidharma appears frequently. Also, in this first Vinaya text, the Abhidharma is used as a point of reference in the explanations of mental states in relation to the observance of the precepts, as it says: 'The literature of the Vinaya and Abhidharma illustrates the correspondence between the precepts (*śīla*) and the man who observes them' (*Lü ming-liao lun*, 665*b* 18-19)[106].

On the other hand, a later tradition claims that the Vātsīputrīyas inherited a book of Abhidharma in nine parts and, not satisfied with that Abhidharma, the descendents of the Vātsīputrīyas subdivided into four lesser schools in order to remedy the discrepancies of that book.

It says in the Mahāprajñāpāramitopadeśa:

> 'Some say: "When the Buddha was in this world, Śāriputra, in order to explain the Buddha's words, compiled the Abhidharma. Later, the *T'u tzŭ* (Vātsīputrīya) monks recited (that work). Until this day, this is what is known as the *Shê-li-fu-a-p'i-t'an* 舍利弗阿毘曇 (Śāriputrābhidharma, T XXVIII 1548)"'[107].

and

> . . . In the *Tu-tzŭ-êrh-a-p'i-t'an* (Vātsīputrīyābhidharma), the *saṃyojanas* are the same, but the *paryavasthānas* are 500 in number'[108].

---

104 The Theravādin Abhidhammapiṭaka consists of seven books: 1. Dhammasaṅgaṇī, enumeration of phenomena; 2. Vibhaṅga, classifications; 3. Dhātukathā, discussion of elements; 4. Puggalapaññatti, description of persons; 5. Kathāvatthu, points of controversy; 6. Yamaka, questions in pairs; 7. Paṭṭhāna, on origination; cf. an analysis of these seven books in Nyanatiloka, *Guide through the Abhidhamma-Piṭaka*, 3rd ed. Kandy 1971; A. Bareau, *Dhammasaṅgaṇi*, annotated tr. Paris 1951, E. Lamotte, *History*, p.181–4; Bareau, *Religions*, p.95.

105 cf. above, Ch.I, n.30.

106 · This stanza and its commentary prove that the Sāṃmitīyas or Pudgalavādins possessed their own Abhidharmapiṭaka. For example, when explaining the stanza, the commentary gives the exact figures of the correspondence between the man and the observance of the rules to be observed in order to dispel defiled thoughts: 588 (= 294 defiled thoughts + 294 observances and, in the totality of defiled thoughts, the observance in relation to the three worlds: 1658 — 972 in the Kāmadhātu + 544 in the Rūpadhātu + 142 in the Ārūpyadhātu (cf. *Lü ming-liao lun*, 665*b–c* 8).

107 *Traité* I, p.112.

108 *ibid.*, p.424. This is further proof that the Vātsīputrīyas possessed their own Abhidharmapiṭaka. The Tds confirms that there are 98 *saṃyojanas*, latent defilements, the same number as with the Sarvāstivādins, *Kośa*, V, p.9 and n.2; Engl. tr., pp.772 and n.21: The 6 *anuśayas* — *rāga*, *pratigha*, *māna*, *avidyā*, *dṛṣṭi*, *vimati* — (*Kośa* V, p.2, Engl. tr., p.767) make 10, according to their nature, divided into five *dṛṣṭis*. They make 98 by counting 36 *anuśayas* in the Kāmadhātu, 31 in the Rūpadhātu and 31 in the Ārūpyadhātu. On the 500 *paryavasthānas*, active defilements, cf. *P'i-ni-mu ching* 毘尼母經 ,(T XXIV, 1463, p.860; *Hōbōgirin*, 'Bonnō', p.124).

The Pudgalavādins distinguished the latent defilements (*anuśaya* = *saṃyojana*) from the active

In Paramārtha's commentary on the 'Treatise of Vasubandhu', the information is more precise:

> 'Śāriputra had developed the Abhidharma in nine parts; that is what is known as the 'Abhidharma of the Characteristics of the Dharma' (Dharmalakṣaṇābhidharma). Rāhula, Śāriputra's disciple, transmitted the Abhidharma to the Arhat Vatsyaputra, and the latter's disciples formed the Vātsīputrīya school. Then, within three hundred years, from the Vātsīputrīya school emerged a further four schools: the Dharmottarīya, Bhadrayānīya, Sāṃmitīya, and Ṣaṇḍa or Ṣaṇṇāgārika. Dissatisfied with the Śāriputrābhidharma, which they considered incomplete, they each compiled śāstras in order to complete [the Śāriputrābhidharma] wherever it was deficient'[109].

In fact, there is now in existence no actual Abhidharma book bearing the title 'Śāriputrābhidharma' or 'Dharmalakṣaṇābhidharma' in nine parts and containing the doctrine characteristic of the Vātsīputrīyas, particularly the thesis of the *pudgala*. There is a voluminous treatise in Chinese entitled Śāriputrābhidharmaśāstra, translated by Dharmayaśas assisted by Dharmagupta in Ch'ang-an 長安 between 407 and 408. The work is divided into four parts and refutes the thesis of the *pudgala* and intermediate existence (*antarābhava*)[110]. In brief, the Śāriputrābhidharmaśāstra did not belong to the Pudgalavādins but most probably to the Dharmaguptakas[111].

Thus we can say that, until now, we have only rediscovered Pudgalavādin śāstras but no Abhidharma texts despite indications that a Pudgalavādin Abhidharma did exist.

3. *The Pudgalavādin Vinayapiṭaka*

The Vinaya, or Basket of the Disciplinary Code of the community of monks, is the collection which preserves the tradition of that community and reflects the break-up of the communities into various schools. After the first Buddhist schism caused by the dispute over the ten disciplinary usages and dissensions caused by doctrinal differentiations, each school retained and developed its collection of disciplinary writings (Vinayapiṭaka).

Consequently, we possess at present different texts concerning the Vinayapiṭaka, namely:

a) that of the Theravādins in Pāli[112],

b) the Chinese translations of those of the Sarvāstivādins (T XXII, 1428), Mahāsāṃghikas (T XXII, 1425), Mahīśākas (T XXII, 1421) and Mūlasarvāstivādins (T

---

defilements (*paryavasthāna*). The former are seeds remaining dissociated from thought, they do not involve moral causality and are neutral in moral conflict. The latter are associated with thought and participate directly in antagonistic moral forces. (Tr. after A. Bareau, 'Richesse et diversité de la pensée bouddhique ancienne', *Présence du Bouddhisme*, p.459.

109 Tr. after Demiéville, 'L'origine', pp.57–8.

110 Cf. Bareau, 'Les origines du Śāriputrābhidharmaśāstra', *Muséon* LXII, 1–2, pp.5–6.

111 Cf. *ibid.*, p.26.

112 The Theravādin Vinayapiṭaka: Suttavibhaṅga, Khandhaka and Parivāra. The five volumes edited by H. Oldenberg in the PTS edition are well presented. A complete English translation by I.B. Horner is also published by the PTS.

XIII, 1442 and following),

c) the Tibetan translation of the latter,

d) Sanskrit fragments of those of the Sarvāstivādins, Mūlasarvastivādins and Lokottaravādins; also commentaries belonging to the Sāṃmitīyas, Kāśyapīyas, Mahāsāṃghikas and other undetermined schools[113].

As for the Vinayapiṭaka of the Pudgalavādins, all we can find is a single treatise of commentaries, the *Lü ming-liao lun*, which is attributed to the Sāṃmitīyas. However, having the highest number of monks and monasteries of the whole community which existed for several centuries, and which were also 'reputed to be more attached to the Vinaya than the other Piṭakas'[114], the Pudgalavādins certainly possessed a considerable Vinaya collection. The *Lü ming-liao lun* commentary supplies us with valuable data on this subject.

I-ching tells us of the existence of a Sāṃmitīya Vinaya which, he says, contained 30,000 *ślokas*[115].

a — *The Vinaya texts*

Due to the *Lü ming-liao lun*, we know in detail a certain number of the Vinaya texts of the Sāṃmitīyas which contained 420 precepts uttered by the Tathāgata as well as a Prātimokṣa treatise:

1. *P'o-shu-tou lü* 婆數斗律
   (Vastuvinaya) (*Lü ming-liao lun*, 666*a* 7) : 200 precepts.
2. *Yu-pa-t'i-she lü* 優波提舍律
   (Upadeśavinaya) (*Lü ming-liao lun*, 666*a* 8) : 121 precepts.
3) *Pi-ch'iu-ni lü* 比丘尼律
   (Bhikṣuṇīvinaya) (*Lü ming-liao lun*, 666*a* 8-9) : 99 precepts.
4. *Po-lo-t'i-mu ch'a lun* 波羅提木叉論
   (Prātimokṣaśāstra) (*Lü ming-liao lun*, 666*a* 13).

Moreover, in this work we find precise ideas of the structure of the Pudgalavādin Vinaya:

b — *The structure of the Vinaya*

The Pudgalavādins divided their Vinaya into nine catgories:

1. Vinaya of the monks (*bhikṣuvinaya*), dealing with the rules specific to monks;
2. Vinaya of the nuns (*bhikṣuṇīvinaya*), dealing with the rules specific to nuns;
3. Vinaya of both communities (*bhikṣubhikṣuṇīvinaya*), dealing with the rules common to the monks and nuns, for example, the first *pārājika*;
4. Vinaya dealing with offences, causes of offences and means of making amends;
5. Vinaya dealing with doubts, the definitive absence of consciousness or death;

113 On the Vinayapiṭakas of the different schools, cf. the analytical description in Lamotte, *History*, pp.165–79.

114 Tr. after Demiéville, *L'Inde classique* II, § 2317.

115 Takakusu, *Record*, pp.XXIV and 8.

6. Vinaya dealing with resolutions, ten types of training (*śaikṣa*)[116] ;
7. Vinaya dealing with non-resolutions, the spontaneous origin of the 42,000 types of training after the end of the formal propositions (*karmavācanā*)[117] ;
8. Vinaya dealing with applications at a single time, practices for receiving ordination, for bathing, etc.;
9. Vinaya dealing with applications at all times of training that should be practised together and at all times (*Lü ming-liao lun*, 666*a* 7 - *b* 11).

The Pudgalavādin Bhikṣuṇīprātimokṣa consists of nine categories of precepts and seven groups of offences.

— Five categories of precepts:

1. *Po-lo-i* 波羅夷 (*Pārājikas*) : 6 offences
2. *Sêng-ch'ih-ti* Shih-sha 僧伽胝施沙 (*Saṅghādisesas*) : 52 offences
3. *Po-lo-i-ni-ka* 波羅逸尼柯 (*Pārāsarnikas*) : 360 offences
4. *Po-ti-t'i-sha-ni* 波胝提舍尼 (*Pratideśanīyas*) : 12 offences
5. *Tu-k'a-to* 獨柯多 (*Duṣkṛtas*) : offences

which are not included in the four preceding categories (*śaikṣa*) or in the offences mentioned in the *P'o-shu-tou-lü* 婆藪斗律 (Vinayavastu). Cf. *Lü ming-liao lun*, 666*b* 13-18).

— Seven groups of offences:

1. *Pārājikas* : 4 offences leading to defeat.
2. *Saṅghādisesas*: 13 offences leading to temporary exclusion from the Community[118].
3. *Sthūlātyayas* (*T'ou-lan-chih-yeh* 偷蘭遮耶, *Lü ming-liao lun*, 666*c* 6): offences not justifying classification in the preceding two groups.
4. *Niḥsargika pārāsarnikas* (*Ni-sa-ch'i-po-lo-i--ni-k'a* 尼薩耆波羅逸尼柯, *Lü ming-liao lun*, 666*c* 8): 30 offences leading to the relinquishment of objects obtained unduly.
5. *Pārāsarnikas*: 90 offences to be declared.

---

116 A detailed commentary is lacking. It could be that these are the well-known ten rules of training (*śikṣāpada* or *sikkhāpada*). The novice should abstain from: 1. taking life (*pāṇātipāta*), 2. theft (*adinnādāna*), 3. sexual relations (*abrahmacariya*), 4. falsehood (*musāvāda*), 5. spirituous drinks (*sūramerayamajjapamādaṭṭhāna*), 6. meals at the wrong time (*vikālabhojana*), 7. attending worldly entertainments (*naccagītavāditavisūkadassana*), 8. the use of unguents, perfume and bodily ornaments (*mālāgandhavilepanadhāraṇamaṇḍanavibhūsanaṭṭhāna*), sleeping on a bed which is too high or wide (*uccāsayanamahāsayana*), 10. accepting gold or silver (*jātarūparajatapaṭigghaṇa*). After *Traité* **II**, p.847, n.3. Cf. Vin. I, pp.83–4; II, p.258; AN I, p.221.

117 The commentary merely mentions 42,000 types of training, without any explanation. It could be that there is a link between them and the 42,000 merits (*puṇya*) which can purify the defilement of the transgression of morality and which are divided as follows: 420 precepts (Vastuvinaya, 200 + Upadeśavinaya, 121 + Bhikṣuṇīvinaya, 99) each of which produces 10 merits; each merit, in turn, produces 10 good factors (5 faculties (*indriya*) + 3 roots (*mūla*) + 2 bodily and vocal observances). That makes 420 precepts x 10 merits x 10 good factors = 42,000 merits. Cf. *Lü ming-liao lun*, 666*a* 5–14.

118 The Pudgalavādin Vinaya uses the term *saṅghādisesa*, reconstructed by the Chinese notes: *sêng-ch'ieh-ti-shih-sha* 僧伽胝施沙 (*Lü ming-liao lun*, 666*c* 5), but not *saṃghāvaśeṣa*, often found in the Sanskrit texts.

6. *Pratideśanīyas*: 4 offences concerning meals not conforming to the rules.
7. *Śaikṣadharmas* (*Hsue tui* 學對 , *Lü ming-liao lun*, 666*c* 11): offences not belonging to the six preceding groups.

It is noteworthy that the commentary on the text does not give the number of articles in the *śaikṣadharma* group. Only the number of articles in the main groups are stated. There are 141 articles in all. By comparing the number of articles in the main categories, other than those of the Prātimokṣa, there is no difference between those of the various Prātimokṣas, except for the Mahīśāsaka Prātimokṣa (T XXII, 1421) which counts 91 *pārāsarnikas* instead of 90. Later, it is in the number of *śaikṣadharmas* which the schools or sub-schools added separately to the Prātimokṣas that the latter differ from each other. The following table shows the similarities and differences of the number of articles of the precepts in the extant Vinayas:

Vinaya of the	Extant today in	Number of *śaikṣadharmas*	Total of precepts
Pudgalavādins	Chinese	unknown	141
Theravādins	Pāli	75	227
Mahāsāṃghikas	Chinese	66	218
Sarvāstivādins (Prātimokṣa)	Chinese	113	263
Vaibhāṣikas (Vinaya)	Chinese	91	241
Dharmaguptakas	Chinese	100	250
Mūlasarvāstivādins	Tibetan	98	248
Kāśyapīyas			
Mahīśāskas	Chinese (*pārāsarnikas*: 91)	100 100	251 251

In the conduct and monastic traditions of the Sāṃmitīyas, apart from the abundance of material found in the *Lü ming-liao lun*, we have discovered details of some of their specific rules:

> 'The lower section of their monastic clothing was cut according to an irregular shape; they slept in kinds of enclosures demarcated by ropes and serving as communal dormitories[119]. Their robes (*cīvara*) were made up of 21 or 24

119 Bareau, *Sectes*, p.122; J. Takakusu, *Record*, p.7.

pieces[120] and their emblems were *sorcika* flowers like those of the Theravādins[121]. They draped their upper robe in the manner of Indian women, gathering the right edge on the left side and leaving the ends floating free'[122].

In brief, although the texts of the Pudgalavādin Vinaya no longer exist, apart from the very informative *Lü ming-liao lun*, we can conclude that the Pudgalavādins possessed a considerable Vinayapiṭaka.

II – *LANGUAGES USED BY THE PUDGALAVĀDINS*

The literature of the Pudgalavādins is virtually entirely lost, except for a few post-canonical treatises. This is why it is difficult to give an idea of the languages used by the Pudgalavādins, particularly to record their writings.

Furthermore, the history of the Personalist schools lasted for more than ten centuries, and their geographical expansion covered all the regions of India. This is the second reason why we cannot determine their method of written expression. A well-known Tibetan tradition records that the Sāṃmitīyas used Apabraṃśa as the language of their texts[123]. This language, in fact, appeared before Sanskrit as the inheritor of Prākrit which it survived for a few centuries[124].

---

120 There are three kinds of *saṅghāti*: the least, middling and best [in quality], each of which are subdivided into three:

1. The least three are made with 9, 11 and 13 bands of material or rags (each band consists of 2 long pieces and 1 short one);

2. the middling three, with 15, 17 and 19 (each band: 3 long and 1 short);

3. the best three, with 21, 23 and 25 (each band: 4 long and 1 short); the Pudgalavādins used only the three best ones.

The Sarvāstivādin Vinaya mentions the three types of *saṅghāti*, whilst the Dharmaguptaka Vinaya only mentions the first two; that is, the Dharmaguptakas differed from the Pudgalavādins by not using the three best robes. Cf. Mochizuki Shinko 望月信亨, *Bukkyō Daijiten* 佛教大辭典, vol. V, 3046 *abc*.

This is the design of a *saṅghāti* consisting of nine bands each of which is made of two long pieces and one short one:

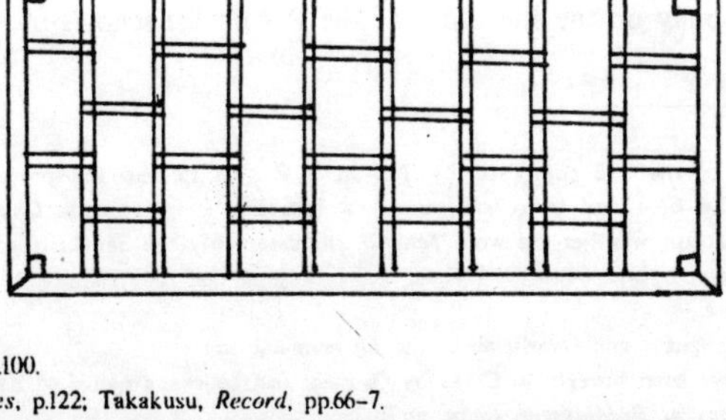

121 *Bu-ston*, II, p.100.

122 Bareau, *Sectes*, p.122; Takakusu, *Record*, pp.66–7.

123 Cf. P.C. Bagchi, 'On the Original Buddhism, Its Canon and Language', *Sino-Indian Studies* II, p.108.

124 *L'Inde classique* II, § 2410.

Notwithstanding, with the literary documentation we have, we can infer that, before the fifth century CE, the Pudgalavādins used Middle-Indian dialects, Prākrit, Sanskrit and hybrid Sanskrit and, from the seventh century onwards, Apabraṃśa.

On the use of languages by the Pudgalavādins before the fifth century CE, we do however have some indications. Among the four treatises from which Chinese translations were made in the fourth and fifth centuries CE, the Sns, translated in 385-431 (?) CE, must have been taken from a text written in a Middle-Indian dialect of the North-West: either Prākrit, or Apabraṃśa, but more likely in mixed or Buddhist Sanskrit, since the transcription and style appear to be the same as those of the languages we find in other treatises.

The Tds, translated in 384-417 CE, and the *Ssŭ*, translated in 382 CE, must have been texts in mixed or Buddhist Sanskrit, a kind of Sanskrit mixing Prākrit and pure Sanskrit, as these texts indicate (*Ssŭ*, 15*b* 27)[125].

As for the *Lü ming-liao lun*, translated in 568 CE, this was a text in Buddhist Sanskrit[126]. On the other hand, the Tds was compiled and preserved in the course of the first centuries CE by monks from Kashmir[127] which was the centre of Buddhist studies in Sanskrit, not only of the Sarvāstivādins but also the Pudgalavādins[128].

The above proposition is reasonable since it is progressively confirmed by the observations of Orientalists, among whom É. Lamotte is one of the most qualified, regarding the use of languages by Buddhists throughout the centuries some hundreds of years after the decease of the Buddha at the beginning of the Common Era: 'During the last centuries of the ancient era, the Buddhist literature used only Middle-Indian Prākrits: Māgadhī, North-Western Prākrit (Gāndhārī) and Pāli. During the first three centuries of the Christian era, these Prākrits were strongly rivalled by the use of mixed Sanskrit. Finally, from the beginning of the Gupta dynasty (fourth cent. A.D.), Buddhist Sanskrit, which was relatively correct, finally replaced the Prākrits and mixed Sanskrit. However, this final stage of evolution had been developing since the second century A.D., during the period of the great Kuṣāṇas'[129].

Hence, it is probable that the Pudgalavādins used Apabraṃśa and mixed Sanskrit for their canonical writings. Nonetheless, in the present state of our knowledge of the Pudgalavādin literature, a firm conclusion cannot be reached.

B — *THE PUDGALAVĀDIN TREATISES*

All that we have today on the literature of the Personalist schools of early Buddhism

---

125 Cf. the preface of the *Ssŭ* composed by Tao-an 道安 *la* 15, and the preface to the Tds by Hui-yüan 慧遠 in the *Ch'u san tsang chi chi* 出三藏記集 (abbrev. *Chu*) X, T LV, 2145, 73*a* 22, 23. It is not certain whether the word *fan* 梵 indicates only the Sanskrit language and not all Indian languages, namely, hybrid Sanskrit, Prākrit, etc., because at that time Chinese knowledge of Indian languages was not precise.

126 See below, 'The language and translation of the *Lü ming-liao lun*'.

127 The Tds must have been brought to China by Gautama Saṅghadeva, a native of Kashmir.

128 *Tāranātha's History of Buddhism in India*, pp.71–2.

129 Lamotte, *History*, p.583.

amounts to four works:

1. The *San fa tu lun* 三法度論, Tridharmakaśāstra, T XXV, 1506.
2. The *Ssŭ a-han-mu ch'ao chieh* 四阿鋡暮抄解, T XXV, 1505.
3. The *San-mi-ti pu lun* 三彌底部論, Sāṃmitīyanikāyaśāstra, T XXXII, 1649.
4. The *Lü êrh-shih-êrh ming-liao lun* 律二十二明了論, Vinayadvāviṃśati-vidyāśāstra, T XXIV, 1461.

They will be studied one by one under the following headings:

1 — Title

2 — Author, commentator and translators

3 — Date

4 — Language and translation

5 — Contents

6 — Original school

I. THE SAN FA TU LUN

I — *TITLE*

The *San fa tu lun* 三法度論 (Treatise on the Three Dharmas) is a treatise of about fifteen pages and 223 questions and answers, in the *Taishō Shinshū Daizō-kyō* 大正新修大藏經 (abbrev. *Taishō* or T) (Vol. XXV, No.1506, pp.15*c* - 30*a*). The reconstruction of the title in Sanskrit is **TRIDHARMAKAŚĀSTRA**[130].

It consists of a systematic elucidation of essential ideas disseminated in the Āgamas[131]. It deals with three doctrinal points based on the theme: 'Knowledge (*jñāna*) of the Good (*kuśala*), the Bad (*akuśala*) and the Support (*niśraya*) constitutes the Dharma access (*dharmaparyāya*) leading to the Supreme Good'.

The treatise is entitled Tridharmakaśāstra because it deals with elements of the teaching which are three in number. Not only are the three points — the Good, the Bad and the Support — dealt with in the three main chapters, they are also dealt with in the nine sections each time they need to be defined. Consequently, the author endeavoured to compress or expand the traditional elements of the teaching and only

130 Cf. Bunyū Nanjio, *A Catalogue of the Chinese Translation of the Buddhist Tripiṭaka* (abbrev. Nanjio), Oxford 1883, p.280; *Répertoire du Canon bouddhique sino-japonais*, fascicule annexe du *Hōbōgirin* (abbrev, *Hōbōgirin, Rép.*), rev. ed., Paris and Tokyo 1978, p.128.

131 Cf. the preface to the Tds composed by Hui-yüan in the *Chu*, X, T LV, 2145, 73*a* 3 and the preface to the *Ssŭ*, T XXV, 1505, 1*a* 6–8.

retained groups of three. For example, instead of counting five aggregates (*skandha*), he retained only three: form (*rūpa*), the formations (*saṃskāra*) and consciousness (*vedanā, saṃjñā, vijñāna*)[132] ; or else he added another, Nirvāṇa — the oneness of the two (Nirvāṇa with a remainder and Nirvāṇa without a remainder)[133] — so as to get the number three[134].

II – *THE AUTHOR, COMMENTATOR AND TRANSLATORS.*

a. The Author:

The *Taishō* edition only mentions the name of the main translator, Gautama Saṅghadeva. However, the notes tell us that the editions from the Yüan 元 (1280-1368) and Ming 明 (1368-1644) dynasties mention the name of the author: the Venerable Shan-hsien (*tsun-chê Shan-hsien* 尊者山賢)[135]. In the preface to the Tds written by Hui-yüan 慧遠 , the name of Shan-hsien is also found[136].

If the translation from Sanskrit into Chinese by Gautama Saṅghadeva and Hui-yüan is correct, the author's name can be reconstructed in Sanskrit as Giri-bhadra[137] or Parvatabhadra, etc., but not Vasubhadra as is often done[138]. There is no doubt over the word *hsien* which translates *bhadra*, as there are in fact several names, such as Dharmabhadra (*Fa-hsien* 法賢), Guṇabhadra (*Kung-tê-hsien* 功德賢), Jñānabhadra (*Chih-hsien* 智賢), Saṅghabhadra (*Chung-hsien* 眾賢), etc., the second part of which (*bhadra*) is also translated by *hsien* 賢 . So there remains only the word *vasu*, the Chinese translation of which should be 'shih', as in the translation of the name of Vasubandhu, which is *shih-ch'in* 世親 . *Vasu* cannot be translated by *shan* which has a different meaning. The hypothesis of the mistaken transformation of the character *shih* 世 into that of *shan* 山 by the copyists cannot be excluded, but neither can it be fully asserted.

Leaving aside the Sanskrit reconstruction 'Vasubhadra' which may correspond to the Chinese transcription *P'o-su-pa-to* 婆素跋陀 (*Ssŭ*, 1*b* 5) which, as the name of the author, appears several times in the *Ssŭ*, the text related to the Tds. We will first of all attempt to justify the reconstruction Giribhadra from the name Shan-hsien

We know that there was a sub-group of the Vātsīputrīyas called Mahāgiriyas, that is, those who reside on great mountains (*mahāgiri*)[139] and that there was an Arhat whose disciples had formed the Bhadrayāniya school in order to complete the Vātsīputrīya Abhidharma[140].

---

132 Cf. Tds, 25*b* 9, 10.

133 Cf. *ibid.*, 24*a* 23–29.

134 Cf. *ibid.*, 22*a* 16.

135 Cf. *ibid.*, 15*c* n.14.

136 Cf. the preface to the Tds in *Chu* X, T LV, 2145, 73*a* 8 sq.

137 Cf. Nanjio, p.280.

138 Cf. *Hōbōgirin, Rép.*, p.128.

139 Bareau, *Sectes*, p.128.

140 *Ibid.*; Demiéville, 'L'origine', pp.23, 58.

Through such information, we can infer that the author of the Tds was Giribhadra (*Shan-hsien* 山賢), a Vātsīputrīya master, named Bhadra, who lived in the mountains (*giri*). (This kind of name was popular, particularly for eminent monks).

Nonetheless, the *Ssŭ* cites different authors' names: *Po-su-pa- t'o* 婆素跋陀 (*Ssŭ*, 1*b* 5), or *Po-su-pa-t'o* 婆蘇跋陀 (*ibid.*, 5*c* 21) or *Po-su-pa-tu* 婆素跋度 (*ibid.*, 8*b* 27), whose Chinese translation by Kumārabodhi or Tao-an is Chin-hsien 今賢[141], and not Shan-hsien 山賢. This leads us to another supposition: the translator of the *Ssŭ*, by defining the name VASUBHADRA 'the sage (BHADRA) precious as goods (VASU = *ts'ai-wu* 財物) of which gold (*chin* 金) is the most valuable element', orally translates Chin-hsien 金賢. Since the phonemes of the Chinese words *chin* 金 and *chin* 金 are the same, it was probably through a misunderstanding of the meaning of the word *chin* 今 that the copyist, instead of copying the character *chin* 金, copied the character *chin* 今; therefore, the name of the author was Chin-hsien 今賢. (It should be noted that Kumārabodhi did not know Chinese).

All the difficulties with the problem of the reconstruction of the name and history of the author oblige us to retain that name as it is mentioned in the texts of the Ming 明 and Yüan 元 dynasties, and in the preface to the Tds by Hui-yüan, that is, Shan-hsien 山賢.

b. <u>The Commentator</u>

According to the writings of Hui-yuän, Saṅghasena (*Sêng-ch'ieh-hsien* 僧伽先) is the commentator of the Tds. Saṅghasena was certainly a Buddhist of the Great Vehicle. We cannot be sure whether he was a monk or merely a devout layman since, in the *San fa tu ching chi* 三法度經記, he is called a monk (*bhi- kṣu*)[142], while in the *San fa tu lun hsü* 三法度論序, he is called a Buddhist layman[143]. Nonetheless, his name Saṅghasena shows that he probably was a monk.

Only a few lines describing the portrait of this commentator are found in the preface to the Tds by Hui-yüan:

> '. . . there was a Mahāyānist layman who was called Saṅghasena. He considered the work of Shan-hsien 山賢 as (a work in which) the idea is profound and simple, but its expression still hidden. That is why he retained the chapters and phrasing of Saṅghasena or Shan-hsien for the teaching, and commented on the text to widen its sense. He greatly emphasised the (doctrinal) elements in order to develop their meaning. To comment on those which are still obscure does not seem possible. Since this commentary was made, the light of the Way (shines) on the world. Such is Saṅghasena's feat of teaching'[144].

This description, however, is not enough reason to conclude that Gautama Saṅghadeva personally knew Saṅghasena in India or that Hui-yüan wrote those lines

---

141 *Ssŭ*, 4*a* 12.

142 Cf. *Chu* X, T LV, 2145, 73*b* 2.

143 *Ibid.*, 73*a* 11–12.

144 *Ibid.*, 73*a* 8–10.

in accordance with what the former had told him. Consequently, the origin of the commentator, Saṅghasena, remains obscure.

c. The Translators

The Tds was translated by Gautama Saṅghadeva and Hui-yüan[145]. This fact is mentioned in the Ming 明 edition and that of the Yüan 元, although the *Taishō* edition only mentions the name of Gautama Saṅghadeva. Further confirmation is given by Hui-yüan's preface to the Tds[146]. In certain texts, Gautama Saṅghadeva's collaborator bears the name Wei-yüan 爲遠 [147], which is surely an error. Although Gautama Saṅghadeva was an Indian monk who knew the Chinese language well, his collaborator, Hui-yüan, a scholar of that time, contributed effectively to the translation of the Tds. This is why, in the biography of Gautama Saṅghadeva as much as in that of Hui-yüan, they are presented as having jointly accomplished this translation.

i) *Gautama Saṅghadeva and his translations*

Saṅghadeva (*Chung-t'ien* 衆天) had the family name of Gautama (*Ch'ü-t'an* 瞿曇)[148]. He was born in Kashmir (*Chi-pin* 罽賓). After entering the Way and having received training, he travelled widely in search of qualified masters. He was well-versed in the three collections of canonical texts (Tripiṭaka) and was very strong in Abhidharma. He always recited 'The Treatise on the Three Dharmas' (Tridharmaka-śāstra) because he considered it an entry into the treasury of the Way[149]. He had a lively and profound intelligence and his conduct, especially his humility, was much appreciated. His travels through all the regions of China enabled him fully to understand the Chinese traditions, Chinese language, as well as languages of bordering areas. He was respectable in appearance and most courteous. He was a good propounder; his talent as such was even famous. He was also a tireless teacher.

In 383 CE, at the end of the Chien-yüan 建元 period (386-385), Saṅghadeva came to Ch'ang-an to disseminate the Buddhadharma. Shortly after his arrival, Saṅghabhūti (*Sêng-ch'ieh-po-ch'êng* 僧伽跋澄)[150] had published[151] the Treatise compiled by Venerable Vasumitra, the *Tsun-p'o-hsü-mi-p'u-sa-so-chi lun* 尊婆須蜜菩

---

145 Cf. Tds, 15*c* 5 and n.14.

146 Cf. *Chu* X, T LV, 2145, Hui–yüan's preface to the Tds, 73*a*.

147 Cf. Minh Chau, *The Chinese Madhyama Āgama* . . ., p.234.

148 According to the *K'ai yüan shih chiao lu* 開元釋教錄 III, T LV, 2154, 505*a* 13–*b* 10; *Kao-sêng ch'uan* 高僧傳 (abbrev. *Kao*) I, T L, 2059, 328*c* 22–329*b* 15; *Biographies des moines éminents (Kao-seng tchouan de Houei-kiao)*, tr. and ann. by R. Shih, pp.51–5; Minh Chau, *Thc Chinese Madhyama Āgama* . . ., pp.323–4.

149 Translation of the phrase 以爲入道之府也 (*Kao*, I, T L, 2059, 328*c* 23). The word is not found in the *Chu* (XIII, 99*c* 2–3) nor in the *Kai yüan shih chiao lu* (III, 505*a* 15). Cf. R. Shih, *Bibliographies des moines éminents*, p.51, n.118.

150 Saṅghabhūti (*Sêng-ch'ieh-po-ch'êng* 僧伽跋澄) was a Buddhist scholar from Kashmir who arrived in China in 381 CE; he translated three works into Chinese in 383. Cf. *Kao*, T L, 2059, 328*a-b*; R. Shih, *op. cit.*, pp.48–51, P.C. Bagchi, *Canon bouddh.* I, p.160.

151 According to R. Shih, Saṅghabhūti published this work in collaboration with Dharmanandī and Saṅghadeva. Cf. R. Shih, *op. cit.*, p.52.

薩所集論 (Āryavasumitra [bodhisattva] saṅgītiśāstra, 10 fascicles, T XXVII, 1549), and Dharmanandīn (*Tan-mo-nan-t'i* 曇摩難提)[152] had published two Āgamas (the Madhyamāgama and Ekottarāgama), the Abhidharma, Vibhāṣa (*Kuang-shuo* 廣說) and the Tridharmakaśāstra (*San fa tu* 三法度) entailing more than an hundred myriad words. However, their translations were deficient.

At that time, political troubles were common. Furthermore, Tao-an, the great Buddhist scholar, was already dead. There was no competent person to revise and correct the translations.

Later, Saṅghadeva, accompanied by the śramaṇa Fa-ho 法和 from Chi-chou[153], went to Lo-yang 洛陽 where he stayed for four or five years in order to revise and explain the translations which had already been made. Fa-ho asked Saṅghadeva to publish the texts of the *A-p'i-t'an* 阿毘曇 (Abhidharma, T XXVI, 1543) and the *Kuang shuo chung ching* 廣說眾經 [154].

In the sixteenth T'ai-yüan 太元 year (391 CE), Saṅghadeva crossed the (Yang-tzŭ 江子) river and went to the South where Yao-hsing 姚興 had mounted the throne and where Buddhist affairs flourished. Saṅghadeva was invited by Hui-yüan to stay in the Lu-shan 廬山 to translate the canonical books. That same year, he translated the Abhidharmahṛdayaśāstra (*A-p'i-t'an hsin lun* 阿毘曇心論) and the Tridharmakaśāstra (*San fa tu lun* 三法度論) on the belvedere of Pan-jo 般若 (*Prajñā*).

In 397 CE, the first Lung-an 隆安 year, he went to Chien-k'ang 建康 (Nanking 南京), the capital, and was greatly admired by the king, the mandarins and nobles of the Chin 晉 court. A devout Buddhist, the high mandarin Wang-Hsün 王珣 , invited Saṅghadeva to stay and teach the Abhidharma in the monastery which he had built. On that occasion, Wang-Hsün invited the śramaṇa Shih Hui-ch'i 釋慧持 [155] and forty other monks to stay in the same monastery. It was in Wang-Hsün's T'ung t'ing 東亭 monastery that Saṅghadeva was asked to translate the Sanskrit texts. He then translated two large works: the *Tsêng-i a-han ching* 增一阿含經 and the *Chung a-han ching* 中阿含經 (Madhyamāgama), with a carefully composed group. There were: the śramaṇa Saṅgharakṣa (*Sêng-chieh-lo-ch'a* 僧伽羅刹)[156], a monk from Kashmir who read the Sanskrit text, the

---

152 Dharmanandī (*Tan-mo-nan-t'i* 曇摩難提) was a monk from Tukhāra and probably a native of India. An Āgama specialist, he reached Ch'ang-an in 384 CE and translated five works into Chinese. Cf. *Kao*, T L, 328*b-c*; Bagchi, *op. cit.*, p.157; Shih, *op. cit.*, pp.48–51.

153 The śramaṇa Fa-ho, a native of Hu-peh 湖北 , was a childhood friend of Tao-an. He was well-versed in the sacred literature and, after Tao-an's death in 385, he continued the work of correcting the translations of canonical texts with foreigners such as Gautama Saṅghadeva. Cf. Bagchi, *op. cit.*, p.336, n.1; *Kao* V, T L, 2059, 254*a*.

154 According to Bagchi, this is the Abhidharmavibhāṣā, T XXVIII, 1547. Cf. *Canon bouddh.*, p.162. This treatise is attributed to Saṅghabhadra. There is another translation, made by Buddharakṣa, of this text recited by memory by Saṅghabhadra in 383 at Ch'ang-an. Cf. Shih, *op. cit.*, p.53, n.196.

155 Shih Hui-ch'i 釋慧持 (337–412) was both the younger brother and disciple of Hui-yüan under the direction of Tao-an. He was probably a collaborator in the field of Chinese language rather than a copyist for Gautama Saṅghadeva. He lived for 76 years and predeceased Hui-yüan. Cf. *Kao* VI, T L, 2059, 361*b*.

156 On the biography of Saṅgharakṣa, cf. *Kao* I and IV, T L, 2059, 329*a* and 361*a*.

śramaṇa Tao-tsu[157] from Yü-chou 豫州 who wrote the Chinese; Li-pao 李寶 and T'ang-hua 唐化[158] from the kingdom of Wu 武 were the translation copyists.

The final days of Gautama Saṅghadeva's life are still unknown to us.

Saṅghadeva's translations in China can be divided into two periods corresponding to two different dynasties:

I. In the first period (385-391 CE) under the dynasty of the Early Chin (*Ch'ien Chin* 前晋 350-391 CE), at Lo-yang, Saṅghadeva translated the following three works:

1. The *A-p'i-t'an pa chien tu* 阿毘曇八犍度 (Abhidharmāṣṭaskandhaśāstra or Abhidharmajñānaprasthānaśāstra);
2. The *A-p'i-t'an hsin lun* 阿毘曇心論 (Abhidharmahṛdayaśāstra), this is the first translation of this work;
3. The *Pi-po-sha-a-p'i-t'an* 鞞婆沙阿毘曇 (Abhidharmavibhāṣā or *Kuang shuo chung ching* 廣說眾經 (lost).

II — In the second period (391-398 CE), under the dynasty of the Eastern Chin (*Hsi Chin* 西晋 317-420), in the Lu-shan and Chien-k'ang, Saṅghadeva translated five works in one hundred and eighteen fascicles:

1. The *Chung a-han ching* 中阿含經 (Madhayamāgama, T I, 26);
2. The *Chung i a-han ching* 增一阿含經 (Ekottarāgama, T II, 125);
3. The *A-p'i-t'an hsin lun* 阿毘曇心論 (Abhidharmahṛdayaśāstra, T XXVIII, 1550);
4. The *San fa tu lun* 三法度論 (Tridharmakaśāstra, T XXV, 1506);
5. The *Chiao-shou pi-ch'ü-ni fa* 教授比丘尼法 (lost).

It is therefore Gautama Saṅghadeva who translated and checked these eight works in all. According to the *Hōbōgirin*, only five works exist in Chinese in the collections of canonical texts.

ii) ***Hui-yüan and his career in Buddhist literature***

Hui-yüan 慧遠 (334-416 ?)[159], whose appelation was Chia 賈, was born in 334 CE in Yen-men 雁門. He was a keen student of Confucianism and Taoism. At the age of thirteen, he accompanied his uncle to study at Lo-yang and Hsü-ch'ang 許昌. At twenty-one, he went to hear Tao-an propound Buddhism and became his disciple. At twenty-four, Hui-yüan began to give lectures on Buddhism, particularly on the doctrine of 'Reality' (*bhūtalakṣaṇa* ? *satyalakṣaṇa* ?) in Buddhism. In 365 CE, Hui-yüan was thirty-two and had lived in the company of Tao-an for more than ten years. He accompanied his younger brother Hui-chih, who was also a disciple of Tao-an, to the South. On their way, they stayed for a time at Hsiang-yang 襄陽. Later,

157 For the biography of Tao-tsu 道慈, cf. *Kao* VI, T L, 2059, 361*b*. He was a disciple of Hui-yüan 慧遠 who, in 419, completed the catalogue of the *Chung ching mu lu* 眾經目錄. Cf. *La Concentration de la marche héroïque (Śūramgamasamādhisūtra)*, tr. É. Lamotte, p.76.

158 Li-pao 李寶 and T'ang-hua 唐化 the copyists cannot be found in the list of monks by Ch'en-yüan 陳垣, *Shi shi i nien lu* 釋氏疑年錄, Peking 1964.

159 Cf. *Kao* VI, T L, 2059, 357*c*-361*b*; Zürcher, *Buddhist Conquest*, p.240 sq. W. Liebenthal, 'Shih Hui-yuan's Buddhism', JAOS 70, 1950. He should not be confused with Hui-yüan 慧遠 (523-592) who lived under the Sui 隋 dynasty.

Hui-yüan settled in the Lu shan, where he remained for thirty years, Lo-yang being a place of retreat much appreciated for its picturesqueness and the beauty of its mountains. It ws there that, in 391 CE, he invited Gautama Saṅghadeva to come and translate the *A-p'i-t'an hsin lun* 阿毘曇心論 (Abhidharmahṛdayaśāstra, T XXVIII, 1550) and the *San fa tu lun* 三法度論 (Tridharmakaśāstra, T XXV, 1506).

In 393 CE, Hui-yüan sent his disciple Fa-lin 法林 to the West to search for approximately two hundred canonical texts. In 402 CE, when he was sixty-nine years old, he founded the Society of the White Lotus (*Po-lien shê* 白蓮社) with 123 members, with the aim of practising the teaching of the Pure Land school (*Ching-t'u tsung* 淨土宗). He had corresponded with Kumārajīva on the doctrine of emptiness (*śūnyatāvāda*).

His life came to a peaceful end in Lo-yang in 416 CE[160]. His portrait can be summarised as follows: 'Hui-yüan was a typical Chinese scholar who converted to Buddhism'[161]. He was not, in fact, a translator but a commentator famous in Buddhist literary history. He wrote and translated (in collaboration with Gautama Saṅghadeva) some thirty works[162], the most important of which are:

1. The *San fa tu lun* 三法度論 (Tridharmakaśāstra, T XXV, 1506);
2. The *A-p'i-t'an hsin lun* 阿毘曇心論 (Abhidharmahṛdayaśāstra, T XXVIII, 1550);
3. The *Chiu-mo-lo-shih fa-shih ta-i* 鳩摩羅什法師大義 (T XLV, 1856)[163].

Among the shorter works by Hui-yüan, his preface to the Tds is important for an understanding of that text. It gives us information on the history of Gautama Saṅghadeva as well as on that of the translation of the Tds.

III — *THE DATE*

In 'L'état actuel des études bouddhiques', Paul Demiéville wrote: 'India has no history, and as regards the beginning of Buddhism and the first period of its history, it would be better to admit straight out that we are still reduced to hypotheses'[164].

In attempting to find the date of the Tds, we get a similar impression, and there is nothing we can do but try to guess from a few vague pointers.

The Tds consists of two parts: one is the original text by Po-su-pa-t'o 婆素跋陀 , and the other is the commentary by Saṅghadeva. That is why two dates need to be determined for the two parts.

---

160 His longevity is indicated by variants: 82, 83, 84 years. Cf. Ch'en-yuan 陳垣 , *op. cit.*, p.6.

161 Cf. P. Demiéville, 'La pénétration du bouddhisme dans la tradition philosophique chinoise', *Cahiers d'histoire mondiale* III (1956), pp.23–4; repr. in *Choix d'études bouddiques*, Leiden 1973, pp.241–60.

162 On Hui-yüan's works, see R.H. Robinson, *Early Mādhyamika in India and China*, pp.100–1.

163 The *Hōbōgirin, Rép.*, p.247, only mentions two works: the Abhidharmahṛdayaśāstra (T XXVIII, 1550) and the *Chiu-mo-lo-shih fa-shih ta-i* 鳩摩羅什法師大義 (T XLV, 1856).

164 Tr. after P. Demiéville, 'L'état actuel des études bouddhiques', *Revue de théologie et de philosophie* XV, 62, p.4.

If we retain the hypothesis according to which the Tds is the work of the founder of the Vātsīputrīya school, we can infer that the original text was composed in the third century EP at the earliest, and more probably towards the beginning of the Common Era, that is, at a time when the Tripiṭaka had already been formed (the existence of the terms Sūtra, Abhidharma and Vinaya as well as extracts in the text prove this) and the Vātsīputrīya school was sufficiently stable and flourishing for it to provoke strong controversy over the theory of the *pudgala* and other theses specific to that school.

As for the date of the commentary, it might be located shortly before 383 CE, at the time of the arrival in Ch'ang-an of Saṅghadeva, who may have studied the teaching under the direction of Saṅghasena and brought the treatise to China.

All this is mere hypothesis.

IV — *THE LANGUAGE AND TRANSLATION*

1. The Language

It is probable that the original text of the Tds was in Sanskrit or hybrid Sanskrit, a kind of Sanskrit mixing Prākrit and pure Sanskrit. In Hui-yüan's preface to the Tds, we find:

'At that time, Saṅghadeva held the text in Sanskrit (?)[165] and translated it into the language of the Chin 晉 '[166]. Equally, in the text of the *Ssŭ*, the contents of which are similar to the Tds, there are indications according to which that text was also in Sanskrit (?)[167]. However, according to Bareau, the difficulties with the Chinese translations of the Tds, as well as the other related texts, the *Ssŭ* and Sns, could well explain in part that they were compiled, not in Sanskrit, a language familiar to Chinese Buddhists of the period, but in highly hybridised Sanskrit, or Prākrit.

With regard to the form of expression, the Tds was written in prose in the form of questions and answers, except for short verses in the introduction, at the beginning of the work, and a few stanzes here and there in long passages. This style of dialogue between master and pupil probably originated in debates and was popularised in the first centuries after the Parinirvāṇa of the Buddha, when the tradition of oral transmission of the holy teachings was still preserved. The Milindapañha, part of the Abhidharmakośa, and of the Vimuktimārgaśāstra, etc., are also in the form of dialogues. Dialogue language is characterised by simplicity and clarity so as to elucidate philosophical problems and polemics. Furthermore, the author and commentator were faithful to this tradition, always using, in all the answers, two methods of expression: 1) the condensed teaching for whomever can reach understanding through condensed teaching, 2) developed teaching for whomever can reach understanding through developed teaching[168]. There is always a sentence which sum-

165 See above, n.125.

166 Cf. *Chu* X, T LV, 2145, 73*a* 22–23.

167 *Ssŭ*, 15*b* 27: *fan pên* 梵本

168 Peṭakopadesa II, p.30: '*uggahantetannu*' and '*nevo*'.

marises the explanations as a conclusion to each heading[169].

It is in the part on the developed teaching that the commentator often used well-known examples to illustrate abstract philosophical ideas[170].

Moreover, a comparison between the two translations, the Tds by Gautama Saṅghadeva and the *Ssŭ* by Kumārabodhi, enables us to think that there was a rearrangement of the doctrinal elements and a perfecting of the style of the text, made by Gautama Saṅghadeva in collaboration with Hui-yüan[171].

2. The Translation

The Tds was translated in the Lu shan in 391 CE, during the sixteen year of the reign of Emperor T'ai-yüan 太元 , under the dynasty of the Eastern Chin 西晉 384-417 CE), a period of acclimatisation of Buddhism in China[172]. This translation belongs to the early period of the translation of the Buddhist Canon into Chinese[173]. At that time, the majority of Hīnayāna texts, namely, the Āgama, Abhidharma and Vinaya, were translated in China[174].

With regard to the translating technique, this is still the period when translations of canonical texts were undertaken by a group of people. The translation groups were well organised, and they were later helped by the emperors of the Sui 隋 , T'ang 唐 , etc., dynasties. It was Hui-yüan and his community who had invited Gautama Saṅghadeva to translate this work. Gautama Saṅghadeva translated orally into the language of the Chin 晉 (Chinese). Hui-yüan's preface does not mention the names of the collaborators but, reading between the lines of this preface by Hui-yüan[175], it is clear enough that the latter was probably Saṅghadeva's main collaborator in respect of the field of language and Chinese Buddhist terms, and that his disciples served as copyists.

As for Saṅghadeva's translating technique, it is mentioned in the preface to the Tds and that to the Abhidharmahṛdayaśāstra, T XXVIII, 1550: 'Although the characters are not difficult, the form does not harm the expression of ideas. Basing himself on the essentials, he rejects literary research. He takes account only of the original meaning'[176], and, 'Deva then took the Sanskrit text and translated orally into the language of the Chin 晉 . When he encountered difficult passages, he retranslated them three times'[177].

However, when comparing it to other Chinese Buddhist translations of the same

---

169 Cf. Tds, 16*b* 13–16.

170 Tds, 18*c* 17–21.

171 Cf. Thien Chau, 'Le Tridharmakaśāstra', Chap.I.

172 Cf. Arthur P. Wright, *Buddhism in Chinese History*, London 1959, repr. New York 1965, p.42 sq.

173 Cf. G.H. Sasaki, 'Hīnayāna Schools in China and Japan' (*Présence du Bouddhisme), France-Asie* 153–7, p.500 sq.

174 *Ibid.*, p.499 sq.

175 *Chu*, T LV, 2145, 73*a* 1 sq.

176 *Ibid.*, 73*a* 23–24.

177 *Ibid.*, 72*c* 26 sq.

period, such as those by Kumārajīva[178] and Fa-hsien 法顯 [179], we can see that the translation of the Tds by Gautama Saṅghadeva contains several inexact and erroneous doctrinal terms, apart from mistakes which may have been made by the copyists, engravers and printers in the course of time[180].

On the whole. despite the defects of Saṅghadeva's translation, the form is light, elegant and rhythmic in the prose and verses. Compared to the translation of the *Ssŭ* by Kumārabodhi, most of which is unclear and the style of which is heavy, neither polished nor rhythmic, this translation is better since it was realised under more favourable conditions: the translators knew the languages and doctrines well. Gautama Saṅghadeva frequently recited the Tds and his knowledge of the Chinese language was good after having lived in China for so long and travelled widely; Hui-yüan, his collaborator, was a scholar of the time.

It seems that Hui-yüan himself, having compared the Tds translation to other bad translations of the time, was satisfied with the work he had written:

> 'From the rise of the Han 漢 dynasty until this Chin 晉 dynasty, among the famous sages, whether religious or lay, who studied and appreciated the holy Canon in order to disseminate Buddhism widely, numerous works were translated. (However, in their translations), the style masked the ideas or the meaning overwhelmed the words. On comparing this translation to others, it surpasses the early works. If the sages of the future were to know the Chin 晉 language and Sanskrit and were good translators, they would be able to find the correspondence of the two texts to judge the contents of this translation'[181].

V – *THE CONTENTS*

The Tds consists of three volumes containing three chapters each with three sections.

---

178 Kumārajīva (344–413) was born into a family living in Kuča, his father being Indian and his mother a princess of Kuča. He entered a Buddhist monastery at the age of eight. He studied in Kashmir and became a famous scholar in Central Asia. Kumārajīva arrived in Ch'ang-an in 401 CE, where he worked until 412 and probably died in 413. He translated 106 works into Chinese.

Cf. *Kao* II, T L, 2059, 330*a*, 333*a*; K. Ch'en, *Buddhism in China*, pp.81–3; P.C. Bagchi, *Canon bouddh.* I, p.178; R. Shih, *op. cit.*, pp.60–81.

179 Fa-hsien 法顯 was born in 340; his family name was Kung 龔, from Wu-yang 武陽 in the command post of P'ing-yang 平陽, a region now known as Shan-si. In order to save him from the death that had overtaken his three elder brothers, his parents put him in a monastery. When he was nearly sixteen, he left Ch'ang-an for India. Accompanied by four colleagues, his journey lasted fifteen years (399–413). The main object of this first-generation pilgrimage was to look for texts on discipline (Vinaya) which were then lacking in China. He was not their translator. Later, Fa-hsien went to Ching-chou 荊州 and died in Hsin ssŭ 辛寺 at the age of 86. He left a long account of his travels through various kingdoms (*Kao-hsing fa-hsien chuan,* 高僧法顯傳 T LI, 2085).

Cf. *Kao* III, T L, 2059, 337b–338*b*; R. Shih, *op. cit.*, pp.108–15; E. Chavannes, 'Voyage de Song yun dans l'Udyāna et le Gandhāra', Appendice, BEFEO III, 1903, pp.435–6; H.A. Giles, *The Travels of Fa-hien*, London 1877, rev. ed. 1923; K.A. Nilakanta Sastri, *Fa-hien, the Chinese Pilgrim*, pp.441–2.

180 Cf. Thien Chau, 'Le Tridharmakaśāstra', Chap.I.

181 *Chu* X, T LV, 2145, 73*a* 24–29.

CHAPTER ONE: THE GOOD (*KUŚALA* ?)
(Vol.I, II, 15*c* 7 - 21*b* 25; verses + questions 1-88)

The first chapter begins with an introduction in verse and prose, in which the purpose for which the work was composed is indicated. It is clear that the author, like the Buddha, envisages helping living beings to eliminate 'the innumerable sufferings caused by rebirth'[182] by explaining the Buddhist teaching to them. The author probably takes as his basis the main theme of this teaching, which amounts to this affirmation: It is knowledge (*chio* 覺, *jñāna* ?) of the Good (*tê* 德, *kuśala* ?), of the Bad (*ê* 惡, *akuśala* ?) and the Support (*i* 依, *niśraya* ?) (which) is the Dharma access (*dharmaparyāya*) leading to the Supreme Good"[183], Nirvāṇa. At question 6 (16*a* 7), the Tds really explains the Good which is related to the qualities and spiritual assets and designates as such merit (*puṇya*), means (*upāya*) and the fruit (*phala*).

First section: Merit (*puṇya*)
(Vol.I, 16*a* 12 - 18*b* 18)

I — Merit (*puṇya*) constitutes the first condition of the Supreme Good:

1. Merit (*puṇya*) consists of three elements:
   — Giving (*dāna*), with reference to the conduct of oneself and others. It consists of three factors:
   a. the relinquishment of possessions (*dhanaparityāga*);
   b. the will to give (*cetanā*)[184] ;
   c. non-intimation (*avijñapti*)[185].
   There are three kinds of gifts:
   1. The gift of the Dharma (*dharmadāna*);
   2. The gift of fearlessness (*abhayadāna*);
   3. The gift of objects (*āmiṣadāna*).
   The fruit obtained by the accomplishment of meritorious action together with the others is greater than the fruit obtained by accomplishing it alone. Pure giving is giving accomplished in total purity of causes and conditions.

---

182 Cf. Tds, 15*c* 7.

183 *Ibid.*, 15*c* 21: *shan shêng* 善勝 . Kumārabodhi's translation: *Chieh-t'uo* (*Ssŭ*, 1*b* 16).

184 AN II, 415: 'I declare, monks, that will is action. Having willed, one acts with body, speech and mind' (*cetanāhaṃ bhikkave kammaṃ vadāmi; cetayitvā kammaṃ karoti kāyena vācāya manasā*). ***Kośa*** III, 1: 'Volition is mental action; it gives rise to two actions, bodily and vocal action' (*cetanā mānasaṃ tajje vākkāya-karmaṇī*, p.2, n.2; Engl tr. p.552).

185 *Wu chiao* 無教 (*avijñapti* = non-intimation, non-manifestation, etc.); this is the old translation (prior to Hsüan-tsang), whilst the 'new translation' of *avijñapti* is *wu-piao* 無表 (without externalisation). According to Lin Lu-kouang, Saṅghadeva translated *avijñapti* by *wu-chiao* 無教 (also in the Abhidharmasāra by Dharmaśrī), as did Narendrayaśa (6th c.) in the commentary by Upaśanta; Dharmagupta and Dharmayaśa, the translators of the Śāriputrābhidharma, did the same. The definition of it is different from that of the Sarvāstivādins, here it means the moral character or wish which precedes intention and will in the relinquishment of possessions. Cf. E.J. Thomas, ***The History of Buddhist Thought***, p.229; T. Stcherbatsky, ***Central Conception of Buddhism***, p.6 and n.4.

2. Morality (*śīla*) is intimation by the body and speech in a positive sense; it is defined as 'leading others, not harming others and increasing the good'. The first two characteristics are aimed at eliminating wrong actions of body and speech[186]. The continual growth of these two characteristics, even during sleep, constitutes the third[187].

3. Cultivation (*bhāvanā*), or mental development, is compared to the action of perfuming sesame seeds with flowers or services rendered to the king who in return necessarily gives a reward. It includes:

a) The four absorptive meditations (*dhyāna*), named after what they obtain:
   1. the discarding of desire (*kāma*);
   2. the discarding of discursive thought (*vicāra*);
   3. the discarding of joy (*prīti*);
   4. the discarding of suffering and happiness (*duḥkhasukha*).

   These correspond to the four stages of the world of form (*rūpadhātu*)[188].

b) The four immeasurables (*apramāṇa*), the spheres of action on living beings, which are immeasurable :
   1. Goodwill (*maitrī*);
   2. Compassion (*karuṇā*);
   3. Altruistic joy (*muditā*);
   4. Equanimity (*upekṣā*)[189].

c) The four formless attainments (*ārūpyadhātusamāpatti*):
   1. The sphere of the infinity of space (*ākāśānantyāyatana*);
   2. The sphere of the infinity of consciousness (*vijñānānantyāyatana*);
   3. The sphere of nothingness (*ākiṃcanyāyatana*);
   4. The sphere of neither-perception-nor-non-perception (*naivasaṃjñānāsaṃjñāyatana*)[190].

II — The Roots (*mūla*).

The word root, the origin of all (means) leading to the Supreme Good, is synonymous with cause (*hetu*). By dealing with the roots in the context of the Good (*kuśala*), the

---

186 Cf. MN I, 415–17.

187 Morality, in the sense given by the first two characteristics, is taken generally; however, the third characteristic expresses the specific Vātsīputrīya theme: see below, 'Secondary theses of the Pudgalavādins'.

188 This is meditation (*dhyāna*) classified according to various mental states, in relation to the four stages of the *rūpadhātu*. Cf. DN I, 73; II, 186, 313; MN I, 139, 181, 276: SN II, 210; V, 307–8; *Kośa* VIII, 1 sq. Meditation in five divisions is based on texts such as AN III, 63. Cf. Dhammasaṅgaṇī, 160–75.

189 The four immeasurables (*apramāṇa*) are practices added to those of the thirty-seven auxiliaries of enlightenment (*bodhipākṣika*, DN II, 119–20). They enable good attitudes to be acquired with regard to beings but do not form part of the way of transcendental accomplishment which leads to enlightenment (cf. DN III, 233). They are also called the four divine abodes (*brahmavihāra*). Cf. DN I, 250; MN II, 76; AN II, 130; IV, 330; SN V, 115; *Kośa* VIII, § 29: '. . .They are called *apramāṇas* because they apply to an immeasurable number of beings, drawing after them an immeasurable merit ('outflowing fruit') and producing immeasurable (retributive) results' (Pruden, p.1264).

190 These four attainments (*samāpatti*) are mental states in respect of the four abodes of the gods of the *ārūpyadhātu*. Cf. DN I, 34, 112; MN I, 41, 159–96; AN IV, 433.

Tds tackles only the three good roots: the absence of craving (*alobha*), hatred (*adveṣa*) and delusion (*amoha*)[191].

The influence of the roots is very strong. The absence of craving increases giving, the gift of objects, the deed of leading others, the absorptive meditations and the abandoning of the bad. The absence of hatred reinforces morality, the gift of fearlessness, the deed of not harming others, the immeasurables and patience. The absence of delusion develops cultivation, the formless attainments and erudition.

In this sense, the roots, like the roots of a tree, support good conduct and become the power (*bala*) of the spiritual life.

III — The Absence of the bad (*apāpa*).

The absence of the bad is a collective term to designate:

1. Patience (*kṣānti*) is a twofold quality: it consists of patience towards oppression caused by the potency of wealth, pardon for wrong actions by the poor, and endurance of suffering provoked by inanimate phenomena such as cold, heat, hunger, etc. The analysis of things which engender anxiety according to the law of causes and conditions (*hetupratyaya*), reinforces endurance. Patience, in this sense, comprises knowledge (*jñāna*)[192] or right view (*samyagdṛṣṭi*).

2. Erudition (*bahuśrutatā*) is wide knowledge of the Sūtras, Abhidharma and Vinaya. He who can destroy craving, hatred and delusion in himself is erudite. Hence, he who is knowledgeable of the Tripiṭaka is erudite because his three bad roots are eliminated.

3. Non-illwill (*avyāpāda*) consists of three factors:
   a. the friendship of virtuous people (*kalyāṇamitra*) is an indispensable condition of the pure life (*brahmacarya*); it is communion in goodwill (*maitrī*), skill (*kausalya*) and capabilities (*sāmarthya*), of the preceptor (*upādhyāya*), disciples (*antevāsin*) and co-disciples (*sabrahmacārin*)[193].
   b. true mastery of thoughts, identical to concentration (*samādhi*), means: the stopping of perturbing thoughts and ideas; the elevation of a weak, soft and unenergetic thought. The protection of a balanced thought to maintain the

---

191 These three good roots (*kuśalamūla*), corresponding to three bad roots (*akuśalamūla*) (cf. DN III, 214; AN I 263), in the sense of negation of the latter, constitute the origin of the good. AN I, 230: *tīn imāni bhikkhave kusalamūlāni. katamāni tīni? alobho kusalamūlaṃ, adoso kusalamūlaṃ, amoho kusalmūlaṃ. imāni kho bhikkhave tīni kusalamūlāni.* Cf. MN I, 49, 489.

192 *Kośa* VI, § 26: 'Immediately after *duḥkhe dharmajñānakṣānti* there arises a *dharmajñāna* having as its object the *duḥkha* of the *kāmadhātu*' (cf. Pruden, p.945).

193 In the Meghiyasutta (AN IV, 354–8), the Buddha commends to Meghiya the important role played by a good friend. The good friend constitutes the first of five conditions, namely: (1) good friend (*kalyāṇamitto*), (2) morality (*sīlavā*), (3) serious conversations which help to open the mind (*yāyaṃ kathā abhisallekhikā cetovivaranasappāya*), (4) purposeful vigorous deportment (*āraddhaviriyo viharati*), (5) wisdom (*paññāvā*), in order to attain liberation.

SN I, 87–8: 'The whole of this religious life, Ānanda, is good friendship, good companionship and good association' (*sakalam eva h'idam Ānanda brahmacariyan yad idam kalyāṇa mittatā kalyāṇa sahāyatā kalyāṇasampavaṅkata*). On the seven qualities of a good friend, cf. AN IV, 32; Vism I, 98.

function of the mind.

c. the right path (*pratipad*), considered as the means which amount to the three preparatory practices (*prayoga*) and lead to the other shore of the flux of existence:

1. the virtue of asceticism (*dhūtaguṇa*)[194], aimed at distancing oneself from inhabited places and opening oneself to serenity and simplicity, consists of twelve practices:

I — The practice of wearing robes made from rags collected from heaps of ordure (*pāṃśukūlika*)

II — That of possessing only three robes (*traicīvarika*);

III — That of wearing coarse robes (*nāmatika*);

IV — That of being content with any seat (*yathāsaṃstarika*);

V — The practice of living in a tranquil place (*araṇyaka*);

VI — That of sheltering under a tree (*vṛkṣamūla*);

VII — That of living in the open air (*abhyavakāśika*);

VIII — That of sitting correctly (*naiṣadika*)[195] ;

IX — The practice of alms-seeking (*piṇḍapātika*);

X — That of eating only one meal (*ekāsanika* ?)[196] ;

XI — That of not eating broth in the afternoon (*khalupascādbhaktika* ?)[197] ;

XII — That of living in a cemetery (*smasānika*)[198].

---

194 Tds, 17*b* 13–14: *shan-hsün chê shih ching po i* 善損者是清薄義 , and *ibid.*, 17*b* 15: *ching kung tê* 淨功得 . These comments enable us to reconstruct the Sanskrit *dhūtaguṇa* behind the Chinese words *shan-hsün* 善損 and to translate them by 'virtue of asceticism' or 'quality of discarding (impurities)' or 'quality of purification'.

Dhūtaguṇa is often found in Sanskrit works, especially those of the Sarvāstivādins, namely: Mahāvyutpatti, p.49; Dharmasaṃgraha, p.63 with lists of twelve articles, whilst *dhutaṅga*, the article of purification, is used in the Pāli texts. According to the Vism (p.61), *dhutaṅga* means: (1) the practices observed by a monk practising austerities with a view to purification (*sabbā'neva pan'etāni tena tena samādānena dhutakilesattā dhutassa bhikkhuno aṅgāni*); (2) knowledge, derived from those practices, of the purification which dispels defilements (*kilesadhunanato vā dhutan ti laddavohāraṃ ñāṇaṃ aṅgaṃ etesan ti dhutaṅgāni*); (3) those practices constitute the path leading to the discarding of defilements (*dhutani ca tani paṭipakkhaniddhunanato aṅgani ca paṭipattiyā ti pi dhutaṅgāni*). Cf. Vin. V, p.193; Thomas, *The History of Buddhist Thought*, p.23, n.1.

195 Although the words *chêng tsê* 正坐 (Tds, 17*c* 22) are translated as 'sitting correctly', the commentary in the Tds (18*a* 3–7) enables us to interpret this practice as being that which consists of sleeping sitting up but never lying down (*naiṣadika*, Pāli *nesajjik'aṅga*).

196 The words *i shih* 一食 (Tds, 18*a* 8–15) with the commentary: 彼乞食已數數食至時，以是廢學，世尊教彼當一食 (Tds, 18*a* 14–15) enables us to understand that this practice is identical to that which consists of sitting down only once for a meal (*ekāsanika*).

197 Tds, 18*a* 8: *kuo chung pu yin chiang* 過中不飲漿 . This practice may mean that which consists of refusing all food after the meal-time (*khalupaścādbhaktika*, Pāli *khalupacchābhattika*).

198 There are other lists of twelve ascetic practices in the original Sanskrit texts (cf. L. Li-kouang, *L'Aide-mémoire*, p.87, n.1), but they do not always give the elements in the same order and they often cite different terms (cf. *L'Inde classique* II, § 2371 (p.599): *Fo shuo shih-êrh t'ou-t'ê ching* 佛說十二頭陀經 , Dvādaśa-dhātasūtra, T XVII, 783, pp.720*b*–722*a*.

2. Restraint of the faculties (*indriyasaṃvara*); this is control of the sense faculties, non-deterioration, protection and submission of the faculties. Furthermore, restraint of the faculties means perception accompanied by correct reflection (*yoniśomanaskāra* ?)[199] ;
3. Adjoining concentration (*upacārasamādhi* ?)[200] is preparatory practice (*prayoga*) in the stage of vision (*darśanabhūmi*). It is in this concentration that, through correct reflection, one gradually examines the truth and obtains a clear comprehension (*abhisamaya*)[201] of it. It is divided into three steps:
   a) patience (*kṣānti*), in which the practitioner profoundly penetrates the reality of compounded things;
   b) name (*nāma*), in which the mind of the practitioner becomes imperturbable in correct reflection.

The list of thirteen practices in Vism, p.59: *pamsukūlika, tecīvarika, piṇḍapātika, sapadānacārika, ekāsanika, pattapiṇḍika, khalupacchābattika, araññika, rukkhamūlika, abbhokāsika, sosānika, yathāsanthatika, nesajjika.* For details, cf. Vism, p.45 sq.; Milindapañha, p.345; Vimuktimārgaśāstra, *Chieh-t'uo tao lun* ,解脱道論 , T XXXII, 1648, p.404*b* 27; N. Dutt, *Early Monastic Buddhism*, pp.153–8.

199 Tds, 18*b* 2, 14, 15: *chêng ssŭ-wei* 正思惟 can be translated as 'correct reflection'. However, the context and the mechanical and erroneous translation by Kumārabodhi: *yin hsing* 婬行 practice of sensual misconduct (*Ssŭ*, 5*a* 13, 16, 18), enables us to guess the Sanskrit word behind the translation: *yoniśomanaskāra* (lit. *yoni*: vulva): reflection coming from the source or womb, profound reflection. See below, 'The *Ssŭ a-han-mu ch'ao chieh*'. It is synonymous with *yoniśovikalpa*. Its opposite is *ayoniśomanaskāra* or *ayoniśomanasikāra* (cf. MN I,7). MN I, 294: 'Friend, there are two conditions through which right view arises: the voice of others and profound reflection' (*dve kho āvuso paccayā sammadiṭṭhiyā uppadāya: parato ca ghoso ca manasikāro*). Cf. AN I, 87; SN I, 105. Peṭakopadesa, 1: 'What is called profound reflection within oneself is that which conforms to the doctrine taught (by the Buddha) and is not drawn to external objects' (*ajjhataṃ yoniso manasikāro nāma yo yathādesite dhamme bahiddhā ārammaṇam anabhiharitvā yoniso manasikāro ayam vuccati yoniso manasikāro*).

Kośa II, 24 (Engl tr. p.190): '*Manasikāra* is the modification (*ābhoga*) of the mind (*cetas*); in other words, 'to bend' or 'to apply' the mind towards an object (*ālambane cetassa āvarjanam avadhāraṇam*). [*Manasikāra* is explained as *manasaḥ kāraḥ* or *manaḥ karoty āvarjayati*]'.

Yoniśomanasikāra is one of four things which are necessary and favourable to the development of wisdom and stream-entry (*sotāppatti*), namely, *sappurisasaṃvesa* (association with virtuous persons), *saddhammasavanam* (hearing the wonderful Dhamma), *yonisomanasikāra* (profound reflection), and *dhammānudhammapaṭipatti* (practice of the Dhamma and its corollaries). DN III, 227; MN II, 17; SN V, 345–411.

200 Tds, 18*b* 7; Tds, 18*b* 8–9 . *Ssŭ*, 4*a* 2–3: 近 定 (Chin Ting)

The Sanskrit term *upacārasamādhi* here indicates the degree of concentration just preceding entry into any meditation (*dhyāna* or *samādhi*) and corresponds to the context of the Tds and *Ssŭ*, which is why it has no connection with access concentration (*upacārasamādhi*): 'the mind becomes concentrated on the level of access through the discarding of obstacles', in the heading 'the two kinds of concentration' in the Theravādin Vism. Cf. *The Path of Purification (Visuddhimagga)*, tr. Ñānamoli, p.131.

201 Translates the words *chên chih shih* 眞知識 (Tds 18*b* 14). This true comprehension is certainly identical to total penetration (*abhisamaya*) of the four noble truths, since the term *abhisamaya* is frequently found linked to the four noble truths (*āryābhisamaya*). Sn 758: *te ve saccābhisamayānicchātāparinibbutā.* Vism, 690: *dukkhaṃ pariññābhisamayena abhisameti, samudayaṃ pahānābhisamayena abhisameti, maggaṃ bhāvanābhisamayena abhisameti, nirodhaṃ sacchikiriyābhisamayena abhisameti.*

c) perception (*hsiang* 想, *saṃjñā*) or clear comprehension; this includes the stage of the supreme worldly dharma (*laukikāgradharma*) since it is so with the perception of the Buddha.

Second section: Means (*upāya*)
(Vol.I, 18*b* 20 - 20*a* 27)

The second question in the first chapter dealing with the Good (*kuśala*) explains means (*upāya*) which include morality (*śīla*), superior calm (*uttaraśamatha*) and wisdom (*prajñā*).

I — Morality (*śīla*).

Morality is divided into two categories:

1. Natural morality (*shou-shêng chieh* 受生戒, *prakṛtiśīla* ?)[202], which includes the precepts which are not connected with the path and transcendental fruits (*lokuttaraphala*).
2. Morality of release (*ch'u-yao chieh* 出要戒, *niḥsaraṇaśīla*)[203] which is composed of what pertains to three factors of the Noble Eightfold Path (*āryāṣṭāṅgikamārga*). Consequently, it consists of:
   a. Right speech (*samyagvāc*): abstention from slander (*paiśunyavāda*), harsh speech (*pāruṣyavāda*), falsehood (*mṛśāvāda*) and frivolous speech (*sambhinnapralāpa*);
   b. Right action (*samyakkarmānta*): abstention from taking life (*prāṇātipāta*), theft (*adattādāna*) and sensual misconduct (*kāmamithyācāra*);
   c. Right livelihood (*samyagājīva*): for monks (*bhikṣu*), to live contentedly with the four necessities (*niśraya*)[204] supplied by devotees (*upāsaka*, *upāsikā*); for devotees, not practising the five types of livelihood which are harmful to others, trading in arms, poisons, intoxicants, flesh and living beings[205].

---

202 Here morality which is natural (*shou shêng chieh* 受生戒, *prakṛtiśīla* ?) is indicated. These are disciplinary rules of the monks or laity prescribed by the Buddha in order to eliminate bad actions of body or speech (see above, First section: merit (*puṇya*), heading 'morality (*śīla*)'.

This idea is identical to prescribed morality (*paññattisīla*), but differs from natural morality (*pakatisīla*) in the Pāli texts (cf. Nyanatiloka, *Buddhist Dictionary*). It is differentiated from the morality of release (*niḥsaraṇaśīla*).

203 *Ch'u-yao chieh* 出要戒, *niḥsaraṇaśīla*, constitutes the morality of release.

DN II, 123: *sīlam samādhi pañña ca vimutti ca anuttarā,*
anubuddha ime dhammā Gotamena yasassinā.

Cf. DN I, 204, 211, 233–4; AN II, 2; SN II, 81.

204 These are: 1) alms-seeking (*piṇḍapātika*); 2) using robes made from rags collected from heaps of ordure (*paṃsukūlika*); 3) sheltering under a tree (*vṛkṣamūlika*); 4) using the concentrated urine of cows as medicament (*pūtimuktābhaiṣajya*). Cf. Vin. I, 58; *L'Inde classique* II, § 2370.

205 The elements and order of the five harmful or forbidden types of livelihood of the Tds are slightly different from those in AN II, 208: *satthavaṇijjā, sattavaṇijjā, maṃsavaṇijjā, majjavaṇijjā*

II — Superior calm (*uttaraśamatha* ?)

Superior calm is full and complete calm, the eradication of the three bad roots; it is the deed of aiming towards the other shore (*pāra*) and staying there. It collectively designates three factors of the Noble Eightfold Path: vigour (*vīrya*), mindfulness (*smṛti*) and concentration (*samādhi*).

1. Vigour (*vīrya*) is also the power (*bala*) which designates action conducive to the Supreme Good, it consists of:
   a. faith (*śraddhā*) which indicates purification (*viśuddhi*) — the destruction of defilements (*āsrava*); aspiration; desire and love for the Dharma; and determination (*adhimokṣa*); commitment to the way;
   b. diligence (*apramāda*) which indicates beginning — beginning to do good; exercise — repetition of action; and perseverance — adhering to an under- taking;
   c. tenacity (*aprahāṇa* ?) which indicates not stopping, not being repulsed and not renouncing.

2. Mindfulness (*smṛti*) is the absence of forgetfulness regarding the four applications of mindfulness (*smṛthyupasthāna*) concerning:
   a. inwardness (*adhyātmika*) — the grasping aggregates (*upādānaskandha*), the elements (*dhātu*) and spheres of one's senses (*āyatana*);
   b. outwardness (*bāhya*) — others; and
   c. a combination of both — grasping (*upādāna*) and non-grasping (*anupādāna*).

   Moreover, the three modalities of mindfulness can be realised through the elimination of three kinds of passions (*kleśa*), craving (*kāma*), anger (恚 *krodha* ?) and delusion (*moha*), which are found inwardly, outwardly and in both.

The Tds lists the twelve modalities of mindfulness after adding feelings (*vedanā*), thoughts (*citta*) and ideas (*dharma*), by multiplying them by the three modalities of mindfulness.

3. Concentration (*samādhi*) designates:
   a. concentration on emptiness (*śūnyatāsamādhi*) which indicates the absence of an agent (*nirahaṃkāra*) and what pertains to an agent (*mamaṃkāra*)[206] and both;
   b. concentration on wishlessness (*apraṇihitasamādhi*) by means of which one understands that compounded things (*saṃskṛta*) are painful and consequently

---

and *viṣavaṇijjā*.

206 Tds, 19*a* 13: *k'ung chieh wo hsing wo tsê chü pu chien* 空者我行我作俱不見 The words *wo hsing wo tsê* 我行我作 probably translate *ahaṃkāramamaṃkāra*.

MN III, 19: 'Monks, for him who knows thus and sees thus, there is no further tendency to pride concerning the agent and what pertains to the agent with regard to a body endowed with consciousness and all outward objects (*evaṃ kho, bhikkhave, jānato evaṃ passato imasmiṅ ca saviññāṇake kāye nahiddhā ca sabbanimittesu ahaṃkāramānānusayā na hontīti*). Cf. MN III, 32; AN I, 112; SN II, 267.

one does not fix (wish for) them. It is noteworthy that this passage informs us of the five categories which are accepted and defended by the Vātsīputrīyas:

1 to 3 — the phenomena of the three time-periods,

4 — Nirvāṇa, and

5 — the *pudgala.*

Of these five categories, the first three are compounded things from the past, present and future; the fourth is Nirvāṇa which is separate from the conditioned world and pertains only to the non-compounded (*asaṃskṛta*); the fifth is that which is not totally separated from the things of the three times as is Nirvāṇa[207].

c. concentration on non-perception (signlessness) (*wu-hsiang* 無想 , *asaṃjñā (samādhi)* or *animitta(sāmadhi)*[208]: this is the renunciation of a perception of deeds, acts and both, compounded things (*saṃskṛta*)[209].

III — Wisdom (*prajñā*)

Wisdom is transcendental knowledge or intuitive comprehension which leads to enlightenment specifically concerning three stages:

1. The stage of vision (*darśanabhūmi*), the process of which includes twelve kinds of knowledge, namely: knowledge of things (*dharmajñāna*), knowledge of investigation (*vicārajñāna* ?) and knowledge of what is not yet known (*ajñātajñāna* ?); these three knowledges relate to the four Truths: suffering (*duḥkha*), its origin (*samudaya*), its cessation (*nirodha*) and the path (*mārga*), in connection with the three worlds[210].

---

207 See below, 'The main thesis of the Pudgalavādins'.

208 Tds, 19*a* 11: *wu hsiang* 無想 ; Tds, 19*a* 27, 28: *wu hsiang chê, shih tsê chü hsiang, li shih tsê chü hsiang, li shih wu hsiang* 無想者，事作俱想，離事作俱想,離是無想 . *Ssŭ*, 4*c* 26: *wu hsiang hsing tsê chü wu hsiang* 無想行作俱無想 . Hence the Sanskrit reconstruction of the term *wu hsiang* 無想 should be *asaṃjñāsamādhi*, not *animittasamādhi* which is translated in Chinese by *wu hsiang* 無相 . However, the ideas do not differ, since the former indicates subjectivity and the latter objectivity.

209 This triad of concentrations, the three subjects of which are emptiness (*śūnyatā*), wishlessness (*apraṇihita*) and non-perception or signlessness (*asaṃjñā* or *animitta*), is the most prescribed and famous. On this subject, see the complete text in EĀ (T II, 125, 630*b*), translated by A. Bareau in *Bouddha*, Paris 1962, pp.162–3. The *Kośa* VIII, § 24, presents a long explanation and notes on this triad of concentrations but the order of the three subjects is not the same: (1) *animitta*, (2) *śūnyatā*, (3) *apraṇihita*. DN III, 219: *suññato samādhi, animitto samādhi, appaṇihito samādhi*. Cf. MN III, 104, 109; AN I, 299; III, 397; SN IV, 360; Vin. III, 93.

210 See below, 'The secondary theses of the Pudgalavādins: thesis No.2'.

I — Duḥkhe	*1 — Dharmajñāna*	*Kāmadhātu*
	2 — Vicārajñāna ?	
	3 — Ajñātajñāna ?	*Rūpadhātu + Ārūpyadhātu*
II — Samudaye	*1 — Dharmajñāna*	*Kāmadhātu*
	2 — Vicārajñāna	
	3 — Ajñātajñāna ?	*Rūpadhātu + Ārūpyadhātu*
III — Nirodhe	*1 — Dharmajñāna*	*Kāmadhātu*
	2 — Vicārajñāna ?	
	3 — Ajñātajñāna ?	*Rūpadhātu + Ārūpyadhātu*
IV — Mārge	*1 — Dharmajñāna*	*Kāmadhātu*
	2 — Vicārajñāna ?	
	3 — Ajñātajñāna ?	*Rūpadhātu + Ārūpyadhātu*

2. The stage of cultivation (*bhāvanābhūmi*): the stage in which the fetters (*saṃyojana*) are destroyed and where one is perfumed with the qualities, including three kinds of knowledge:
   a. Knowledge of marks (*lakṣaṇajñāna* ?) concerning the three marks — arising (*utpāda*), duration (*sthiti*) and disappearance (*vyaya*)[211]. It may be noted that the Tds says about this: 'The living being (*sattva* = *pudgala*) and Nirvāṇa are not identical to the marks'[212]. This adherence, according to the Tds, avoids belief in extreme views: eternity and annihilation; existence and non-existence. The Tds also admits that these three marks are objects (*viṣaya*) of wisdom; consequently, they no longer pertain to compounded things (*saṃskṛta*) but become qualities (*guṇa*);
   b. Knowledge of aspects (*ākārajñāna*) is integral comprehension which discerns the marks known by aspects: impermanence (*anitya*), suffering (*duḥkha*) and impersonality (*fei wo* 非我, *anātmaka*)[213];
   c. Knowledge of varieties is:
      1. Comprehension of the flavour (*rasa*) of the happiness of mankind (*manuṣya*) and the gods (*deva*);
      2. Comprehension of unhappiness, suffering in the three bad destinies (*durgati*) and,

211 AN I, 152: Monks, there are three marks of compounded things pertaining to compounded things. What are those three? They are arising, disappearance and change (*tīṇ' imāni bhikkhave saṃkhatassa saṃkhatalakkhaṇāni. katamāni tīni? uppado paññāyati vayo paññāyati ṭhitassa aññatatthataṃ paññāyati*).

Kośa II, § 45 counts four marks: the marks are birth, old-age, duration, impermanence (*lakṣaṇāni . . . jātir jarā sthitir anityatā*).

212 See below, 'The main thesis of the Pudgalavādins'. See also Bareau, *Sectes*, p.117.

213 These are the three marks of existence which constitute the basic teaching of Buddhism. They are also aspects of reality. The Buddha is only a 'revealer' of these aspects, not their creator or inventor: 'All compounded things are impermanent (*sabbe saṅkhārā aniccā*), all compounded things are suffering (*sabbe saṅkhārā dukkhā*), all things are impersonal (*sabbe dhammā anattā*)'. Cf. AN I, 286. *Kośa* VII, § 13: 'The aspects, *ākāras*, are, in their mental nature, *prajñā*, a discernment'.

3. Renunciation of both, demerit and merit[214].
Due to right views (*samyagdṛṣṭi*) in relation to the realities explained above, one understands that all defilements (*āsrava*) should be renounced.

3. The stage of him-who-has-no-more-to-train-in (*aśaikṣabhūmi*), identical to the Arhat, possesses:
   a. Higher knowledge (*vidyā*), including:
      1. Knowledge of the recollection of former existences (*pūrvanivāsānusmṛtijñāna* ?);
      2. Knowledge of the births and deaths of beings (*shêng shê chih* 生死智, *upapādacyutijñāna* ?);
      3. Knowledge of the destruction of the defilements (*āsravakṣayajñānā*)[215].
   b. Superknowledges (*abhijñā*); the Tds lists only three elements of these since the others are counted under higher knowledge (*vidyā*). They are:
      1. Supernormal power (*ṛddhi*) — mastery of displacement (*gamana-aiśvārya*), mastery of transformation (*nirmāṇa-aiśvārya*) and mastery of holiness (*ārya-aiśvārya*);
      2. The divine ear (*divyaśrotra*) and,
      3. Knowledge of others' thoughts (*paracittajñāna*)[216].

      It may be noted that, in this passage, the Tds mentions only five superknowledges, excepting the knowledge of the destruction of the defilements (*āsravakṣayajñāna*), which can be obtained by worldlings (*pṛthagjana*)[217] ;
   c. Analytical knowledge (*pratisaṃvid*) including:
      1. analytical knowledge of the Dharma (*dharmapratisaṃvid*);
      2. analytical knowledge of the meaning (*arthapratisaṃvid*);
      3. analytical knowledge of languages (*niruktipratisaṃvid*);
      4. analytical knowledge of eloquence (*pratibhānapratisaṃvid*)[218].

---

214 Dhp. 412: In the world he who has transcended the two attachments: that of merit and that of demerit, will be free of sadness, unblemished and pure, him I call brahman (*yo dha puññan ca pāpañ ca ubho saṃgaṃ upaccayā asokaṃ virajaṃ suddhaṃ tam ahaṃ brūmi brāhmaṇaṃ*).

215 On the three higher knowledges (*vidyā*), cf. DN III, 28; MN I, 22–4, 482. *Kośa* VII, § 45: Three *abhijñās* are higher knowledge, because they bring about the cessation of non-knowledge concerning the past, etc. (*tiśro vidyā avidhyāya, pūrvāntādau nirvartanāt*).

216 On the six superknowledges (*abhijñā*), cf. DN I, 8; III, 110; MN I, 34; II, 238; AN I, 254–5.

The attaining of the six superknowledges by the Buddha is described in MN I, 69; by his disciples in SN II, 217–22. It is said that, of the 500 monks living with the Buddha, 60 monks attained the six superknowledges. Cf. SN I, 191.

In fact, the first five are qualities common to worldlings (*pṛthagjana*) and holy ones (*ārya*), the sixth (*āśravakṣayajñāna*) is the quality specific to the holy ones. See below, 'The secondary theses of the Pudgalavādins, thesis No.5'. Cf. La Vallée Poussin, 'Les Buddha et les Abhijñā', in *Le Muséon*, 1931, pp.335–42.

217 See below, 'the secondary theses of the Pudgalavādins, thesis No.5'.

218 On the four analytical knowledges (*pratisaṃvid*), cf. AN II, 160; III, 113, 120; *Kośa* VII, §§ 37–40.

Third Section: The Fruit (*phala*)
(Vol.II, 20*b* 5 - 21*b* 25)

The third section of the first chapter on the Good (*kuśala*) deals with the fruit. These fruit pertain to Nirvāṇa with a remainder (*sopadhiśeṣa*) which is differentiated from Nirvāṇa without a remainder (*nirupadhiśeṣa*)[219]. Nirvāṇa, identical to liberation (*vimukti*), is divided into three: it is related to the level and career of its aspirants: Buddha, Pratyekabuddha and Śrāvaka.

I — The Buddha, Pratyekabuddha and Śrāvaka

The Buddha is a perfectly and fully Enlightened One (*samyaksaṃbuddha*). All the Buddhas are equal not only in their accomplishments (*śīla, samādhi, prajñā*), but also in the domains of their attributes (*buddhadharma*)[220]. The Pratyekabuddha is a solitary Buddha. He realises his enlightenment (*bodhi*) by himself and does not

---

219 Nirvāṇa with a remainder (*sopadhiśeṣanirvāṇa*) is obtained through the elimination of the passions (*kleśa*). We understand by 'remainder' (*upadhi*) what is left, i.e., the five grasping aggregates (*pañca upādānaskandha*), which still remain although Nirvāṇa has already been attained. Nirvāṇa without a remainder (*nirupadhiśeṣanirvāṇa*) is the elimination of the passions; at the same time, the five grasping aggregates are also destroyed. In other words, it is Nirvāṇa without the psycho-physical process of existence. Nirvāṇa without a remainder (*nirupadhiśeṣa*) occurs on the death of an Arhat or Buddha. Cf. Itivuttaka, 41; Udāna VIII, 9; MN II, 257; *Kośa* VI, p.211, n.2 (Engl tr. p.1063).

220 Tds, 20*b* 10–11, mentions: the ten powers (*bala*), four confidences (*vaiśāradya*), and all the Buddha attributes (*buddhadharma*). In the Pāli texts, the ten powers and four confidences are also found. Cf. MN I, 69–72; AN II, 8; IV, 83.

According to the *Kośa*, the Buddha attributes are eighteen in number: the ten powers (*bala*), four confidences or absences of fear (*vaiśāradya*), three mindfulnesses (*smṛtyupasthāna*) and great compassion (*mahākaruṇā*). Cf. *Kośa* VII, §§ 28-33.

L'Inde classique II, §2278, summarises as follows the ten powers through which the Buddha knows:

1. The established and the non-established (*sthānāsthāna*),
2. the fruition of actions (*karmavipāka*),
3. the path where it leads (*sarvatragāmanī pratipad*),
4. the world with various bases (*nānādhātu*),
5. the various tendencies [of beings] (*nānādhimukti*),
6. the raising and lowering of their faculties (*indriyavarāvara*),
7. the affliction, purification and establishment of the meditations (*sarvadhyānavimokṣasamādhisamāpattikleśavyavadānavyutthāna*),
8. the recollection of former abodes (in existences, *pūrvanivāsanysmṛti*),
9. deceasing and arising (*cyutyutpatti*),
10. the destruction of the defilements (*āsravakṣaya*).

Cf. MN I, 69–70; AN V, 33; X, 21; Kathāvatthu (*Points of Controversy*) 140, §§ 3-12. Also, *L'Inde classique* II, summarises the four absences of fear or confidences as follows:

The Tathāgata does not fear (1) that anyone will say that he does not possess supreme Enlightenment, (2) that his defilements are not destroyed, (3) that he did not clearly announce the removal of obstructions, and (4) that the Dharma he proclaimed does not lead to the cessation of suffering. Cf. AN II, 8; IV, 83.

teach others[221]. The Śrāvaka, the listener, is the disciple of the Buddha, his liberation comes from teaching by others.

Liberation (*vimukti*) is the common goal of the Buddha, Pratyekabuddha and Śrāvaka[222]. Nevertheless, the means which they use are not the same. The Buddha attains liberation through compassion (*karuṇā*), whilst the Pratyekabuddha and Śrāvaka acquire liberation through repugnance (*nirvidyata*); the difference is that the Pratyekabuddha obtains repugnance by himself, the Śrāvaka through others.

Moreover, they have all attained the elimination of defilements and, furthermore, the Buddha is an Omniscient One (*sarvajña*)[223] ; the Pratyekabuddha is not an Omniscient one, his qualities are not equal to the Buddha's; the Śrāvaka does not possess all the qualities and his career depends on others.

---

221 The Pratyekabuddhas are a kind of intermediate person between Arhats and perfect Buddhas (Bareau, *Religions*, p.62; cf. MN III, 86). They only appear in the world at times when there are no Buddhas (cf. *Le Compendium de la super-doctrine . . . d'Asaṅga*, tr. and ann. by W. Rahula, p.146 and n.3). It is through timidity and lack of courage that the Pratyekabuddhas do not teach the Dharma (*Kośa* III, § 94). The Isigilisutta (MN III, 69–71) gives a long list of names of Pratyekabuddhas (Pāli, Paccekabuddhas), and DN II, 142–3, and AN I, 77, mention their importance. There are two types of Pratyekabuddha: those who live in groups (*vargacārin*) (who appear during the period of increase) and those who are like the rhinoceros [Tr.: or 'rhinoceros horn', i.e. solitary] (living alone, *khaḍgaviṣāṇakalpa*) (*Kośa* III, § 94; cf. Sn (Gavisāṇasutta), p.6. On the difference in their wisdom and acquisition, the Pug, pp.14, 73, declares: The Paccekabuddha and the Sammāsambuddha both attain the truth without receiving instruction from others but the former attains neither omniscience nor mastery of the fruit. Cf. Miln, pp.104–5; Ria Kloppenborg, *The Paccekabuddha, A Buddhist Ascetic*, Leiden 1974, pp.13–35.

222 The Buddhas are Arhats in the sense of having exhausted the fetters of existence (*parikṣṇīnabhavasaṃyojana*). Cf. DN I, 87; MN I, 29. On the other hand, SN III, 66, says that the Tathāgata and a monk liberated by wisdom (*paññavimutta-bhikkhu*) are equal with regard to their liberation (*vimutti*), but the Tathāgata is different from the monk liberated by wisdom because he discovered and showed the Path (*magga*) which was previously unknown.

It is the Buddha himself who declared: 'I am truly an Arhat in the world' (*ahaṃ hi arahā loke* — MN I, 171), when he replied to Upaka, a man he met on the road from Gayā to Bārānasī. MN I, 179: *tathāgato arahaṃ sammāsambuddho*.

Consequently, Arhat is one of the ten epithets of the Buddha: He is, in truth, the Blessed One, the Liberated One, the Perfectly Enlightened One. Endowed with knowledge and conduct, the Auspicious One, the Knower of worlds, the incomparable guide of men to be tamed, the Master of gods and mankind, the Enlightened One, the Blessed One (*iti pi so bhagavā, arahaṃ, sammāsambuddho, vijjācaraṇasampanno, sugato, lokavidū, anuttaro purisadammasārathi, satthā deva manussānaṃ, buddho, bhagavā ti* — DN I, 49, 87, 224; Vin. I, 35).

223 The Buddha is called the Omniscient One since he possesses the threefold knowledge: *pūrvanivāsānusmṛti, divyacakṣus, āsravakṣaya*. MN I, 482: Vaccha, the monk Gotama truly possesses the threefold knowledge. It is right to say so, in relation to what has been said about me and I am not accused of what is false (*tevijjo samaṇo Gotamo ti kho Vaccha byākaramāno vuttavādi c'eva me assa ca man abhūtena abbhācikkheyya . . .*). In reality, the Buddha is not possessed of a knowledge or vision which encompasses everything at all times as has falsely been attributed to him. MN I, 482: The monk Gotama is all-knowing, all-seeing; he claims to possess unlimited vision; he says 'Whether I am moving or standing still, awake or asleep, my knowledge is always and constantly with me. Those people do not say what has been said of me, and accuse me without foundation' (*samaṇo Gotamo sabbaññu sabbadassāvī, aparisesaṃ ñāṇadassanaṃ paṭijānāti: carato ca me tiṭṭhato ca suttassa va jāgarassa ca satataṃ samitaṃ ñāṇadassanam paccupaṭṭhitanti, na me te vuttavādino, abbhācikkhanti ca pana man'te asatā abbhūtenāti*).

II – The Śrāvaka

The Buddha is incomparable. The Pratyekabuddha is unique. As for the Śrāvaka, he is the disciple of the Buddha[224]. Because of the degree of their five faculties[225] which are either soft, middling or sharp, numerous categories of them are known, corresponding to three stages:

1. the stage of not yet abandoned desires (*avītarāgabhūmi*);
2. the stage of abandoned desires (*vītarāgabhūmi*);
3. the Arhat.

Here, the reversal of the order of the three stages, as described in the Tds, is made to assist comprehension.

1. *The stage of not yet abandoned desires*

The stage of not yet abandoned desires consists of three main fruit: each of these fruit is further divided into three categories:

1a. The eighth[226], the first Śrāvaka fruit is he who has realised the Path of Stream-entry (*srotaāpattipratipannaka*)[227] consisting of:

1. he who has pursued the truth through faith (*śraddhānusārin*)[228] ;

---

224 Śrāvaka: the disciple, in a restricted sense, in relation to the four fruit of the eight categories of noble disciples (*āryapudgala*). Cf. MN I, 181; AN I, 208; SN V, 202.

225 SN V, 227: Monks, the faculty of faith is favourable to enlightenment; the faculty of vigour. . ., the faculty of mindfulness. . ., the faculty of concentration. . ., the faculty of wisdom is favourable to enlightenment. That is why they are called the auxiliaries of enlightenment, the qualities of enlightenment (*saddhhiyindriyan bhikkhave. . ., viriyindriyam. . ., satındriyam. . ., samādhinariyam. . ., paññindriyam bodhipakkhiyo dhammo tam bodhāya saṃvattati*). Cf. also AN II, 149.

Kośa II, § 35: 'the five faculties, faith, power, mindfulness, recollection, discernment (*prajñā*), are the support (*āśraya, pratiṣṭhā*) of Nirvāṇa'.

226 *Kośa* VI, § 35: '. . . the eighth holy one is *srotāapanna*'. Also, *Kośa* VI, § 36: 'the "eighth" *aṣṭamaka*. *Pu-kuang* indicates two explanations: 1) the *srotaāpannaphalapratipannaka*; 2) the man possessed of the *duḥkhe dharmajñānakṣānti*'. The second explanation has the same meaning as that of the eighth in the Tds. Cf. Kathāvatthu, 243–51; Mahāvagga, Vin. I, 159.

227 It is also called *sotāpannamagga*, a term explained in the Aṭṭhasālinī as: 'The path of Sotaāpanna is called *dassana* because it is the seeing of Nirvāṇa for the first time. . .' (cited and tr. in *Kośa* VI, p.191, n.3; Engl. tr., p.1059; cf. Aṭṭhasālinī, 43).

228 Tds, 20c 20, 21: 信，信勝慧隨 *śraddhānusārin*: he in whom faith prevails and wisdom is secondary.

MN I, 479: Monks, who is he who has pursued the truth through faith? Monks, there is a certain person who has not touched with his body the peaceful liberations relating to the formless world which are beyond the world of subtle form, dwells there, and when he has seen deliverance through his wisdom, his defilements are completely exhausted; furthermore, he has faith in and affection for the Tathāgata, and also posseses these qualities, namely: the faculties of faith, vigour, mindfulness, concentration and wisdom. That person, monks, is called him who has pursued the truth through faith (*katamo ca bhikkhave puggalo saddhānusārī? idha bhikkhave ekacco puggalo ye te santā vimokkhā atikkamma rūpa āruppā te na kāyena phassitvā viharati, paññāya c'assa disvā āsavā aparikkhīṇā honti, tathāgate c'assa saddhāmattaṃ hoti pemamattam, api c'assa ima dhammā honti, seyyathīdaṃ: saddhindriyaṃ, viriyindriyaṃ, satindriyaṃ, samādhindriyaṃ, paññindriyaṃ ayaṃ vuccati bhikkhave puggalo saddhānusārī*). Cf. MN–A III, 190. The translation of the phrase '. . . *ekacco puggalo ye te santā vimokkhā atikkamma rūpe āruppā* . . .' is made in consultation with the commentary in MN–A III, 188: '. . .

2. he who has pursued the truth through wisdom (*prajñānusārin*)[229] ;
3. he who has pursued the truth through faith and wisdom (*śraddhāprajñānusārin*)[230].

These three categories are differentiated once the practitioner is at the stage of maturity (*gotrabhūmi*) where the knowledge of things (*dharmajñāna*) appears. They depend on the dominant faculty (*indriya*). The first category, in which faith (*śraddhā*) prevails, is that of the soft faculty (*mṛdvindriya*); the second, in which wisdom prevails, is the middling one (*madhyendriya*) and the third, in which both faculties are equally powerful, is the sharp (*tīkṣṇendriya*).

1b. He who has entered the stream (*śrotaāpanna*) or he who has stood on the path[231] consisting of:

4. he who has no more than seven rebirths at the most (*saptakṛdbhavaparama*), soft faculty[232] ;

---

arūpasamāpattiyā rūpakāyo vimutto'. Cf. DN III, 105; SN V, 200–5; Pug, 15; Vism, 659.

Kośa VI, § 29: '. . . he who is in this pursuit, or whose habit is to pursue by reason of faith, is called *śraddhānusārin* because, at first (*pūrvam*: at the *pṛthagjana* stage), he pursued the truth (*arthānusevana*) (. . .) under the impulse of others, through trust in others (*parapratyayena*).

229 Tds, 20*c* 20, 21, 22: 慧，慧勝信隨: *prajñānusārin*: he in whom wisdom prevails and faith is secondary. DN–a, 890: *dhammo = paññā*.

MN I, 479: Monks, who is he who has pursued the truth through the doctrine? There is, monks, a certain person who has not touched with his body the peaceful liberations relating to the the formless world which are beyond the world of subtle form, dwells there, and when he has seen deliverance with his wisdom, his defilements are completely exhausted; futhermore, he partially consents through his wisdom to profound reflection on the doctrines expounded by the Tathāgata, and also possesses the following qualities, namely: the faculties of faith, vigour, mindfulness, concentration and wisdom. That person, monks, is called him who pursued the truth through the doctrine (*katamo ca bhikkhave puggalo dhammānusārī? idha bhikkhave ekacco puggalo ye te santā vimokkhā atikamma rūpe āruppā te na kāyena phassitvā viharati paññāya c'assa disvā āsavā aparikkhīnā honti, tathāgatappaveditā c'assa dhammā paññāya mattaso nijjhānam khamanti, api c'assa ime dhammā honti, seyyathīdam: saddhindriyaṃ, viriyindriyaṃ, satindriyaṃ samādhindriyaṃ, paññindriyaṃ. ayam vuccati bhikkhave puggalo dhammānusārī*). Cf. MN–A III, 190.

230 This is a category combining the two preceding ones.

231 Tds, 21*a* 4–5: 須陀洹者是道；升是道故曰洹. *Srota* is the path (*mārga = srota*) (the word *huan* 洹 in the first phrase is probably superfluous). Because he stands on the path, he is called *āpanna*.

Kośa VI, § 34: '*Srotaāpanna*: the stream (*srotas*), the stream of Nirvāṇa, the path, since one moves (*gamyate*) by means of a stream. The ascetic who has entered it, who has arrived at and reached it, is named = stream enterer (*srota-āpanna*)'. MN I, 142: All monks who have eliminated the three fetters are *sotāpannas* who do not again fall into the bad destinies and are definitively destined to enlightenment (. . . *yesaṃ bhikkhūnaṃ tīni saṃyojanāni pahīnāni sabbe te sotāpannā avinipātadhammā niyatā sambodhiparāyanā*). Cf. DN III, 227. Dhp, 178, speaks of the highest value of the Sotāpanna fruit by comparing the values of this world and those of the heavenly worlds.

232 Tds, 21*a* 6: . . 受天人樂要般涅槃 = (he) enjoys happiness among the gods and mankind before attaining Parinirvāṇa. A similar definition is found in AN I, 233, 235; IV, 381 = *sattakkhataparamaṃ deve ca mānuse ca sandhāvitvā saṃsāritvā dukkhass'antaṃ karoti*.

Kośa VI, § 34: '. . . as he can be reborn seven times but no more, he is a "maximum seven times" (*saptakṛtvaḥ paramaḥ*). On the disagreement between the different schools concerning the number of rebirths in this fruit, cf. *Kośa* VI, § 36 (tr., pp.201–2, Pruden, pp.958–60).

5. he who is reborn in several families (*kulaṃkula*)[233], middling faculty;
6. he who is middling, sharp faculty.

1c. The stage of the refining of desire (*tanūbhūmi*) is the stage of those who possess all the Srotaāpanna qualities and have reduced the passions to be destroyed by cultivation which relate to the world of desire (*kāmadhātu*), consisting of:

7. he who is a once-returner (*sakṛdāgāmin*)[234], soft faculty;
8. he who will not be reborn again (*ekabījīn*)[235], middling faculty;
9. he who is middling, sharp faculty.

2. *The stage of the abandoning of desire (vītarāgabhūmi)*

The stage of the abandoning of desire is the stage in which the practitioner has eliminated the passions of the world of desire or the five lesser fetters (*pañcadhāvarabhāgīya*)[236] ; they consist of three main fruit; each of those main fruit is divided into three categories:

2a. He who is freed by faith (*śraddhādhimukta*) is the fruit in which faith predominates in the attainment of Parinirvāṇa[237], consisting of:

---

233 Tds, 21*a* 7–8: 三結盡思惟所斷少盡。。。從家至家而般涅槃 : having exhausted the three fetters (*saṃyojana*) and refined the passions to be destroyed through cultivation (*bhāvanāheyakleśa*) . . ., he passes from family to family before attaining Parinirvāṇa. The Pāli texts give a precise description of the Kolaṃkola category as follows: *tiṇṇaṃ saṃyojanānaṃ parikkhayā kolaṃkolo hoti, dve vā tīṇi vā kulāni samdhavitvā samsaritvā dukkhassantaṃ karoti* — AN I, 233; IV, 381.

Kośa VI, § 34, gives a similar definition and divides the *kulaṃkula* into two types: 1) *devakulaṃkula*, the holy one who, having been reborn in two or three families among the gods, attains Nirvāṇa in the same heaven or in another; 2) *manuṣyakulaṃkula*, the holy one who, having been reborn in two or three families among men, attains Nirvāṇa in that *dvīpa* or another'.

234 Tds, 21*a* 12–13: 此終生天上，一來而般涅槃 : having deceased in this world, he is reborn in the world of the gods, then returns once more before attaining Parinirvāṇa.

Kośa VI, § 35: 'The *sakṛdāgāmin*, "who returns once", having gone to the gods, returns among mankind, and has no further rebirth, hence his name'.

235 Tds, 21*a* 13–14: 一種者，受一有而般涅槃，增益功德故: he who will be reborn once only is he who receives only one existence before attaining Parinirvāṇa in order to increase his merit. Probably the Sanskrit word behind the Chinese *i-chung* 一種 should be *ekabījīn*, lit. he who would have only one seeding, since *bīja*: seed, grain, germ, but not *ekavīcika* the definition of which in the *Kośa* VI, § 36, recalls: *vīci* signifies interval, separation. Nirvāṇa is separated from that holy one by one rebirth; the fruit of *anāgāmin* is separated (*vyavahita*) from that holy one by one category of passion: he is therefore called *ekavīcika*. AN I, 233: 'he who has only one "seeding" is he who has eliminated the three fetters, being born once only as a human being, he puts an end to suffering' (*tiṇṇaṃ saṃyojanānaṃ parikkhayā ekabījī hoti, ekaṃ yeva mānusakaṃ bhavaṃ nibbattitvā dukkhassantaṃ karoti*). Cf. Pug, 16.

236 *Satkāyadṛṣṭi, śīlavrataparāmārśa, vicikitsā, kāmacchanda* and *vyāpāda*, are called the five lesser fetters (*avarabhāgīyasaṃyojana*) because they bind beings to the lower destinies of the world of desire (*kāmadhātu*), namely: those of the hells (*naraka*), hungry ghosts (*preta*) and animals (*tiryag*). Cf. AN II, 5, 134; *Kośa* V, § 43.

237 Tds, 20*b* 22–23: 以信為首度故曰信解脱 : because faith is dominant in his liberation, that is why he is called he who is liberated through faith. MN I, 478: Monks, who is he who is liberated through faith? There is, monks, a certain person who has not touched with his body the peaceful

1. he who goes upstream (*ūrdhvasrota*)[238] ;
2. he who attains Parinirvāṇa through compounded things (*sābhisaṃskāraparinirvāyin*)[239] ;
3. he who attains Parinirvāṇa through the uncompounded (*anabhisaṃskāraparinirvāyin*)[240].

2b. He who is endowed with correct views (*dṛṣṭiprāpta*) is the fruit in which the element of correct views is dominant in liberation[241], consisting of:

---

liberations relating to the formless world which are beyond the world of subtle form, dwells there, and when he has seen deliverance with his wisdom, some of his defilements are completely exhausted; furthermore, his faith in the Tathāgata is fixed, rooted, established. That person, monks, is called he who is liberated through faith (*katamo ca bhikkhave puggalo saddhāvimutto? idha bhikkhave ekacco puggalo ye te santā vimokkhā atikkamma rūpe āruppa te na kāyena phassitvā viharati, paññāya c'assa disvā ekacce āsavā parikkhīṇā honti, tathāgate c'assa saddhā niviṭṭhā hoti mūlajātā patiṭṭhitā. Ayaṃ vuccati bhikkhave puggalo saddhāvimutto*). Cf. MN-A III, 189-90.

Kośa VI, § 31: 'When faith (*śraddhā*) predominates [in the ascetic with weak faculties], the ascetic is "informed" by his aspiration (*adhimokṣa*): he is therefore called a *śraddhā-adhimukta*'. Cf. Vism XXI, § 74; Bareau, *Religions*, p.59.

238 Tds, 20*b* 25--27:上流者愛彼將至上，復次流者道，彼於 欲界將至上故曰上流: he who goes upstream (*ūrdhvasrota*) is he who, through aspiration, is on the point of attaining the higher stages. Moreover, the stream (*srota*) designates the path (*mārga*). The practitioner, living in the world of desire, is on the point of attaining the higher stages, that is why he is called he who goes upstream.

DN III, 237 = *uddhaṃsota Akaniṭṭha-gāmī*: he who goes upstream towards the Akaniṭṭhā heaven and there attains Parinirvāṇa.

Kośa VI, § 37: 'The *ūrdhvasrotas* is the saint for whom there is *srotas*, that is, *gati* or movement upwards. *Srotas* and *gati* have the same meaning. He does not obtain Nirvāṇa wherever he is reborn on leaving the Kāmadhātu, because he goes upwards'; that is to say, the Akaniṣṭhas consist of three kinds: (1) the jumper (*pluta*), (2) the half-jumper (*ardhapluta*) and (3) the one who dies everywhere (*sarvacyuta*) (cf. *Kośa* VI, § 38).

239 Tds, 20*b* 28–29:行般涅槃者，行謂之有爲，多方便及道緣行至無爲 : he who attains Parinirvāṇa through compounded things (*sābhisaṃskāraparinirvāyin*): The *saṃskāras* are compounded (*saṃskṛta*) things, and it is with numerous means (*upāya*) and the path (*mārga*) and through compounded things (*saṃskāra*), that he reaches the uncompounded. Cf. Pug, 17; *Kośa* VI, § 37. The *sābhisaṃskaraparinirvāyin* attains Nirvāṇa via a path whose object is the compounded (*saṃskṛta*) (= *saṃskāra*), namely, suffering, its origin and the path (*duḥkha, samudava, mārga*).

240 Tds, 20*b* 29–20*c* 2:無行般涅槃者，無行謂之無爲，少方便及道，緣無爲至無爲: he who attains Parinirvāṇa through the uncompounded (*anabhisaṃskāraparinirvāyin*): *anabhisaṃskāra* is the uncompounded; it is with few means (*upāya*) and the path (*mārga*), and through the uncompounded (*asaṃskṛta*) that he attains the uncompounded.

Kośa VI, § 37: The *anabhisaṃskāraparinirvāyin* attains Nirvāṇa via a path which has as its object the Unconditioned (*asaṃskṛta*), namely, cessation or the third Truth (*nirodha*).

241 Tds, 20*b* 23: 以慧爲首度故見到 : because wisdom dominates his liberation, that is why he is called he who is endowed with correct views (*dṛṣṭiprāpta*). MN I, 478: Monks, who is he who is endowed with correct views? There is, monks, a certain person who has not touched with his body the peaceful liberations relating to the formless world which are beyond the world of subtle form, dwells there, and when he has seen deliverance with his wisdom, some of his defilements are completely exhausted; furthermore, he has seen and understood the doctrines expounded by the Tathāgata. That person, monks, is called he who is endowed with correct views (*katamo ca bhikkhave puggalo diṭṭhipatto? idha bhikkhave ekacco puggalo ye te santā vimokkhā viharati, paññāya c'assa te na kāyena phassitvā viharati, paññāya c'assa disvā ekacce āsavā parikkhīṇā honti, tathāgatappaveditā c'assa dhammā paññāya vodiṭṭhā honti*

4. he who attains Parinirvāṇa in the interval (*antarāparinirvāyin*)[242] ;
5. he who attains Parinirvāṇa by being reborn (*upapadyaparinirvāyin*)[243] ;
6. he who goes upstream (*ūrdhvasrota*)[244].

2c. The bodily witness (*kāyasākṣin*)[245] pertains to the formless world (*ārūpyadhātu*). That is why he attains Parinirvāṇa without an intermediate existence. The bodily witness also includes three categories identical to those of the two preceding groups (*śraddhādhimukta and dṛṣṭiprāpta*):

7. he who attains Parinirvāṇa through compounded things (*sābhisaṃskāraparinirvāyin*);
8. he who attains Parinirvāṇa through the uncompounded (*anabhisaṃskāraparinirvāyin*);
9. he who attains Parinirvāṇa in rebirth (*upapadhyaparinirvāyin*)[246].

---

vocaritā. ayaṃ vuccati bhikkhave puggalo diṭṭhipatto). Cf. MN-A III, 189.

Kośa VI § 31: The ascetic with sharp faculties, who was *dharmānusārin*, takes the name of *dṛṣṭiprāpta*. . . When *prajñā* dominates [in the ascetic with sharp faculties], the ascetic is 'informed' by speculative view: he is therefore called *dṛṣṭiprāpta*. Cf. also *Kośa* VI, §§ 61, 63.

242 TDs, 20*c* 46:中般涅槃者，此命終未生餘得道，中般涅槃如小迸未墮已滅 : he who attains Parinirvāṇa in the interval (*antarāparinirvāyin*) is he who, his life having come to an end and whose rebirth in another (world) has not yet occurred, obtains the path (*mārga*) and attains Parinirvāṇa in the interval; he is like a spark which is extinguished before reaching the ground. Cf. Pug, 16. The *Abhidharmakośa* and *Abhidharmasamuccaya* explains the *antarāparinirvāyin* differently as he who attains Nirvāṇa (*parinirvāti*) in an intermediate existence (by going to the *rupadhātu*). Cf. *Le Compendium de la super-doctrine (philosophie) (Abhidharmasamuccaya) d'Asaṅga* (abbrev. *Compendium*), tr. and ann. W. Rahula, p.115; below, 'The secondary theses of the Pudgalavādins: thesis No.14'.

243 Tds, 20*c* 6–7: 生般涅槃者，如火迸墮地即滅，如是始生次第得道般涅槃 : he who attains Parinirvāṇa by being reborn is he who obtains the path (*mārga*), then attains Parinirvāṇa at the moment of rebirth (*utpannamātra*) like a spark which is extinguished the moment it touches the ground.

Kośa VI, §37: The second (*upapadyaparinirvāyin*) acquires Nirvāṇa immediately he is reborn (*utpannamātra*), quickly by means of *sopadhiśeṣa*– (or, according to other masters, *nirupadhiśeṣa*–) Nirvāṇa, because he is zealous (*abhiyukta*) and because the path is spontaneous, realising it himself (*abhiyuktavahimārgatvāt*).

244 This is the same category as that of the *ūrdhvasrota in the śraddhādhimukta* group. See above, n.237.

245 Tds, 20*b* 23–24: 二俱（信慧）是身證 : (liberation) through two elements (faith and wisdom) together is the bodily witness (*kāyasākṣin*). MN 1, 478: Monks, what is the bodily witness? There is, monks, a certain person who has touched with his body the peaceful liberations relating to the formless world which are beyond the world of subtle form, dwells there, and when he has seen deliverance with his wisdom, some of his defilements are completely exhausted. That person, monks, is called bodily witness (*katamo ca bhikkhave puggalo kāyasakkhī? idha bhikkhave ekacco puggalo ye te santā vimokkhā atikamma rupe āruppā te kāyena phassitvā viharati, paññāya c'assa disvā ekacce āsavā parikkhīṇā honti. ayam vuccati bhikkhave puggalo kāyasakkhī*). Cf. MN-A III, 189; AN IV, 451; Pug, 14.

Kośa VI, § 43: The Anāgāmin, whichever he may be, who has acquired *nirodha* — as he has, in his body, seen the absence of thought, immediately experienced (*sākṣātkaroti*) a dharma similar to Nirvāṇa, namely the *nirodhasamāpatti* — is called *kāyasākṣin*, a bodily witness. For details, see *Kośa* VI, § 43 (pp.223-5; Pruden, pp.977-8).

246 The three categories have already been explained above. The characteristic of these fruits is that they pertain to the formless world (*ārūpyadhātu*) in which the intermediate existence (*antārabhava*) does not occur. That is why those who possess them attain Parinirvāṇa without an intermediate existence (Tds,

3. *The Arhat*

The Tds maintains that the Arhat is susceptible to regression[247] and, consequently, it deals with the nine categories corresponding to the three faculties:

3a. Sharp faculty (*tīkṣṇendriya*):
1. he who is stable (*sthitākampyadharman*), he who eliminates the passions by renouncing means (*upāya*)[248].
2. he who progresses (*prativedhanādharman*): he who by eliminating the passions seeks and obtains the excellences[249].
3. he who is immovable (*akopyadharman*): he who possesses an immovable analytical knowledge[250].

3b. Weak faculty (*mṛdvindriya*):

4. he who regresses (*parihānadharman*): he who regresses from comprehension of the Noble Truths (*satyābhisamaya*) or the stage of cultivation (*bhāvanā-bhūmi*)[251].
5. he who thinks (*cetanādharman*): he who thinks of abandoning his existence after having attained Arhatship[252].

20*c* 10–12).

247 See below, 'The secondary theses of the Pudgalavādins: thesis No.13'.

248 Tds, 21*a* 20–21: 住法者，離方便除煩惱故 : lit. he who is stable is he who renounces means by eliminating the passions. *Kośa* VI, § 57: the *sthitākampya* is the Arhat who, while lacking strong causes for regression, even without taking care is subject to not moving, that is, remaining in the fruit; and who, by not regressing, lacks effort (*abhiyoga*) and is not able to progress (*vardhayitum*). Cf. Rahula, *Compendium*, p.157.

249 Tds, 21*a* 21–22: 升進者，除諸煩惱，求上勝能得，勝者達通辯: lit. he who progresses (*prativedhanādharman*) is he who eliminates the passions, seeks the excellences and obtains them; . . . the excellences are higher knowledge (*vidyā*), superknowledge (*abhijñā*) and analytical knowledge (*pratisaṃvid*).

Kośa VI, § 57: The *prativedhanādharman* (= *prative dhanābhavya*) is the Arhat able to penetrate (*prativedhum*) without effort (*abhiyoga*) the Immovable Ones. Cf. Rahula, *Compendium*, p.158.

250 Tds, 21*a* 24: 不動法者，己得勝果，一切談論不動辯才 : he who is immovable (*akopya-dharman*) is he who, having obtained the excellent fruits, possesses analytical knowledge (*pratisaṃvid*) which no discussion can move. *Kośa* VI, § 57: the *akopyadharman* or Immovable One is the Arhat not subject to regression. The *Compendium* gives a similar definition. Cf. Pug, 11.

251 Tds, 21*a* 25: 退法者，或差降退非聖諦。。。或於修地退 . Cf. below, 'The secondary theses of the Pudgalavādins: thesis No.13' and n.752.

252 Tds, 21*a* 19–21*b* 3: 念法者，己得阿羅漢，劣行故及身劣便作是念，我所作己作，我何爲住，如是念恩 : he who thinks (*cetanādharman*) is he who after having become an Arhat, due to the lessening of practice and weakening of the body, thinks that, having accomplished all the tasks to be done, it is useless to remain. Thus does he think.

Kośa VI, § 57: The *cetanādharman* is an Arhat who is capable of putting an end to his existence at will (*cetayitum*), without being an *anurakṣaṇādharman*, etc. It is interesting to note the different interpretation of the Arhat *cetanādharman* in *Compendium*, p.157 (tr.): This is a person by nature having weak faculties, whether distracted or not, who regresses from his state of happiness in this life if it is not reflected upon, but does not regress if it is reflected upon. According to *Kośa* VI, § 57 (p.253, n.5; Pruden, n. 348, p.1072): the *cetanādharman* is he who, fearing falling away, always thinks of putting an end to his existence. Thus, the thera Godhika who, having regressed six times from abounding mental liberation (*samādhika cetovimutti*), committed suicide so as not to regress when he realised it for the seventh time (SN I, 120), was probably a *cetanādharman*. Cf. Pug, 12: *cetanābhabho*.

6. he who preserves (*anurakṣaṇādharman*): he who protects what he has attained with all available means[253].

3c. <u>Middling faculty</u> (*madhyendriya*):

7. he who is liberated through wisdom (*prajñāvimukta*): he who attains liberation through wisdom pertains to the lower category[254] ;

8. he who attains complete liberation[255] ;

9. he who attains incomplete liberation[256].

The last two categories together are also called he who is doubly delivered (*ubhayatobhāgavimukta*), who possesses both faith (*śraddhā*) and wisdom (*prajñā*) and pertains to the excellent category[257].

---

253 Tds, 21*b* 3–4: 護法者，不退亦不思念，但極大方便護。如貪多方便得才守 : he who preserves (*anurakṣaṇādharman*) is he who does not regress and does not think but (mobilises) all available means (*upāya*) to protect himself, just as a poor man acquires a fortune through numerous means and guards it.

Kośa VI, § 57: The *anurakṣaṇādharman* is an Arhat capable of guarding. *Compendium*, p.157; cf. Pug, 12: *anurakkhanābhabho*.

254 Tds, 21*b* 4 does not give a definition of the *prajñāvimukta*, except for the indication of the lower category. MN I, 477: Monks, who is he who is liberated through wisdom? There is, monks, a certain person who, not having touched with his body the peaceful liberations relating to the formless world which are beyond the world of subtle form, dwells there, and when he has seen deliverance through wisdom, his defilements are completely exhausted. That person, monks, is called he who is liberated through wisdom (*katamo ca bhikkhave puggalo paññāvimutto? idha bhikkhave ekacco puggalo ye te santā vimokkhā atikkamma rūpe āruppā te na kāyena phassitvā viharati, paññāya c'assa disvā āsavā parikkhīṇā honti. ayaṃ vuccati bhikkhave puggalo paññāvimutto*). Cf. MN–A III, 188; pug, 14. According to *Kośa* VI, § 64, he who is delivered from the *kleśavaraṇa* through the power of wisdom is a *śraddhādhimukta*.

255 See next note.

256 Tds, 21*b* 5 does not give a definition of these two fruits. *Kośa* VI, § 65: 'The *ubhayatobhāgavimukta* who is *samayavimukta* is complete from the point of view of his attainment. The *ubhayatobhāgavimukta* who is *asamayavimukta* is complete from the point of view of his faculties and attainment'. Cf. Pug, 11.

Kośa VI, § 57: or else *samaya* means 'time': the first five Arhats are susceptible to falling from deliverance (*vimukta*), they are therefore delivered for a time (*kālāntara*), and so are *samayavimukta*; the sixth Arhat (cf. *Kośa* VI, § 56) is not susceptible to falling from deliverance, he is therefore definitively delivered (*atyantavimukta*), and so is *asamayavimukta*.

Hence, he who attains complete liberation 'from the point of view of his faculties and attainment' is probably identical to the *asamayavimukta*, while he who attains incomplete liberation 'from the point of view of his faculties and attainment' is identical to the *samayavimukta*. For, moreover, the two pairs of fruits pertain to the *ubhayatobhāgavimukta* at Tds, 21*b* 6 as well as in *Kośa* VI, § 65: the Asaikṣa is complete from two points of view (faculties and attainment).

257 Tds, 21*b* 7: 俱解脱者，信及慧，已得此二故勝 : lit. he who is doubly delivered is he who (possesses) faith and wisdom; having acquired those two elements, he is excellent. MN I, 477: Monks, who is he who is doubly delivered? There is, monks, a certain person who, having touched with his body the peaceful liberations relating to the formless world which are beyond the world of subtle form, dwells there, and when he has seen deliverance with his wisdom his defilements are completely exhausted. That person, monks, is called he who is doubly delivered (*katamo ca bhikkhave puggalo ubhatobhāgavimutto? idha bhikkhave ekacco puggalo ye te santā vimokkhā atikkamma rūpe āruppā te kāyena phassitvā viharati, paññāya c'assa disvā āsavā parikkhīṇā honti. ayaṃ vuccati bhikkhave puggalo ubhatobhāgavimutto*). Cf MN–A III, 188, Pug, 14.

III — Liberation (*vimokṣa*)

Liberation means the elimination of all passions (*kleśa*) relating to the triple world. Consequently, it consists of the following three categories divided into eight levels[258]:

1 — Liberation in relation to the world of desire (*kāmadhātuvimokṣa*) includes three liberations:

1. Liberation accomplished through the contemplation of the repulsive (*aśubhabhāvanā*), in the perception of beings endowed with internal forms: meditation on the decomposition of a corpse in a cemetery[259] ;
2. Liberation accomplished through contemplation of the repulsive, in the perception of beings devoid of form: without perceiving any form and entering the meditation in which the body of another is perceived like that described earlier[260] ;
3. Liberation accomplished through contemplation of the lovely (*śubhābhāvanā*): meditation on detachment from colours[261].

2 — Liberation in relation to the world of subtle form (*rūpadhātuvimokṣa*) includes four liberations in which the desires of the world of subtle form are already eliminated. These are the four attainments (*samāpatti*) related to the formless world (*ārūpyadhātu*)[262] ;

3 — Liberation through cessation (*nirodhavimokṣa*) is liberation accomplished through the cessation of thoughts (*citta*) and concomitant mental actions (*cittasamprayukta*)[263].

These eight levels of liberation designate the lowest to the highest degrees of meditation practice.

---

258 The eight liberations (*vimokṣa*) constitute one of the best known methods of meditation and are described in all the canonical texts; for example: DN II, 262; MN II, 12–13; AN I, 40; IV, 306. The *Kośa* VIII, §§ 32–4, gives a detailed analysis of this subject.

259 See next note.

260 Among the eight liberations, the first are accomplished through contemplation of the repulsive (*aśubhābhāvanā*) aimed at eliminating desire, and practised in the first two absorptions (*dhyāna*). On the contemplation of the repulsive, cf. DN II, 296; MN III, 82; *Kośa* VI, § 9.

261 This is liberation accomplished by the contemplation of the lovely (*śubhābhāvanā*), practised in the fourth absorption (*dhyāna*). Cf. *Kośa* VIII, § 32.

262 These four liberations are identical to the four attainments (*samāpatti*) of the formless world .

263 This liberation is none other than the attainment of the cessation of perception and feeling (*saṃjñāveditanirodhasamāpatti*). It is considered as true Nirvāṇa in this world.

AN IV, 454: Moreover, a monk, having gone completely beyond the sphere of neither perception nor non-perception, enters the cessation of perception and feeling, dwells there and, when he has seen deliverance, his defilements are completely exhausted. In that sense, the Blessed Lord calls it Nirvāṇa in this world, in the real sense (*puna ca param. . . bhikkhu sabbaso nevasaññānāsaññāyatanaṃ samatokkamma saññāvedayitanirodham upasampajja viharati, paññāya c'assa disvā āsavā parikkhīṇā honti. Ettavatā pi kho. . . diṭṭha dhammanibbānam vuttam bhagavatā nippariyāyena*).

CHAPTER TWO: THE BAD (*AKUŚALA*)
(Vol.II, 21*b* 26 - 25*a* 26; questions 89-150)

In the second chapter, the Tds deals with the Bad (*akuśala*). The bad is defined as 'blemish', that which blemishes good conduct. It consists of misconduct (*duścarita*), thirst (*tṛṣṇā*) and ignorance (*avidyā*).

First section: misconduct (*duścarita*)
(Vol.II, 21*b* 28 - 23*a* 7)

Instead of dealing with the ten kinds of misconduct as do other canonical books[264], the Tds lists only nine of them, grouped into three main categories:

I — Misconduct of body (*kāyaduścarita*)

Misconduct of body is of three kinds:

1. Taking life (*prāṇātipāta*), the action of killing beings, accomplished with:
   a) the intention of killing which consists of: 1) mental desire: the idea of killing; 2) the desire to be killed by another: inciting others to kill; 3) joy at the action of others: feeling joy at killing by others;
   b) the order to kill which consists of: 1) advising; 2) ordering others to kill; and 3) approving the killing of others;
   c) the deed of killing, the realisation of killing which consists of: 1) the idea of living beings; 2) the idea of relinquishing life; and 3) the destruction of life[265].

2. Theft (*adattādāna*) is the action of voluntarily taking the possessions of others, accomplished with: a) the idea of the possessions of others; b) the idea of stealing, and c) appropriation with intention[266].

---

264 *Kośa* IV, § 65: Bad actions of body, speech and mind are regarded as being the three bad practices. On the ten kinds of misconduct, cf. MN I, 44, 360; III, 23; AN I, 111; Vin.V, 138.

265 *Kośa* IV, § 73: Taking life is to kill another, consciously, without making an error (*prāṇātipātaḥ saṃcintyābhrāntyaiva parāmaraṇam*, p.153, n.1; cf. Pruden, p.649). The Aṭṭhasālinī, 97, lists the five conditions necessary for taking life: 'a living being, consciousness that there is a living being there, the intention of killing, the attack and the death resulting therefrom' (*tassa pañca sambhārā honti: pāno, pānasaññitā, vadhakacittam, upakkamo, tena maraṇan'ti*), and the six methods of achieving it: with one's own hand, by instigation, by a projectile, by stratagem, by ruse or by supernormal means (*cha payogā: sāhatiko, āṇattiko, nisaggiko, thāvaro, vijjāmayo, iddhimayo ti*). Cf. *Traité* II, p.784, n.1.

266 *Kośa* IV, § 73: 'Theft, taking what is not given (*adattādāna*) — is to appropriate the possessions of another by force or in secret' (*adattādānaṃ paravasvīkaraṇaṃ balacchalāt*, p.155, n.4; cf. Pruden p.651). Aṭṭhasālinī, 98, analyses theft into five constituents: possessions of others, consciousness that they are the possessions of others, the intention to steal, the execution and taking away resulting therefrom (*pañca sambhārā honti: parapariggahītam, parapariggahītasaññitā, theyyacittam, upakkamo tenāharanaṃ*). There are six methods of stealing: with one's own hand, etc. One or another of these methods will be implemented according to circumstances, through stealing by false weights and measures, by force, by concealing, by intrigue or by counterfeiting (*chappayogā sahatthikādayo va. te ca kho yathānurūpaṃ theyyāvahāro pasayhāvahāro paṭicchannāvahāro parikappāvahāro kusāvahāro ti imesam avahārānaṃ vasena pavattā*). Cf. *Traité* II, p.795, n.1.

3. Sensual misconduct (*kāmamithyācāra*) is forbidden sensual relationships, practised with: a) the women of others; b) persons observing the law[267], and c) through forbidden paths (*amārga*)[268].

On this subject, the Tds shows that sexual acts by lay people are not necessarily misconduct (*duścarita*), but that sexual wrong action is misconduct; whereas, for monks, all sexual relations constitute misconduct because they should observe continence (*brahmacarya*).

Next, the Tds affirms that all wrong things arise from three bad roots: it is possible that wrong things arise either from attachment (*rāga*), or from hatred (*dveṣa*) or from attachment alone since from attachment comes hatred. That is why there can be no confusion between the 'initial resolve' and the sequence of events. For example, 'it is through covetousness of the teeth and skin (of animals) that hostility (towards them) ensues, then the action of killing'.

II — Misconduct of Speech (*vāgduścarita*)

Traditionally, misconduct of speech is of four kinds[269], but the Tds abridges them to three:

1. Lying (*mṛśāvāda*) is discourse which dissimulates the truth, it is motivated by covetousness of a gain: a) for oneself; b) for another or c) for reasons of self-interest[270].

2. Speech which is too frank is speech which possesses the following three qualities: a) speech devoid of grace, harmful speech (*pāruṣyavāda*)[271] ; b) speech

---

267 The commentary in the Tds on the women of others and persons subject to the law is very clear and rich; cf. Tds 22*a* 5–18. MN I, 286: In sensuality, there are illicit practices: relationships with girls under the guardianship of a mother, father, mother and father, brother, sister or relatives; with girls who are under the protection of the law, already promised to a husband and protected by a stick, or even with girls crowned with the flower-garlands of betrothal (*kāmesu micchācārī kho pana hoti, yā tā māturakkhitā piturakkhitā (mātāpiturakkhitā) bhāturakkhitā bhaginirakkhitā ñātirakkhitā sassāmikā saparidaṇḍā, antamaso mālāguṇaparikkhittā pi, tathārūpāsu cārittaṃ apajjitā hoti*). Translated in É. Lamotte, *Traité* II, p.799, n.1; cf. AN V, 176; *Kośa* IV, § 74.

268 According to the Tds, 22*a* 18–21, sexual relations through forbidden paths consist of sexual intercourse with (1) a woman after her confinement, (2) a young girl by force, (3) a man (= homosexuality) and (4) a hermaphrodite. *Traité* II, p.799, n.1, b : Intercourse with one's own wife through a forbidden pathway (*amārga, anaṅga*), that is to say, anywhere that is not the *yoni*. Cf. *Kośa* IV, § 74 (p.157, n.3; cf. Pruden, pp.652, 739, n.330).

269 These are: (1) lying (*musāvāda*), (2) slander (*pisuṇāyavāda*), (3) harmful speech (*pharusāya*), (4) frivolous speech (*samphappalāpa*); cf. MN I, 44.

270 Aṭṭhasālinī, p.99: Lying has four constituent factors: (1) a false thing, (2) the intention to deceive, (3) a corresponding effort and (4) communication of the thing to another (*tassa cattāro sambhārā honti: atathaṃ vatthu, visaṃvādanacittaṃ, tajjo vāyāmo, parassa tadatthavijānan ti*). Translated by É. Lamotte in *Traité* II, p.804, note. *Kośa* IV, § 74: Lying is discourse held, with differing thoughts, with a person who understands its meaning.

271 *Kośa* IV, § 76: Harmful speech is abusive discourse.

which provokes separation, slander (*paiśunyavāda*)[272] ; c) speech which possesses both characteristics of the first two, combined harmful and slanderous speech.

3. Frivolous speech (*saṃbhinnapralāpa*) consists of: a) inopportune discourse; b) untruthful discourse and c) senseless discourse[273].

III — Misconduct of thought (*manoduścarita*)

Misconduct of thought designates three mental actions:

1. Covetousness (*abhīdyā*) is desire for other peoples' goods, a wish to seize others' possessions; it is differentiated from intention which is the desire to act, because it is desire limited to itself[274].
2. Ill-will (*vyāpāda*) is malevolent thought which is disposed to oppress others[275].
3. False view (*mithyādṛṣṭi*) is heresy, of which there are three kinds: a) opinions denying actions (*karman*)[276] ; b) opinions denying results (*vipāka*)[277] and c) nihilism (*nāstidṛṣṭi*)[278].

   The three preceding categories of mental misconduct include all bad causes opposed to all good causes.

Second section: thirst (*tṛṣṇā*)
(Vol.II, 23*a* 9 - 24*a* 8)

The second section of the second chapter deals with thirst (*tṛṣṇā*) which, according to the Tds, is pursuit[279], consisting of three elements: attachment (*rāga*), hostility (*hui* 恚 , *pratigha*?) and conceit (*māna*).

I — Attachment (*rāga*)

---

272 *Ibid.*, malicious or slanderous speech is the discourse of a person with a defiled mind with a view to dividing.

273 Frivolous speech (*saṃbhinnapralāpa*) is inconsiderate speech. It is all defiled discourse which is not lying, slander or harmful. Cf. *Kośa* IV, §§ 76–7.

274 *Kośa* IV, § 77: Covetousness is the desire to appropriate, through illegal ways, the goods of others.

275 *Kośa* IV, § 78: Malevolence is hatred of living beings.

276 It is opinion that denies moral causality (*ahetudṛṣṭi*) or non–action (*akiriyavāda*). For example, Makkhali–Gosāla denied will and all causes of corruption predestined by fate. He accepted rebirth but denied that man can modify his destiny. Cf. DN I, 53–4. MN I, 250: The Buddha criticised him as one of the most harmful persons. Cf. AN I, 33.

277 This is the opinion of Pūraṇa–Kassapa who denied merit and demerit or all the results of good or bad actions (*akiriyavāda*). Cf. DN I, 5, 35, 52; MN II, 404.

278 This is the opinion of ethical nihilism (*natthikavāda*) of Ajita–Kesakambali, asserting that all belief in a good action and its recompense is pure delusion because, according to him, life is nothing but a combination of the four great elements, namely: earth, water, fire and air, and after death, there is nothing. Cf. DN I, 55; MN I, 515; III, 71; *Kośa* IV, § 78.

279 *Kośa* III, § 23 gives the same definition: *tṛṣṇā*, the state of him who desires sense pleasures and sexual union.

Attachment[280] consists of:

1. Attachment to sense-desire (*kāmarāga*)
   a) five kinds of attachment corresponding to five sense-objects (*kāmaguṇa*)[281] ;
   b) three kinds of attachment: 1) attachment to desire for a man (weak category); 2) attachment to desire for a woman (middling category); and 3) attachment to desire for a hermaphrodite (strong category).

2. Attachment to existence (*bhavarāga*) which corresponds to the triple world:
   a) attachment to the world of desire (*kāmarāga*);
   b) attachment to the world of subtle form (*rūparāga*);
   c) attachment to the formless world (*ārūpyarāga*)[282].

3. Attachment to the pure life (*brahmacaryarāga*)
   a) attachment after having obtained the desired object;
   b) desire before obtaining the desired object[283] and
   c) sorrow following the loss of the desired object.

Attachment to existence has as its object the living beings and things of the triple world, whilst attachment to sense-desire concerns the passions (*kleśa*). The process consisting of the three phases of attachment to the pure life can be applied to the other two attachments. As for attachment to sense-desire, this process applies to a woman, a man and a hermaphrodite; hence there are nine kinds of attachment in all. This number is equally valid for the last two attachments. In all, twenty-seven kinds of attachment are counted.

II — Hostility (*hui* 恚 , *pratigha*?)

Hostility is discontent caused by oneself, by those close to one or by one's adversaries[284]. The Tds deals with hostility in the section on thirst by explaining it as ill-will which also forms part of thirst.

Wishing ill occurs in four circumstances:

(1) for oneself, (2) for those close to one, (3) one seeks happiness which one has not yet obtained, and (4) happiness having been obtained, one does not wish to lose it; unhappiness which has descended on one, one wishes to escape, and the unhappiness which still spares us one wishes to avoid. As for the adversary, while unhappiness still does not affect him, one wishes that it will descend on him, and, unhappiness having reached him, one desires it to endure; happiness not having

280 Cf. DN III, 254; MN I, 433; AN IV, 9. *Kośa* V, §§ 1, 2, defines attachment as a tendency (*anuśaya*) associated with pleasure.

281 These are: form (*rūpa*), sound (*śabda*), odour (*gandha*), taste (*rasa*) and the tangible (*spraṣṭavya*).

282 On the triple world (*dhātu*), cf. MN III, 63; AN IV, 67–8; *Kośa* II, § 73; E. Lamotte, *History*, pp.32–3.

283 MN I, 102: Based on thirst (*taṇhā*) means that sort of morality aroused by desire for a happy life; for example, 'because of this moral habit, custom, austerity, pure life, I will become a heavenly being or another god (*iminā haṃ sīlena vā vatena vā tapena vā brahmacariyena vā devo vā bhavissāmi devaññataro vā ti*).

284 W. Rahula, in his *Compendium*, p.9, translates *pratigha* as 'repugnance'; the definition of the former in the text is: 'It is ill-will (*āghāta*) towards living beings, suffering, and conditions of suffering'.

been obtained by him, one wishes that he never obtain it, and, when he does obtain it, one wishes that he lose it quickly.

Amongst the three kinds of hostility, hostility caused by oneself or hostility caused by those close to one have the same nature: they are manifested in the three time-periods: the past, present and future, during which all pursuit is in vain. Hostility caused by an adversary is also manifested in the three times-periods, but it ensues from the success of the foe. Hence, there are nine kinds of hostility in all.

Hostility, in this sense, is different from ill-will (*vyāpāda*), described in the three kinds of misconduct, since the former has external causes, whilst the latter is anger caused by ignorance.

The Tds divides hostility into three categories, based on their duration:

1. The weak is compared to patterns which appear on the surface of water and which disappear instantaneously;
2. The middling, to patterns made by oneself, and which endure for a while;
3. The strong, to patterns engraved on stone, which only vanish along with it.

III — Conceit (*māna*)

Conceit is arrogance, originating in a thought of comparing oneself to others[285] There are nine kinds of conceit in all:

1. Conceit of inferiority (*unamāna*), arising from the idea: 'I am not like others'; this conceit is manifested according to the following characteristics: a) mistaken conceit (*mithyāmāna*); b) unreal conceit (*abhūtamāna*); c) very lowly conceit (*adhihīnamāna*);

2. Conceit of equality (*samamāna*), arising from the idea: 'I am equal to others'. It also has three characteristics: a) conceit due to oneself (*asmimāna*); b) conceit due to arrogance; c) conceit due to disdain;

3. Conceit of superiority (*adhimāna*), arising from the idea: 'I am superior to others'. It is divided into three categories: a) profound conceit; b) extremely profound conceit (*matimāna*); excessive conceit (*abhimāna*)[286].

---

285 *Kośa* II, § 33: *Māna*, conceit-scorn, is arrogance; *Compendium*, p.9,: It is mental exaltation (*cittasyonnatiḥ*) which is based on the idea of the self.

286 Similarly, the Jñānaprasthānaśāstra, T XXVI, 1544, 1028*b* 26-28 teaches nine types of *māna*, *mānavidhā*, or simply *vidhā*, namely:

1. 'I am better (*śreyān*)'; 2. 'I am equal'; 3. 'I am less good';
4. 'Another is better than myself'; 5. 'He is my equal'; 6. 'He is less good than I';
7. 'Another is no better than myself'; 8. 'He is not equal to me'; 9. 'He is no less good than I'.

These nine types come from three *mānas*, namely: *māna*, *adhimāna* and *ūnamāna*, while the *Kośa* counts only seven *mānas*, namely: *māna*, *adhimāna*, *mānātimāna*, *asmimāna*, *abhimāna*, *ūnamāna*, *mithyāmāna*. Cf. *Kośa* V, § 10.

Third section: Ignorance (*avidyā*)
(Vol.II, 24*a* 10 - 25*a* 24; questions 135 - 150)

According to the Tds, ignorance (*avidyā*)[287] consists of: non-knowledge (*ajñāna*), erroneous knowledge (*mithyājñāna*) and doubt (*vicikitsā*).

I — Non-knowledge (*ajñāna*)

Non-knowledge designates:

1. Non-comprehension of compounded things (*saṃskṛta*), that is, non-comprehension of:
   a. appropriation (*upādāna*) — of the aggregates (*skandha*), elements (*dhātu*) and spheres (*āyatana*) of oneself and others, that is, attachment to the self (*ātman*) and attachment to what pertains to the self (*ātmīya*);
   b. non-appropriation (*anūpādāna*) — grass, trees, a wall, etc., and the appropriation of others as an object;
   c. both together.

2. Non-comprehension of the uncompounded (*asaṃskṛta*) designates non-comprehension of:
   a. Nirvāṇa with a remainder (*sopadhiśeṣa*);
   b. Nirvāṇa without a remainder (*nirupadhiśeṣa*);
   c. a combination of both[288].

3. Non-comprehension of the ineffable (*avaktavya*) designates non-comprehension of:
   a. the designation of appropriation (*upādānaprajñapti*): the living being (*sattva*) who, not having appropriated the aggregates, elements and spheres, is considered as both identical to them and different from them[289] ;
   b. the designation of the past (*atītaprajñapti*): the teaching based on the aggregates, elements and spheres of the past;
   c. the designation of cessation (*nirodhaprajñapti*): the teaching based on the cessation of appropriation, for example, the Parinirvāṇa of the Buddha[290].

---

287 Tds, 24*a* 12–13: 如人有惡子說無子，如是無明惡明故說無明 : Just as having one's chi!dren devoured is equivalent to not having any at all, so, because ignorance (induces) aberrant knowledge, it is that which is called ignorance. The canonical texts give precise definitions: 'Ignorance is what hides the four Noble Truths' (cf. SN II, 4), the origin and disappearance of the aggregates (cf. SN III, 162, 171). Being one of the defilements (*āsrava*) and one of the tendencies (*anuśaya*), it constitutes the original condition of the process of the twelve links of the cycle of birth and death.

Kośa III, § 28: '*Avidyā* is an entity (*dharma*) apart, the contrary of *vidyā*, 'knowledge', like non-friend, not-true, etc.' (*vidyā-vipakṣo dharmo 'nyo vidyāmitrānṛtadivat*).

288 Cf. above, n.219.

289 Tds, 24*b* 2–3: 受施設者，眾生已受陰界入，計一及餘 The translation is based on the following meaning: appropriation (受 *upādāna*) is synonymous with the living being (*sattva*) who, in turn, is synonymous with the *pudgala*.

290 See below, 'The main thesis of the Pudgalavādins'.

Moreover, the designation of the past has as its aim the remedying of the false views on annihiliation (*ucchēdadṛṣṭi*) of living beings, the designation of cessation as remedying false views on eternalism (*śāśvatadṛṣṭi*), the designation of appropriation as remedying non-existentialism (*nāstidṛṣṭi*), and the designation of non-appropriation as remedying existentialism (*astidṛṣṭi*).

II — Erroneous knowledge (*mithyājñāna*)

Erroneous knowledge designates:

1. Belief in individuality (*satkāyadṛṣṭi*)[291]:
   a. belief in the reality of the self (*ātman*),
   b. belief in the reality of what pertains to the self (*ātmīya*), and
   c. belief in the reality of freedom (*aiśvarya*)[292].

2. Extreme views (*antagrāhadṛṣṭi*):
   a. belief in annihilation (*ucchedadṛṣṭi*),
   b. belief in eternity (*śāśvatadṛṣṭi*), and
   c. belief in a combination of both[293].

3. Attachment to views (*dṛṣṭiparāmarśa?*)[294]:
   a. attachment to rules (*śīla*);
   b. attachment to views (*dṛṣṭi*)[295] ;
   c. attachment based on the two preceding ones[296].

---

291 This is the first of the ten fetters (*saṃyojana*), consisting of twenty categories obtained by applying four categories of belief in individuality to each of the aggregates (*skandha*): (1–5) belief in being identical to the body (*rūpa*), feelings (*vedanā*), perceptions (*saṃjñā*), formations (*saṃskāra*) or consciousness (*vijñāna*); (6–10) belief of being known in them; (11–15) belief of being independent from them; (16–20) belief in being their possessor.

Kośa V, § 7: Believing in me and mine (*ātmātmīyagrāha*) constitutes *satkāyadṛṣṭi*.

292 Tds, 24*b* 14–16: 'Belief in the reality of freedom is the illusion regarding the five sense-objects (*pañcakāmaguṇa*) which are similar to the trunk of a banana tree, to balls of foam on water; they are considered as freedom (*aiśvarya*), (whereas they are) like heavenly cities'.

293 According to the Tds, 24*b* 18–22, the first two views (*antagrāhadṛṣṭi, ucchedadṛṣṭi*) maintain that: (1) the universe is eternal and non-eternal or is neither eternal nor non-eternal; (2) the universe is limited and unlimited or is neither limited nor unlimited; (3) the body and life (*jīvita*) of living beings have an end and do not have an end or neither have an end nor do not have an end; and the last view (combination of both the above) maintains that: (1) the universe is simultaneously eternal, limited and unlimited; (2) living beings are simultaneously eternal and non-eternal.

294 Tds, 24*b* 23: *taochien* 盗見 . The translation of the Sanskrit word *dṛṣṭiparāmarśa* (*chien* 見 = *dṛṣṭi*, *tao* 盗 = *parāmarśa*) is probably mechanical. Here, the word means attachment to views.

295 Tds; 24*b* 26: 此眞實餘虛非眞，是謂見盗(= 盗見) This (opinion) is true, the others are false and untruthful, that is attachment to views (*dṛṣṭiparāmarśa*). Similar phrases are found in the canonical texts, for example: '. . . the world is eternal, that is the truth, any other (opinion) is foolish (*sassato loko, idam eva saccaṃ, mogham aññan ti* — Udāna, p.67).

296 According to Tds, 24*b* 27–29, attachment based on the two preceding ones is attachment which rests either on rules or on views, by considering that they constitute means of purification, such as the five elements of purification, namely: morality (*śīla*), concentration (*samādhi*), wisdom (*prajñā*), deliverance (*vimukti*) and the knowledge of deliverance (*vimuktijñāna*). Cf. AN III, 57.

The Tds also classes these three elements of erroneous knowledge as follows: belief in individuality and extreme views are found in the Truth of suffering, in relation to the triple world; attachment to rules is found in the Truth of suffering and the Truth of the Path in relation to the triple world.

Satkāyadṛṣṭi *Antagrāhadṛṣṭi*	*duḥkhasatya*	*Kāmadhātu* *Rūpyadhātu* *Ārūpyadhātu*
Śīlaparāmarśa	*duḥkhasatya* *mārgasatya*	*Kāmadhātu* *Rūpyadhātu* *Ārūpyadhātu*

III — Doubt (*vicikitsā*?):

Doubt[297] is indecision, hesitation:

1. Not understanding the jewels (*ratna*):
   a) the Buddha; b) the Teaching (*dharma*); c) the Community (*saṃgha*);

2. Not understanding the truth (*satya*):
   a) conventional truth (*saṃvṛtisatya*) - the traditional habits, customs of society, and the rules of training;
   b) characteristic truth (*lakṣaṇasatya*) — suffering (*duḥkha*), the origin of suffering (*samudaya*), and the Path (*mārga*);
   c) absolute truth (*paramārthasatya*) — Nirvāṇa[298].
   According to the Tds, only a single truth exists on the absolute level[299].

3. Not understanding concentration (*samādhi*) which consists of:
   a. Concentration in relation to the world of subtle form (*rūpyadhyāna*), the absorptions (*dhyāna*)[300], immeasurables (*apramāna*)[301], spheres of mastery

---

297 This is the translation of the expression *huo chih* 惑智 (Tds, 24*a* 10, 11, 24*c* 1). It is probable that the word *chih* 智 is necessary for the first two elements: *fei chih* 非智, *hsieh chih* 邪智, but is not needed for the third: *huo* 惑, where the Sanskrit word is *vicikitsā*.

298 Nirvāṇa is the absolute because it is the only reality which actions of body, speech and mind cannot attain or conceive. Cf. Tds, 25*a* 1–5.

299 See below, 'The secondary theses of the Pudgalavādins, thesis No.10'.

300 These are the four absorptions (*dhyāna*); see above, n.188.

301 These are the four immeasurables; see above, n.189.

(*abhibhvāyatana*)[302], three deliverances (*vimokṣa*)[303], the first eight of the ten spheres of totalisation of the object (*kṛtsṇāyatana*)[304] ;

b. attainment in relation to the formless world (*ārūpyasamāpatti*), the four attainments in relation to the formless world, the last two of the ten spheres of totalisation of the object (*kṛtsṇāyatana*)[305] ;

c. undefiled concentration (*anāśravasamādhi*): this is concentration leading to the exhaustion of the defilements. It consists of the concentrations on emptiness (*śūnyatāsamādhi*), on wishlessness (*apraṇihitasamādhi*) and on nonperception (or signlessness — *wu hsiang* 無 相 , *asaṃjñāsamādhi*: *animittasamādhi*)[306].

Moreover, there are twelve categories of doubt by including noncomprehension of the four Noble Truths in relation to the triple world. The influence of doubt is very powerful, that is why doubt is also mentioned under the preceding headings

Further on, the Tds states that in all there are ninety-eight tendencies; if thirst (*tṛṣṇā*) is analysed in detail[307].

---

302 The spheres of mastery (*abhibhvāyatana*) are eight in number: (1) having a notion of visible forms internally, one sees limited (*parītta*) forms externally and masters them; (2) similarly, one sees unlimited (*apramāṇa*) forms; (3) having a notion of formlessness internally, one sees limited forms externally and masters them; (4) similarly, one sees unlimited forms; (5) having a notion of formlessness internally, one sees forms that are blue. . . (6) . . . yellow . . . (7) . . . red . . . and (8) . . . white, and masters them. The first two spheres of mastery are identical to the first deliverance (*vimokṣa*); the next two to the second; and the last four, to the third. Cf. DN II, 110 sq.; MN II, 11, 13; IV, 305, 348; AN I, 40; IV, 305; *Kośa* VIII, § 35; Vism, p.175; Dhs, p.52; Bareau, *Religions*, p.57; Rahula, *Compendium*, p.167, n.1.

303 These are: (1) deliverance through emptiness (*śūnyatāvimokṣa*) resulting from the elimination of the conception of self (*ātman*), (2) deliverance through signlessness (*animittavimokṣa*), from the illusion of the impermanence of things; (3) deliverance through wishlessness (*apraṇihitavimokṣa*), from attachment to objects of craving, hatred and delusion. Paṭisambhidāmagga II, 35: *tayo me bhikkhave vimokkhā suññato vimokkho animitto vimokkho appanihito*. *Kośa* III, § 25: Immaculate, they are the three *vimokṣamukhas*. Cf. also p.187, n.2; Vism XXI.7).

304 The first eight of the ten spheres of totalisation of the object (*kṛtsṇāyatana*) are the spheres of totalisation of (1) earth (*pṛthivīkṛtsṇāyatana*), (2) water (*ap-*), (3) fire (*tejas-*), (4) wind (*vāyu-*), (5) blue (*nīla-*), (6) yellow (*pīta-*), (7) red (*lohita-*), (8) white (*avaaāta-*). These spheres, which present elements of the whole universe, constitute an external means of arousing and developing concentration and attaining the four absorptions (*dhyāna*) pertaining to the world of subtle form (*rūpadhātu*). Cf. DN III, 268; MN II, 14; AN V, 46; Vism, p.110, *Kośa* VIII, § 36.

305 The last two of the ten spheres of totalisation of the object (*kṛtsṇāyatana*), namely, space (*ākāśa-*) and consciousness (*vijñāna-*), relate to the last two formless attainments (*ārūpyasamāpatti*).

306 See above, n.209.

307 There are 6 *anuśayas*: *rāga, pratigha, māna, avidyā, dṛṣṭi, vimati* (*Kośa* V, p.9). They make 98 by counting 36 *anuśayas* in the world of desire (*kāmadhātu*), 31 in the world of form (*rūpadhātu*) and 31 in the formless world (*ārūpyadhātu*) (*Kośa* V, p.9) Cf. *Traité* I, p.424, n.4.

CHAPTER THREE: THE SUPPORT (*NIŚRAYA*)
(Vol.III, 25*b* 5 - 30*a* 14; questions 151-223)

The third chapter deals with the Support (*niśraya*). The support signifies the criteria on which beings base their existence and knowledge. It includes the aggregates (*skandha*), elements (*dhātu*) and spheres (*āyatana*). These three elements constitute the Support of the Good (*kuśala*) and Bad (*akuśala*).

First section: The Aggregates (*skandha*)
(Vol.III, 25*b* 26 - 26*b* 24)

The image the Tds uses to illustrate the word 'aggregate' (*skandha*) is 'heap', 'pile'. Generally, the aggregates are five in number[308]. Here, the Tds reduces them to three: form (*rūpa*), pyschological formation (*saṃskāra*) and knowledge (*vijñāna*). Although they are three in number, they encompass all the psycho-physical phenomena of existence.

I — Form (*rūpa*)

Form designates the group of corporeality. It consists of:

a) the four great elements (*mahābhūta*): earth (*prithividhātu*): solidity (*khakkhatatva*); water (*abdhātu*): liquidity (*dravatva*); fire (*tejodhātu*): heat (*uṣṇatva*); wind (*vayudhātu*): mobility (*laghusamudīranatva*). These are the separate and mixed elements.

b) derived form (*upādāyarūpa*):

1. the visible (*sanidarśana*): colours: blue (*nīla*), yellow (*pīta*), red (*lohita*), white (*avadata*); shapes: rough (*karkaśatva*), silky (*kasāya*), tall (*dīrgha*), short (*hrasva*), square (*caturaṅga*), round (*parimaṇḍala*);
2. the invisible (*anidarśana*): sound (*sabda*), odour (*gandha*), taste (*rasa*), the tangible (*spraṣṭavya*), the five sense-organs (*pañcendriya*) and four great elements (*mahābhūta*).

The Tds also counts smoke (*dhuma*), clouds (*abhra*), mist (*mahika*), etc., as derived form[309].

II — Formation (*saṃskāra*)

Formation designates the group of psychological elements, supported by the body, speech and mind, and which constitute bodily activities, vocal activities

308 These are the aggregates of (1) form (*rūpaskandha*), (2) feeling (*vedanā-*), (3) perception (*saṃjñā-*), (4) the formations (*saṃskāra-*), and (5) consciousness (*vijñāna-*). They designate all the psycho-physical phenomena, as the Buddha declared, of the existence of a man or a being. Cf. SN III, 59-61.

309 The aggregate of form designates all that is form or matter in the universe. SN III, 86: All that is effected materially is called form (*ruppati ti kho bhikkhave tasmā rūpaṃ iti vuccati*); cf. MN I, 53. *Kośa* I, § 12 sq., gives a detailed explanation of this subject.

and mental activities[310].

Accomplished activities pertain to the sphere of compounded things (*saṃskṛta*), which is formation (*saṃskāra*). In reality, the five aggregates are formations from the sphere of compounded things (*saṃskṛta*)[311]. There are innumerable kinds which act according to these combinations and innumerable ways. By analysing it according to the three worlds (*dhātu*), formation (*saṃskāra*) consists of:

a. meritorious formation (*puṇyābhisaṃskāra*);
b. demeritorious formation (*apuṇyābhisaṃskāra*);
c. immovable formation (*āneñjyābhisaṃskāra*)[312].

III — Knowledge (*jñāna*)

Knowledge is synonymous with the factors of the Path (*margāṅga*)[313]. Knowledge is a collective term to designate: (1) feeling (*vedanā*), (2) perception (*saṃjñā*) and (3) consciousness (*vijñāna*).

1. Feeling (*vedanā*) is merely feeling associated with life (*jīva*), but it is not life. It is nothing but itself. According to its nature, three categories of feeling can be distingushed:
a. pleasant feeling (*sukhavedanā*), arising from sense-pleasures, non-illwill and non-attachment;
b. unpleasant feeling (*duḥkhavedanā*), arising from birth, old-age and death;
c. Neither pleasant nor unpleasant feeling (*aduḥkhasukhavedanā*), contrasted

---

310 The aggregate of psychological formations (*saṃskāraskandha*) includes different mental actions which it is difficult to reduce to a precise definition. The Theravādin Abhidhamma masters analyse this aggregate into 50 mental functions (*cetasika*), among which is volition (*cetanā*), with the sense of motivation, activity, attitude, etc. (cf. SN III, 60). This volition is manifested in three kinds of activity: bodily, vocal and mental (cf. MN I, 301). In this sense, this aggregate is identical to action (*karman*) (cf. AN III, 415; VI, 13, 15) and constitutes a force which influences the process of rebirth (cf. DN III, 258).

311 SN III, 87: What is it, monks, that you call the formations? Because they form all that is compounded, that is why they are called formations. What is the compounded that they form? They form form as the compound of form; they form feelings as the compound of feelings; they form perceptions as the compound of perceptions; they form mental functions as the compound of mental functions; they form consciousness as the compound of consciousness. Hence, monks, they form compounded things, that is why they are called formations (*kiñca saṅkhāre vadetha? saṅkhataṃ abhisaṅkharontīti, bhikkhave tasmā saṅkhārā ti vuccati. kiñca saṅkhataṃ abhisaṅkharonti, rūpaṃ rūpattāya . . ., vedanaṃ vedanattāya . . ., saññaṃ saññattāya . . ., saṅkhare saṅkhārattāya . . ., viññānaṃ viññāṇattāya saṅkhatam abhisaṅkharonti; saṅkhataṃ abhisaṅkharontīti kho bhikkhave tasmā saṅkhārā ti vuccanti*).

Kośa I, § 7: Compounded things (*saṃskṛta*) constitute the pentad of the *skandhas*, form, etc.

312 Amongst these three formations of action, the first two, meritorious formation extends from the world of desire to the world of subtle form; immovable formation, to the formless world. On the three formations of action, and their cessation, cf. SN II, 80–4.

313 See below, 'The secondary theses of the Pudgalavādins: thesis No.12'.

to the two preceding ones[314].

Taken as a whole, feelings exist in the three worlds, but whilst pleasant feelings exist the the world of desire and the world of subtle form, unpleasant feelings only exist in the world of desire.

On the subject of the origin of feelings, pleasant feeling relies on an abundance of desire, unpleasant feeling on the magnitude of hate, and neither pleasant nor unpleasant feeling on the depth of ignorance.

Moreover, there is pleasant feeling without craving, which can eliminate desires, such as the third absorption; unpleasant feeling without hatred, such as the Buddha who, suffering from a headache and wound in his foot, did not arouse hatred; and neither pleasant nor unpleasant feeling, which exists in the fourth absorption and the attainments of the formless world.

All feelings arise from action (*karman*), restraint and the elements (*dhātu*).

1. Feelings arising from action consist of:
   a. pleasant feelings which arise from meritorious action (*puṇyakarman*), which exist in the four absorptions, etc.; they can dispel misconduct (*duścarita*);
   b. unpleasant feelings which arise from demeritorious actions (*apuṇya-karman*) constitute misconduct;
   c. immovable feelings which arise from immovable actions (*āneñjya-karman*) such as the fourth absorption and the attainments of the formless world.

2. Feelings arising from restraint consist of:
   a. restraint by oneself, for example when, having harmed ourselves with a knife, we tend our wound;
   b. restraint by others, for example when someone, having given us a head-wound, tends us, and,
   c. restraint by oneself and others, for example when a man, having asked another to harm himself, tends him afterwards.

3. Feelings arising from of the elements (*dhātu*), understood in the sense of fundamental constituent parts, consist of:
   a. feelings arising with time (*kāla*) — because of changes in time, one has pleasant or unpleasant feelings;
   b. feelings arising from the ill — physical illness which consumes the body; and
   c. feelings arising from misfortune — material or natural things which

---

314 On the three conditions, cf. DN III, 275; SN III, 86; IV, 232. They arise immediately on contact. Consequently, there are six kinds of feeling which are based on the five senses and the mind; cf. MN I, 51).

Kośa I, § 14: Feeling (*vedanā*) is a painful impression, etc. Cf. *Compendium of Philosophy* (Abhidhammatthasaṅgaha) by S.Z. Aung and C.A.F. Rhys Davids, London 1890, p.111 sq. Furthermore, there are other classifications of 36 or 108 feelings. Cf. Vibhāṣā, 139, T XXVIII, 1545, 715*a*.

give rise to misfortune.

2. Perception (*saṃjñā*) implies the receptivity of images[315]. Because the field of action of knowledge relates to the three worlds, there are three kinds of perception:

a. perception (*saṃjñā*) is the receptivity of images, relying on two elements: subject and object;
b. the absence of perception (*asaṃjñā*) is the absence of receptivity, the state of non-reliance on two elements: subject and object; and
c. the attainment of non-perception (*asaṃjñāsamāpatti*); this is the total abandoning of receptivity of objects, namely, sound, form, etc.

The Tds adds:

a. perception also designates the attainment in the sphere of the infinity of consciousness (= *vijñānānantyāyatanasamāpatti*)[316] ;
b. the absence of perception is the attainment in the sphere of neither perception nor non-perception (*naivasaṃjñāsaṃjñāyatanasamāpatti*);
c. the attainment of non-perception is the attainment in the sphere of nothingness (*ākiṃcanyāyatanasamāpatti*)[317].

3. Consciousness (*vijñāna*) is knowledge of different things[318]. It consists of:

a. what is born; it is at the moment of conception, by entering the mother's womb, that the different kinds of formation (*saṃskāra*) together produce consciousness[319] ;
b. what forms the sense spheres (*āyatana*); it is consciousness, continually increasing even in the mother's womb, which gradually forms the sense

---

315 SN III, 87: What is it, monks, that you call perception? Because it perceives, monks, it is called perception. What does it perceive? It perceives (colour): blue, green, yellow, red, white . . . (*kiñca bhikkhave saññaṃ vadetha? sañjānāti kho bhikkhave tasmā saññā ti vuccati. kiñca sañjānāti? nīlam . . ., pītakaṃ . . ., lohitakaṃ . . ., odātam pi sañjānāti . . .*). On the six kinds of perception which are aroused by contact, cf. AN III, 413.

Kośa I, § 4: notion (*saṃjñā*) consists of the apprehension of signs.

316 Tds, 26*b* 10: *Kuan shan shih ch'u* 觀善識處 . The translation here is adapted to the context, since it cannot be translated otherwise despite the meaning of the Chinese words.

317 Perception, in Buddhism, implies not only the fact of receiving the qualities of objects, but also the knowledge of internal objects, ideas, memory, imagination, illusion, ideation, etc. Cf. MN I, 410, AN V, 105; Sn, 874.

318 SN III, 87: What is it, monks, that you call consciousness? It is conscious, monks, that is why it is called consciousness. Of what is it conscious? It is conscious of bitter (taste), etc. . . . (*kiñca bhikkhave viññānaṃ vijānāti? vijānātīti kho bhikkhave tasmā viññānam ti vuccati. kiñca vijānāti? ambilam pi vijānāti . . .*).

Kośa I, § 14: Consciousness (*vijñāna*) is the impression relating to each object. Cf. Aṭṭhasālinī III, 185.

319 I.e., consciousness (*vijñāna*) which is formed in the course of past lives and descends into the mother's womb at the moment of rebirth (*saṃskāra pratītya vijñāna*). See below, 'The main thesis of the Pudgalavādins: *pudgala*-designated-by-transmigration, and n.581.

spheres[320] of four kinds: (1) disturbed spheres, (2) undisturbed spheres, (3) fixed spheres, and (4) unfixed spheres[321] ; and,

c. what is not formed by the sense spheres; this is consciousness, after birth, which is conditioned by the faculties and objects of the faculties (*indriyārtha*)[322].

Consciousness, according to the Tds, is the point of support (*āśraya*) of wisdom (*prajñā*), what is supported (*āśrita*)[323].

Second Section : The Elements (*dhātu*)
(Vol.III, 26*b* 26 - 28*c* 28)

As from the second section of the third chapter, the Tds deals with the elements of the three worlds. They include all living beings up to those who have attained

---

320 It is consciousness (*vijñāna*) which conditions the production of mentality and corporeality (*vijñāna pratītya nāmarūpa*) which, in turn, conditions the production of the six sense spheres (*nāmarūpa pratītya ṣaḍāyatana*). The Tds shortens the process and merely emphasises the function of consciousness. SN II, 114: Just like, friend, two bunches of reeds stay upright supporting each other, so, friend, consciousness depends on name-and-form, and name-and-form is conditioned by consciousness, the ten sense spheres are conditioned by name-and-form, contact by the ten sense spheres, etc. Such is the origin of this whole mass of suffering (*seyyathāpi āvuso dve naḷakalāpiyo aññam nissāya tittheyyum. evam eva kho āvuso nāmarūpapaccayā viññāṇaṃ viññaṇapaccayā nāmarūpaṃ, nāmarūpapaccayā saḷāyatanaṃ saḷāyatanapaccayā phasso, pe. evam etassa kevalassa dukkhakkhandhassa samudayo hoti*). Cf. DN II, 63.

321 Tds, 26*b* 19: *chêng pu chêng ju, ting pu ting ju* 諍不諍入，定不定入. The translation is based only on the interpretation.

322 MN I, 11-12: By reason of the eye and the visible, friend, visual consciousness arises . . . And, friend, by reason of the ear and sounds auditory consciousness arises, . . . by reason of the nose and odour olfactory consciousness arises, . . . by reason of the tongue and taste gustatory consciousness arises, . . . by reason of the body and the tangible bodily consciousness arises, . . . by reason of the mind and mental objects mental consciousness arises . . . (*cakkhuñcāvuso paṭicca rūpe ca uppajjati cakkhuviññāṇaṃ, . . . sotañcāvuso, paṭicca sadde ca uppajjati sotaviññāṇaṃ, . . . ghānañcāvuso paṭicca gandhe ca uppajjati ghānaviññāṇaṃ, . . . jivhañcāvuso paṭicca rase ca uppajjati jivhāviññāṇaṃ, . . . kāyañcāvuso paṭicca phoṭṭabbe ca uppajjati kāyaviññāṇaṃ, . . . manañcāvuso paṭicca dhamme ca uppajjati manoviññāṇaṃ*). *Kośa* III, § 32, *Traité* II, p.747, n.1.

323 In general, consciousness is discrimination (*vijānāti vijānāti ti . . . tasmā viññāṇam ti vuccati* — MN I, 292); it is discrimination of the pleasant, unpleasant and neutral (*kiñca vijānāti: sukhan ti pi . . . dukkhanti pi . . . adukkhamasukhanti pi vijānāti* — MN I, 292); or one knows things through consciousness (*tena viññāṇena jānāti* — MN III, 242); whilst wisdom is comprehension ((*prajānāti pajānātīti . . . tasmā paññāvā ti vuccati* — MN I, 292); it is the comprehension of suffering, its origin, cessation and the Path (*kiñca pajānāti: idam dukkhan-ti . . ., ayaṃ dukkasamudayo ti . . ., dukkhanirodho ti . . ., dukkhanirodhagāminī pajānāti* — MN I, 292). The difference between these two mental factors is that wisdom is cultivated, whereas consciousness is cognition, knowledge (*paññā bhavetabhā viññāṇaṃ pariññeyyaṃ, idam nesaṃ nānākaraṇaṃ* — MN I, 293). Furthermore, wisdom pertains to the aggregate of the formations (*saṇkhārakhandha*), whilst consciousness pertains to the aggregate of consciousness (*viññāṇakhandha*). However, in reality it is difficult to distinguish one from the other; as it is said in the text: . . . such is wisdom, such is consciousness; these things are intermingled or are not intermingled. Can the difference between these things be demonstrated after having analysed them so many times? What one comprehends one knows, what one knows one comprehends (*yā ca paññā yañca viññāṇaṃ ime dhammā saṃsaṭṭhā no visaṃsaṭṭhā, na ca labhā imesaṃ dhammānaṃ vinibbhujitvā vinibbhujitvā nānākaraṇaṃ paññapetuṃ. yaṃ pajānāti taṃ vijānāti, yaṃ vijānāti taṃ pajānāti* — MN I, 292).

Parinirvāṇa without a remainder (*nirupadhiśeṣa*) and consist of:

1. the elements of the world of desire (*kāmadhātu*);
2. the elements of the world of subtle form (*rūpadhātu*); and
3. the elements of the formless world (*ārūpyadhātu*).

I — The world of desire (*kāmadhātu*)

Because sensual desire (*kāma*) dwells there and because sensual desire is maintained there, it is called the world of desire; it consists of five destinies[324], namely:

1. Mankind (*manuṣya*) consisting of:
   a. man (*puruṣa*),
   b. woman (*strī*), and
   c. the hermaphrodite — all live on the four continents (*catvārodvīpa*) surrounded by the ocean: (1) Jambudvīpa, to the south[325]; (2) Pūrvavideha, to the east; (3) Aparagodānīya, to the west; (4) Uttarakuru, to the north[326].

2. The gods of the world of desire (*kāmadeva*) who are gods who arouse sensual desire (*yü shêng t'ien* 欲生天) with goddesses (*apsarā*)[327]; this distinguishes them from the gods who have abandoned sensual desire (*li yü t'ien* 離欲天, *vītarāgadeva*. They are of three kinds:
   a. gods whose sensual desire is expressed by conversation (*shuo yü shêng t'ien* 說欲生天), the Nirmāṇaratis;
   b. gods whose sensual desire is expressed by look (*ch'in yü shêng t'ien* 親欲生天): the Paranirmitavaśavartins:
   c. gods whose sensual desire is expressed by contact (*hsi hua yü shêng t'ien* 細滑欲生天) are of three kinds: (1) gods whose sensual desire is expressed by entwining: the Yāmas; (2) gods whose sensual desire is expressed by holding hands: the Tuṣitas; (3) gods whose sensual desire is expressed by coupling: that is, the Trāyastriṃśas, who dwell on the summit of Mount Sumeru; the Cāturmahārājakāyikas, who dwell in the middle of Mount Sumeru; the Bhūmidevas, who dwell in the forests of that land.

   All these gods obtain their sensual satisfaction as a man does, but in their case there is no emission of impurities, only of breath. Their longevity is great.

3. The bad destinies (*durgati*) are places where there is more suffering than joy. Beings in those destinies always tend towards the Bad. They are considered as

---

324 *Kośa* III, § 1: Hell, *pretas*, animals, mankind, six [spheres of] gods: such is the Kāmadhātu. On the five destinies, see below, 'The secondary theses of the Pudgalavādins: thesis No.11'.

325 According to ancient Indian geographical knowledge, Jambudvīpa is the triangular continent or rose-apple continent in which India is situated. Cf. Bareau, *Religions*, p.43; A. Foucher, *La vie du Bouddha*, p.33.

326 On the four continents, dimensions and life-spans of living beings of those continents, cf. *Kośa* III, pp.175–7 ff (Pruden, p.473 ff).

327 Tds, 26c 18: *t'ien nü* 天女 : goddesses who are the equal of the gods in the six levels of the world of desire (*kāmadhātu*).

afflicted and there are three:

a. hells (*naraka, niraya*);
b. animals (*tiryagyoni*);
c. hungry ghosts (*preta*).

3a. The hells are places where one cannot be happy[328]. There are many of them, which are divided as follows:

1. Cold hells (*śītanaraka*) which consist of:
    a) hells with distinctive lamentations: (1) the Arbuda, (2) the Nirarbuda, and (3) the Ababa;
    b) hells with non-distinctive lamentations: (4) the Hahava, (5) the Huhuva, and (6) the Utpala;
    c) hells without lamentation: (7) the Kumuda, (8) the Sogandhika, (9) the Puṇḍarīka, and (10) the Padma[329].

    The ten cold hells are located between the four continents and touch the bottom of the great circle of the iron mountain (*mahācakravāda*). They are all hells destined for those who have spoken and thought ill on meeting the holy ones.

2. Hot hells (*uṣṇanaraka*), which consist of:
    a) hells provided with torturers: (1) the Saṃjīva, (2) the hell of 'the aligned', and (3), the Kālasūtra;
    b) hells with a small number of torturers: (4) the Saṃghāta, (5) the Mahāraurava, (6) the Prātāpana. The guardians (*narakapāla*) of the two preceding hells are not burnt by fire, as are the hell-bound, because of their mission; as for the consequences of their actions, that cannot be contemplated[330] ;
    c) hells without torturers: (7) the Ṛaurava, (8) the Tāpana, and (9) the

---

328 The Buddha denounced popular, superstitious belief in hell during his time; but he spoke of repugnant, nauseous and ugly worlds. On the hells (*naraka, niraya*) in the canonical texts, cf. J. Masson, *La religion populaire dans le canon bouddhique pāli*. p.96 sq.; L. Feer, 'L'enfer indien', IA, 1892, II, p.213 sq.

329 SN I, 152, AN V, 172 also count ten cold hells, but their names are not the same: (1) *Abbuda*, (2) *Nirabbuda*, (3) *Ababa*, (4) *Aṭaṭa*, (5) *Ahaha*, (6) *Kunuda*, (7) *Sogandhika*, (8) *Uppala* (AN V, 172): *Uppalakā*, (9) *Puṇḍarīka*, (10) *Padma*. *Shih chi ching* 世記經 (T I, 1, 125*c*); *Ta liu t'an ching* 大樓炭經 (T I, 23, 286*c*); *Ch'i shih ching* 起世經 (T I, 14, 329*a*) also count ten cold hells. The Saṃyuktāgama, T II, 99, 351*c*–352*a*; Divyāvadāna, p.47, and *Kośa* III, § 59, accept only eight cold hells: (1) *Arbuda*, (2) *Nirarbuda*, (3) *Aṭaṭa*, (4) *Hahava*, (5) *Huhuva*, (6) *Utpala*, (7) *Padma*, (8) *Mahāpadma*. Cf. Lin Li-kouang, *L'Aide-mémoire*, p.10 sq., with a good and long note on the cold hells.

330 On the problem of the infernal guardians (*nirayapāla*), the Tds does not supply satisfactory explanations. According to a Viṃśaka commentary, the Sāṃmitīyas believed that the guardians of the hells were real beings (*Kośa* III, § 59 — pp.152–3, n.3; Pruden, p.534, n.409). In contrast, the Sarvāstivādins accepted that the guardians of the hells were not living beings (*Kośa*, ibid, p. 153, n.1; Pruden. p.534, n.410). The Theravādins affirmed that there certainly existed infernal guardians just as executioners and punishments existed in this world; cf. Kathāvatthu (*Points of Controversy*), pp.345–7.

Avīci[331].

3. Frontier hells (*pratyantanaraka*) which are hells found under water, in mountains and in deserts[332]. The hell-bound undergo, alone, the consequences of their bad actions there.

3b. Animals (*tiryak*) are all the species which are born as animals because of various criminal actions[333], that is to say:
a) beings which walk on the ground;
b) beings which swim in water; and
c) beings which fly in the air.

According to another classification, animals are distributed into: (1) apods, like the snake, etc.; (2) bipeds, like birds, etc.; (3) multipeds, like oxen, horses, bees, myriapods, etc.

3c. Hungry ghosts (*preta*) are living beings reborn in a particularly wretched condition in fruition of their bad actions [334]. They consist of:
1. The wretched, those who are most wretched: (a) hungry ghosts whose mouths spit fire; (b) hungry ghosts whose mouths are as small as the prick of a needle; (c) the deceased whose mouths are malodorous;
2. The poor, those who sometimes obtain a little impure food: (a) hungry ghosts with pointed hair like needles; (b) the deceased with putrid hair; (c) the goitrous deceased;
3. The rich: (a) the deceased who live off rejected things; (b) hungry ghosts living off lost things; (c) hungry ghosts who possess great power (the Yakṣas, Rākṣasas and Piśācas)[335].

II — <u>The world of subtle form</u> (*rūpadhātu*)

The world of subtle form is the world in which are reborn living beings who, due to meditation, obtain a wonderful form. It consists of:

---

331 Hence, the Tds, 27*b* 24–28*a* 17 counts nine hot hells, including the hell of 'the aligned' (*hsing ti-yü* 行地獄) that is not found in other texts, which accept only eight hot hells; cf. Jātaka V, pp.266–71; Divyāvadāna, p.67; *Ch'i shih ching* 起世經 T I, 14, 320*c* sq; *Mahāvastu* I, tr. J.J. Jones, London 1949, pp.6–13; *L'Aide-mémoire*, p.3. According to the Tds, 27*c* 12–14, the hell of the aligned is a hell in which 'the hell-bound are arranged in lines, as in abattoirs, (their) hands, feet, ears, noses and heads are severed. Those hell-bound were butchers, which is why they undergo such sufferings'.

332 On the frontier hells (*pratyantanaraka*) which are often sixteen in number, cf. *Shih chi ching* 世記經 (T I, 1, 121*c*), *Ta liu t'an ching* 大樓炭經 (T I, 23, 283*c*), *Ch'i shih ching* 起世經 (T I, 1, 320*c*). *Kośa* III, § 59: The sixteen hells are created by the power of actions of all beings (. . .); there are hells, the *prādeśika* hells, created by the power of individual actions, the actions of one being, two beings, several beings. Their variety is great; their place is undetermined: river, mountain, desert, or elsewhere. Cf. also *Kośa*, p.155, n.1; Pruden, p.535, n.415.

333 Cf. AN II, 72–3; Vin II, 10.

334 *Kośa* III, 9: They (the *pretas*) are of two kinds, apparitional and also chorion-born. Cf. also *Kośa*, p.29, n.3; Pruden, p.504–5, n.75.

335 On the Yakṣas, Rākṣasas, Piśācas, cf. J. Masson, *La religion populaire dans le canon bouddhique pāli*, pp.126 sq., 134 sq.

1. The level of joy (*prīti*):
   a) the spheres endowed with reasoning (*savitarka*) of the Brahmapurohitas, Brahmakāyikas and Brahmapāriṣadyās;
   b) the spheres endowed only with investigation (*savicāramātra*) of the Mahābrahmas who are experienced in the intermediate absorption (*dhyānāntara*)[336] ;
   c) the spheres devoid of reasoning (*avitarka*) of the Parīttābhas, Apramāṇābhas and Ābhāsvaras;

2. The level of joylessness (*aprīti*): the spheres devoid of joy of the Parittaśubhas, Apramāṇaśubhas and Śubhakṛtsnas;

3. The level of equanimity (*upekṣā*):
   a) the sphere with perception of the Bṛhatphalas;
   b) the sphere without perception of the Asaṃjñins;
   c) the sphere associated with the awakened mind of the Suddhāvāsikas: namely, Sudṛśas, Sudarśanas and Suddhas[337].

III — The formless world (*ārūpyadhātu*)

The formless world consists of the four stages in which are reborn those who have practised the right attainments (*samāpatti*). This is explained under the heading of cultivation (*bhāvanā*) in the first chapter.

Third Section - The Domains (*āyatana*)
(Vol.III, 29*a* 9 - 30*a* 14)

The domains (*āyatana*) are the basis of the Good (*kuśala*) and Bad (*akuśala*). There are three domains: the domain of the tangible (*hsi hua ju* 細滑入 , *spraṣṭavyāyatana* ?); the domain of reasoning (*tu ju* 度入 , *tarkāyatana* ?) and the domain of liberation (*chieh-t'uo ju* 解脱入 , *vimokṣāyatana* ?). Among them, the domain of liberation is that of the Good, the domain of reasoning is that of the Bad and the domain of the tangible is that of both.

I — The domain of the tangible (*hsi hua ju* 細滑入 , *spraṣṭavyāyatana* ?)

The domain of the tangible is based on objects (*ālambana*) and is divided into three fields of action (*ching chieh* 境界 , *viṣaya* ?):

1. The nearby field of action (*chin ching-chieh* 近境界 , *saṃnikṛṣṭaviṣaya* ?) is the field of action which is the origin of the different kinds of tangible which

---

336 On the intermediate absorption (*dhyānātara*), see below, 'The secondary theses of the Pudgalavādins: thesis No.9'.

337 Generally, the canonical texts count five levels of Śuddhāvāsikas (those of the pure abode), namely: (1) Avṛhas (the not-large), (2) Atapas (the heatless), (3) Sudṛśas (the good-looking), (4) Sudarśanas (those of good aspect), and (5) Akaniṣṭhas (the not-inferior). Cf. DN III, 237; MN III, 103; *Kośa* VI, § 37; *L'Inde classique* II, § 2261.

are attained through knowledge;

2. The not-nearby field of action (*pu chin ching-chieh* 不近境界, *viprakṛṣṭiviṣaya* ?) is the field of action the objects of which are not in contact with the organs and which depends on the power of the faculty of perception of external objects;

3. The domain of the absence of a field of action (*wu ching-chieh* 無境界, *aviṣayāyatana* ?) is the domain in which no correspondence exists between the objects and the senses[338].

II — The domain of reasoning (*tu ju* 度入, *tarkāyatana* ?)

The domain of reasoning is the domain of innumerable non-Buddhist opinions on the cause of compounded things (*saṃskṛtadharma*). Generally, three theories exist in relation to this domain:

1. The theory of a single cause (*i ch'u yin shuo* 一處因說, *ekahetudṛṣṭi*)[339] ; is belief in only one cause — actions (*karman*)[340] among the three causes, namely (past) actions, (present) action by oneself and action performed by others;

2. The theory of the incorrect cause (*pu chêng.yin shuo* 不正因說, *visamahetudṛṣṭi* ?) is the attribution of the origin of the world as well as of the good and bad to (1) creators — Brahmā, Iśvara, Viṣṇu[341], (2) things — time

338 According to the Tds, 29*a* 28–29*b* 4, the domain of the absence of a field of action (*wu ching-chieh* 無境界, *aviṣayāyatana*) is that of lack of contact between the sense faculties and their objects, i.e.: form, sound, odour, taste and tangible (無緣說無境界 — Tds, 29*a* 9; 此五境界無緣 — Tds, 29*b* 2).

339 Accepting dependent origination (*pratītyasamutpāda*) as the principal law, all Buddhist schools deny the theory of a Primal Cause as well as that of a single cause. Cf. MN I, 92–3; AN III, 61; Aṭṭhasālinī, 59: *ekakāranavādo paṭisedhito hoti.*

340 The expression 'actions' here indicates actions from the past; this is a belief according to which present existence is caused only by what was done in the past (*pubba-kata hetu*). This opinion was criticised by the Buddha as being the doctrine of passivity — fatalism. Cf. AN III, 61; MN II, 214 sq., Jā V, 208.

341 Brahma, Iśvara or Maheśvara, and Viṣṇu are the gods of the brahmanic Trimurti; cf. *Traité* I, p.137, n.2. The belief according to which the world was created by Brahmā or Iśvara (*issara-nimmāna-hetu*) was criticised by the Buddha as being theistic determinism.

DN III, 28: Certain monks and brahmans believe, according to their traditional doctrine, that (the beginning of the universe) is the work of the Lord or of Brahmā (*eke samaṇabrāhmaṇā issarakuttaṃ brahmakuttaṃ ācariyakaṃ aggaññaṃ paññapenti*). MN II, 227: Monks, if living beings, having been created by a creator, receive pleasant or unpleasant feelings, then, monks, the Nigaṇṭhas are truly created by a cruel creator, since, in the present, they receive such painful, severe, sharp feelings (*sace, bhikkhave, sattā issaranimmānahetu sukhadukkham paṭisaṃvedenti, addhā, bhikkhave, nigaṇṭha pāpakena issarena nimīnitā, yaṃ etarahi evarūpā dukkhā tippā kaṭukā vedanā vediyanti*).

On the criticism of theism, cf. also Jā V, 238; VI, 208, or K.N. Jayatilleke, *Early Buddhist Theory of Knowledge*, pp.410–11; Gunapāla Dharmasiri, *A Buddhist Critique of the Christian Concept of God*, Colombo 1974; Helmuth von Glasenapp, *Buddhism — A Non-Theistic Religion*. tr. Irmgard Schloegel, London 1970.

(*kāla*)[342], breath (*prāṇa*)[343] and spontaneity[344], and (3) both;

3. The absence of a cause (*ahetudṛṣṭi*)[345] is the opinion which denies any cause of the good and bad, such as the theory of inherent nature (*svabhāvadṛṣṭi*)[346], the

---

342 Tds, 29*c* 7–8: Time creates everything,
Everything ripens with time,
Everything is destroyed by time,
All worlds are created by time.

Time (*kāla*) is thus a force outside compounded things and considered like Iśvara, Puruṣa, Prajāpati and Prakṛti, who are supposed to create living beings and the universe (Ud-a, 345: *atthato parena issarena vā purisena vā pajāpatina vā kālena vā pakatiyā vā atthā ca lokoca nimmito ti attho*). In the Atharvaveda (19, 53, 54), Kāla, conceived as an hypostatised entity having everything under its control and 'beyond which there is no other greater force' (*tasmād vai nā 'nyatparamasti tejaḥ*, 53–4), is said to have produced both the past and the future (*kālo ha bhūtaṃ bhavyañ ca . . . ajanayat*, 19, 54–3), while it is itself eternally existent (*ajaraḥ*, 19, 53–1; *amṛtaṃ nyasaḥ*, 19, 53–2), according to Jayatilleke, *op. cit.*, p.142 and the notes. The *Traité*, when criticising the opinion according to which time (*kāla*) is considered as the cause of all things, gives a stanza similar to that of the Tds:

Time passes by and beings ripen,
Time advances and beings burgeon.
Time can understand men,
That is why Time is a cause.

Cf. *Traité* I, pp.76–9. Clearly, the two preceding stanzas are variants of a well-known verse of the Kālavāda: Time ripens beings; time embraces creatures . . .
Time watches for those who sleep; Time, in truth, is difficult to overcome.

(*kāla paccati bhūtāni kālaḥ saṃharate prajāḥ, kālaḥ sypteṣu jagarti kālo ti duratikramaḥ* — extracted from Madhyamakavṛtti, p.386). On the subject of time, cf. Lilian Silburn, *Instant et Cause*, Paris 1955, pp.137–42.

343 The word breath (*prāṇa*), according to the Veda, designates physical life (since as long as there is breath, there is life), which is identical to the Ātman and Brahman as life and cosmic priniciple. Cf. Bṛhadāraṇyaka Upaniṣad, 1, 5, 3; 3, 9, 26; Chāndogya Up., 3, 13, 5, etc.; J. Gonda, *Les religions d'Inde (Vedisme et Hindouisme ancien)*, p.241; L. Silburn, *op. cit.*, 'le souffle vital et cosmique, principe de continuité', pp.106, 108.

344 Tds, 29*c* 5: *tsê-jan* 自然 . There is no commentary concerning this theory. However, due to the criticism of the commentator: 'If spontaneity produces (things), it no longer makes sense (自然若生非自然義— Tds, 29*c* 16), we may suppose that this is the theory maintaining that things are produced by the very initiative of agents, without the intervention of other conditions.

345 The theory of the absence of a cause (*ahetudṛṣṭi*) is one of the three false opinions criticised by the Buddha (cf. AN III, 61). It was the doctrine of Maskarin Gośāliputra, a contemporary of the Buddha, who was also a fatalist (cf. DN I, 53). Jā V, 237: If actions have no cause, then who would be responsible for wrongs: (*akāma-karaṇīyasmiṃ kuvidha pāpena lippati?*).

346 Tds, 29*c* 20–22: 性者言萬物性中生非因他，所以者何。如棘刺利無能利也 : The theory of inherent nature (*svabhāvadṛṣṭi*) says that all things are engendered by their own nature and not by other causes. Why? For example, a pointed spine is sharp, there does not exist (any other thing) which made it sharp. L. Silburn, *op. cit.*, p.133: [tr] 'For the Svabhāvavādins, things spring into existence without the intervention of an internal or external final cause such as actions performed previously by each or by divine will. Things evolve in a mechanical way, through their own nature: if the spines which I come up against are therefore sharp and if they are found on my path, it is their nature to prick; it is not in any way through divine decree, nor because of faults I might have commited'. Cf. *ibid.*, pp.132–5: 'Svabhāvavāda'.

theory of chance[347] and non-existentialism (*nāstidṛṣṭi*)[348].

III – The domain of liberation

Liberation (*vimukti*) is the elimination of the bad and the reaching of the other shore (*pāra*). This domain consists of:

1. Perception (*saṃjñā*) — the penetration of the truth;
2. Absorptive meditation (*dhyāna*), and
3. Erudition (*bahuśrutatā*) — knowledge in conformity with the teaching of the Buddha.

In brief, the comprehension and application of the three doctrinal points (*tridharma*) are essential to the obtaining of liberation.

VI – *THE ORIGINAL SCHOOL*

By minutely examining the main thesis, the *pudgala*, and fourteen secondary theses of the Tds[349], it can be concluded that it is a treatise of the Pudgalavādins, in general, and of the Vātsīputrīyas in particular. It might be possible to attribute it to the Sāṃmitīyas, but the former hypothesis is preferable for the following reasons:

I. Although very little is known about the Vātsīputrīya schism, the majority of Orientalists agree in thinking that the Vātsīputrīyas were those who provoked the first schism among the Sthaviras through their personalist doctrine (*pudgalavāda*), in about 200 EP, that is, 280 BCE, whilst the Sāṃmitīya school, one of the first derived from that of the Vātsīputrīyas, appeared between the third century BCE and the first century CE, a more precise date not being possible. Moreover, the

---

347 Tds, 29*c* 22–23:偶者，言萬物偶生，如大水泉源草墮中合在一處 : The theory of chance says that all things arise by chance, just as blades of grass fall into the source of a large river, meet and accumulate. It is the opinion which maintains that the arrival of beings in the world has no objective nor subjective reason. In other words, the existence of life is undetermined; consequently, man is not responsible for his actions. It might be wondered if this theory is the same as that criticised by the Buddha in MN II, 222, under the title of *diṭṭhadhammupakkamahetu*: Monks, if living beings, by chance as a cause, receive pleasant or unpleasant feelings, then, monks, the Niganṭhas fall into the chance of the bad since, at present, they receive such painful, severe and sharp feelings (*sace, bhikkhave, sattā diṭṭhadhammupakkamahetu sukha dukkhaṃ paṭisaṃvedenti, addhā, bhikkhave, nigaṇṭha pāpadiṭṭhadhammupakkamā, yaṃ etarahi evarūpā dukkhā tippā kaṭukā vedanā vediyanti*). The translation has been made by consulting *Ni-kan ching*. T I, 26, 442*b*.

348 Tds, 29*c* 25–26:無者，言審爾此中無所有，云何生由何生何處生，此非有所有 : Non-existentialism (*nāstidṛṣṭi*) affirms that nothing exists in the world; birth, the cause of birth, and place of birth: these things never existed. MN I, 71: This world does not exist, neither does the other world (*natthi ayaṃ loko, natthi paraloko*). Cf. DN I, 55; SN II, 26.

In AN I, 173, 175; III, 61–2, the Buddha grouped the doctrines of contemporary religious and philosophical schools into three theories: (1) The first admits that all happiness, suffering and neutral feelings are engendered by former actions (*pubbe katahetu*). (2) the second admits that everything is the creation of a Supreme God (*issaranimmānahetu*). (3) The third admits that everything is uncaused and unconditioned (*ahetu-appacaya*). He rejected them since they lead to passivity and regression; those three theories do not lead to the good life; according to them the religious life is futile.

349 See below, Chapter Three.

main reason for the Sāṃmitīya schism among the Vātsīputrīyas, according to Vasumitra, was not the *pudgala* theory but the different explanations given by the four schools of the stanza common to the Pudgalavādin schools[350].

Beyond this information from Vasumitra, it is not known what provoked the appearance of the Sāṃmitīya school[351].

II. The lists of the fruits of the two schools — Vātsīputrīyas and Sāṃmitīyas — are totally different:

1. Acording to the Tds, 20*b* 18 - 21*b* 71, there are twenty-nine categories of Śrāvakas[352], whilst the Sns (472*a* 13-21), which does indeed belong to the Sāmmitīya school, notes only ten or twelve of them that are different from the stanza mentioned which provoked the Sāṃmitīya schism[353]. According to the commentary on the stanza, the four fruits of the Sāṃmitīyas in the Sns correspond to six kinds of persons[354].

By comparing this list with the Vātsīputrīya one of the Śrāvaka fruits, in the Tds, 20*b* 18 - 21*b* 7, the latter is more complicated and prolix[355].

In this connection, it can be stated that neither did the Tds belong to three other schools, namely, the Dharmottarīya, Bhadrayānīya and Ṣaṇṇāgārika, because their list of the fruits, according to the interpretations of the stanza cited by K'uei-chi, are totally different from that of the Vātsīputrīyas[356].

III. Nearly all the theses found in the Tds correspond to those attributed to the Vātsīputrīya school by the treatises, namely, the Mahāvibhāṣāśāstra, Samayabhedopacanacakra, Abhidharmakośa, etc., and the Buddhist literature of Kashmir.

IV. The Tds does not mention the basic theses of the Sāṃmitīya school:

1. The thesis treating the ontological problem, cited by Bhavya, the absence of a commentary to which does not permit the obscurity to be cleared[357].

2. The thesis of the existence of an indestructible thing (*avipraṇāśa*), which plays an important role in the process of action and fruition, which is found

350 See above, Chapter One, 'The Vātsīputrīya sub-schools: the Sāṃmitīyas', and n.44.

351 Bareau, *Sectes*, p.33: [tr] 'We do not know who provoked their appearance (the appearance of the four schools: Sāṃmitīyas, Bhadrayānīyas, Dharmottarīyas and Ṣaṇṇāgārikas) and we know little of what differentiated them'.

352 See below, 'The Pudgalavādin lists of Śrāvakas'.

353 See previous note.

354 See above, Chapter One, 'The Vātsīputrīya sub-schools: the Sāṃmitīyas', and n.45.

355 See below, 'The Pudgalavādin lists of the Śrāvakas'.

356 Bareau, *Sectes*, pp.127, 128, 129, 130.

357 *Ibid.*, p.123: [tr.] 'What should exist (*bhavanīya*) and what exists (*bhava*), what should cease (*nirodhavya*) and what has ceased (*niruddha*), what should be born (*janitavya*) and what has been born (*jāta*), what should die (*maranīya*) and what is dead (*mṛta*), what should be liberated (*muktavya*) and what is liberated (*mukta*), what should go (*gantavya*) and what goes (*gāmin*), what should be cognised (*vijñeya*) and consciousness (*vijñāna*) exist'.

in the Sns, 462*a* 13-16[358].

V. The Tds gives us details of the essential doctrinal points included in several theses concerning the whole of the Pudgalavādin doctrine, whilst the Sns attributed to the Sāṃmitīyas reveals only a few fundamental Pudgalavādin theses, namely: 1) the indestructible thing *(pu-mie* 不滅 , *avipraṇāśa* ?), 2) the *pudgala*, 3) the intermediate existence (*antarābhava*), etc.

In brief, all the preceding information enables us to conclude that the Tds is a basic work of the Pudgalavādin mother school, that is, the Vātsīputrīya school[359].

II. THE SSŬ A-HAN-MU CH'AO CHIEH

I — *TITLE*

Ssŭ a-han-mu ch'ao chieh 四阿鋡暮抄解 (Fragmentary commentary on the four Āgamas) is a work which has come down to us only in Chinese translation. It occupies fifteen pages of the *Taishō* edition, volume XXV, No.1505, pages 1*b*-15*b*. The title was probably giveṇ by Tao-an (312-285), who wrote the preface, in order to conform to Chinese tradition: the title of the book is always placed at the beginning of the text[360]. The original title is certainly the 'Treatise on the Three Dharmas', the Chinese translations of which, found in the text, differ: *San fa chieh t'uo tu* 三法解脫度 (the Treatise on the Three Dharmas) *Ssŭ*, 7*a* 12; 8*b* 27) which can also be reconstructed as *Tridharmakaśāstra*. The existence of a new title can be explained as follows: Tao-an wished to emphasise the importance and essence of the work which, according to him, is a 'necklace of pearls' of the four Āgamas[361].

The *Ssŭ* was assuredly based on the same text as the Tds since the contents of the former are similar to those of the latter.

II - *THE AUTHOR, COMMENTATORS AND TRANSLATORS*

a. The Author

The *Ssŭ* was composed by the Arhat P'a-su-pa-t'o 婆素跋陀 (*Ssŭ*, 1*b* 5), the Sanskrit reconstruction of which, made by Orientalists, is Vasubhadra. Since there is no historical certainty concerning the author of the *Ssŭ*, it is better to retain the Chinese translation Chin-hsien 今賢 (*Ssŭ*, 4*a* 12) as the name of the author. It is noteworthy that the Chinese translation of the name of the author of the Tds, translated by Saṅghadeva, is Shan-hsien 山賢 Obviously, the author of the

358 See below, 'The secondary theses of the Pudgalavādins, thesis No.1'.

359 E. Zürcher considers that the *San fa tu lun* 三法度論 belonged to the Sarvāstivādin school. Cf. Zürcher, *Buddhist Conquest* II, p.408, n.73.

360 Cf. the preface to *Ssŭ*, 1*a* 2.

361 Cf. *ibid*., 1*a* 6, 10.

Ssŭ gives only the essential messages which are followed by headings written by the commentator. The most developed section could have been written later by the commentator, Saṅghadeva.

b. <u>The Commentators</u>

Unlike the preface to the Tds written by Hui-yüan, that of the *Ssŭ* by Tao-an does not mention the name of the commentator, Saṅghasena. Nonetheless, through the words *ch'ao chieh* (fragmentary commentary) included in the title and through the language forms, it is easy to recognise the existence of passages of commentaries and sub-commentaries in the text. It is possible that the commentary was written by Saṅghasena. The comparison of similar passages in the Tds and *Ssŭ* admits of this supposition. The sentences of sub-commentaries were written by the collaborators of Kumārabuddhi in consultation with the latter. This section is very short and printed in small characters at the end of passages and obscure words[362].

c. <u>The Translators</u>

It was Kumārabuddhi who, on the invitation of Tao-an, translated this work from Sanskrit into Chinese[363] in the eighth month of the eighteenth Chien-yüan 建元 year (382 CE). He completed the translation at the monastery of Yeh 鄴 (Chang-tê 漳德 prefecture in Honan 河南) in the space of two months. Kumārabuddhi belonged to the royal family of Turfan and had come with his master to Chang-an in 382 CE. This is the only work that he translated. The rest of his history remains virtually unknown to us.

Unlike Gautama Saṅghadeva, who was extremely familiar with the Chinese language after his long journeys in China, Kumārabuddhi, whose knowledge of that language was unsure, undertook the translation in the same year that he arrived in Chang-an (383 CE). Furthermore, the preface written by Tao-an indicates that Kumārabuddhi translated the work from the Sanskrit text[364]. Tao-an does not mention that he translated orally into Chinese, as did Hui-yüan in his preface to the Tds, by indicating Saṅghadeva's method of translating[365].

It was Fo-nien 佛念 [366] and Fo-hu 佛護 who then translated the Chinese

362 Cf. *ibid.*, 1*a* 21–22.

363 Cf. *ibid.*, 1*a* 15–20; 15*b* 27.

364 Cf. *ibid.*, 1*a* 15.

365 Cf. the preface to Tds, 73*a* 22, 23.

366 Fo-nien 佛念 or Chu Fo-nien 竺佛念 . A native of Liang-chou 涼州 , he left home in his youth. He learnt and recited the canonical texts and he knew perfectly the languages of various countries, since his family came from Hsi ho 西河 . Having gained mastery of Sanskrit, he became a translator-intermediary and cooperated with Saṅghabhadra and Dharmadaṇḍin. He himself published the following texts:

1. *P'u sa ying lo ching* 菩薩瓔珞 (Bodhisattvamālā), T XVI, 656.
2. *Shih chu tuan chieh ching* or *Tsui shêng wen p'u sa shih chu ch'u kou tuan chieh ching* 十住斷結經 or 最勝問菩薩十住除垢斷結經 , T X, 309.
3. *Ch'u yao ching* 出曜經 (Dharmapada, Udānavarga), T IV, 212.
4. *T'ai king* or *P'u sa ts'ung tou shu t'ien chiang shên mu t'ai shuo kuang p'u ching* 胎經 or

Ssŭ[367] after having understood the Sanskrit text explained by Kumārabuddhi. It is probable that these two important collaborators knew Sanskrit partially. The other collaborators, such as Sêng-tao 僧導, T'an-chiu 曇究 and Sêng-jui 僧叡 were transcribers[368].

III - *THE DATE*

We have no information concerning the date of the *Ssŭ*. Since the identity of the *Ssŭ* and the Tds is recognised, we should have two dates for the *Ssŭ*: one for the original text which must have been composed between the beginning of the third century BCE and the third century CE. The other, for the commentary which should date to the first half of the fourth century CE. The date of the sub-commentary is the same as that of the translation, 382 CE.

IV - *THE LANGUAGE AND TRANSLATION*

a. The Language

Apparently the *Ssŭ* was in Sanskrit, as is indicated at the end of the text: 'The Sanskrit text consists of forty-six folios, each folio containing twenty-eight *slokas*'[369]. This information is confirmed by the preface to the *Ssŭ* written by Tao-an: 'Kumārabuddhi took (the text) in Sanskrit in his hands'[370]. Nonetheless, we cannot be sure that the treatise was in pure Sanskrit since it is certain that, at that time, the word *fan* 梵, for the Chinese, meant any language used in Buddhist books originating from eastern countries. A. Bareau's idea concerning the language of the Tds, namely that it was probably compiled in highly hybrid Sanskrit or Prakrit[371], can equally well be applied to this text.

b. The Translation

The translation of the *Ssŭ* was directed by Tao-an, who asked the translators to render it literally from Sanskrit into the Ch'in 秦 language (Chinese), that is to say, only a verbatim translation was made, whilst the style and substance of the text was preserved as much as possible[372].

If we compare this translation to that by Gautama Saṅghadeva, we see that it is

---

菩薩從兜術天降神母胎說廣普經, T XII, 384.

5. *Chung yin ching* 中陰經 (Antarābhavasūtra), T XII, 385.

Cf. *Kao* I, T L, 2059, 329*a-b*; R. Shih, *op. cit.*, pp.55–6; E. Zürcher, *Buddhist Conquest*, n.1 of the first chapter.

367 Cf. the preface to *Ssŭ*, 1*a* 15.

368 Cf. *ibid.*, 1*a* 15, 16.

369 *SSŭ*, 15*b* 27.

370 The preface to *Ssŭ*, 1*a* 15.

371 See above, n.125. Note 6 of the preface to *Ssŭ* (1*a* 15) reinforces the idea that the *Ssŭ* was probably written in the *hu* 胡 language rather than *fan* 梵. The word *hu* 胡 has a very general meaning and designates all foreign languages west of China.

372 The preface to *Ssŭ*, 1*a* 19–21:

faithful to the Sanskrit text but that it is not clear and lacks the elegance of the Chinese language. The verses are transformed into prose and several passages are incomprehensible.

These weaknesses can be explained by the following facts:

1) The translators, Kumārabuddhi and Fo-hu 佛護, were not familiar with foreign languages or the characteristic doctrines of the Vātsīputrīya school;

2) The translation was made in a very short time: two months — from the eighth month to the eleventh month of the eighteenth Chien-yüan 建元 year (382 CE);

3) The translation is the first and only one made by Kumārabuddhi[373].

In the *Yüeh tsang chih chin* 閱藏知津, Chih-hsü 智旭 (1599-1655), a very famous commentator, also declares that is it very difficult to read this text[374].

V – *THE CONTENTS*

Whilst the Tds is divided into three fascicles of three chapters or nine sections, the *Ssū* consists of two fascicles containing nine sections which occupy fifteen pages in the *Taishō* edition: the first fascicle (1*b* 7 - 8*b* 28) is composed of five sections which constitute three chapters dealing respectively with the Good (*kuśala*), the Bad (*akuśala*) and the Support (*niśraya*). This division into nine sections probably conforms to the division of the original Sanskrit text[375] which consisted of forty-six folios each containing twenty-eight *ślokas* or units of thirty-two syllables; in all, there are one thousand, two hundred and eighty-eight *ślokas*[376]. As for the doctrinal elements of the work, they are, on the whole, the same as those of the Tds. Consequently, it is not necessary to give details here of the contents of the *Ssū*. However, the contents of both texts — Tds and *Ssū* — are not absolutely identical; furthermore, the two translations are different. That is why it is interesting to examine separately, in the order in which they appear, the characteristic theses of the Pudgalavādins in the *Ssū*, noting their differences in relation to those of the Tds.

It is useful to consult the translation of the passages concerning these theses in the Tds[377], before reading the passages of the translation of the theses and their critical comparisons which follow. Obviously, the *Ssū* discusses practically all the theses presented in the Tds, which are as follows:

THESIS I — 'Morality (*śīla*) designates action of body and action of speech'.

373 Cf. Bagchi, *Canon bouddhique* I, p.156–7.

374 Cf. Chih-hsü 釋智旭 *Yüeh tsang chih chin* 閱藏知津, The Commercial Press, Shanghai 1931, vol.VI, p.89: 文甚難讀. The title of this work is not found in the catalogue of the *Taishō shinshū daizokyō mokuroku* 大正新修大藏經目錄, new ed., Tokyo 1969, or in Nanjio. Nevertheless, a summary of the work is found in *Bussho-Kaisetsu Daijiten* 佛書解說大辭典 (12 vol.), editor-in-chief Ono Gemmyō 小野玄妙 Tokyo 1932, vol.I, pp.262–3.

375 The number of the divisions is always accompanied by the title of the work.

376 Cf. *Ssū*, 15*b* 26 sq.

377 See below, 'the Pudgalavādin theses'.

and

THESIS II — 'Merit (*puṇya*) increases continually even during sleep'.

These two theses are explained in the same passage in *Ssŭ*, 1*a* 26 - 2*a* 6:

'Morality (*śīla*) consists of actions of body (*kāya*) and speech (*vāc*) in relation to the life of others[378], what is not the life of others, and the increase (of merit)[379] (Sūtra).

Morality designates the three elements which are associated with the body and speech and which arise together.

Question: What does that mean? *Answer*: (With regard to morality concerning) the life of others, what is not the life of others and the increase (of merit, morality concerning) the life of others indicates the fact that, being hungry and weak, knowing ourselves, we do not harm the life of others; living beings, if they know themselves, do not harm (other) living beings. (Sub-commentary: this is not killing). It is the same for not taking (with a defiled mind) the possessions and women of others.

(Sub-commentary: hence, whatever is said about life (*shou* 受), it should be understood that it also encompasses all that is not life; outside body and speech, everything is what is not life)[380]. This is (respecting) what is not the life of others (?). Falsehood (*mṛṣāvāda*), slander (*paiśunyāvāda*), harmful speech (*pāruṣyāvāda*) and frivolous speech (*sambhinnapralāpa*) constitute the fact of not being interested in the life of others. If the seven factors[381] do not harm others, power is used to help the poor by thinking that we ourselves and others are the same (?).

Merit increases continually if one makes the following resolve: 'Henceforth, I shall abstain from killing living beings'. During that time, (merit) increases abun- dantly, just as invested capital yields interest. Merit grows in the element of consciousness[382] just as seeds, once sown, produce stalks and leaves and grow until they bear fruit. It is the same for (merit) which continues to grow abundantly even during sleep. That is why the increase (of merit) is morality. (Sub-commentary: (merit) is not lost (even) during sleep).

The explanations concerning these two theses are quite clear in both texts, *Ssŭ*,

---

378 *Ssŭ*, 1*c* 26: *t'a shou* 他受 ; the term is unclear. In this context, we can suppose it means the 'life of others' since the word *shou* 受 (*upādāna* ?) also means life.

379 The word *huai* 壞 (*Ssŭ*, 1*c* 26) is meaningless in this context. After consulting the phrase *t'a shou t'a pu shou tsêng* 他受他不受增 (*Ssŭ*, 1*c* 27–28) and the word *tsêng* 增 in the Tds, 16*b* 3, we propose the translation given here.

380 The phrase *chih fen shen ch'ou pu yeh* 直分身口不受也 (*Ssŭ*, 2*a* 1) is far from clear.

381 These are the three good bodily actions (*kāyakarman*), namely: 1) not killing living beings (*prāṇātipātāvirati*); 2) not stealing (*adattādānāvirati*); 3) not indulging in sensual misconduct (*kāmamithyācāravirati*), and the four good vocal actions, namely: 1) not lying (*mṛśāvādaprativirati*); 2) not slandering (*paiśunyāprativirati*); 3) not using harmful words (*pāruṣyāprativirati*); 4) not speaking frivolously (*saṃbhinnaprālāpāprativirati*).

382 *Ssŭ*, 2*a* 4–5: *shan shêng chieh shou* 善生覺受 ; this expression is not clear. However, in this context, we can propose the following translation: 'possessions grow in the element of consciousness'. The word *chieh* 覺 means consciousness in this translation as in other old translations.

1c 26 - 2a 6, and Tds, 16b 3-13, with the exception of the following sentence in *Ssŭ*, 2a 4-5: '(Merit) grows in the element of consciousness, just as seeds, once sown, stalks and leaves grow until they bear fruit'. In Tds, 16b 11-12, the word 'consciousness' (*chieh* 覺) is missing from the phrase: 'When the resolve to observe morality is taken, the element of the good develops continually, just as, in a rotten fruit, the seed begins to germinate and grow.

Thus, the two translations do not have the same meaning. On the other hand, the sub-commentary of the *Ssŭ*, 2a 6, also states the meaning of the second thesis: '(Merit) is not lost even during sleep'.

THESIS III — 'The adjoining concentration (*upacāra-samādhi* ?) consists of patience (*kṣānti*) name (*nāma*) and perception (*saṃjñā*)'.

This thesis is explained in *Ssŭ*, 4a 2-12:

'The adjoining concentration (*chin sh'an* 近定, *upacārasamādhi* ?) is adjoining meditation which includes patience (*kṣānti*), name (*nāma*)[383], perception (*hsiang* 想, *saṃjñā*)' (Sūtra).

That is why it (is called) adjoining concentration, (which adjoins) liberation, as was said earlier.

Question: If they have already been defined, why are the absorptions (*dhyāna*) explained here?

Answer: The earlier ones were worldly, (whilst if) one practises here, one will surely obtain a liberation which is the supreme liberation.

It is in this adjoining concentration that one obtains (clear comprehension) of the four Noble Truths (*āryasatya*). It is like a man who, having crossed a desert, finds a park, dwellings, fruit trees, flowers and fruit, and thinks that he will certainly not suffer any longer from hunger since he is so close to such an accumulation. Being tormented by craving (*rāga*), anger (怒, *krodha* ?) and delusion (*moha*), he is guided in meditation by a good friend (*kalyāṇamitra*). He assiduously practises the contemplation of the impermanence (*anityatā*), insubstantiality (*anātmaka*) and suffering (*duhkha*) of the aggregates (*skandha*), elements (*dhātu*) and domains (*āyatana*). If he practises it with delight, that increases patience (*kṣānti*). (When he) reinforces the meditation and becomes unshakeable (*aneñja*), that is the name (*nāma*). When clear comprehension of suffering (*duḥkhābhisamaya* ?)[384] is as lucid as in a dream in which one sees pleasant images, that is an increase of perception (*saṃjñā*). The supreme worldly dharma (*laukikāgradharma*) is perception of the Blessed Lord. In the practice of that concentration, (if one attains) enlightenment, comprehension and joy, that is

---

383 The word *wu* 無 (*Ssŭ*, 4a 2) has no meaning here. Consulting Tds, 18b 7, we take from it the word *ming* 名 and translate as 'name' (*nāma*).

384 *Ssŭ*, 4a 10: *ku shih* 苦時. This is probably a mistranslation of the Sanskrit term *duḥkhābhisamaya*. Consequently, the translation 'true comprehension of suffering' is a correction based on Tds, 18b 16: *ku kuan hsiang* 苦觀想.

clear comprehension of the Noble Truths (*āryasatyābhisamaya*)[385].

The formulation of this thesis and the examples which illustrate it in *Ssū*, 4*a* 2-12, are as clear as those in Tds, 18*b* 9-18. However, the preceding paragraph does not contain elements which are found in the same paragraph of the Tds, such as: 'In concentration, one progressively examines the truth (*satya*)' (Tds, 18*b* 10), and 'It resembles, because of its successive levels, (the state one is found in) when coming out of a dream . . .; (Tds, 18*b* 17-18). Consequently, the *Ssū* lacks a thesis in the Tds: 'Clear comprehension of the Noble Truths (*āryasatyābhisamaya*)' (*Ssū*, 4*a* 11-12). Is this a shortening of the original text or an error of translation?

THESIS IV - 'There are five things subject to being known, the first three of which are compounded things (*saṃskṛta*); the fourth, the *pudgala*, which is neither identical to nor different from compounded things; and the fifth, Nirvāṇa, which is devoid of causes and conditions (*ahetupratyaya*)'.

This thesis is explained in *Ssū*, 4*c* 20-25:

'That means the absence of attachment to the three (time-periods): the present (*pratyutpanna*)[386], the past (*atīta*) and the future (*anāgata*). These are all compounded things (*saṃskṛta*), as it is said in the 'Discourse on the Place of Teaching' (*shuo-chu hsiu-tu-lu* 說處修妒路 Deśanasthānasūtra) and the 'Discourse on the Past' (*kuo-ch'ü hsiu-tu-lu* 過去修妒路 Atītasūtra). Are consciousness, the *pudgala* and Nirvāṇa included in the three (time-periods)? Are those three things identical (to the three time-periods) or different (from them)? The Nirvāṇa of relinquishing the body is devoid of causes and conditions (*ahetupratyaya*). When consciousness, in the present, ceases all reflection, that is the infinite consciousness, in the present, of Nirvāṇa[387]. (As for the) *pudgala*, 'whether it is different (from the three times-periods) or not', is impossible to say'.

The contents of the preceding paragraph are quite similar to that in Tds, 19a 22-26. It is noteworthy that Kumārabuddhi, in *Ssū* 4*c* 22, translates the Sanskrit word *pudgala* by 'our body' (*chi shen* 己身), whilst Saṅghadeva, in Tds, translates it as 'self' (我) (Tds, 19*a* 23). The interpretation thus given of the word *pudgala* in the *Ssū* is as clear as that in the Tds. The *Ssū*, 4*c* 24-25 writes: 'Whether the *pudgala* is different (from the three time-periods) or not, is impossible to say'. While the Tds,

385 The words *shih shêng ti shih* 是聖諦時 (*Ssū*, 4*a* 12) are mistranslations; they doubtless mean 'true comprehension of the Noble Truths' (*āryasatyābhimasaya*). Tds, 18*b* 18: *shêng ti kuan* 聖諦觀 .

386 Translation based on the sub-commentary *hsiang ying hsien tsai yeh chu chih yeh* 相應現在也住止也 (*Ssū*, 4*c* 20) and n.25 *hsien tsai* 現在 *ming* 名

387 On consulting the sub-commentary 相應現在也住止也 (*Ssū*, 4*c* 20), we think this is a mistranslation: the characters *hsiang ying* 相應 probably translate the Sanskrit word *pratyutpanna*. Consequently, the characters *hsiang ying* in the phrase 彼覺相應一切思惟滅是涅槃無盡覺想應 (*Ssū*, 4*c* 23-24) should probably be translated as 'the present'. Furthermore, this proposition is significant for the Pudgalavādins in the establishment of the '*pudgala* designated by cessation', since it makes Nirvāṇa infinite consciousness rather than annihilation. See below, 'The main thesis of the Pudgalavādins'.

19*a* 26 explains this idea in the following way: 'Whether the *pudgala* is separate from the three time-periods or not, is impossible to say[388].

THESIS V — 'There are twelve knowledges (*jñāna*) in the path of vision (*darśanamārga*)'.

This thesis is explained in *Ssŭ*, 5*a* 9-22:

'The path of vision consists of knowledge of things (*fa chih* 法智, *dharmajñāna*), knowledge of investigation (*kuan chih* 觀智, *vicārajñāna* ?) and knowledge of what is not yet known (*wei chih chih* 未知智, *ajñatajñāna* ?)' (Sūtra).

These three knowledges constitute knowledges of the stage of vision (*darśanabhūmi*). With regard to the meaning of the knowledge of things and knowledge of investigation, it is comparable to a surgeon who discovers an abcess at its outset and as it develops, and who opens it with a lancet. With his fingers he prods the direction of the vessels in order not to harm them. It is only after that that he opens it fully. It is the same for the practitioner who makes use of correct reflection[389] on suffering (*duḥkhatā*), impermanence (*anityatā*) etc.

By practising (correct reflection on) impermanence (*anityatā*), he enters (the stage of) vision (*darśanabhūmi*); his sufferings cease, his fetters are abandoned: 'Through those two knowledges, are the fetters broken or not broken?', so reflects the practitioner (this expresssion applies to the knowledge of what is not yet known)'.

'Since the world of desire (*kāmadhātu*) is subject to impermanence (*anityatā*), it is the same for the world of subtle form (*rūpadhātu*) and the formless world (*ārūpyadhātu*)'. Having gained this knowledge from reflection, one abandons the fetters pertaining to the world of subtle form and the formless world.

'Hence, the attainment of correct reflection on suffering in the domain of suffering constitutes knowledge of investigation (*vicārajñāna*) and knowledge of what is not yet known (*ajñātajñāna*) relating to the world of subtle form and the formless world. Similarly, there are three knowledges relating to the origin (*samudaya*) of suffering. The attainment of correct reflection and the cessation (of suffering)[390] is knowledge of things (*dharmajñāna*). The cessation (of the origin) is (also) knowledge of investigation. When the fetters are abandoned[391] that is knowledge of things; partial liberation is knowledge of investigation. It is the same for the knowledge of what is not yet known relating to the world of subtle form and the formless world'.

'It is the same for the three knowledges relating to cessation (*nirodha*) and the Path (*mārga*). The attainment of correct reflection and the cessation of suffering constitute the knowledge of things (*dharmajñāna*); and also the knowledge of investigation (*vicārajñāna* ?). It is likewise for the knowledge of what is not yet

---

388 See below, 'The main thesis of the Pudgalavādins'.

389 It is certain that Kumārabuddhi mistranslated the Sanskrit word *yoniśomanaskāra*. Saṅghadeva translated it as *chêng sê-wei* 正思惟 (Tds, 19*b* 18, 19).

390 *Ssŭ*, 5*a* 18: *yin hsing li mie hsi* 婬行利滅息. The Chinese translation is completely word for word, hence the need for modification.

391 *chêng* 正 (*Ssŭ*, 5*a* 19) is a mistake for *chih* 止

known relating to the world of subtle form and the formless world'[392].

'It is the same for the three knowledges relating to the Path (*mārga*)'.

Such are the twelve knowledges which should be understood in detail. Each of the four Truths relates to three (knowledges). That makes twelve (knowledges).

On the whole, the explanation of this thesis, both in the doctrinal elements and literary expression, is similar in the two treatises. We can note that Kumārabuddhi mechanically mistranslated the doctrinal term, the original Sanskrit of which is *yoniśomanaskāra* (lit. reflection which goes to the source), by 'practice of lust' or 'giving way to lust' (*yin hsing* 婬行) (*Ssŭ*, 5*a* 13, 16, 18), whilst Saṅghadeva rightly translated it as 'correct reflection' (*chêng sê-wei* 正思惟) (Tds, 19*b* 18, 19). The first translation is incorrect both from the philological and doctrinal point of view.

THESIS VI — 'It is impossible to say that the *pudgala* (= living being, *sattva*) and Nirvāṇa are different from the characteristics (*lakṣaṇa*) or that they are identical to them'.

This thesis is explained in *Ssŭ*, 5*a* 25 - 5*b* 2:

'(Is it) not said, furthermore, that the Living Being (*sattva* = *pudgala*) and Nirvāṇa are classed among the characteristics (*lakṣaṇa*) (?). If it is said that the Living Being and Nirvāṇa are (characteristics), that is a great mistake, (since) they are impermanent (*anitya*). If it is not said, the mistake lies in the Sūtra. It should be said that the characteristics of compounded things (*saṃskṛtalakṣaṇa*) include arising (*utpāda*), enduring (*sthiti*) and disappearance (*vyaya*). In the increase of merit (*puṇya*), which is the merit of the characteristics of the person (*pudgala*)? Whether the *pudgala* is different or is not different (from the characteristics), is impossible to say. If it is different from them, it is permanent (*nitya*). If it does not differ from them, it is impermanent (*anitya*). Hence, those two theses are wrong. It is not said that Nirvāṇa is the absence of characteristics[393]. That is why one is happy to say more about the characteristics of compounded things (*saṃskṛtalakṣaṇa*) as such. That is what is called the increase of merit. What are the merits of the characteristics? We must speak of knowledge (*jñāna*)'.

On the whole, despite everything, the explanation in the *Ssŭ*, is less clear and rythmic than that in the Tds, but there are no fundamental differences between the two treatises in respect of the doctrinal points..

THESIS VII — 'The five superknowledges (*abhijñā*) can be obtained by worldlings (*pṛthagjana*)'.

This thesis is explained in *Ssŭ*, 5*c* 11-12:

'. . . Flying, supernormal hearing and the knowledge of other's intentions

392 A proposition is obviously missing before the two words *shih tao* 是道

393 See below, 'The secondary theses of the Pudgalavādins, thesis No.10'.

(*paracittajñāna* ?) constitute the superknowledges, (which, with the knowledge of the recollection) of former lives (*pūrvanivesānusmṛtijñāna* ?) and knowledge of births and cessations, are the five superknowledges of worldlings (*pṛthagjanābhijñā*)'.

With the exception of minor literary differences in the two translations, there is nothing to remark.

THESIS VIII — 'The intermediate existence (*antarābhava*) and Parinirvāṇa in the intermediate existence (*antarāparinirvāṇa*) exist in the world of desire and in the world of subtle form, but they do not exist in the formless world'.

This thesis is explained in *Ssŭ*, 6*a* 27-28:

'Liberation in the world of desire and liberation in the world of subtle form, (due to) these two (liberations), all Parinirvāṇas in the intermediate existence (*antarāparinirvāṇa*) are abandoned'.

On comparing the two texts, we find the main point of the thesis is the same. However, the doctrinal elements which constitute it in the *Ssŭ* are richer than those found in the Tds. Since, apart from the element of the intermediate existence, the *Ssŭ* also mentions another element, namely, Parinirvāṇa in the intermediate existence (*antarāparinirvāṇa*). The *Ssŭ*, 6*a* 27-28 states: '. . . Due to these two (liberations), all Parinirvāṇas in the intermediate existence are abandoned', whilst the Tds, 20*c* 10-12, recognises only the intermediate existence, which is defined as follows:

'Being delivered from the world of desire and the world of subtle form, one completely abandons the intermediate existence; there is no intermediate existence in the formless world'.

THESIS IX — 'The Arhat is susceptible to regression'

This thesis is explained in *Ssŭ*, 6*c* 12-16:

'The weak faculty (*mṛdvindriya*) includes him who regresses (*parihāṇadharma*) . . .' (Sūtra).

'. . . Because of the diminution of thought which is called he who regresses. Regression does not mean falling among living beings (眾生 *sattva*)[394], (but) falling to the stage of cultivation (*bhāvanābhūmi*). Cultivation (*bhāvanā*) means regular practice. It is the same with paragraphs (of discourses) which one forgets through not reciting them. (Equally), if one does not practise cultivation, one regresses. Regression (is

394 *Ssŭ*, 6*c* 14: *chien fa pu chung shêng chien* 減法不眾生減. Regression does not mean falling among living beings. This translation is made in consultation with the following phrase from the text: *fên pieh ti chien* 分別地減 : falling to the stage of cultivation — Kumārabuddhi translated *fĕn pieh ti* 分別地 from the word *bhāvanābhūmi*, whilst Saṅghadeva translated it as *hsiu ti* 修地. The interpretation, according to the *Ssŭ*, is that when the Arhat falls from *aśaikṣa* to *śaikṣa*, he remains in the stage of cultivation — the fruits of *sakṛdāgāmin* and *anāgāmin*, and does not fall to the lower states of living beings.

caused by) suffering, business, arguments, long journeys and walking. Those are the five things which cause regression. They are also (the causes susceptible) to leading to falling to the stage of cultivation'.

On comparing the translation of the *Ssŭ* with that of the Tds, we see that there is a notable difference from the doctrinal point of view. With regard to the regression of the Arhat pertaining to the 'he who regresses' category, the *Ssŭ*, 6*a* 14, says: 'Regression does not mean falling among living beings (衆生 , *sattva*), it is falling to the stage of cultivation', whilst the Tds, 21*a* 25-26, says: 'He who regresses is he who falls either to a lower state, (but) not (from comprehension of) the Noble Truths[395], or to the stage of cultivation (*bhāvanābhūmi*). The difference in the two texts is that the *Ssŭ* admits that the Arhat does not fall among living beings whilst the Tds maintains that the Arhat falls to a lower state, apart (from comprehension of) the Noble Truths (*satyābhisamaya*). Nonetheless, both texts have a point in common: falling to the stage of cultivation. It might be asked whether there is some difference in interpretation between the two texts in relation to the theory of the Arhat's regression.

THESIS X — 'There is an ineffable (*avaktavya*), indicating:

a) the designation of appropriation (*upādānaprajñapti*), the *pudgala*, which is both identical to and different from the elements;
b) the designation of means (*upāyaprajñapti*) associated with the past, present and future; and,
c) the designation of cessation (*nirodhaprajñapti*) concerning Parinirvāna'.

This thesis is explained in *Ssŭ*, 10*a* 4-29:

'The ineffable (*avaktavya*) includes the designation of appropriation (*shou chieh-shou* 受教授 , *upādānaprajñapti*), the designation of means (*fang-pien chieh-shou* 方便教授 *upāyaprajñapti* ?) and the designation of cessation (*mieh chieh-shou* 滅教授 *nirodhaprajñapti*)' (Sūtra).

'If one ignores these three designations, that is non-comprehension of the ineffable. The designation of appropriation is the designation of life (*jīva*). (Subcommentary: as a phoneme from India the word [meaning] life and [that meaning] living being are the same). (Life is) internal appropriation (*upādāna*) in the present and consists of the aggregates (*skandha*), elements (*dhātu*) and domains (*āyatana*) (?).

395 Tds, 21*a* 25–26:退法者，或差降退非聖諦故曰敍h法或於修地退 : He who regresses is he who falls either to a lower state, (but) not (from comprehension of) the Noble Truths, or to the stage of cultivation (*bhāvanābhūmi*). It is probable that the text lacks essential characters which were found between the character *fei* 非 and the two characters *shêng ti* 聖諦 . We therefore propose the preceding translation (or rather, interpretation), in consultation with *Kośa* VI, pp.256–8 (Pruden pp.1003–12) and the notes on the subject. The Arhat does not fall from the *srotaāpanna* fruit which is established by the abandoning of the passions abandoned through the vision of the Truths. For a detailed explanation, see below, n.756.

That is to say, the objects of appropriation concerning internal life in the present (?), which is formed by compounded things (*saṃskāra*) and fetters (*saṃyojana*); that is what is called the designation of appropriation (?); it does not pertain to either the past or the future'.

'(With regard to) the designation of appropriation in relation to life (*jīva* = *sattva* = *pudgala*), it is not identical to (the body; that) cannot be confirmed (?). If life and the body are identical, (life is) impermanent (*anitya*) and suffering (*duḥkha*). If it is not different, it is eternal (*śāśvata*) and (not) suffering. If (life is) eternal, the pure life (*brahmacarya*) is not practised. In eternity, it is not necessary to lead a pure life; the harvesting of fruit, receiving and giving have no meaning. (If life is) impermanent, neither would that make any sense. Since in both cases[396], either eternalism[397], or annihilation[398], neither suffering nor happiness exist. (Sub-commentary: the master is explaining [this idea] by saying that this is the answer of the Buddha whose aim is to satisfy sectaries so that they obtain this or that)[399]

'The designation of means signifies designation based on the past (*atīta*), future (*anāgata*) and present (*pratyutpanna*). It is associated with the three time-periods. As (the Buddha said): 'In the past, I was King Sunetra[400]. (Sub-commentary: The Sanskrit Sunetra corresponds to ten names: goat, eye, earth, sky, water, speech, direction, light, scissors, reality. These are ten comparisons. That man does not under- stand that he belongs to some [thing] in the ten births). In the future, there will be (a man) who will be named Ajita[401]. In the present period, it is Gautama Siddhārtha[402]. Compounded things (. . . is appropriation (*upādāna*) in the future, (and) appropriation in the past. By

---

396 *Ssŭ*, 10*a* 11: *fang pien* 方便 (*upāya, prayoga*), which means 'the means' or 'preparatory exercise', is not indicated here; that is why the modification in meaning is necessary.

397 *Ssŭ*, 10*a* 11: *pien tuan* 遍斷 ; in this context, these words should be translated as 'eternalism and annihilation'.

398 See previous note.

399 It is probable that Kumārabuddhi is referring to the attitude of the Buddha who remained silent when Vacchagotta asked him questions about the existence or non–existence of the self (*ātman*); cf. SN IV, 400 sq.; Udāna, 67. See below, 'The main thesis of the Pudgalavādins'.

400 *Ssŭ*, 10*a* 14: *Ch'ü tien wang* 衠點(點)王, these characters cannot be reconstructed in Sanskrit. It may be that they are a wrong transcription of the name of a king — Sunetra, who appears in several works concerning the former lives of the Buddha. Cf. *Kośa* IX, §§ 271, 272, and the long note on Sunetra in *Traité* I, pp.319–21.

401 *Ssŭ*, 10*a* 16: *wu shêng* 無勝 : these characters can be reconstructed in Sanskrit as Ajita, another name of Maitreya, the future Buddha, as the Buddha predicted: 'At the time, monks, when humans will live to the age of eighty thousand years, there will appear in the world the Perfect One, the Fully Enlightened One, the Blessed One named Metteyya . . . (. . . just as I appeared in the present, Perfect, Fully Enlightened . . .) (. . .That man, through his superior knowledge, will understand and make known this world with its devas, Māras, Brahmās, this world with its monks and brahmins, with its devas and humans, just as at present I, through my superior knowledge, have understood them and made them known. He will teach the Dhamma, he will proclaim the pure life (*brahmacariya*), lovely in the beginning, lovely in the middle, lovely at the end, with its aim and its meaning, full and realisable in an absolutely pure way, as I do at present. He will head a community of several thousand monks, just as I at present head a community of several thousand monks' (D III, 76).

402 *Ssŭ*, 10*a* 16: *kung shih ta* 工師達, these characters are probably a mistransliteration of the Sanskrit words Gautama Siddhārtha, the name of the Buddha.

convention, this designation (is established) in order to (cure opinions) on annihilation (*uccheda*) and eternity (*śāśvata*). If (King) Sunetra had been annihilated, how would I exist (now)? If he had not been, how could I exist? Based on conventional truth (*saṃvṛtisatya*), this designation of means is spoken of[403].

Question: What does the designation of cessation mean?

Answer: 'It is the designation of cessation in which appropriation is exhausted and where nothing further is appropriated' (Sūtra).

'Appropriation has been explained above. That appropriation is exhausted; nothing further is appropriated, no other (life) is assumed; having ceased, nothing further remains, the other shore has been reached; that is the designation of cessation (by means of which false) views of annihilation and eternity are cured. Hence, it is certainly nothing but the synonym of the designation of Parinirvāṇa (?) which is also the ineffable (*avaktavya*). If (the ineffable) is different (from the body), there is no Parinirvāṇa. If it is not different, there is equally no Parinirvāṇa. Hence, having understood the suffering of birth and the ineffable (*avaktavya*), one inevitably attains Parinirvāṇa which is like a lamp which goes out. Internal appropriation undergoes no further suffering[404].

The designation of means (*upāyaprajñapti*) concerns the aggregates (*skandha*), elements (*dhātu*) and domains (*āyatana*) of the past; as the Buddha said above: 'I was King Sunetra'. It is the same for (the designation of means, of the future). 'The designation of cessation signifies, in the first place, the cessation of appropriation (*upādāna*) (as when it is said): 'The Blessed Lord attains Parinirvāṇa'. The designation of means (teaches us) that life (*jīva*) is not annihilated. The designation of cessation (teaches us) that life is (both) continuous and changed. The designation of appropriation eliminates the opinion according to which life exists or does not exist'[405].

Amongst the three designations of the ineffable (*avaktavya*), what is written on the designation of appropriation and the designation of cessation in the *Ssŭ* is no different from what is said in Tds, 24*b* 2-3, 4-5. Only, the designation of means has a very particular import, since it signifies the designation not only associated with the past, but also with the present and future (*Ssŭ*, 10*a* 12-19); this designation expresses the continuity of life (*jīva*) or of the Living Being (*sattva*) in relation to the three time-periods, whilst the Tds, 24*a* 29 and 24*b* 1 sq., speaks of the designation of the past (*atītaprajñapti* ?) which only presents the link between the past and the present.

THESIS XI — 'Only one absolute truth exists: Nirvāṇa'.

This thesis is explained in *Ssŭ*, 10 *c* 9-10:

'Conventional truth (*saṃvṛtisatya*), characteristic truth (*lakṣaṇasatya* ?) and

403 These phrases are obscure. The translation is based on the three designations of *pudgala*. Cf. *Ssŭ*, 10*a* 17–19.

404 *Ssŭ*, 10*a* 24–26: 如是見生苦已不説己，應般涅槃如燈滅，内受一若干苦不著受
The propositions should be modified in order to have the meaning conform to the text.

405 See below, 'The secondary theses of the Pudgalavādins: thesis No.8'.

absolute truth (*paramārthasatya*)'.

The *Ssŭ* does not contain the passage on the explanation of the three truths, in particular the absolute truth (*paramārthasatya*), as does Tds, 24*c* 16 - 25*a* 12. The latter gives a definition of the absolute truth, arguments for the singleness of Nirvāṇa, and even rejects adherence to several kinds of Nirvāṇa (Tds, 25*a* 2-12).

THESIS XII — 'Knowledge which consists of feeling (*vedanā*), perception (*saṃjñā*) and consciousness (*vijñāna*) forms part of the elements of the Path (*mārgāṅga*)'.

This thesis is explained in *Ssŭ*, 11*a* 12-13

'(Knowledge) includes feeling (*vedanā*), perception (*saṃjñā*) and consciousness (*vijñāna*)' (Sūtra).

'These three elements constitute things of the Dharma.'

There is not much difference between the doctrinal commentary in the *Ssŭ* and that in Tds, 25*b* 27-28, concerning this thesis. It is certainly difficult to understand the explanations in the *Ssŭ* because the translation is very obscure; this is equally so for the sub-commentary in Chinese (cf. *Ssŭ*, 11*a* 13).

THESIS XIII — 'There are only five destinies (*gati*)'.

This thesis is explained in *Ssŭ*, 12*a* 9-24:

'The world (*dhātu*) consists of the world of desire (*kāmadhātu*), the world of subtle form (*rūpadhātu*) and the formless world (*ārūpyadhātu*)' (Sūtra).

'. . . The world of form consists of mankind (*manuṣya*), gods (*deva*) and the (bad) destinies (*durgati*)' (Sūtra).

'. . . The (bad) destinies are the hells (*naraka, niraya*), animals (*tiryak*) and hungry ghosts (*preta*)' (Sūtra).

There is no difference between the two texts on the subject of this thesis.

THESIS XIV — 'There is an intermediate absorption (*dhyānāntara*) between the first and second absorption'.

This thesis is explained in *Ssŭ*, 14*a* 7-10:

'(The stage endowed with thought[406] consists of (the level) endowed with reasoning (*savitarka*), (the level) devoid of reasoning (*avitarka*)[407], and the (level) endowed with investigation (*savicāra*)' (Sūtra).

'The stage connected with reasoning (*savitarka*) (is the stage) endowed with

---

406 *Ssŭ*, 14*a* 7: *shih nien* 及念 . This is a stage in which coarse and subtle thoughts exist.

407 *Ssŭ*, 14*a* 7: *chih chieh chih hsing* 自覺自行 . In doctrinal terminology, these terms correspond to the Sanskrit *savitarka* and *savicāra*.

reasoning. (The stage) which eliminates reasoning (is the stage) devoid of reasoning. (The stage devoid of) joy (*prīti*) is the same (?). Hence, by classing it with the absorptions (*dhyāna*): (the stage) endowed with reasoning is the first (absorption), the stage devoid of investigation is the second one, (the stage) devoid of reasoning (but endowed with investigation) is placed between the first and second (absorptions)[408]. (If one) practises those absorptions, one is reborn in the world of subtle form'.

Generally speaking, the doctrinal elements of this thesis are similar in the two texts. However, the translation, or rather the doctrinal terms of both texts are not identical. For example, the *Ssŭ* uses the expression 'endowed with thought' (*chih nien* 及念) to indicate the stage which consists of the three other levels, namely:

the level endowed with reasoning (*savitarka*),

the level devoid of reasoning (*avitarka*) and

the level endowed (only) with investigation (*savicāra*),

whilst Tds, 28*b* 23, uses the term 'endowed with joy' (*yu hsi* 有喜, *prīti*) to indicate them. The latter is more precise than the former. Nonetheless, further on at *Ssŭ*, 14*a* 8, there is the term 'happiness', or rather 'joy' (*lo* 樂) which perhaps indicates the joy (*prīti*) which characterises the three stages mentioned and which is often found in the canonical texts.

VI – *THE ORIGINAL SCHOOL*

Because the *Ssŭ* contains nearly all the doctrinal points — especially the theses of the Vātsīputrīyas or Pudgalavādins — contained in the Tds, and because the Tds, through its indications, is attributed to the Vātsīputrīya school, it is permissable to believe that the *Ssŭ* is equally a Vātsīputrīya work.

III. THE SAN-MI-TI PU LUN

I – *THE TITLE*

San-mi-ti pu lun 三彌底部論, the Sanskrit equivalent of which is Sāṃmitīya-nikāyaśāstra (abbrev. Sns — The Treatise of the Sāṃmitīya School, found in *Taishō*, volume **XXXII**, No.1649, pp.462*a* - 473*a*). This new title, very general in meaning, scarcely conveys the particular contents of the treatise which has another name, given at the end of the text, *i-shuo lun* 依說論 (Sns, 473*a* 14), and which corresponds to the Sanskrit Āśraya-prajñaptiśāstra. This designation probably concerns the contents of the work, the largest part of which attempts to explain the theory of the *pudgala* as a designated person.

---

408 Modifications and additions in the translation are needed in order to make the meaning conform to the doctrine concerning the absorptions, particularly the intermediate absorption (*dhyānāntara*) which comes between the first and seond absorptions.

II – *THE AUTHOR AND TRANSLATOR*

In the Chinese translation, we find no trace of the names of the author and translator of the treatise. It seems this silence over the name of the author of a literary work was very common in India in early times. In some cases, the author was either a well-known personality whose name it was unnecessary to indicate, or a person advanced on the Path whose humility prevented him from quoting his name in a description of the Noble Truths. Another possibility cannot be excluded: this is that the treatise was a joint composition, compiled by several persons — masters or co-disciples — belonging to the same — Sāṃmitīya — school after studies and discussions which lasted for a long time. In consequence, the completed book was considered as a joint work and could not be attributed to a particular person.

The absence of the name of the translator in this treatise is equally a fact quite often noted in Chinese Buddhist translations.

III – *THE DATE*

The date of composition of the Sns is not indicated in the treatise. However, it is evident that it was composed after the schism which separated the Sāṃmitīyas from the Vātsīputrīyas, possibly at the beginning of the Common Era[409]. Since place-names, Pañcha-Mathurā, Mathurā, are found in the text (Sns, 471*a* 1) in connection with an illustration of the doctrine, it might be asked whether this treatise was written in that area of India. Furthermore, the Sns was probably composed after the Tridharmaka-śāstra, as arguments in defence of the *pudgala* doctrine are more profound and detailed in the Sns than in the Tds. Moreover, the supposed date of the Chinese translation, in the period of the Western Chin (*Hsi Chin* 西晉, 385-431 CE) dynasty, informs us that the Sns must have been composed in the very early years of the fifth century, and possibly even some time before.

VI – *THE TRANSLATION*

The author of the *K'ai yüan shih-chiao lun* 開元釋教錄 (T LV, 2059, 518*c* - 621*b*) supposes that this translation was made under the Ch'in 秦 dynasty (265-313 CE). Until now, we have found no proof of this date. However, it seems certain that this translation belonged to the early period of the history of the translation of Buddhist texts in China, because the technical terms are similar to those of translations from the same period, for example: *yin* 陰 (*skandha*, 462*b* 4); *t'ung* 痛 (*vedanā*, 463*a* 2), *shêng yin* 盛陰 (*upādānaskandha*, 464*a* 24), etc. In any case, it is certain that this translation was made before the time of Hsüan-tsang (602-664).

With regard to the language of the original Sns text, it appears to have been in Prākrit or Āpabhraṃśa rather than Sanskrit or hybrid Sanskrit. In fact, the expression and syntax in this work differ from those of the other treatises.

The translation is somewhat obscure. Furthermore, the join between phrases and

---

409 This date is deduced from the contents of the work, in which are found extracts from the Buddha's discourses, and doctrinal divergencies of the schools.

propositions is found with difficulty because the necessary propositions are missing. Chih-hsü 智旭 criticised it: 'The style has little continuity'[410].

V — *THE CONTENTS*

Whilst the Tds and *Ssŭ* describe all the doctrinal elements which encompass the specific theses of the Vātsīputrīya school, the Sns, in contrast, deals only with theses characteristic of the Sāṃmitīya school, namely: the indestructible thing (*avipraṇāśa* ?), the *pudgala*, the intermediate existence (*antarābhava*), etc., which formerly caused strong controversy.

The Sns occupies more than ten pages of the *Taishō* edition and consists of three fascicles which do not correspond to any discernible logical division. That is why we can divide the text into four parts according to the subjects.

FIRST PART

The first part (462*a* 6 - 466*a* 27) deals with major subjects such as the thesis of the indestructible (*avipraṇāśa* ?). the seven opinions concerning the person[411] and its relationship with the aggregates (*skandha*), and the Sāṃmitīya position in relation to these seven opinions.

I — <u>The introduction and thesis of the indestructible</u> (*avipraṇāśa* ?)

The treatise begins with an introduction (462*a* 6 - *b* 5) explaining the existence of a thing (*dharma*), called 'the increase' (*shêng* 生 , *upacaya*) or 'the indestructible' (*pu-mieh* 不滅 , *avipraṇāśa* ?)[412]. This is the thing which preserves actions (*karman*) by means of which results are produced in future existences; the intermediate existences (*antarābhava*) of the holy ones (*ārya*) can notably be explained in this way.

II — <u>The seven adverse opinions</u>

After the introduction, the Sns (462*b* 6 - 464*a* 15) presents seven contradictory opinions concerning the person, its nature identical with or different from the aggregates (*skandha*) and its permanence or impermanence. It is noteworthy that all these opinions are based on the words of the Buddha contained in the Sūtras. Here are these seven differing opinions:

1. *There is no person, since:*
   a. only aggregates (*skandha*) and domains (*āyatana*) exist, and only suffering (*duḥkha*) exists; but no person that suffers exists[413] ;

---

410 Chih-hsü 释智旭 *Yüeh tsang chih chin* 閲藏知津 , *op. cit.*, vol.IV, p.89: 久不甚聯絡.

411 The translation sometimes mentions the word *jên* 人 , and sometimes *wo* 我 . In order to facilitate the distinction from the word self, translated from the Sanskrit *ātman*, the meaning of which is totally heretical in Buddhism, we always translate by person (*pudgala*) the words *jen*, *wo* 人我 which, in this text, indicates a designated individual (*pudgala*) rather than that of an absolute self (*ātman*).

412 See below, 'The secondary theses of the Pudgalavādins, thesis No.1'.

413 The same idea is found in SN I, 135:

There is only suffering which appears,

b. the person does not exist[414] ;
c. only the ignorant consider the body as the person;
d. the reality of the person and what pertains to it is not proved;
e. the person is unreal.

2. *It is impossible to say that the person exists or does not exist, since*:
   a. the character of the person cannot be defined in relation to compounded things (*saṃskṛta*) and the uncompounded (*asaṃskṛta*)[415] ;
   b. the existence or non-existence of the person is a question which the Buddha avoided (*avyākṛta*)[416] ;
   c. the fact of the indetermination of the person with regard to compounded things (*saṃskṛta*) and the uncompounded (*asaṃskṛta*);
   d. the confusion between permanence (*nitya*) and impermanence (*anitya*);
   e. the fact of not pertaining to existence, nor to non-existence[417].

3. *The person really exists, since*:
   a. it is the person bound to the five aggregates who wanders from one life to another;
   b. it is because the vision of the person is right view (*samyagdṛṣṭi*) just as the vision of spontaneously born beings (*aupapātika*) is right view[418] ;
   c. the teaching on the four applications of mindfulness (*smṛtyupasthāna*) indicates that there is a person who contemplates the body (*kāya*), feelings

---

that suffering remains and disappears.
There is no other thing, only suffering which appears.
When it ceases, there is no further thing.
(*dukkhaṃ eva hi sambhoti / dukkhaṃ tiṭṭhati veti ca // nāññatra dukkhā sambhoti / nāññaṃ dukkhā nirujjahtī //*); Vism XVI, 90: *dukkhaṃ eva hi, na koci dukkhito.*

414 This refutation of the existence of the self is based on arguments which are often found in the canonical texts, for example: the Chachakkasutta (MN, No.148/III, 280–7); Natumhākasutta (SN XXII, 33/III, 33–4).

415 It seems this position is similar to that of the *pudgala* thesis. However, it is refuted by the Pudgalavādins themselves, as it does not affirm the existence of the person, while the Pudgalavādins admit it. See below, 'The Sāṃmitīya position in relation to the seven opinions'.

416 On the questions to be rejected, see above, 'The theses of the Pudgalavādins: the original teaching of the Buddha'. Cf. SN IV, 393; MN I, 484; Ud VI, 4. According to DN III, p.229, there are four types of conversation, namely: 1) the questioner's doubt are dispelled by answers (*paṭipucchāvyākaraṇīya*); 2) direct answers are given to questions without discussion with the questioner (*ekaṃsavyākaraṇīya*); 3) answers are given in part, that is, one aspect of the question is taken up, then another (*vibhajjavyākaraṇīya*); 4) the indeterminate nature of the problem leads to infinity; that is why all discussion (*ṭhapanīya*) should be avoided. 'The order of questions to be rejected' corresponds to the fourth category above.

417 This position is based on two extremist ideas, existence and non-existence, in order to deny the existence of the self. Cf. SN II, 15.

418 The canonical texts recognise the existence of living beings 'born spontaneously' (*aupapātika*, Pāli: *opapātika*), that is, born without the intervention of parents. These are heavenly beings and infernal beings. MN I, 34: . . . After having eliminated the five lesser fetters, I shall be reborn spontaneously (in such and such a world), there I shall immediately attain Parinirvāṇa and shall not return to this world (. *pañcannaṃ orambhāgiyānaṃ saṃyojānaṃ parikkhāya opapātiko as:.aṃ tatthaparinibbhāyī anāvattidhammo tasmā lokā ti . . .*).

(*vedanā*), the mind (*citta*) and mental objects (*dharma*)[419] ;

d. the word of the Buddha to the disciples (*śrāvaka*) on fire worship causes a belief that there is a person who directs the action of burning the body and who accepts the order to burn;

e. the term 'person' used by the Buddha in the sentence: 'a virtuous person (*pudgala*) who appears in the world brings happiness to many men'[420].

4. *The person is identical with the aggregates* (skandha), *since the Buddha said that*:

   a. the six sense organs and six objects constitute the person[421] ;

   b. these are form, character, etc. (the aggregates) of a person which constitute the person, there is nothing beyond that[422].

5. *The person is different from the aggregates, since*:

   a. the Buddha said that the burden — the five aggregates — differs from the bearer of the burden — the person[423] ;

   b. the Buddha said that the person appropriates thirst (*tṛṣṇā*) as second nature in the cycle of birth and death (*saṃsāra*)[424] ;

---

419 The Satipaṭṭhānasutta (MN, No.10/I, 55–63) deals with the fixing of attention on four objects: the body, feelings, the mind and mental objects, for example saying: . . . and furthermore, monks, a monk going, knows: 'I am going'; standing, he knows: 'I am standing'; etc. (*puna ca paraṃ bhikkhave bhikkhu gacchanto vā: gacchāmīti pajānāti, ṭhito vā: ṭhito'mhīti pajānāti* . . . — MN I, 56).

420 This sentence is certainly invested with the same contents as the Pāli phrase in AN I, 22: Monks, there is a person whose appearance in the world is for the welfare of many, for the happiness of many, through compassion for the world, for the benefit, welfare and happiness of gods and mankind. Which is that person? It is the Tathāgata, the Arhat, the Perfectly Enlightened One (*ekapuggalo bhikkhave loke uppajjamāno bahujanahitāya bahujanasukhāya lokāya sukhāya devamanussānam. katamo ekapuggalo? tathāgato araham sammāsambuddho*). Cf. *Kośa* IX, p.259 (Pruden, p.1330).

421 See below, n.437

422 This idea conforms with what the Buddha said about the identification of the person and the five aggregates. This is the first of the following four attachments to the self: Monks, all recluses and brahmins who admit the self in different ways consider the five aggregates, or one or another of them, as being the self. Which are those five? Monks, an uneducated worldling who does not discern the holy ones considers form . . . feeling, perception, the formations and consciousness as being the self, or else the self as being the possessor of one of those groups, or else those aggregates are included in the self, or else the self is included in those aggregates. Hence the view: it occurs to him to think 'I am' (*ye hi keci bhikkhave samaṇāvā brāhmaṇā vā anekavihitam attānam samanupassamānā samanupassanti, sabbe te pañcupādānakkhande samanupassanti etesaṃ vā aññataraṃ. katame pañca? idha bhikkhave assutavā puthujjano ariyānaṃ adassāvī, la, sappurisadhamme avinīto rūpam attato samanupassati, rūpavantaṃ vā attānam attanī vā rūpam rūpasmiṃ vā attānaṃ; vedanaṃ; saññaṃ; saṅkhāre; viññāṇam attato samanupassati; viññāṇavantaṃ vā attānam attani vā viññāṇaṃ viññāṇasmiṃ vā attānam. iti ayam ceva samanupassanā asmīti cassa adhigataṃ hoti* — SN III, 46). The translation is slightly modified by abbreviation.

423 Cf. the Bhārahārasutta (SN III, 25). It is noteworthy that there is another opinion also based on this discourse in order to show that the person and the aggregates differ from each other.

424 This is an opinion resulting from a misunderstanding of the Buddha's words on the importance of thirst. For example, Itivuttaka, p.8: Monks, I do not see any other fetter which fetters (beings) and through which beings wander for a very long time and hasten through the cycle of existences as this fetter of thirst. Evidently, monks, being fettered by that fetter of thirst, beings wander and hasten through the cycle of existences (*nāhaṃ bhikkhave aññaṃ ekasaṃyojanaṃ pi samanupassāmi yeneva*

c. the rebirth of a person in another life in order to undergo or enjoy the results of actions (*karman*) in this life[425] ;
d. the identity of the person in different lives; for example, the identity of the Buddha and personages in his former lives under the names of Sunetra, Mahādeva, etc;
e. the Buddha does not affirm that the nature of the person is impermanent or permanent, whilst he does affirm the impermanent nature of the aggregates.

6. *The person is eternal*
   a. since it has no beginning, as the origin of the cycle of birth and death is inconceivable. (In consequence, the person is eternal[426]) ;
   b. the knowledge of the recollection of former lives[427] ;
   c. because of the existence of an eternal plane where suffering and regression no longer exist[428] ;
   d. and the existence of imperturbable joy which can be enjoyed[429].

7. *The person is impermanent, since* :
   a. it has an origin, for example, the birth of the Buddha which brings happiness to so many people[430] ;
   b. this life is transformed into a heavenly existence;
   c. conditions of life change in different lives;
   d. living beings appear and disappear;
   e. the states of birth (*jāti*), old-age (*jarā*), disease (*vyādhi*) and death (*maraṇa*) are manifestations of impermanence.

III — The Sāṃmitīya position in relation to the seven opinions.

Next, the Sns (464*a* 16 - 466*a* 27) explains the Sāṃmitīya position in relation to the preceding seven opinions.

1. *The person exists since*:
   a. the Buddha does not deny the person, but he wishes to illustrate the nature of suffering, the arising and cessation of suffering, by emphasising the

---

saṃyojanena saṃyuttā sattā dīgharattaṃ sandhāvanti saṃsaranti yathayidaṃ bhikkhave taṇhā-saṃyojanaṃ. taṇhāsaṃyojanena hi bhikkhave saṃyuttā sattā dīgharattaṃ sandhāvanti saṃsarantīti).

425 This proposition rests on the false opinion according to which the person having produced actions in a former life is different from the person receiving the fruits in a later life.

426 On the impossibility of conceiving the origin of the cycle of birth and death, see earlier, 'The literature of the Pudgalavādins' and notes 99, 100, 101.

427 On the knowledge of the recollection of former lives, see below, 'The secondary theses of the Pudgalavādins, thesis No.5'. Cf. DN I, 81; AN III, 99.

428 This is Nirvāṇa or Parinirvāṇa. See below, 'The secondary theses of the Pudgalavādins, thesis No.10'.

429 See below, 'The main thesis of the Pudgalavādins: the *pudgala* designated by cessation'.

430 See above, n.420. Here, it is the argument concerning the impermanence of the person which is manifested in this world for a certain time.

existence of suffering[431] ;

b. the Buddha declares to the sectaries that there is a person as a designation which rests on compounded things (*saṃskāra*)[432] ;

c. (consequently), the opinion on the substantiality of the five aggregates is a false view[433] ;

d. the Buddha does not deny the person but, in order to dispel attachment to another, he teaches the insubstantiality of the person and what pertains to it;

e. certainly, the person is unreal but, in order to dispel attachment to existence, the Buddha responds with non-existence; that does not mean that he denies the person.

2. *It is possible to say that the person exists, since*:

a. although it is impossible to say that the person is permanent (*nitya*) or impermanent (*anitya*), it is possible to say that the person exists since the Buddha said: 'There are persons who burn their bodies, etc.' or 'the ignorant take bad actions (*akuśalakarman*) as their nature, the intelligent take good actions (*kuśalakarman*) as theirs';

b. the questions to be rejected (*avyākṛta*) are those which are not correctly asked, since the Buddha never rejects propositions such as this: the ignorant are bad and the intelligent are good;

c. the fact of indetermination forms part of the person because the person is equally non-identical with compounded things not different from compounded things[434] ;

d. to admit that the person does not exist is to express a wrong view (*mithyādṛṣṭi*), because the Buddha declares that attachment to the two ideas, existence and non-existence, is wrong, since this pertains to a question to be rejected (*avyākṛta*) and leads to ideas of permanence and impermanence. It is right view (*samyagdṛṣṭi*) if it is admitted that the person exists unconditionally and does not belong to either impermanent compounded things nor the permanent compounded thing[435] ;

e. it is possible to say that the person exists (conditionally) because the Buddha

---

431 This is a defence of the Sāṃmitīya thesis of the *pudgala* in relation to the Theravādins who categorically deny the existence of a person undergoing suffering. See above, n.413.

432 Here the Sns, 464*b* 6–7, asserts that the Buddha taught that a designated person exists which rests on the impure aggregates, or person designated by the support (*i-shuo-jên* 依説人 *āśrayaprajñaptapudgala*).

433 This is clear proof that the Pudgalavādins themselves also rejected the concept of a substantial self (*ātman*). This is why the definitions of *pudgala* as a real and permanent substance are unfounded.

434 Sns, 464*c* 10–11: 我等今説，若我驗者應是行爲異行，如是正説爲是行爲異行應説 : we declare that: if the person is examined [in order to know] if it is identical with compounded things or different from them, it should correctly be stated that it is neither identical with compounded things nor different from them. —
This proposition is indeed the essential position of the *pudgala* thesis.

435 These are also the main arguments with which the Pudgalavādins established the *pudgala* thesis, the position of which lies between two extremist ideas: existence (permanence) and non-existence (impermanence). Cf. Sns. 464*c* 15–24 and the translation below, 'The main thesis of the Pudgalavādins'.

says that the basis exists[436].

3. *The person does not exist as a reality, since*:
   a. although there is no chained person, the chain exists just as there are chains in prisons even when there are no prisoners;
   b. an opinion on the existence of the person is a right view (*samyagdṛṣṭi*) because the Buddha, relying on the defiled aggregates (*sāśravaskandha*), declares that the person exists; since it a man who sees the person[437] ;
   c. in reality, only the mind (*citta*) exists which intervenes in the practice of the four applications of mindfulness (*smṛtyupasthāna*), and nothing else[438] ;
   d. the Buddha said to the disciples (*śrāvaka*) that it is things (*dharma*) which are based on the elements (*āyatana*), and that there is nothing else[439] ;
   e. the Buddha declares that the person exists as a designation (*prajñapti*). The refutation of the person entails the refutation of morality (*śīla*), the four Noble Truths (*āryasatya*) taught by the Buddha, etc.[440].

4. It is impossible to say that the person is identical with the aggregates or that the aggregates are identical with the person, since the person is ineffable (*avaktavya*) but the aggregates are not. Moreover, if the person were identical with the aggregates, when the aggregates disappear or appear, the person should also disappear or appear[441].

5. *It is impossible to say the person is different from the aggregates, since*:
   a. the discourse never teaches the separation between the life of man[442] and the

---

436 Sns, 464*c* 27–28: 若都無我，佛不應說有依止，佛說有依止故，是故有我可說。

The words *i-chih* 依止 are translated by 'the basis' with the meaning of the basic elements, i.e., the aggregates.

437 Sns, 465*a* 18: 依有漏陰，佛說有人，以人見有人故名正見: basing himself on the defiled aggregates, the Buddha spoke of the existence of the person. Because of the fact that a man perceives the existence of the person, that is called right view. This translation is more of an interpretation, since the text makes no distinction between the two words *jên* 人 .

438 This refutation in the Sns proves that the Pudgalavādins never admitted that the *pudgala* was what observes the four objects in the practice of the four applications (*smṛtyupasthāna*).

439 SN IV, 15: What is the totality of things? It is the eye and visibles; the ear and sounds, the nose and odour, the tongue and taste, the body and the tangible, the mind and mental objects. Those things, monks, are called the totality. — Monks, if someone says: 'Rejecting that totality, I shall make known another totality', that is mere speculation on his part and, when questioned, he cannot give an explanation; furthermore, he is in a dilemma. Why? Because, monks, that is beyond his capacity (*sabbaṃ vo bhikkhave dessissāmi, taṃ suṇātha. kiñca bhikkhave sabbaṃ? cakkhuṃ ceva rūpā ca sotañca saddā ca ghānañca gandhā ca jivhā rasā ca kāyo ca phoṭṭhabbā ca mano ca dhammā ca. idaṃ vuccati bhikkhave sabbaṃ. yo bhikkhave evam vadeyya. ahaṃ etaṃ sabbaṃ paccakkhāya aññaṃ sabbaṃ paññāpessāmīti, tassa vācāvatthur evassa, puṭṭho ca na sampāpeyya, uttariñca vighātaṃ āpajjeyya. taṃ kissa hetu, yathā taṃ bhikkhave avisayasmiṃti*). Cf. *Kośa* IX, p.248 and n.1 [Pruden, pp.1324, 1364].

440 It is obvious that the Sns is promoting vigorous and convincing arguments in favour of the existence of the *pudgala*; cf. Sns, 465*a* 17 – *b* 1, or below, 'The main thesis of the Pudgalavādins'.

441 These too are arguments on which the essential position of the *pudgala* thesis is based.

442 This translates the words *jên ming* 人命 (= *jīva*?) (Sns, 465*b* 5).

person, but it says that there is a person who bears the burden; that is why the burden exists;

b. when thirst (*tṛṣṇa*) is eliminated, there is no further transmigration in the cycle of birth and death; this means that the person and the aggregates are not separate;

c. it is by being based on the aggregates that this life and the future life receive the results of actions (*karman*); this means that the person and the aggregates are not separate;

d. the 'I' of which the Buddha speaks is a designation marking transmigration between the different existences of a person[443] ;

e. the characteristic of things (*dharmalakṣaṇa*) cannot be defined as permanent or impermanent. It is the same for the person[444]. If the person were different from the aggregates:

a) the person would either be found in the body, or enclose the whole;

b) when the sense organs are destroyed, the five objects should still be known;

c) the person could go from this body to another, then return to the first body;

d) the person should not be reborn in different destinies; otherwise it would be reborn in all the destinies at a given moment; consequently, it should not always reside in the body; hence, liberation would be difficult to obtain; if the person were to pass from one destiny to another, it should not create actions (*karman*); if there were no actions or results, neither would there be any merit (*puṇya*); equally, there would be no detachment from the bonds, nor the practice of meditation; it is thus that liberation should operate.

6. *The person is not eternal, since:*

a. it cannot be said that the cycle of birth and death is eternal because its origin is inconceivable. Equally, it is impossible to maintain that the person is eternal because it has no origin;

b. the knowledge of the recollection of former lives does not allow a conclusion that the person is eternal, since the person is different from the aggregates; when the aggregates disappear, the person would not disappear. Thus the recollection of the past does not concern this life and does not extend to other lives, whilst the cycle of life and death is unceasing.

---

443 It is with this idea that the Pudgalavādins established the *pudgala* designated by transmigration (*tu-shuo-jên* 度説人 , *saṇkramaprajñaptipudgala*).

444 Sns, 465*b* 29: 我等今説陰我異不異不可説， 是故法相以常無常爲首不可説

: we declare that it is impossible to say that the aggregates and the person are either different or identical. That is why it is impossible to say, in the first place, that the characteristic of things is either permanence or impermanence. Thesis IIc of the Vātsīputrīyas by Vasumitra: 'Compounded things (*saṃskṛta*) either endure temporarily or disappear in a single instant (*ekakṣaṇika*)'. According to their doctrine, this is a specific property not only of compounded things in general but also of the Pudgala in particular. See below, 'The secondary theses of the Pudgalavādins; thesis No.8'.

c. certainly, the Buddha spoke of Nirvāṇa with a remainder (*sopadhiśeṣa-nirvāṇa*) and of Nirvāṇa without a remainder (*nirupadhiśeṣanirvāṇa*), but he did not speak of an eternal person;
d. imperturbable joy exists in Nirvāṇa without a remainder[445], but, for the eternal person, there is no imperturbable joy because, for it, joy and sorrow are not important.

7. *The person is not (absolutely) impermanent, since*:
a. the person is designated on the basis of the appearance of the aggregates. This does not mean that the aggregates are different from the person. Hence, it is impossible to speak of the appearance of a person, only its designation can be spoken of;
b. if the person were totally impermanent, then there would be no relationship between the former life and the later life. Consequently, there would be no results of actions, merit, recollection, etc. The impermanence of the person is based on the disappearance of the aggregates of one destiny and their appearance in another destiny[446].

SECOND PART

In the second part (466*a* 28 - 469*a* 28), the Sns deals with the *pudgala* thesis, questions concerning life after death and the origin of the course of existence.

I — The *Pudgala*

The theory of the *pudgala* is presented from 466*a* 28 to 466*c* 28. The *pudgala* is a conditioned person whose nature, connection with the elements, rôle in the round of rebirth (*saṃsāra*) and cessation (*nirodha*) are progressively defined in conformity to the Buddhadharma.

The thesis of the *pudgala* is based on the following three kinds of designations (*prajñapti*):

1. The *pudgala* designated by the support (*i-shuo-jên* 依說人, *āśrayaprajñapti-pudgala*?). The support here consists of compounded things (*saṃskāra*). This relationship is similar to that of fire in relation to fuel[447], or to milk in relation to its colour[448]. In this sense, the person and form (*rūpa*) are two things which are neither identical nor different. They exist and perish together;

2. The *pudgala* designated by transmigration (*tushuo-jên*, 度說人 ,

445 On the imperturbable joy in Nirvāṇa without a remainder, cf. below, 'The main thesis of the Pudgalavādins: the *pudgala* designated by cessation' and n.692.

446 This position is certainly consistent with the preceding thesis concerning compounded things: it is impossible to say that the characteristic of things is either permanence or impermanence (Sns, 465*b* 29).

447 The relationship between fire and fuel is difficult to explain; cf. *Kośa* IX, 234, or above, 'The main thesis of the Pudgalavādins, the position of the *pudgala*'.

448 It is impossible to say that milk is identical with colour or different from colour. Cf. *Kośa* IX, 239, or above, 'The main thesis of the Pudgalavādins, the position of the *pudgala*'.

saṅkramaprajñaptipudgala?). Transmigration is the continuity of a living being in the three time-periods: past, present and future. Without this designation, there are no means of recognising the identity of living beings from one existence to another;

3. The *pudgala* designated by cessation (*mieh-shuo-jên* 滅說人 , *nirodhaprajñaptipudgala*?). Cessation is the extinction of the five aggregates or defilements (*āśrava*). In other words, this designation shows that the cessation of the cycle of birth and death does not signify annihilation.

The *pudgala* is therefore only a designation (*prajñapti*), the existence of which is based on the first idea. The second explains the continuity of the process of the life of a person. With the third, it is intended to demonstrate that a 'state' exists after Parinirvāṇa in which the five aggregates are no longer present.

II — The problem of life after death

From 466*c* 28 to 467*c* 14, the Sns deals with questions and answers on the subject of what happens after death. There are divergent opinions which are opposed by the affirmations of the Sāṃmitīyas in relation to the doctrine of the *pudgala* and the intermediate existence (*antarābhava*).

1. Who transmigrates? The *pudgala* in the intermediate existence (*antarābhava*).

With regard to the different opinions on the subject of the question of what transmigrates and the answer of the Sāṃmitīyas, the Sns (467*a* 1 - *b* 18) explains:

a. *The three adverse opinions*:

1 — Only the five aggregates pass from one existence to another. They are consciousness (*vijñāna*) and actions (*karman*) which determine rebirth;

2 — It is the person (alone) who goes from one life to another, and not the aggregates.

3 — There is no person which transmigrates because, according to the Buddha, new divine persons exists, the name one receives depends on actions accomplished here and there; when virtuous persons appear in the world, many people delight in the happiness they have brought. Hence, those who are born are not reborn again.

b. *The Sāṃmitīyas' answer.*

1 — When the aggregates disappear, the *pudgala*, by means of the intermediate existence (*antarābhava*), passes on and is reborn in another destiny. The divine eye alone is capable of perceiving the intermediate existence.

2 — It is impossible to say that the person alone goes to the other destiny, since the opinion according to which there is a real person separate (from the aggregates), whether it be eternal or non-eternal, is a wrong view (*mithyādṛṣṭi*).

2. How does the intermediate existence (*antarābhava*) appear?

The Sns (467*b* 19 - *c* 14) explains the manner in which the intermediate existence appears as follows: at the moment when a man is about to die, the intermediate existence is on the point of manifesting itself. That person consisting of the intermediate aggregates cannot be considered as the same as the one which is designated by the support (*āśrayaprajñaptipudgala*?). It is not true that a person first assumes the five intermediate aggregates then abandons the human aggregates, since a person cannot have two existences at the same time. Neither is it to the contrary, because, if a person were first to abandon the human aggregates, then assume the five aggregates of the intermediate existence, there would be a void between two destinies. Hence, the actions are taken simultaneously. This means that the very instant when the mind (*citta*) of the last moment of that human existence has just expired, the mind of the intermediate existence begins to exist. That state is called the state of the appearance of the mind. It is thus that one abandons the five human aggregates and receives the five aggregates of the intermediate existence.

III — <u>Is there an origin to the series of existences</u> ?

From 467*c* 15 to 469*a* 28, the Sns describes opinions concerning the question: Basing themselves on the teaching of the Buddha, the Sāṃmitīyas affirm that the absolute origin of the cycle of birth and death is inconceivable. It is impossible to say that it exists or that it does not exist because, if there were a real origin, it would be inconceivable. It is, however, impossible to say that it is absolutely real or unreal. The Buddha declares that the question of the origin of the cycle of birth and death is a question to be rejected (*avyākṛta*) since, if one says that existences have no origin, one falls into the false view of nihilism and, if one says that existences do have an origin, one then falls into the false view of eternalism. Here are the reasons for which the origin of the series of existences is inconceivable:

1. The beginning of thirst (*tṛṣṇā*) in relation to existences is inconceivable;
2. If there were no cycle of birth and death, there would be no Nirvāṇa. Although Nirvāṇa has a beginning, the origin of the cycle of birth and death is inconceivable;
3. It is the evolution of causes which constitutes the cycle of birth and death. It is not men who are provided with original persons; if they were so provided, the cycle of birth and death would be infinite;
4. The lives of the past which can be remembered are innumerable; that is why the origin of the cycle of birth and death is inconceivable;
5. If an origin of the cycle of birth and death were to exist, the origin of one life in the past would also have to exist;
6. Due to the evolution of thirst (*tṛṣṇā*), the Buddha declares that the origin of lives in the past is inconceivable. It is because the origin of the cycle of birth and death does not exist that there is no name for that origin.

It is thus that the absolute origin of the cycle of birth and death is inconceivable. Nonetheless, that does not mean that no origin exists at all, since the cycle is conditioned; consequently, it is not eternal. As conditions evolve, consequences also evolve. The inconceivable fact of the origin, middle and end of the cycle of birth and death does not mean that cycle does not exist. For example, the

Sāṃmitīyas always affirm: 'The *pudgala* exists in relation to the aggregates and transmigration'.

It is noteworthy that, according to the school's doctrine, the Sāṃmitīyas distinguished between the elements (*dharma*) of the person (*pudgala*). From the point of view of the elements, they say that the origin of the cycle of birth and death is inconceivable, but that does not encompass the point of view of the person. The person is veiled by ignorance (*avidyā*), consequently, it transmigrates. In other words, 'when the elements reach the mind (*citta*), rely on it and (then) transmigrate, the Buddha calls that the person (*pudgala*)'. The *pudgala* is thus something 'separate' from the elements, then it is possible to say that the elements are impermanent, but it is impossible to say whether the *pudgala* is permanent or impermanent. Hence, we can understand the expressible or inexpressible nature of the origin of life. The cycle of birth and death therefore does not possess any origin.

THIRD PART

The third part of the work is very long (469*b* - 471*c* 3). In this section, the Sns first presents ten of the adversaries' arguments aimed at denying the intermediate existence; it then affirms the intermediate existence by refuting the adverse arguments and by reinforcing its own.

I — Ten opposing arguments

From 469*b* 5 to 469*c* 26, the Sns describes the arguments of different schools, based on the words of the Buddha and which are opposed to the intermediate existence:

1. The absence of any mention by the Buddha of the intermediate existence, of the being who goes to the intermediate existence and the path leading to the intermediate existence.
2. The Buddha does not speak of the intermediate existence in the context of the destinies of birth (the five destinies) or the categories of living beings.
3. The Buddha does not speak of actions (*karman*) leading to the intermediate existence when he speaks of actions in the five destinies.
4. The Buddha clearly specifies the number of the five destinies but he does not mention the intermediate existence.
5. The Buddha says that rebirth in the Avīci hell, after death, is immediate.
6. If there were an intermediate state between death and birth, there would be another intermediate state between the intermediate existence and birth, etc.
7. Due to the uselessness of the intermediate existence which does not posssess any of the specific charactersitics of life.
8. Due to the impossibility of conceiving the birth of the elements which are both identical with and different from those of the birth existence (*upapattibhava*).
9. The Buddha does not speak of the characteristics of the intermediate existence whilst he does describe the characteristics of the five destinies.
10. The Buddha says that birth takes place an instant after the decease of the present body.

II — Ten answers from the Sāṃmitīyas

By answering the ten preceding arguments, the Sns (469*b* 27 - 470*b* 15) justifies its support of the thesis of the intermediate existence with the following reasons:

1. The intermediate existence is like the vehicle of the five destinies. That is why the Buddha does not speak of it in the context of the five destinies.
2. The intermediate existence is not a destiny in which one stays, but it is a stage for the transfer of the faculty of life (*jīvitendriya*). That is why the Buddha does not speak of it in the context of the five destinies[449].
3. A man receives the results of his actions and undergoes rebirth in the six destinies[450], but not in the intermediate existence. That is why the Buddha does not speak of actions in the intermediate existence.
4. What is not mentioned by the Buddha nonetheless exists. The Buddha himself says that there are many things to be taught but that he cannot speak of them all.
5. It is in order to reject the opinion according to which there is no intervening destiny in the course of rebirth that the Buddha speaks of immediate rebirth in the Avīci hell. That means that there is no intermediate existence.
6. The intermediate existence cannot be demonstrated in a conclusive manner by the existence, for example, of intermediate meditation (*dhyānāntara*)[451].
7. The intermediate existence enables a person to reach and be reborn in another destiny.
8. After having passed into the intermediate existence, one receives the birth existence (*upapattibhava*). These two existences are similar because the former is the vehicle and the latter the destination. That is why the intermediate existence exists.
9. It is because the Buddha wishes to avoid disputes on the existence or non-existence of that intermediate stage that he does not speak of it.
10. It is because the birth existence has not yet appeared that the body must pass through the intermediate existence to reach the other existence.

III — Ten arguments used to demonstrate the intermediate existence

Further on, the Sns (470*b* 16 - 471*a* 5) again cites the words of the Buddha aimed at demonstrating the intermediate existence. Here are the basic ideas:

1. The Buddha teaches that attachment to the intervening stage (which, according to the Sāṃmitīyas, is the intermediate existence) should be abandoned.
2. The Buddha affirms that there exists an individual composed of a mind-made

449 On the five or six destinies, see below, 'The secondary theses of the Pudgalavādins: thesis No.11'.

450 See preceding note.

451 On the intermediate meditation (*dhyānāntara*), see below, 'The secondary theses of the Pudgalavādins, thesis No.9'.

body (*manomayakāya*), of thirst (*tṛṣṇā*) and of appropriation (*upādāna*)[452].

3. The intermediate existence from which one attains Parinirvāṇa, among the five categories of the non-returner (*anāgāmin*)[453].
4. The fact that the body cannot reach the other existence; it is therefore necessary to have another subtle body so that consciousness (*vijñāna*) can reach the other existence.
5. The supernormal power of the divine eye (*divyacakṣus*) can see the disappearance and appearance of living beings. (That is why there is an intermediate existence.)
6. The Buddha speaks of the existence of the *gandharva*, one of the three elements which constitute the embryo[454]. That is an affirmation of the intermediate existence.
7. Because of mutual relations, the intermediate existence is necessary for a transitionary domain to exist (between death and rebirth).
8. The example of the seeds and seedlings: seeds give rise to seedlings and seedlings yield seeds. The seed corresponds to the previous existence, the seedling corresponds to the intermediate existence and the seed produced by the seedling corresponds to the birth existence.
9. The illumination of the world by the Bodhisattva (the Buddha before his last birth), when he descended from the Tusita heaven and entered his mother's womb[455].
10. The existence of the changing of the mind (*citta*) which occurs at the moment when one is on the point of receiving the new birth. Without the intermediate existence, this changing cannot be accomplished.

IV — Criticism of the adversaries

Once again, the Sns, 471*a* 6 - *b* 20, presents the counter-attacks of the adversaries of the thesis of the intermediate existence:

1. The intervening state (in argument No.1) consists of the six consciousnesses

452 This idea is found in the Vātsyāyanasūtra, which is mentioned by the Sns, 471*a* 12 sq. This person is considered to be that of the intermediate existence provided with attachment to the taste of meditation at the moment of leaving the world of desire, but who is not yet reborn in the world of subtle form.

453 On the five categories of the non-returner (*anāgāmin*), see below, 'The Pudgalavādin Lists of Śrāvakas'. As for the idea of attaining Parinirvāṇa in the intermediate existence, cf. below, 'The secondary theses of the Pudgalavādins, thesis No.14'.

454 See below, notes 640–2.

455 Clearly, this proposition is based on a paragraph in the Acchariyabbhutadhammasutta (MN III, 120): Ānanda, when the Bodhisatta, having left the Tusita heaven, descends into his mother's womb, an immense and marvellous radiance, surpassing even the power of the gods, appears in the whole universe, including the world of the gods, the world of Māra and of Brahmā and the world of the recluses, Brahmins, gods and mankind . . . (*yadā, Ānanda, bodhisatto tusitā kāya cavitvā, mātu kucchim okkami, attha sadevake loke samārake sabrahmake sassamaṇabrāhmaṇiyā pajāya sadevamanussāya appamāno ulāro obhāso pātubhavati atikkam'eva devānaṃ devānubhāvaṃ*). Cf. *Romantic Legend of Sākya Buddha* (佛本行集經), tr. S. Beal, pp.36–7.

(*vijñāna*), but not of the intermediate existence[456].

2. The combination of the mind-made body (*manomayakāya*), thirst (*tṛṣṇā*) and appropriation (*upādāna*) means the combination of attachment to the taste of meditation (*dhyāna*) and thirst, but not to the intermediate existence.
3. Attaining Parinirvāṇa in the intervening state[457] does not mean attaining Parinirvāṇa in the intermediate existence.
4. The fact of reaching the other existence is comparable to the appearance of a shadow or of an impression of being lightly touched. This is the manner in which the death existence (*maraṇabhava*) precedes the birth existence (*upapattibhava*). That is why the intermediate existence is not necessary.
5. The supernormal power of the divine eye (*divyacakṣus*) enables it to perceive subtle destinies[458], but not the intermediate existence.
6. The Buddha speaks of the *gandharva* by giving that word the meaning of a being which aims at its destiny or is guided by the power of good or bad actions. The *gandharva* does not imply the intermediate existence.
7. Mutual relations can be manifested from the death existence (*maraṇabhava*) to the birth existence (*upapattibhava*), but not from the death existence to the intermediate existence.
8. The example of the seeds and seedlings is dangerous (for your position) because, according to that example, on leaving a human existence, if one were reborn in the intermediate existence, one would not be able to be reborn in another human existence.
9. The citation is wrong. The illumination of the Bodhisattva takes place while he is in the process of becoming a Buddha, that is, during the time which separates the Bodhisattva state from that of Buddhahood, but not in the intermediate existence[459].
10. The changing of the mind (*citta*) which occurs at the moment of rebirth is similar to the following example: One dreams of Pañca-Mathurā and one perceives Mathurā: there is no intervening country[460]. That proves that there is no intermediate existence.

V — The confirmation by the Sāṃmitīyas

After having described the criticisms, the Sns, 471*b* 21 - *c* 3, also deals with the confirmation of the intermediate existence by the Sāṃmitīyas:

---

456 According to Vasumitra, the Mahāsāṃghikas, Ekavyāvahārikas, Lokottaravādins, Kukkuṭikas and (early) Mahīśāsakas denied the existence of the intermediate existence. Cf. *Kośa* III, p.32, n.1 [Pruden, p.372].

457 Cf. below, 'The secondary theses of the Pudgalavādins, thesis No.14'.

458 Sns, 471*a* 26–27: *hsi tao* 細道 or *yu tao hsi wei* 有道細微.

459 On consulting the proposition in the Acchariyabbhutadhammasutta (MN III, 120), we can conclude that the citation is not wrong; only the illustration of the intermediate existence could be criticised from the doctrinal point of view.

460 Mathurā was a town in which medieval Buddhism flourished. It neighboured on Pañca–Mathurā or Pañcāla. On Pañcāla, see B.M. Law, *Geography of Early Buddhism*, London 1932, pp.18–19.

1. According to the discourse, the intermediate existence certainly exists. It is the Buddha who, with his divine eye, sees living beings who come and go with their actions (*karman*) in the cycle of birth and death.
2. Leaving the human destiny, after death, one is reborn in other destinies.

FOURTH PART

The last part (471*c* 4 - 473*a* 13) deals with the different destinies of life, including the various states of evolution of persons, from the ordinary man to the arhat. This section is very obscure, not only because of its language, but also because of its ideas. However, we can grasp the following classification of the two kinds of person:

The first, that of the worldling (*pṛthagjana*) is divided into three categories:

1. He who is not yet disgusted with the world of desire (*kāmadhātunirvedita*) and who possesses the ninety-eight tendencies (*anuśaya*)[461] and all the passions (*kleśa*) in connection with the three worlds (*dhātu*).
2. He who is disgusted with the world of desire (*kāmadhātu*) and who is reborn in the destiny of the non-perceptive gods (*asaṃjñideva*).
3. He who is disgusted with the world of subtle form (*rūpadhātunirvedita*) and who is reborn in the world of desire (*kāmadhātu*) after having fallen from the world of subtle form (*rūpadhātu*).

The second, that of the holy one (*ārya*), is divided into ten or twelve categories:

1. He who undergoes seven deaths and seven births (*saptakṛtabhavaparama*);
2. He who is a once returner (*sakṛdāgāmin*);
3. He who is a once returner (attains Parinirvāṇa) by being reborn into several families (*kulaṃkulasakṛdāgāmin*);
4. He who is a once returner (separate from Parinirvāṇa) by the interval (of one birth) (*ekavīcikasakṛdāgāmin*)[462] ;
5. He who is a once returner (attains Parinirvāṇa) by being disgusted with the world of desire and by being reborn in the higher stages (*kāmadhātunirvedha ūrdhvasrotasakṛdāgāmin*);
6. The category which includes three categories:
   a — He who attains Parinirvāṇa in rebirth (*upapadyaparinirvāyin*);
   b — He who attains Parinirvāṇa through compounded things (*sābhisaṃskāra-parinirvāyin*);
   c — He who attains Parinirvāṇa through the uncompounded (*anabhisaṃskāra-parinirvāyin*);
7. He who attains Parinirvāṇa in the intermediate existence (*antarāparinirvāyin*);
8. He who is disgusted with the world of subtle form and is reborn in the higher

461 The number 98 of the *anuśuayas* agrees with that of the Tds, cf. above, n.307.

462 Sns, 472*a* 17: *i-chien hsi-t'o-han* 一間斯陀含 (*ekavīcikasakṛdàgāmin?*); whereas Tds 21*a* 13 has *i-chung* 一種 (*ekabījin*), See above, n.235.

stages (*rūpadhātunirvedha ūrdhvasrota*);

9. He who attains Parinirvāṇa through compounded things in rebirth (*upapadya-saṃskāraparinirvāyin*?)[463].
10. The arhat.

The majority of passages in this part are devoted to a detailed explanation of these categories of persons. Nonetheless, the obscure style and doctrinal points, or rather, incoherent ideas contained in these passages, prevent us from citing the continuation of the series of these categories.

The Sns concludes the treatise with a stock phrase aimed at encouraging the practice of the Buddha's teaching.

VI — *THE ORIGINAL SCHOOL*

The important element which first makes us think that the Sns belongs to the Sāṃmitīya school is the title of the treatise itself. Nonetheless, we might wonder if this title was given by the author himself or attributed to it later by the translator. However it may be, by examining the characteristic doctrinal points of the treatise, the conclusion can be reached that it is a work of the Pudgalavādins in general and the Sāṃmitīyas in particular for the following reasons:

Firstly, the Sns defends their specific theses, namely:

1. The *pudgala*;
2. The indestructible thing (*avipraṇāśa*?);
3. The intermediate existence (*antarābhava*);
4. The six destinies (*gati*);
5. The characteristic of things (*dharmalakṣaṇa*) which is both permanent and impermanent;
6. An intermediate meditation (*dyānāntara*) exists.

Secondly, among the above theses, only No. 2 and No.4 are theses specific to the Sāṃmitīya school, the others are common to various other Pudgalavādin schools and are also found in the Tds. It is noteworthy that the common theses are better formulated and better explained in the Sns than in the Tds. For example, the thesis of the *pudgala* is dealt with, in the Sns, with the refutation of adverse arguments and described in vigorous style. It is the same for the thesis of the intermediate existence. Conversely, these theses are described in a general way, but not in detail, in the Tds. This tends to prove that the Sns was composed late in the period when the Pudgalavādin school was flourishing and the Sāṃmitīyas were eclipsing the Vātsīputrīyas.

Thirdly, it is impossible to attribute the Sns to the Vātsīputrīyas or other sub-schools, such as the Dharmottarīyas, Bhadrayānīyas and Ṣaṇṇāgārikas, because:

1. The title of the work indicates that it is of Sāṃmitīya origin;
2. The work contains theses specific to the latter, namely: the indestructible thing

463 On the fruits, cf. above, the Tds, third section: the fruits (*phala*) (Vol.II, 20*b* 2 - 21*b* 25).

(*avipraṇāśa*?) and the six destinies (*gati*);

3. The list of the ten or twelve categories of fruits is totally different from that of the Vātsīputrīyas in the Tds and those of the other sub-schools[464].

In conclusion, we have every right to believe that the Sns is indeed a work of the Sāṃmitīyas.

IV. THE LÜ ÊRH-SHIH-ÊRH MING-LIAO LUN

I - *TITLE*

The *Lü êrh-shih-êrh ming-liao lun* 律二十二明了論 (Treatise dealing with twenty-two stanzas explaining the Vinaya) is a treatise concerning the Vinaya. This work is so-entitled because it consists of twenty-two stanzas encompassing all the essential ideas disseminated in the canonical books of the Basket of the Vinaya and the unrecorded disciplinary traditions of the Sāṃmitīya school. The meaning of the title is quite clear, as the text itself confirms: 'The reason for entitling the text *Lü ming-liao lun* is because it can analyse and explain the Vinaya'[465]. The treatise which we have to hand is published in the Taishō edition, Vol.XXIV, No.1461, pp.665*b* - 673a.

II — *THE AUTHOR*

All that we know of the author of the *Lü ming-liao lun* is his name transcribed in Chinese, Fu-t'o-to-lo-to 弗陀多羅多. or Fo-t'o-to-lo-to 佛陀多羅多, the Sanskrit reconstruction of which is Buddhatrāta. He was certainly an Indian monk who was well-versed in the Tripiṭaka in general, as is indicated by the title 'Dharma-master' (*fa-shih* 法師) which accompanies his name; furthermore, he was also a Vinaya master whose knowledge of the discipline is illustrated by the present very succinct and learned treatise. No biography of him seems to have been preserved.

III - *THE TRANSLATOR*

The translator of this treatise is Paramārtha (Chen-ti 真諦) or Kulanātha (*kou-lo-na-t'o* 拘羅那陀) (500-569)[466]. He was born in a brahmin family in Ujjayinī (Ujjain, central India) where he did his studies. Once proficient in Buddhist literature, he went to northern India and probably settled in Pāṭalīputra. He went to China as a cultural and religious messenger for the king of Magadha at the request of a Chinese mission. He was welcomed in Nanking 南京 in the year 548 of the

---

464 See below, 'The Pudgalavādin Lists of Śrāvakas'.

465 *Lü ming-liao lun*, 665*b* 17 : 如本二十二明了論，能分別 解釋律所立名

466 *Hsü kao sêng chuan* 續高僧傳, T L, 2050, 429*c*–431a; cf. P. Demiéville, 'Sur l'authenticité du *Ta tch'eng k'i sin louen*', pp.15–28.

emperor Wu 武 (502-550) who wished to name him head of the programme of translating Buddhist books. Unfortunately, this programme was not realised because of internal disorders. Paramārtha went to southern China where he led a wandering life while translating Buddhist texts in those regions. Dissatisfied with his mission in China, he aimed to return to India. In 562, he embarked on a boat for India but a typhoon obliged him to return to Canton.

From then on he remained in China and continued to translate Buddhist texts. He died at the age of 71.

Paramārtha was the most cultivated and erudite of all the Indian missionaries in China. He was the only master of Buddhism to whom Hsüan-tsang bowed. Half of the seventy works which he translated have survived. Of them, only this treatise pertains to the Vinaya, the other major translations are basic works of the Yogācāra school, namely:

1. *Ta-ch'êng mei-shih lun* 大乘唯識論 (T XXXI, 1589);
2. *Shê ta-ch'êng lun*攝大乘論(Mahāyānasaṃgraha) (T XXXI, 1593);
3. *Chuan-shih lun*轉識論 (T XXXI, 1587);
4. *Hsien-shih lun*顯識論 (T XXXI, 1618);
5. *San wu-hsing lun*三無性論(T XXXI, 1617).

Two other translations concerning the history of the Buddhist schools deserve notice:

6. *Shih pa pu lun*十八部論(Samayabhedoparacanacakra) (T XLIX, 2032);
7. *I pu tsung lun lun* 異部宗輪論 (Samayabhedaoparacanacakra) (T XLIX, 2031).

IV — *THE DATE*

The date of composition of the treatise is unknown, as is the history of its author. The contents of the treatise prove that it was not composed until after the compilation of the three Vinaya, Sūtra and Abhidharma collections of the Sāṃmitīya school, that is, between the second century BCE and the fifth century CE. This hypothesis on the date of compostion of the treatise can be reinforced by the fact that it was probably composed at the time when the Sāṃmitīya school was flourishing.

V - *THE LANGUAGE AND TRANSLATION*

It is difficult to discover the language of the original text of the *Lü ming-liao lun* through the Chinese translation. Nonetheless, it can be assumed that it was Sanskrit or hybrid Sanskrit for the following reasons:

Firstly, the language of the treatise, throughout the translation, is clear and precise. Even the stanzas give us condensed and clear ideas, and the prose is elegant.

Secondly, Paramārtha, the translator, was a scholar with a perfect mastery of Sanskrit and well-versed in Sanskrit Buddhist literature, as his translations demonstrate.

The translation was made by Paramārtha, one of the four great translators of Buddhist texts in China. That is why the translation is marked by its clarity, not only from the point of view of language, but also of doctrine.

As to the history of the translation, the colophon says: 'In the second Kuang-ta year of Ch'en 陳光大, on the twentieth day of the first month of the year Mou tsê 戊子 (568 CE), the Vinaya master Fa-t'ai 法泰 of the Ting-lin 定林 temple in the capital, who was to be found at the Nanhai 南海 command post in the prefecture of Kuang-chu 廣州, asked the Tripiṭaka master Chü-na-lo-t'o 俱那羅陀 or t'a 他 to translate the treatise. (The monk) Hui-k'ai 慧愷 of the Aśoka temple in the capital repectfully held the brush. The translation of this treatise is in one scroll. The notes and explanations are in five scrolls' (*Lü ming-liao lun*, 672*c* 5-9).

VI - *THE CONTENTS*

The treatise consists of twenty-two stanzas with commentary. Basing ourselves on the stanzas and their meaning, we summarise the essential ideas here:

Stanzas I-II are devoted to part of the introduction which explains:

1. The agreement between the Vinaya and Abhidharma of the Sāṃmitīyas on the two numbers which explain the correspondence of defiled thoughts and the observances[467].
2. The Buddhas' praise of the practice of the three trainings (*śikṣā*).
3. The basis of morality (*śīla*), consisting of knowledge of the eight precepts[468] and the obtaining of ninety-six merits[469].
4. The purification engendered by the merits[470] of the observance of the precepts.

Stanzas III-XXI constitute the main part of the treatise. With their commentary, they mention and clarify all the elements of the disciplinary code of the Sāṃmitīya community without any special classification. Consequently, we can do no more than summarise the essential points, paragraph by paragraph.

1. Five characteristics of a precept (666*a* 16-27).
2. Nine parts of the Vinaya (666*a* 27 - 666*b* 11).
3. Five categories of *prātimokṣa* (666*b* 12-18).

---

467 See above, n.106.

468 According to the *Lü ming-liao lun*, 665*c* 19–24, 8 precepts: 4 wrong bodily actions (abstaining from taking life, theft, sexual misconduct and other wrong actions), and 4 wrong vocal actions (abstaining from false speech, slander, harsh speech, useless speech). These eight are not the same as the 8 precepts advocated in MN I, 360: abstaining from (1) taking life, (2) theft, (3) falsehood, (4) slander, (5) avarice, (6) acrimonious blame, (7) anger, and (8) vanity. Cf. *Traité* II, p.771 and n.2.

469 *Lü ming-liao lun*, 665*c* 25 – 666*a* 1-5: 96 merits which can be counted in two ways:

1. (24 merits: 8 precepts x 3 bodily, vocal and mental observances). Due to the observance of oneself, the teachings of others, the delight in observance of others, and the practice of 8 precepts before receiving them, one obtains 96 merits in all; (8 x 3) x 4 = 96.

2. (24 merits = 8 merits obtained through abstention from 8 wrong bodily actions in the absence of hatred and delusion, 8 through abstention from 4 wrong vocal actions in the absence of the same two roots, 8 through abstention from 8 wrong bodily and vocal actions in the absence of craving). By multiplying these 24 merits by the four preceding methods, there are, in all, 96; (4 x 2) + (4 x 2) + (8 x 1) x 4 = 96.

470 Here the merits number 42,000 (420 x 10 x 10). Cf. *Lü ming-liao lun*, 666*a* 5–15. See above, n.117.

4. Eight kinds of transgresssion (666*b* 18 - 666*c* 21).
5. Seven groups of offences (666*c* 4-12).
6. Five methods of *prātimokṣa* recitation in the bi-monthly ceremonies of confession (*poṣadha*) (666*c* 13-17).
7. Four defeats and four gains (666*c* 18-26).
8. Undefined (*aniyata*) offences (666*c* 27 - 667*a* 6).
9. Precepts based on conviction and reality (667*a* 8-19).
10. Natural offences described in the Vinaya (667*a* 20-28).
11. Judicial acts (*karmavācanā*) of the two communities (667*b* 1-9).
12. Schism, non-schism and circumstances (667*b* 10-27).
13. Minor, sub-minor and non-minor precepts (667*b* 28 - 667*c* 3).
14. Correct conduct for entering lay people's houses (667*c* 4-11).
15. Three ways of making amends for faults (667*c* 12-24).
16. Three methods of confession (667*c* 25 - 668*a* 1).
17. Precepts established on these three bases: diminution, development and equilibrium[471] (668*a* 2-5).
18. Transgression and non-transgression (668*a* 7-24).
19. Five methods of making amends for offences (particularly the *saṅghādiśeṣas*) (668*a* 25 - 668*b* 15).
20. Four categories of forfeiture[472] (668*b* 16-18).
21. Application of six prescriptions concerning the pardoning of offences consisting in the temporary forfeiture of the three robes (*cīvara*) (668*b* 19 - 668*c* 1).
22. Four kinds of offences[473] (668*c* 2-6).
23. Among the thirty *parasarnikas*, six precepts requiring the forfeiture of objects before confession (668*c* 7-13).
24. Four kinds of relationship authorised by the precepts concerning the category of *parasarnika*[474] (668*c* 13-16).
25. Seven methods for receiving full ordination (*upasampadā*) due to others: four for monks, three for nuns (668*c* 17-22).
26. Two methods of creating merit: that of the Pratyekabuddhas is limited, while that of the Buddha is unlimited and perfect (668*c* 22-23).

---

471 The inadequacies of the commentary impede clarification of these terms. However, it is possible to make a provisional translation of the passage in the commentary as follows: 'In the Vinaya, the precepts are established on three different notions: the establishment of the precepts rests on the basis (1) of development (of purification), (2) on equilibrium (in the monastic life) and (3) on the diminution (of wrong actions)'. Cf. *Lü ming-liao lun*, 668*a* 2–4.

472 These are modalities of the forfeiture of objects, such as clothing and bowls, obtained improperly.

473 *Lü ming-liao lun*, 668*c* 2–6: According to the Vinaya there are four kinds of offences encompassing all offences; they are: (1) offences the same in origin but different in character; (2) offences the same in character but different in origin; (3) offences the same in character and origin; (4) offences not the same in character and origin.

474 They are: (1) the maternal relatives of the mother; (2) the paternal relatives of the mother; (3) the maternal relatives of the father; (4) the paternal relatives of the father. Cf. *Lü ming-liao lun*, 668*c* 13–15.

27. Five kinds of falsehood[475] (668*c* 24-28).
28. Natural things and things produced by the practice of the Path (668*c* 29 - 669*a* 16).
29. Four manners of receiving nourishment (669*a* 16-24).
30. Three conditions for receiving alms (669*a* 26 - 669*b* 6).
31. Ten kinds of food kept after nightfall (669b 7-11).
32. Seven causes of loss of assistance (669*b* 13-26).
33. Three ways of touching and moving (an alms-bowl) before eating (669*b* 26-29).
34. Five cases when not seeking alms from door to door is allowed (669*b* 29 - 669*c* 3).
35. Five cases of offences destroying probation[476] (669*c* 3-14).
36. Nine cases of interruption of the retreat during the rainy season (*varṣa*) which can be summarised in three cases: leaving for seven days, the existence of dangers and voluntary interruption (669*c* 14-24).
37. Five conditions for accomplishing the retreat during the rainy season (669*c* 25-29).
38. Eight cases of danger in the retreat during the rainy season (669*c* 29 - 670*a* 5).
39. Merits and demerits of the five judicial acts (*karma*) (670*a* 5-18).
40. Through four kinds of prohibition concerning the precepts, the intention of the Buddha in establishing the precepts can be understood (670*a* 18 - 670*b* 1).
41. Three categories of alms-bowls and clothing to be transmitted, retained at will, the places and prescribed times (670*b* 2-15).
42. Constituents of offences of forfeiture (*nisargika*): place, means, ownership and object (670*b* 15- 670*c* 4).
43. Eight manifestations of respect of nuns (670*c* 4-16).
44. Relationship between the two communities concerning the teachings by monks on a mission to nuns (670*c* 16-29).
45. Four kinds of dwelling (671*a* 1-2).
46. Five judicial acts based on five cases (671*a* 2-12).
47. Five categories of acquisitions (671*a* 12-17).
48. Five groups of persons who transgress the Vinaya (671*a* 17-20).
49. Judgements particular to offences engendered by the domains (*āyatana*) and elements (*dhātu*) (671*a* 20-27).
50. Eight deeds of destruction of the efficacity of the *kaṭhina* robe (671*a* 27 - 671*b* 2).
51. Five merits for whoever observes the *kaṭhina* robe (671*b* 2-6).
52. Two methods of preserving the *kaṭhina* robe (671*b* 6-8).
53. Twenty categories of persons who cannot receive ordination (*Upasaṃpadā*) (671*b* 9-13).
54. Ten ways of leaving the monkhood (671*b* 13-19).
55. Two methods of preserving things (671*b* 19-26).
56. Four judicial acts (*karman*) concerning the seven methods of calming disputes

475 Since circumstances and intentions differ, there are five kinds of falsehood: those leading to *pārājika, saṅghādiśeṣa, sthūlātyaya, parasarnika, duṣkṛta.* The nature of these offences can be ascertained from the Vinaya. Cf. *Lü ming-liao lun,* 668*c* 24-28.

476 These are circumstances which cause the inefficacity of the 17 kinds of probation practised by the monks.

(*adhikaraṇaśamatha*) (671*b* 26 - 671*c* 13).
57. Four judicial acts concerning confession in the bi-monthly ceremony (*poṣadha*) (671*c* 13-20).
58. Five judicial acts concerning the celebration at the conclusion of the retreat (*pravāraṇā*) (671*c* 20-25).
59. Transmission of the alms-bowl and three monastic robes (671*c* 25-25).
60. Five kinds of fruit which are purified[477] (671*c* 25-29).
61. The purification of vegetables is feasible by oneself, others or both (671*c* 29 - 672*a* 6).
62. The preceptor (*upādhyāya*) and teacher (*ācārya*) qualified from the viewpoint of the Vinaya should be chosen from among those who possess five merits in the five groups of fifty merits (672*a* 6 - 672*b* 20).

The last stanza (XXII) is the conclusion affirming that clear comprehension, recitation and practice of the preceding disciplinary codes enable us to grasp all the significations of the Vinaya and to explain them easily without consulting others.

VI – *THE ORIGINAL SCHOOL*

The text concerning the disciplinary codes in the treatise gives us no positive proof enabling us to identify its original school. Nonetheless, we have found many clear indications confirming that the *Lü ming-liao lun* pertained to the Sāṃmitīya school, apart from the assertion, mentioned with the name of the author in the first lines of the text, in particular that the author of this work belonged to that school.

Here are the doctrinal indications due to which it can be confirmed that this treatise is a work of the Sāṃmitīya school in particular, and of the Pudgalavādin school in general:

> 'The four stages of "entry into the predestination of rightness (*samyaktvaniyāma*), namely: patience (*jên* 忍 , *kṣānti*), the name (*ming* 名 , *nāma*), the characteristic mark (*hsiang* 相 , *lakṣaṇa*)[478] and the supreme worldly dharma (*shih ti i* 世第一 , *laukikāgradharma*)' (*Lü ming-liao lun*, 665c 13).

It is certainly difficult to rediscover the origin of the school in the Vinaya treatises but, owing to these indications, it can be concluded that the *Lü ming-liao lun* is a work of the Sāṃmitīyas or, more generally, of the Pudgalavādins.

---

477 These are methods of purifying fruit which the monks should observe before eating them.

478 Instead of using the word *hsiang* 想 (*saṃjñā*: perception), as in other Pudgalavādin works, the *Lü ming-liao lun*, 665*c* 13, mentions the word *hsiang* 相 (*lakṣaṇa*: characteristic).

CHAPTER THREE

THE THESES OF THE PUDGALAVĀDINS

A — *THE ORIGINAL TEACHING OF THE BUDDHA*

Before embarking on the Pudgalavādin theses themselves, we should recall some of the main doctrines of Buddhism with regard to the reality of a man or a being in relation to his fetters and liberation. We need to refer to the original teaching propounded by the Buddha in order to grasp and judge the doctrinal ideas presented by the Pudgalavādins.

To this end, we will briefly describe some doctrines considered to be the essence of Buddhism from the point of view of knowledge and its applications.

I - *Essential doctrines*

1. The doctrine of dependent origination

Among the doctrinal principles (*dharma*) advocated by the Buddha, the doctrine of dependent origination (*pratītyasamutpāda*) is essential[479]. Overall, this doctrine explains that everything is both conditioned (*pratītyasamutpanna*) and conditioning (*pratītyasamutpāda*); therefore it is relative and interdependent. Being endowed with non-determinist characteristics, this doctrine opposes theories of determinism through past actions or an all-powerful deity and

---

479 Vin. I, 40: Of things which are engendered by a cause, the Tathāgata explains the cause. As regards their cessation, the Great Recluse speaks (*ye dhammā hetuppabhavā, tesaṃ hetuṃ tathāgato āha. tesañca yo nirodho, evaṃvādi mahāsamaṇo*, Cf. MN II, 32; SN II, 28; Sanskrit: *ye dharmā hetuprabhavaḥ hetuṃ teṣaṃ tathāgataḥ hyavadat. teṣaṃ ca yo nirodha evaṃ vādī mahāśramaṇaḥ*). As this stanza says, the essence of the Buddha's teaching is summarised in the doctrine of dependent origination (*pratītyasamutpāda*). This law was discovered by the Buddha on his attainment of perfect enlightenment (cf. Vin.I, 1, 2: Udāna I, 2). The Buddha discerned that 'whoever sees the law of dependent origination sees the teaching; whoever sees the teaching sees the law of dependent origination' (*yo paṭiccasamuppādaṃ dhammaṃ passati so paṭiccasamuppādaṃ dhammaṃ passatīti* — MN I, 190–1). The following verse to a certain degree summarises the principle of this doctrine:

When this is, that is,
This arising, that arises;
When this is not, that is not,
This ceasing, that ceases.

(*imasmiṃ sati idaṃ hoti / imassupàdā idaṃ uppajjati / imasmiṃ asati idaṃ na hoti / imassa nirodhā idaṃ nirujjhati //* — MN III, 63; SN II, 23, 70, 95; Ud 2).

This law is manifested everywhere and in everything, as SN III, 103, writes: I have taught you, monks, to see dependent origination everywhere and in everything (*paṭicca vinītā kho me tumhe, bhikkhave, tatra tesu tesu dhammesu*). MN II, 197: In truth my teaching is analytical, it does not support a singie thesis (*vibhajjavādo kho ahaṃ ettha, māṇava, nāhan ettha ekaṃsavādo*). Hence, the law of dependent origination is supplied with the characteristics of 'objectivity, necessity, invariability and conditionality' (*tathatā avitathāta anaññāthatā idappaccayatā ayaṃ vuccati . . . paṭiccasamuppādo* — SN II, 26).

theories of non-determinism[480].

2. The two corollary doctrines

In order to develop the doctrine of dependent origination, particularly at the level of a man or a being, the Buddha advocated the doctrine of insubstantiality (*anātmavāda*) and that of impermanence (*anityavāda*).

The first rejects the concept of a soul endowed with a permanent substance (*ātman*) and maintains that a man is merely a psycho-physical complex which, like everything else, is insubstantial[481]. This doctrine is an analysis of phenomena in space: 'All compounded things are impermanent'[482]. Compared to form or the body, the mind is even more impermanent[483].

---

480 Being endowed with non-determinate characteristics, the doctrine of dependent origination opposes theories of determinism through past actions (*pubbekatahetu*), through an all-powerful deity (*issaranimmānavāda*), and the theory of non-determinism (*ahetu-apaccaya-vāda*). Cf. AN I, 173 sq.

481 Dhp 279: *Sabbe dhammā anattā*. This doctrine constitutes the special teaching of the Buddhas (*buddhānaṃ sāmukkaṃsikā desanā* — MN I, 380) which rejects the concept of a soul with permanent sub- stance (*ātman*). Similarly, this doctrine analyses what is conventionally called a 'man' or 'person' in their different physical and mental aspects. To show that a man is merely a composite of psycho-physical elements, the Buddha, basing himself on these two foundations: name-and-form (*nāmarūpa*) (cf. SN II, 100; IV, 124), used several systems of analysis, namely:

1. the five aggregates (*skandha*) (cf. SN III, 59–61);
2. the six elements (*dhātū*) (cf. MN I, 140; III, 239)';
3. the twelve bases (*āyatana*) (cf. DN II, 302);
4. the eighteen elements (*dhātu*) (cf. SN II, 72);
5. the five nourishments (*āhāra*) (cf. MN I, 48), etc.

Of these analyses, that of the five aggregates appears frequently in the canonical texts. It emphasizes the insubstantiality of the mental aspect, particularly that of a man. These constituents are unreal, empty and insubstantial (cf. SN IV, 54). That is why a man or a being is only a conventional designation. If there were a permanent absolute self, the ideal life leading to the cessation of suffering could not be established (cf. SN III, 143).

482 Dhp 277: *Sabbe saṅkhārā aniccā*; SN II, 49: *Yaṃ bhūtaṃ tam nirodhadhammaṃ*. This doctrine demonstrates that the world is like a mountain stream which flows fast and is forever changing (cf. AN IV, 137). There is no existence, there is only becoming (*bhava*). The arising (*uppāda*), disappearance (*vyaya*) and changing of what exists (*aññatattha*) are the three signs of compounded things (cf. AN I, 152). Things appear and disappear from instant to instant (cf. SN II, 49). The five aggregates which constitute a man or a being are impermanent (cf. SN III, 143), but they are not transformed and they do not totally dissolve, that is why there is continuity (cf. MN I, 40). Nonetheless, it is because things are impermanent and life changeable that the ideal life leading to the cessation of suffering can be established (cf. SN III, 143).

483 Generally, the belief in the permanence of phenomena is based on the view that the mind is something lasting which does not change. In reality, the mind is less permanent than form or the body, as the Buddha said in AN I, 10: Monks, I know no other thing that changes as rapidly as the mind; truly, monks, it is not easy to find a thing which can be compared to the mind in the rapidity of change (*nāhaṃ bhikkhave aññaṃ ekadhammaṃ pi samanupassāmi yaṃ evaṃ lahuparivattaṃ yathayidaṃ cittaṃ yāvañ c'idaṃ bhikkhave upamā pi na sukarā yāva lahuparivattaṃ cittan ti*).

By means of dialectical analysis, the Buddha demonstrated the impermanence of the six kinds of consciousness, of contact (*sparśa*), of feeling (*vedanā*), of mental factors (*saṃskāra*), of perception (*saṃjñā*), by explaining that even their conditions are impermanent:

'Owing to the eye and the visible, visual consciousness arises. The eye is impermanent, changeable,

II — *The Application of these doctrines.*

The three preceding doctrines explain what is the reality of the world in general and of a person in particular.

1. The denial of a soul.

   With regard to the person, these doctrines accept that that which we conventionally call a person or a being is no other than a simple pyscho-physical process of five aggregates without a substantial subject and which changes perpetually. In this sense, nothing exists except consciousness, feeling, etc., but never anyone that is conscious, feels, etc.[484].

2. Rebirth without a person

   As long as a person clings to existence, despite the cessation of conditions of existence in the present, his continuity is manifested in the next life. In this process there is no person which transmigrates, but only name-and-form (*nāma-rūpa*)[485], linked indissolubly to craving (*tṛṣṇā*) as vital force[486], continues to exist

---

unstable. Thus, that duality is ephemeral and transitory. That cause, that condition which gives rise to visual consciousness is also impermanent, changeable, unstable; and how, monks, is it possible that visual consciousness, having arisen in dependence on impermanent conditions, could become permanent? Hence, the meeting, the convergence, the coming together of these three things, — that, monks, is called eye contact. Eye contact is also impermanent, changeable, unstable. That cause, that condition which gives rise to eye contact, that is also impermanent, changeable, unstable; and how, monks, could eye contact, having arisen in dependence on impermanent conditions, become permanent? Experiencing contact, monks, one feels. Experiencing contact, one perceives. Those states are ephemeral and transitory — impermanent, changeable, unstable'. The other six kinds of consciousness are examined in the same way (SN III, 67–9).

On the other hand, the Buddha used impermanence, along with the other two signs, as a basis of argument for rejecting belief in a permanent soul or self:

'What do you think, monks, is the body (or other psycho-physical phenomena), permanent or impermanent? — Impermanent, Lord. — But what is permanent, is that suffering or joy? — Suffering, Lord. — Then what is impermanent, full of suffering, subject to change, can one, when considering it, say: this is mine, I am this, this is my self? — One cannot, Lord. — Consequently, monks, with regard to body (and other phenomena), everything that never has been, will be nor is, whether it be in us or in the external world. . ., whether it be weak or strong, high or low, far or near, all that is not mine, I am not it, it is not my self: this is what should be seen by whomever possesses true knowledge' (SN III, 67–8; Vin. I, 14).

484 SN II, 13: I (the Buddha) do not speak of anyone who touches (*phusatīti aham na vadāmi*). I do not speak of anyone who feels (*vediyatīti aham na vadāmi*). Cf. MN I, 293; Vism, 460.

485 In this context, name–and–form (*nāma-rūpa*) indicates the five aggregates, since name is a collective term for the four mental aggregates, that is: feeling, perception, mental factors and consciousness; whilst form indicates the body. It is this phenomenon of name–and–form which reappears in another existence, but the self does not transmigrate.

486 Craving (*tṛṣṇā*) is the vital force of the cycle of birth and death; consequently, it is the cause of suffering in its three aspects. DN II, 308: Monks, what is the Noble Truth of the origin of suffering? It is craving which always incurs new births and which, attached to pleasure and covetousness, sometimes here, sometimes there, always finds new joy. It is craving for sensuality, craving for existence and craving for annihilation (*yāyaṃ taṇhā ponobhavikā nandi-rāga-sahagatā tatra tatrābhinandinī, seyyathīdam kāmataṇhā bhavatāṇha vibhavataṇhā*).

in one of the five destinies. Because the life of a person is unique, he who is born in the later existence and he who died in the preceding existence are not the same, nor another[487]. Hence there is continuity but not identity.

3. The responsibility for actions

'Beings are the possessors of their actions, inheritors of their actions, action is the womb from which they are born, action is their friend, their refuge. Whatever action they accomplish, good or bad, they are the inheritors of it'[488]. The manifestation of actions and their results (*karmavipāka*) is not limited to the present life or to humanity, but extends over the five destinies and three times: past, present and future[489]. Here, a problem arises: the identification of him who performs the actions and the identification of him who receives their fruit. Are they identical or different? — The person who performs the actions and the one who experiences their results are neither the same nor different[490].

Hence, a person is responsible for his actions and will inherit their consequences, even though he is neither the same nor other than himself in relation to the earlier existence.

4. Liberation without anyone to be liberated

Beings are attached to the wheel of existence by fetters (*saṃyojana*). Due to practice in accordance with the Path (*mārga*), liberation (*nirvāṇa*) is attained. If

---

Craving, being comparable to what kindling is to fire, is an element necessary to the rebirth of a being (cf. SN IV, 400). Dhp 334: In a negligent man, craving grows like a climbing plant. It jumps from one existence to another like a monkey greedy for fruit in the forest. (trans, after A. Bareau in *Bouddha*, p.138) (*manujassa pamatta cārino taṇhā vaḍḍhati māluvā viya, so plavati hurāhuraṃ phalam icchaṃ, va vanasmiṃ vānaro*).

487 During the process of existence across different times, only the person composed of the five aggregates appears and disappears successively, but there is no fixed being; consequently, the identity or difference between two existences cannot be affirmed. It is said in Miln, p.40:

— Venerable Nāgasena, is he who is reborn the same as he who died or another?

— Neither the same, nor another (*na ca so na ca añño*).

Cf. SN II, 20, or below n. 490.

488 MN III, 203: *kammassakā sattā kammadāyādā kammayonī kammabandhū kammapaṭisaraṇā. kammaṃ satte vibhajati yadidaṃ hīnappanītatāyāti.*

489 AN III, 415: There exists an action, monks, which ripens in the hells, an action which ripens in the womb of animals, an action which ripens in the domain of hungry ghosts, an action which ripens in humanity . . ., an action which ripens in the heavenly world. . . . Monks, I declare that the result of action is threefold: ripening during this life, ripening during the next rebirth and ripening during successive births (*atthi bhikkhave kammaṃ nirayavedaniyaṃ, atthi kammaṃ tiracchānayonivedaniyaṃ, atthi kammaṃ pittivisayavedaniyaṃ, atthi kammaṃ manussalokavedaniyaṃ, atthi kammaṃ devalokavedaniyaṃ*) . . . (*tividhāhaṃbhikkhave kammānaṃ vipākaṃ vadāmi: diṭṭh'eva dhamme upapajje vā apare vā pariyāye*).

490 SN II, 20: He who performs (the actions) experiences (the results) — that, Kassapa, which you first called 'suffering created by oneself constitutes eternalism. One performs (actions), the other experiences (the results)': that, Kassapa, for what is affected by feelings, expressed by 'suffering caused by another person', constitutes nihilism (*so karoti so paṭisaṃvediyatīti kho Kassapa ādito sato sayaṃkataṃ dukkhanti iti vadaṃ sassataṃ etan pareti. añño karoti añño paṭisaṃvediyatīti kho Kassapa vedanābhitunnassa sato paraṃkataṃ dukkhanti iti vadaṃ ucchedaṃ etaṃ pareti*).

the defilements (*kleśa*) are eliminated, Nirvāṇa is realised, even in this life[491]. Nirvāṇa pertains to the uncompounded (*asaṃskṛta*); it is ultimate reality. That is why it is immeasurable, unknowable by ordinary people and only the holy ones actualise it. Nirvāṇa realised by a holy one who is still alive with his old aggregates is Nirvāṇa with a remainder (*sopadhiśeṣanirvāṇa*). Nirvāṇa without a remainder (*nirupadhiśeṣa*) is Nirvāṇa without the psycho-physical process which occurs on the death of the holy ones. It is also called Parinirvāṇa. What happens to an Arhat or a Tathāgata after Parinirvāṇa? That is a question which the Buddha refused to answer (*avyākṛta*)[492]. To prevent his disciples from engaging in interminable polemics and harmful speculations, the Buddha spoke very little of Nirvāṇa, especially of Parinirvāṇa. On this avoided subject, the Buddha said: 'This teaching is profound, difficult to see, difficult to understand, calm, excellent, beyond the domain of reason, subtle, intelligible to the wise'[493].

Nevertheless, it is certain that there is no person who accedes to Nirvāṇa, since the remainder of the aggregates which form the existence of a being is totally extinguished after the death of an Arhat or a Tathāgata; it is like a fire or a lamp which goes out after the fuel is consumed[494].

III — *The Characteristics and Efficacy of these Doctrines*

1. Pragmatic teaching

What we have seen constitutes the main points of the truth taught by the Buddha concerning the person or being with its fetters and its liberation. The Buddha only taught:

'truths which are profitable, fundamentally linked to the pure life, leading to aversion, to detachment, to cessation, to tranquillity, to supernormal knowledge, to perfect enlightenment, to Nirvāṇa'[495].

In this sense, original Buddhism is a pragmatic doctrine[496], which never

491 Cf AN I, 58.

492 On this subject, see below and n. 499.

493 MN I, 487: *Gambhīro h'ayam . . . dhammo duddaso duranubodho santo paṇito atakkāravacaro nipuno paṇḍitavedanīyo . . .*

494 See below, 'The main thesis of the Pudgalavādins: *Pudgala*–designated–by–cessation'.

495 MN I, 431: *Etaṃ hi mālunkyāputta atthasaṃhitaṃ, etaṃ ādibrahmacariyakaṃ, etaṃ nibbidāya virāgāya nirodhāya upasamāya abhiññāya sambodhāya nibbānāya saṃvattati, tasmā taṃ mayā byākataṃ.*

496 The pragmatic nature of Buddhism is clearly summed up in the simile of the poisoned arrow (cf. MN I, 429) by the fact that the Buddha did not reply to insoluble problems (*avyākata*) because they are not profitable, not being fundamentally linked to the pure life, nor leading to aversion, to detachment, to cessation, to tranquillity, to supernormal knowledge, to perfect enlightenment, to Nirvāṇa (*na h'etaṃ atthasaṃhitaṃ n'ādibrahmacariyakaṃ, na nibbidāya na virāgāya na nirodhāya na upasamāya na abhiññāya na saṃbodhāya na nibbānāya* — MN I, 431); and in the simile of the raft serving to reach the other shore (cf. MN I, 134), the conclusion of which is as follows: Equally, monks, I have taught a doctrine resembling a raft — it is made for crossing and not for relying on. You, monks, who understand the doctrine resembling a raft, you should abandon good things and, even more so, bad ones (*evam-eva*

touches on metaphysical and non-profitable problems such as those of a Creator[497], or a Primal Cause[498] or other questions to be avoided (*avyākṛta*), namely:

1. Is the universe eternal, or
2. is it non-eternal;
3. Is the universe finite, or
4. is it infinite;
5. Is the soul the same thing as the body, or
6. is the soul one thing and the body another;
7. Does the Tathāgata exist after death, or
8. does he not exist after death, or
9. does he (both) exist and not exist after death, or
10. does he (both) neither exist nor not exist after death?[499].

These are questions engendered by false views about the concept of an absolute self to which the Buddha never replied[500]. His silence was very often misinterpreted. However, when we re-examine these questions, opinions become much less opposed to each other. In particular, the discussion of these points has nothing to do with the search for truth. In other words, the Buddha was concerned only with the profitable, immediate and urgent problem which is directed at the happiness and liberation of mankind, and knowledge of which is the most important point.

---

kho bhikkhave kullūpamo mayā dhammo desito nittharanatthāya no gahaṇatthāya. kullūpamam vo bhikkhave ājānantehi dhammā pi vo pahātabbā, pag-eva adhamma — MN I, 135). In fact, Buddhism is only preoccupied with the problem of 'suffering and the cessation of suffering'. On the other hand, Buddhism itself should be considered as a means of application and not as a thing to which one should cling.

497 There is no metaphysical problem concerning a Creator and creation in Buddhism. The Buddha considered belief in an almighty God (*issaranimmānavāda*) as a false view. Cf. AN I, 173 sq.

498 The doctrine of dependent origination renders void the search for a primal cause, since in reality a primal cause never existed. The origin of the existence of a being and the universe is inconceivable (*anamatagga*) (cf. SN II, 179). Furthermore, speculation on a primal cause can lead to mental trouble (cf. AN IV, 77).

499 MN I, 426: 1. *sassato loko* 2. *asassato loko* 3. *antavā loko* 4. *anantavā loko* 5. *taṃ jīvaṃ tam sarīraṃ* 6. *aññaṃ jīvaṃ aññaṃ sarīraṃ* 7. *hoti tathāgato paraṃ maraṇā* 8. *na hoti tathāgato paraṃ maraṇā* 9. *hoti ca na ca hoti tathāgato paraṃ maraṇā* 10. *n'eva hoti na na hoti, tathāgato paraṃ maraṇā*. Cf. DN I, 191; II, 68, III, 135; MN I, 484–5; SN III, 257; IV, 393; AN II, 41. The Pāli texts only mention ten questions, whereas the Buddhist literature in Sanskrit, such as Kośa V, 22, refer to fourteen *avyākṛtavastus*: 1) the world is eternal, 2) non-eternal, 3) eternal and non-eternal, 4) neither eternal nor non-eternal, 5) the world is finite, 6) infinite, 7) finite and infinite, 8) neither finite nor infinite, 9) the Tathāgata exists after death, 10) does not exist after death, 11) exists and does not exist after death, 12) neither exists nor does not exist after death, 13) the life principle is the same as the body, 14) different from the body. Cf. T.R.V. Murti, *The Central Philosophy of Buddhism*, p.36, n.2.

500 On the reasons for which the Buddha did not answer the questions to be avoided, see below, 'The main thesis of the Pudgalavādins: Position of the *pudgala*'. Also cf. SN IV, 391–7; MN I, 484; Udāna VI, 4.

2. The middle way

Alongside the pragmatic aspect of the teaching, the doctrinal points mentioned above are characterised as being the middle way (*madhyamapratipad*) which avoids all extreme notions both from the point of view of knowledge[501] as that of practice[502].

It is right view (*samyagdṛṣṭi*), according to the doctrine of dependent origination, of insubstantiality and of impermanence, which dispels false views (*mithyādṛṣṭi*) of the reality of the being such as the belief in a substantial and permanent soul which gives rise to non-profitable things (*akuśaladharma*): 'sorrow, grief, suffering, lamentation and despair[503]. Furthermore, he who, with right view, sees that the five aggregates are not a self, do not pertain to a self, is he who is detached, freed by the absence of the acquisiton of impurities[504].

In consequence, knowledge in conformity with the reality of a being constitutes 'the pure life (*brahmacarya*), for the total cessation of suffering'[505].

---

501 MN I, 65: There are, monks, two theories — the theory of existence and that of non-existence. Monks and brahmaṇas who adhere to the theory of existence are intimate with it, cling to it and strongly oppose the theory of non-existence; monks and brahmaṇas who adhere to the theory of non-existence are intimate with it, cling to it and are strongly opposed to the theory of existence (*Dve'ma bhikkhave diṭṭhiyo: bhavadiṭṭhi ca vibhavadiṭṭhi ca. ye hi keci bhikkhave samaṇā vā brahmaṇā va bhavadiṭṭhim allīnā bhavadiṭṭhim upagatā bhavadiṭṭhiṃ ajjhositā, vibhavadiṭṭhiyā te paṭivirudhā. ye hi keci bhikkhave samaṇā vā brahmaṇā va vibhavadiṭṭhim allīnā vibhavadiṭṭhim upagatā vibhavadiṭṭhim ajjhositā, bhavadiṭṭhiyā te paṭivirudha*). In the canonical texts, the following pairs of extremist theories are found:

1. The theory admitting that everything exists (*sabbaṃ atthī ti*) and the theory admitting that nothing exists (*sabbaṃ natthī ti*). Cf. SN II, 76; III, 134.

2. Eternalism (*sassatadiṭṭhi*) admitting that the life of beings is eternal, and annihilation (*ucchedadiṭṭhi*) (cf. SN II, 20) admitting that the life of beings ends after death (III, 98). Eternalism admits that he who performs actions is the same as he who experiences the results, and annihilation admits that he who performs actions is different from him who experiences the results (cf. SN II, 20).

3. The materialist concept saying that the body and the life principle are identical (*taṃ jıvaṃ taṃ sarīram*. Cf. SN II, 61.

4. Determinism admitting that the happiness and suffering of beings are determined by actions from the previous life (*sabbaṃ pubbekatahetu*), and non-determinism admitting that things never relate to causes and conditions (*sabbaṃ ahetu apaccaya*). Cf. AN I, 173.

502 In the introduction to the first discourse (Dhammacakkapavattanasutta), addressed to his five former companions in Banaras, the Buddha said: There are, monks, two extremes with which a monk should not be associated. Which are they? Clinging to sense pleasures, which is base, vulgar, common, ignoble and associated with disadvantage, and devoting oneself to self-mortification, which is painful, ignoble and associated with disadvantage (*Dve'me bhikkhave antā pabbajitena na sevitabbā. katame dve? yo cāyam kāmesu kāmasukhallikānuyogo, hīno, gammo, pothujjaniko, anariyo, anatthasamhito; yo cāyaṃ attakilamathānuyogo dukkho, anariyo, anatthasaṃhito* — SN V, 421).

503 MN II, 138: Well now, monks! So I do not see, monks, any theory of the self in which attachment does not give rise to sorrow, grief, suffering, lamentation and despair (*Sādhu bhikkhave, ahaṃ pi kho taṃ bhikkhave attavādupādānaṃ na samanupassāmi yaṃ sa attavādupādānaṃ upādiyato na upajjeyyum sokaparidevadukkhadomanassupāyāsā*).

504 SN III, 45: For him who sees (things as they are) with perfect wisdom, his mind is detached, freed by the absence of the acquisition of impurities (. . . *evaṃ etaṃ sammappaññaya passato cittaṃ virajjati vimuccati anupādāyā āsevehi*).

505 SN III, 147: . . . *tasmā brahmacariyavāso paññayati sammādukkhakkhayāya.*

B — *THE THESES OF THE PUDGALAVĀDINS*

Due to the absence of any Pudgalavādin canonical literature, nearly all the interpretations of their doctrinal position are badly defined or have been exaggerated. By considering the Pudgalavādins as heretics[506], their theses, which are doctrinal solutions to explain ever-outstanding problems, have not been properly appreciated.

Nonetheless, due to the four works accessible in Chinese, we have attempted to indicate the main thesis, that of the *pudgala*, fifteen secondary theses and two lists of śrāvakas of the Pudgalavādins.

I - *The main thesis: the pudgala*

We intend to explain here the main thesis of the Pudgalavādins — the *pudgala* — in detail, since it is the main thesis of the school. In Pudgalavādin literary works, the thesis is presented as a characteristic doctrine of the school. The author of the Tds emphasises that non-comprehension of that ineffable thing (*avaktavya*) constitutes an aspect of non-knowledge (*ajñāna*) which, in turn, is one of the three elements of non-higher-knowledge (*avidyā*). (Cf. Tds, 24*a* 29, 24*b* 8). In the same work, the explanation of this thesis is repeated frequently in varying ways. Equally, the Sns devotes a considerable number of passages to refuting adverse arguments before establishing the existence of the *pudgala* (cf. Sns, 462*b* 5 - 466*c* 29).

Moreover, indirect sources such as the Samayabhedoparacanacakra (*I pu tsung lun lun*異部宗輪論), T XLIX, 2031, by Vasumitra, the *Shih-pa pu lun*十八部論, T XLIX, 2033, translated by Paramārtha, and the Mahāvibhāṣā (*Ta-p'i-p'o-sha lun*大毗婆沙論), T XXVIII, 1545, also present the existence of the *pudgala* as the main thesis of the Vātsīputrīyas. The Kathāvatthu attributes to the latter two theses, namely: the *pudgala* and the downfall of the arhat[507] ; this last is also accepted by the Sarvāstivādins[508]. Furthermore, only the *pudgala* thesis is subjected to refutation in a large part of the Kathāvatthu[509] and the whole of Chapter Nine of the Abhidharmakośa[510]. It is therefore evident that the existence of the *pudgala* is the main thesis of the Vātsīputrīya doctrine, the mother school of the Pudgalavādins.

1. Definitions of the *pudgala*

The etymology and meaning of the word *pudgala* are not clear from the philological and philosophical points of view.

1. The *Buddhist Hybrid Sanskrit Dictionary* defines it: '*pudgala*, often written *puṃgala* . . . = Skt. puruṣa, *person, man, creature, soul* (often in the latter sense

---

506 Kośa IX, p.273 and n.1. The Pudgalavādins are heretics and do not win deliverance. According to Kośa IX, p.273, Preliminary Notes, Lcan-skya hu-thug-tu (Wassilief, p.270), Śāntideva (Bodhicaryāvatāra VI, 60) and Candrakīrti (Madhyamakāvatāra VI, 86) condemn the Pudgalavādins as infidels, outside the Saddharma.

507 Cf. Kathāvatthu I, I, 2; Bareau, *Sectes*, p.115 n.4 and p.118, n.1.

508 Cf. Kośa VI, 58; Kathāvatthu I, 2.

509 Kathāvatthu, pp.8–63.

510 Kośa V, pp.227–79.

= ātman)'[511].

2. The explanation by H. Kern [tr.]: '*pudgala* (*saṃskrit*): sometimes an atom, a monad, an individual; sometimes an assemblage of atoms, considered as a unity. In the ordinary sense of 'a person, an individual', the word is used by Nāgasena, for example, in the Milindapañha. In metaphysics, it is less profound yet useful to leave several meanings to a single word, especially without a more precise definition of the meaning used in a given case. It is therefore easy to juggle with words'[512].
3. According to L. de La Vallée Poussin, *pudgala* is an obscure term because, among the Jains, *pudgala* or *pudgalāstikāya* is matter, part of things which constitute a non-living being (*ajīva*), whereas among the Buddhists it designates a self with a soul (*ātman*), a man (*puruṣa*), the life principle (*jīva*), a living being (*sattva*), etc.[513] ;
4. A. Bareau, in 'La notion de la personne dans le Bouddhisme indien', clarifies it as follows [tr.]: 'The term which designates (the notion of a person) is *pudgala*, a word of which the origin is obscure but of which the traditional Buddhist definition and etymology, which identify it with or have it derive from the names *puruṣa* and *puṃs*, both meaning «man» in the two senses of «a human being» and «a person of the masculine sex», are clear. We should note in passing that the word *puruṣa* also serves to designate the three persons in the language of Indian grammarians. In non-Buddhist Sanskrit, the term *pudgala* often designates the human body and even, in the doctrine of the Jains, matter in general, a meaning which it has never had in Buddhism but which may be older than that of «person» with which the latter always uses it'[514].

In consequence, in order to understand the notion of the *pudgala* of the Pudgalavādins, it is first of all necessary to differentiate it from the concepts of the metaphysical self (*ātman*) of a man such as the universal *ātman* of Vedānta or the *puruṣa* of the Sāṃkhya.

'The *ātman* represents the «self» in a physical and psychic sense, the centre of the personality which makes an individual what he is and, moreover, designates a reality, such a breath, eyes, etc., which pertains to a man by nature, an element of pyschophysical personality which has a determined function in his life'[515]. The *ātman* persists and passes through different existences (under the appearance of an animal or, more generally, a human being) as a function of *karman* which is attached to it[516]. In this sense, the *ātman* is the creator of actions, it receives their results and constitutes the agent in rebirth. Furthermore, the *ātman* is Reality

---

511 F. Edgerton, *Buddhist Hybrid Sanskrit Dictionary*, New Haven 1953, repr. Delhi 1993, p.347*a*.

512 H. Kern, *Histoire du Bouddhisme dans l'Inde*, Paris 1901, p.376, n.2.

513 La Vallée Poussin, *Nirvāṇa*, p.35, n.3.

514 A. Bareau, 'La notion de la personne dans le Bouddisme indien', pp.83–97.

515 J. Gonda, *Védisme et Hindouisme ancien*, Paris 1962, p.242.

516 *Ibid.*, p.249.

identical to the Absolute, the Brahman[517].

With regard to the notion of a self (*ātman*) in Vaiśesika philosophy, this is expressed by J. Filliozat as follows [tr.]: 'He (the Vaiśesika: one realism, and dualist) in fact admits, on the one hand, combined material atoms for composing all things; on the other hand, multiple *ātmans* which, associated with compounds of atoms, are engaged in the phenomenal world and led into the circle of Saṃsāra. However, these *ātmans* are freed by the knowledge of the true nature of things which causes them to see their own essence, distinct from that of the compound of atoms and other realities. More simply, the Vaiśesika offers the exact determination of the *ātman* through the exclusion of the rest (*viśeṣa*); hence, it is isolated and frees itself'[518].

As for the *puruṣa*, this is a notion implying the domain of beings in the Sāṃkhya system. The Ṛg Veda describes this cosmic, primordial, archetypal being as follows:

> 'The *puruṣa* is all that,
> All that has been, all that will be,
> The Lord of Immortality'[519].

In fact, the *puruṣa* 'is to *prakṛti* what the being is to becoming (Oltramare), immobility to movement. Pure spirituality (*cinmātra*), a torch (*prakāsa*) which lights the activity of Nature, it is on contact with it that the *tattvas* develop, that the *guṇas* function, that life is formed and everywhere suffering. However, it is merely a spectator: unqualified, unqualifiable, it neither acts nor thinks, has neither volition nor perception.

Single in essence, it is innumerable in its manifestations: there are as many «souls» as there are bodies, all the same, omnipresent'[520]. Indeed, 'That being is a gigantic man who, in the beginning, completely covered the earth, even surpassing it. That man was the world, the world of the past as well as the world to come; he was also the master of immortality'[521].

According to Radhakrishnan, the *puruṣa* of the Sāṃkhya is not a person but a subtle body which is the essence of rebirth as well as the priniciple of individual identity across various existences[522]. Furthermore, S. Dasgupta, in *A History of Indian Philosophy*, gives his idea on the notions of *ātman*, *puruṣa* and *jīva* in the

---

517 'You are that' (*tat tvam asi*): the *Ātman* and the *Brahman* are the same thing; the Brahman manifests itself in all selfs. It is the essential spirit of the Upaniṣads (700–600 BCE). 'The sum and substance of Upaniṣad teaching is involved in the equation Ātman = Brahman' — S. Dasgupta, *A History of Indian Philosophy* I, p.45. On this subject, G.P. Malalasekera wrote: Every human being had in him a part of Brahman, called *ātman* or the little self. Brahman and Ātman were one, and of the same 'substance'. — *The Truth of Anattā*, Kandy 1966, p.4; cf. K. Bhattacharya, *L'Ātman-Brahman dans le Bouddhisme ancien*, pp.7–9 and notes.

518 *L'Inde classique* II, § 1481.

519 Ṛg Veda, 10, 90.

520 *L'Inde classique* I, § 1434.

521 Gonda, *Védisme et Hindouisme ancien*, pp.225–6.

522 Cf. S. Radhakrishnan, *Indian Philosophy*, p.284.

context of Indian philosophy as follows:

> 'All the Indian systems except Buddhism admit the existence of a permanent entity variously called *ātman*, *puruṣa* or *jīva*. As to the exact nature of this soul there are indeed divergences of view. Thus while the Nyāya calls it absolutely qualityless and characterless, an indeterminate unconscious entity, Sāṃkhya describes it as being of the nature of pure consciousness, the Vedānta says that it is that fundamental point of unity implied in pure consciousness (*cit*), pure bliss (*ānanda*), and pure being (*sat*). But all agree in holding that it is pure and unsullied in its nature and that all impurities of action or passion do not form a real part of it. The summum bonum of life is attained when all impurities are removed and the pure nature of the self is thoroughly and permanently apprehended and all other extraneous connections with it are absolutely dissociated'[523].

Furthermore, from several discourses attributed to the Buddha, we know in a general way the various speculations concerning the opinion of a self at the time of the Buddha. For example:

1. The Alagaddūpamasutta points out concepts of self to which an illiterate and ordinary man may adhere, namely: the life principle of an individual identified with the five aggregates, and the points of view concerning a persisting self, unchanged at death. There are six points of speculation which the text describes as follows:

   1. '. . . (he) considers his body (and says to himself): this is mine, I am that, that is my self',
   2. considers his feelings . . .,
   3. his perception . . .,
   4. his mental factors . . .,
   5. whatever is seen, heard, thought, known, apprehended, desired and followed by his mind (and says to himself): 'that is mine, I am that, that is my self', and
   6. whatever point of speculation, saying: 'that is the world, that the self; after death I shall become permanent, stable, eternal, I shall not be subjected to change, I shall always remain thus', (and says to himself): 'that is mine, I am that, that is my self'[524].

2. The Poṭṭhapādasutta gives a summary of concepts which admit the existence of an entity, a real ego forming the permanent substance behind the activities of a person, be it subtle or gross, that is, three aspects of the self:

   1. the gross self (*olārīko attapaṭilābho*), endowed with form, made of the four elements of nature, nourished by material food;
   2. the self based on the assemblage of an incorporated mind-being (*manomaya attapaṭilābho*), endowed with all its senses directed by the mind; and

---

523 Dasgupta, *A History of Indian Philosophy* I, p.75.

524 Cf. MN I, 135-6.

3. The formless self (*arūpa attapaṭilābho*), made of feelings, a purely psychic nature in itself corresponding to the consciousness of the formless world[525].

Thus, the concepts of self (*ātman*), according to the systems of non-Buddhist Indian thought, are considered to be principles, more or less vital and cosmic, identified with the consciousness of a man who, in turn, constitutes part of the *brahman*. Whereas, the *pudgala* or Being (*sattva*) of the Pudgalavādin school is quite another thing than the self (*ātman*) of the Sāṃkhyas, Vaiśesikas and other later brahmanical systems[526].

Furthermore, it is evident that the thesis of the *pudgala* must be different from the sixty-two views concerning the self and the universe taught by monks and brahmins contemporary with the Buddha in the Brahmajālasutta[527].

It is clear that *pudgala* and *sattva* are not terms invented by the Pudgalavādins. They are terms which are found in the canonical texts, but with the meaning (individual, person, being) of mere designations and simple conventional means of expression (*vohāravacana*), but not of absolute truth (*paramārtha-*

---

525 DN I, 195; after the wording of J. Filliozat in *Les philosophies de l'Inde*, Paris 1970, p.25.

526 The other later brahmanical systems uphold the idea of the identity of the Brahman and Ātman. For example, Saṃkara (788–820 CE) develops this notion in his doctrine of integral (*kevala*) or 'unspecified' (*nirviśeṣa*) non-duality (*advaita*), admitting that the ineffable Brahman — an essence which ia ineffable, omniscient, omnipresent, eternally pure (*śuddha*), enlightened (*buddha*), and free (*mukta*), eternally immovable (*kūṭastha*), devoid of forms, parts, attributes (*nirviśeṣa, nirguṇa*) — is identical to the *ātman*, a term which combines the notion of 'person' and that, reflexive and somewhat grammatically, of 'self': the *brahman* is none other than the 'supreme self' (*paramātman*). The *ātman* is not the sum of individual 'souls' but an infinite essence, one like the *brahman*, basically spiritual, neither moving nor suffering. It is absolute consciousness, which is not the object of the notion of self, but is its witness (*sākṣin*) (cf. *L'Inde classique* II, § 1404); beings are defiled seeds or atoms, but which can, by means of purification, become united with the *brahman* or *paramātman* (cf. S. Dasgupta, *A History of Indian Philosophy*, pp.429–39; G.P. Malalasekera, *The Truth of Anattā*, pp.7–8).

527 These are the opinions of non-Buddhist philosophers at the time of the Buddha:

A — on the beginning of phenomena:

1) some maintain, on four grounds, that the self (*ātman*) and the world (*loka*) are eternal;
2) some maintain, on four grounds, that the self and the world are partly eternal and partly non-eternal;
3) some maintain, on four grounds, that the world is finite, infinite, finite and infinite, non-finite and non-infinite;
4) some evade the question like an eel, on four grounds, and refuse to give a precise answer;
5) some admit, on two grounds, that the self and the world appear without cause.

B — on the future of phenomena:

6) some admit, on sixteen grounds, that the self exists, consciously, after death;
7) some maintain, on eight grounds, that the self exists, unconsciously, after death;
8) some maintain, on eight grounds, that the self is neither conscious nor unconscious after death;
9) some admit, on seven grounds, the annihilation of the individual;
10) some admit, on five grounds, that Nirvāṇa consists of bliss in this life, either in the sense-pleasures or in one of the four absorptions (*dhyāna*). Cf. DN I, 22 sq. (Brahmajālasutta); Kośa IX, p.282 sq.; J. Masuda, *Origin and Doctrines of Early Buddhist Schools*, p.54; S. Dasgupta, *A History of Indian Philosophy* I, pp.195–6, 238–9; 'The Theory of Soul in the Upanishads' JRAS 1899, pp.71–87.

satya)[528]. For example:

— 'A person (*puggala*), monks, who is born in the world, is born for the welfare of many people, for the happiness of gods and mankind in the world. Who is that person? It is the Tathāgata, Arhat, Sammāsambuddha'[529].

— 'The Order of disciples of the Blessed One consisting of the four pairs of men, eight persons (*puggala*) . . .'[530].

— 'All living beings (*satta*) will come to be; and all living beings will travel on, after having abandoned their bodies'[531].

— 'If all the bones that a person had during his existences in the course of an aeon were assembled, they would make a mountain.'[532].

By relying on the three texts of Indian origin preserved in their Chinese translation, the Tds, *Ssŭ* and Sns, we can understand how the *pudgala* is conceived as a designation of a person, more or less synonymous with the terms designating an individual principle such as *sattva* (being), *nara* (man), *manuja* (born of Manu), *mānava* (youth), *poṣa* (who feeds himself), *jīva* (life principle), *jantu* (who is born), etc., and *yakkha* or *yakṣa*, an interesting term found in the Suttanipāta[533].

2. The *pudgala* according to extant Pudgalavādin works

However it may be, when the Pudgalavādins wished to make known the real existence of the *pudgala* by enhancing the principle of individualisation in the constituent impersonal elements, they did not fail to raise all kinds of questions and restart debate on basic doctrines. This is indicated in the following passages. For example:

1. The Tds, when describing the concentration on emptiness (*śūnyatāsamādhi*), implies that the Pudgalavādins clearly understood the Buddha's teaching on the nature of the five aggregates in conformity with conventional truth and absolute truth: 'Emptiness (*śūnyatā*) is the absence of Me, of Mine (*ahaṃkāra-mamaṃkāra*) and of both, the absence of these three things is what is called emptiness (*śūnyatā*)'. '. . . How can Me and Mine not exist (when) the Blessed One has said: «At the time, I was the brahmin Sunetra»? He also said: «Monk, my hand appears in space». It cannot be thus (since) Me and Mine are conventional designations (*chia-hsao* 假號, *prajñapti*). However if the five aggregates (*skandha*) are considered, the self (*ātman*) would be Me (*ahaṃkāra*).

---

528 On the two truths, cf. DN I, 202; MN I, 181; SN IV, 273; AN I, 222; III, 213; Udāna, 48; Ñāṇananda, *Concept and Reality in Early Buddhist Thought*, Kandy 1971, pp.40–1.

529 See above, n.420.

530 AN III, 212: *Bhagavati sāvakasaṅgho, yad idaṃ cattāri purisayugāni aṭṭha purisapuggalā . . .*

531 Udāna 48: *Ye keci bhūtā bhavissanti ye c'āpi sabbe gamissanti pahāya dehaṃ . . .*

532 Itivuttaka, § 24: *Ekasa-ekena kappena puggalassa — aṭṭhissancayo siyā pabbatasamo rāsi iti vuttaṃ mahesinā.*

533 Cf. Sn 875–6. The questioner and the Buddha used the term *yakkha* to indicate the empirical person.

That the Blessed One never admitted. If the objects (*ching-ch'ieh* 境 界, *viṣaya?*) are considered as possessions, that would be Mine (*mamaṃkāra*). That the Buddha did not admit either. As it is said in the *Shêng fa yin ching* 聖 法 印 經 (Āryadharmamudrāsūtra): «Emptiness (*śūnyatā*) is contemplation of the empty (*śūnya*)».

Hence, emptiness (*śūnyatā*) and Me and Mine (*ahaṃkāramamaṃkāra*) can be established together. That is why there is no error. That is what is named emptiness' (Tds, 19*a* 13-20).

2. The same ideas are expressed in another Pudgalavādin work, the Sns: 'The characteristics (*hsiang* 相 , *lakṣaṇa*) of the self (*ātman*), etc., are accepted through faith. As the Buddha said to the sectaries (*tīrthika*): «Although a Me exists, it is only a designation, it is not a reality. It is based on defiled aggregates (*āsrava-skandha*)». In seeing (impermanent) things which come and go, the Buddha calls that the self, (but) it is not a real self. As the Buddha said: «(The self) relies on compounded things (*saṃskāra*)». The term (of self) is derived from compounded things». That is why the Buddha speaks (of a self). Such is the explanation of the term self' (Sns, 464*b* 5-10).

'Being blinded by ignorance (*avidyā*)', one considers the five aggregates (*skandha*) which are not the self as being the self. (It is like) an uncomprehending baby which sees the mother of others and calls her its mother. It is the same for those who call self the five aggregates which are not the self. Such is the teaching of the Buddha' (Sns, 464*b* 12-16).

These ideas are confirmed by an extract by Vasubandhu in the Abhidharma- kośa devoted to the argument in defence of the Vātsīputrīyas when they are attacked over the concept of attachment to the Me and Mine and affection for the Me and Mine:

'When one recognises a self in what is not a self, as do the sectaries, one feels affection for that supposed self; however, when one sees the self in the ineffable *pudgala*, as do the Buddhas, no affection is aroused regarding the self'[534].

Thus, the Pudgalavādins had understood the fundamental teachings of the Buddha, particularly the doctrine of insubstantiality which vigorously rejects belief in a substantial, permanent self (*ātman*). Indeed, the Buddha is specifically called 'the master of the doctrine of insubstantiality' (*anātmavādī*). Only the doctrine of insubstantiality, not being found in other systems of Indian thought, constitutes the fundamental teaching of the Buddha. Consequently, without a correct understanding of this doctrinal notion, it is impossible to have knowledge and practice in conformity with Buddhism.

In the Saṃyuttanikāya III, 147, the Buddha, having taught that there is no substantial entity by means of an analysis of the five impermanent aggregates, takes a small quantity of dust on the tip of his nail and says to a monk:

'. . . Even if this small quantity of matter, monk, were permanent, stable, eternal, unchangeable by nature, then the pure life for the total destruction of suffering

534 Kośa IX, p.273.

could not be established (by me)'[535].

Similarly, in the Saṃyuttanikāya III, 103, the Buddha reproached a monk for doubting the denial of an absolute self by saying:

'It is possible, monks, that someone senseless, sunk in ignorance, led astray by craving, thinks that he surpasses the teaching of the master (by questioning) thus: Since you say that the body is not the self, that feelings . . ., perception . . ., mental factors. . . and consciousness are not the self, what, then, is affected by the actions which the non-self has done?'[536]

Although the Pudgalavādins have clearly understood the essence and importance of the doctrine of insubstantiality, they established the thesis of the *pudgala*. This doctrinal invention probably had two aims, namely:

a — to reintroduce the existence of a person in order to modify the dogmatic interpretation of the doctrine of insubstantiality by categorically denying the existence of the life principle of an individual.

In this sense, G.P. Malalasekera, having understood the necessity for this notion, wrote in *The Truth of Anattā*: '. . . the Sāṃmitiyas and the Vajji- puttakas (?) held the conception of a person (*puggala*) which for all practical purposes may be regarded as an effective self'[537].

Furthermore, T.R.V. Murti demonstrated the Pudgalavādins' motive in their adherence to the theory of the *pudgala* as follows:

'Universally condemned by all the other Buddhistic schools as heretical, the Vātsīputrīyas held tenaciously to the doctrine of the *pudgalātman* (the individual) as a quasi-permanent entity, neither completely identical with the mental states, nor different from them. However halting this conception may be, it is evidence of the awareness of the inadequacy of a stream of elements to account for the basic facts of experience, memory, moral responsibility, spiritual life etc. The Vātsīputrīyas showed the hollowness, at least the inadequacy, of the doctrine of elements; the states (*skandhas*) cannot completely substitute the *ātman*; a permanent synthetic unity must be accepted'[538].

b — to respond to attacks by non-Buddhists who affirmed the existence of a self (*ātman*). With regard to the first aim, Th. Stcherbatsky held the same opinion, and he goes even further by saying: 'Had not the denial of the *ātma* been so categorical, the Vātsīputrīya would have certainly invented another . . .'[539].

In this respect, A. Bareau explains [tr.]: 'In order to answer attacks by

---

535 SN III, 147: *Ettakaṃ ce pi bhikkhu rūpaṃ abhavissa niccaṃ dhuvaṃ sassataṃ aviparịnāmadhammaṃ, na yidam brahmacariyavāso paññāyetha sammādukkhakkhayāya.*

536 SN III, 103–4: *Ṭhānaṃ kho panetaṃ bhikkhave vijjati yaṃ idhekacco moghapuriso avidvā avijjāgato taṇhādhipateyyena cetasā satthusāsanaṃ atidhāvitabbaṃ maññeyya. iti kira bho rūpaṃ anattā, vedanā, saññā, saṅkhārā, viññanaṃ anattā anattakatāni kammāni katamattānaṃ phusissanti.*

537 Malalasekera, *The Truth of Anattā*, p.24.

538 T.R.V. Murti, *The Central Philosophy of Buddhism*, p.81.

539 Th. Stcherbatsky, *The Conception of Buddhist Nirvāṇa*, p.31, n.1.

non-Buddhist schools and calm intellectual anxiety which engendered in them a consciousness of that contradiction, certain Buddhist scholars were not slow to seek an explanation for it which, while remaining in conformity with the original doctrine, was able to satisfy logic. Thus it was that, about two centuries after the Parinirvāṇa, the Vātsīputrīya school appeared, the basic thesis of which was the recognition of a personal principle and, so as not to fall into flagrant heresy which would have been an affirmation of the existence of the *ātman* or the *jīva*, the Vātsīputrīyas called it *pudgala*. This was not sufficient to win them an assurance of orthodoxy; they developed a whole theory round this notion, declaring that the *pudgala* was neither identical to the various constituent elements of an individual, which would have identified them as materialists, nor different from them, which would have assimilated them with Brahmanic and Jaina spiritualists. Pressed by their adversaries to supply clarification, they added that this *pudgala*, which transmigrates and subsists even in the eternal bliss of Nirvāna, was neither permanent nor impermanent, neither relative nor absolute, in a word inexpressible, which served somewhat badly in hiding the embarrassment into which this halting solution plunged them, which various others did not fail to demonstrate to them. None of this, however, prevented the Vātsīputrīyas and others from developing and prospering for nearly a thousand years, as is confirmed by the narratives of the travels of Hsüan-tsang and I-ching'[540].

Furthermore, A. Berriedale Keith, in *Buddhist Philosophy in India and Ceylon*, also appreciated the thesis of the *pudgala*: 'Its merits, however; are obvious; it mediates, in the best Buddhist manner, between phenomena with a basis and the permanent unchanging self of the Brahmanic tradition '[541].

These appreciations seem to be reinforced by the fact that the Vātsīputrīya school was one of the western schools in Kauśāmbi and Mathurā which developed in a society dominated by Brahaminism, since 'the doab between the Ganges and the Yamunā is the territory of choice of the Brahmarṣi', whilst the eastern schools were not subjected to the same confrontation as the brahminical influence in the eastern lands was not so old[542].

Other schools were based on similar ideas, themselves also attempting to resolve the problem to which the Pudgalavādins claimed to give a solution. For example:

1. The Sarvāstivādins, instead of establishing an ego-entity, upheld the theory that 'everything exists' (*sarvamasti*), that is, phenomena from the past and the future as well as phenomena from the present. This thesis was intended to explain the continuity of a phenomenon across the three times; in consequence, problems concerning a being, a person, consciousness, memory, rebirth, the fruition of actions, etc., were similarly resolved[543].

---

540 A. Bareau, 'Richesse de la pensée bouddhique ancienne', *France-Asie* 153–157, Saigon 1959, p.453.

541 A. B. Keith, *Buddhist Philosophy in India and Ceylon*, Oxford 1923, repr. New Delhi 1993, p.83.

542 Cf. J. Przyluski, *Le Concile de Rājagṛha*, p.309–10.

543 Cf. Bareau, *Sectes*, pp.131–52; Kośa, 'Introduction to the seven Abhidharma treatises', and V, 25–7; Kathāvatthu I, 6.

2. The Abhidhamma masters of the Theravādin school maintained a sort of consciousness as an element of existence (*bhavaṅga*) constituted of ignorance (*avidyā*) and the power of actions (*karman*), which subsisted across various existences and which Nyanatiloka described as follows:

   '*Bhavaṅga* (*bhava-aṅga*) which, in the canonical works, is mentioned twice or thrice in the Paṭṭhāna, is explained in the Abhidhamma-commentaries as the foundation or condition (*kāraṇa*) of existence (*bhava*), as the *sine qua non* of life, having the nature of a process, lit. a flux or stream (*sota*). Herein, since time immemorial, all impressions and experiences are, as it were, stored up, or better still said, are functioning, but concealed as such to full consciousness, from where however they occasionally emerge as subconscious phenomena and approach the threshold of full consciousness, or crossing it become fully conscious. This so-called «subconscious life-stream» or undercurrent of life is that by which might be explained the faculty of memory, paranormal psychic phenomena, mental and physical growth, Karma and Rebirth, etc.'[544].

3. The Sautrāntikas affirmed that there were two aggregates, 'the basic aggregate and the functional aggregate: the former is permanent, the latter impermanent. According to their interpretation, these two aggregates, despite their differentiation, purportedly join and constitute a living being. Hence, one can remember past experiences because what is done by the functional aggregate is memorised by the basic aggregate'[545].

4. The Mahāsāṃghikas admitted that basic consciousness (*mūlavijñāna*) constitutes the essence of life by serving as a foundation for the six sense consciousnesses[546].

---

544 Nyanatiloka, *Buddhist Dictionary*, p.33. Ñāṇamoli translates *bhavaṅga* as 'life–continuum' in *The Path of Purification (Visuddhimagga)*, p.515. According to P.S. Jaini, the Theravādins interpreted the luminous mind (*prabhāsvara-citta*) as *bhavaṅga-citta* (AN–aṭṭhakathā I, 60); i.e. the *paṭisandhi citta* is thought which links the previous life to the later life; cf. Abhidhammatthasaṅgaha, Ch.III, § 10. Cf. P.S. Jaini, 'The Sautrāntika theory of Bījā' (*Bulletin of the School of Oriental and African Studies* XXII, part 2, 1959), p.249.

545 Mahāvibhāṣā, XI, T XXVII, 1545, 55*b* 23–26:

一根本蘊，二作用蘊，前蘊是常，後蘊非常，彼作是說，
根本作用二蘊雖別，而共和合爲一有情，如是可能
憶本所作，以作用蘊所作事，根本蘊能憶故

The definition of these two aggregates by J. Masuda is not the same; in his *Origin and Doctrines of Early Indian Buddhist Schools . . . of Vasumitra's Treatise*, p.68, n.1., he writes: '. . . The *ekarasaskandha* (or the *skandha* of *one* taste) continues to exist (lit, turns) from time immemorial without changing its nature (lit. in *one* taste): it is the «subtle consciousness» (細 意識) which is intermittent and which possesses the four *skandhas* . . . The *mūla* (or original) of the *mūlāntikaskandha* means the aforementioned subtle consciousness. (This) is the origin (of a sentient being who) transmigrates (lit. abides) in the *saṃsāra*. Therefore it is called *mūla*. From this origin there arise the five *skandhas*, which are also spoken of by (other) schools. Now the *ekarasaskandha*, being the origin, is not called *antika* (or end). The other five *skandhas* which are intermittent spring out of this origin: hence the name *mūlāntikaskandha*'.

546 . Bareau, *Sectes*, p.111; Mahāyānasaṃgrahabhāṣya (*Shê ta ch'êng lun shih* 攝大乘論釋) II, T XXXI, 1595, 160*c* 7–8: 根本識

5. The Mahīsāsakas maintained that there is an aggregate which continues until the end of births and deaths[547].

6. Alongside doctrinal deviations and the schools of Early Buddhism or the Small Vehicle (*hīnayāna*), the Mahāyānists established the doctrines of the *Ālayavijñāna*[548],

---

547 Mahāyānasaṃgrahabhāṣya, *op. cit.*, 160*c* 1–4 and 8: 'Since these impressions impregnate, always exist and never perish in the aggregate which continues until the end of births and deaths'; later, form–and–mind (name–and–form) reappear because of that (由此熏習種子於窮生死陰恆在不盡故，後時色心因此還生).

And 'Before Nirvāṇa without a remainder (*nirupadhiśeṣanirvāṇa*), that aggregate does not disappear; that is why it is called the aggregate which continues until the end of birth and death' (於無餘涅槃前此陰不盡故名窮生死陰).

548 On this subject, J. Masuda gives his point of view in his *Origin and Doctrines of Early Buddhist Schools*, pp.53–4, n.1: 'Though the Vijñaptimātrasiddhiśāstra tries to refute the Vātsīputrīya view, yet it seems to me that the Yogācāra Theory is much indebted to the idea of the Vātsīputrīya'.

The concept of *ālayavijñāna*, which is capable of retaining the *bījas* (these have always existed naturally (*prakṛti*) but are created and impressed anew by pure or defiled actions (Siddhi, p.103) and the fact that they do not perish reveals that the *ālayavijñāna* is a 'substratum' which exists from one life to another. Cf. Siddhi of Hsüan–tsang, § 1. *Ālayavijñāna*, pp.94–9, and § 2. Theory of the *Bījas*, pp.100–23. On this subject, the *Hōbōgirin* writes:

'. . . The *ālayavijñāna* constitutes the cohesion in each autonomous series of conditioned instants through the development of one and the same causality, it thus gives us the illusion of an individual, of a personality; it is therefore both a safeguard against absolute nihilism as proposed by the Mādhyamika school, and it is also a trap into which a common adherent of the Self risks falling'.

The idea of *ālaya* has its very origin in a Sanskrit text (the Ekottarāgama) as well as in the corresponding Pāli text (Aṅguttara, *Catukkanipāta*, No.128) and was widely developed in Mahāyānist literature, i.e.: Abhidharmamahāyānasūtra, Laṅkāvatārasūtra, Sandhinirmocanasūtra, Mahāyānaśraddhotpādaśāstra, etc. (cf. *Hōbōgirin*, fasc. I, pp.35–37.

Although the Theravādins did not recognise the theory of the *bījas* as maintained by the Sautrāntikas and developed by the Mahāyānists, there exists in the Aṅguttara a long discourse concerning this idea:

Ānanda, there is a person who possesses wholesome and unwholesome qualities. In the course of time, his wholesome qualities disappear and unwholesome qualities appear. Nonetheless, since his wholesome roots are not completely eliminated, new wholesome qualities grow from the wholesome (roots). Thus, that person becomes one who (in the future life) will not fall (from the pure life). His wholesome qualities are like good seeds sown in cultivated and fertile ground, and which are able to bear abundant fruit (*idhāhaṃ pajānāmi: imassa kho puggalassa vijjamānā kusalā pi dhammā akusalā pi dhammā. tam enaṃ aparena samayena evaṃ . . . pajānāmi imassa kho puggalassa kusalā dhammā antarhitā. akusalā dhammā samukhībhūtā, atthica khvā'ssa kusala-mūlaṃ asamucchinnaṃ, tamhā tassa kusalā kusalaṃ pātubhavissati. evam ayaṃ puggalo āyatiṃ aparihāna-dhammo bhavissatīti. seyyathā pi bījāni akhaṇḍāni . . . sukhette suparikammakatāya bhūmiyā nikkhittāni . . . vepullaṃ āpajjissanti* — AN III, p.404).

Here is the verse on the *ādānavijñāna* (= *ālayavijñāna*) often cited in the Sanskrit texts: Appropriating consciousness, profound and subtle like a rushing stream, proceeds with all the seeds. Fearing that they imagine it is the Self I have not revealed this to fools (*Ādānavijñāna gambhīrasūkṣmo ogho yathā varati sarvabījo / bālāna eṣo mayi na prakāśi mā haiva ātmā parikalpayeyuḥ*). Translated after L. de La Vallée Poussin, *Vijñānamātrasiddhi (La Siddhi de Hiuan-tsang)* I, Paris 1928, p.173.

the *Tathāgatagarbha*[549] and the *Tathāgatātman*[550].

All these theories were aimed at answering non-Buddhists who affirmed the existence of the Self (*ātman*) and draw them to Buddhism[551].

Th. Stcherbatsky remarks: 'The Vātsīputrīyas and others assume a kind of surviving *pudgala*; this tendency is the forerunner of Mahāyāna'[552].

Already at the time of the Buddha, there were various beliefs about the self, the most important of which are the six false views which are as many radical errors over the self:

1. 'I have a self'.
2. 'I do not have a self'.
3. 'Through the self, I know the self'.
4. 'Through the self, I know the non-self'.
5. 'Through the non-self, I know the self'.
6. 'It is my self which speaks, feels, and which sometimes here, sometimes

---

549 Laṅkāvatārasūtra (*Ta-ch'êng ju-lêng-ch'ieh ching* 大乘入楞伽經), T XII, 672, 599, 15–28: The Buddha said: Mahāmati, my teaching on the Tathāgatagarbha is not comparable to the doctrine of Self (*ātman*) as professed by the sectaries. Mahāmati, the Tathāgata, the Arhat, the Perfectly Enlightened One teaches the Tathāgatagarbha in the sense of emptiness (*śūnyatā*), reality (*tathatā*), Nirvāṇa, non-arising (*anutpāda*), signlessness (*animitta*), wishlessness (*apraṇhita*). It is in order to avoid the terror inspired in ignorant people (*bāla*) by the doctrine of insubstantiality (*anātmavāda*) that (the Tathāgata) teaches the doctrine of the Tathāgatagarbha, the domain of which transcends discrimination and imagination. The Bodhisattva–Mahāsattvas, in the present and the future, should not be attached to it as a self (*ātman*). It is like a potter who makes different pots from a single mass of clay, using means such as manual skill, water, a stick, wheel and cord. Similarly, the Tathāgata applies various kinds of wisdom, skilful means, by relying on the doctrine of insubstantiality which is free from all signs of discrimination, and sometimes teaches the Tathāgatagarbha, sometimes insubstantiality, with different and varied terms. Mahāmati, I teach the Tathāgatagarbha in order to attract the groups of sectaries attached to the Self (*ātman*) and help them to avoid false views, to penetrate the three deliverances (*vimokṣa*) and rapidly attain supreme and perfect Enlightenment. (This translation is based on the Chinese text, which is why it differs slightly from K. Bhattacharya's tr. from the Sanskrit in *L'Ātman-Brahman dans le Bouddhisme ancien*, pp.131–2.)

550 Going even further, the Mahāyānists even used the term sectary — *ātman*, and identified the Tathāgatagarbha with the *ātman*: 'The *ātman* is the *tathāgatagarbha*. All beings possess the Buddha Nature: this is what the *ātman* is. This *ātman*, from the start, is always covered by innumerable passions (*kleśa*): this is why beings are unable to see it. It is as if, in a poor woman's hut, there was a treasure of pure gold without absolutely anyone in her family knowing anything about it . . . The Tathāgata, today, reveals to beings that precious treasure, that is, the Buddha Nature. When all beings have seen it, they experience great joy and take refuge in the Tathāgata. The Tathāgata is he who excels in skilful means (*upāya*); the poor woman represents the innumerable beings; the treasure of pure gold is the Buddha Nature'. Translation after É. Lamotte of the *Ta-pan-nieh-p'an ching* (大般涅槃經 Mahāparinirvāṇasūtra), T XII, 375, ch.8, 648*b*, in *The Teaching of Vimalakīrti*, pp.lxxvii–lxxviii.

551 The arguments in the Laṅkāvatāra: 'Mahāmati, I teach the Tathāgatagarbha in order to attract the groups of sectaries attached to the Self (*ātman*) and help them to avoid false views . . .' (above, n.549) could also be used by the Pudgalavādins who tried to attract others through the designation of the *pudgala*. On the need to invent such a concept in order to modify or clarify the Buddhist teaching concerning the existence of an individual, cf. E. Conze, *Buddhist Thought in India*, pp.132–4; Kimura Taiken Zenshū, 木村泰賢全集 V, pp.385–90.

552 Th. Stcherbatsky, *The Conception of Buddhist Nirvāṇa*, p.240.

there, experiences the fruit of good or bad actions; this self is permanent, stable, eternal, unchanging, and it remains so forever'[553].

All concepts of the self can be summarised in twenty kinds of belief in individuality (*satkāyadṛṣṭi*), that is, four for each of the five aggregates:

I — (1-5) the aggregates are identical to the self,
II — (6-10) the self is the possessor of the aggregates,
III — (11-15) the aggregates are in the self,
IV — (16-20) the self is in the aggregates[554].

These four propositions only represent two main notions: the first is that the self is identical to the aggregates (I), the second, that the self is different from the aggregates (II, III, IV). Obviously, the last three propositions are the various possibilities of the notion expressing the self as being different from the aggregates.

It is probable that the adherents of these philosophical views had met the Buddha who refused to recognise the existence of a central and permanent personal element. The Buddha taught: 'the abolition of false ideas, stubborness, prejudice, tendencies, addictions, the appeasing of all actions, the rejection of all the elements of rebirth, the destruction of craving, the absence of passion, cessation, Nirvāṇa'[555]. Such a teaching could but elicit a painful reaction in those who were attached to a belief in the self: 'Assuredly I shall be annihilated, I shall be destroyed and shall no longer exist'[556].

They reproached the Buddha for demolishing the existence of a being. Protesting against this accusation, the Buddha explained that adherence to the theory of a permanent self was an absolutely false belief, that the five impermanent and painful aggregates did not constitute a self, that he who understands that is freed from the world, and that the consciousness of a monk thus freed could not be accessible to Indra, Brahmā and Prajāpati in his present life[557] nor after his death:

'Māra cannot find the path of those who are perfect in morality,
who dwell in diligence and free themselves through perfect knowledge'[558].

This is how the Buddha clarified this subject:

'. . . Although I speak and teach in this way, some monks and brahmins accuse me

---

553 MN I, 8: 1) *atthi me attā ti* . . ., 2) *natthi me attā ti* . . ., 3) *attanā va attānaṃ sañjānāmīti* . . ., 4) *attanā va anattānaṃ sañjānāmīti* . . ., 5) *anattāna va attānaṃ sañjānāmīti* . . ., 6) *yo me ayam attā vado vedeyyo tatra tatra kalyāṇapāpakānaṃ kammānaṃ vipākam paṭisamvedeti, so kho pana me ayaṃ attā nicco dhuvo sassato avipariṇāmadhammo sassatisamam ṭath'eva thāssatīti.*

554 SN III, 3–4, 46; MN I, 300: . . . *rūpam attato samanupassati, rūpavantaṃ vā attānaṃ attani vā rūpaṃ rūpasmiṃ vā attānam.* The other aggregates are illustrated in the same way.

555 MN I, 136: . . . *sabbesaṃ diṭṭhitthānādiṭṭhithāna pariyuṭṭhānābhinivesānusayānaṃ samugghātāya sabbasaṅkhārasamathāya sabbūpadhipaṭinissaggāya taṇhakkhaya virāgāya nirodhāya nibbānāya* . . ..

556 MN I, 136: . . . *Ucchijjissāmi nāma su, vinassissāmi nāma su, na su nāma bhavissāmīti.*

557 MN I, 140: . . . *Evaṃ vimuttacittaṃ kho bhikkhave bhikkhuṃ sa-Indā devā sa Brahmakā sa Pajāpatikā anvesaṃ nādhigacchanti: idaṃ nissitaṃ tathāgatassa viññāṇam ti.*

558 Dhp 57: *Tesaṃ sampannasīlānaṃ appamādavihārinaṃ / sammadaññāvimuttānaṃ Māro maggaṃ na vindati //.*

wrongly, falsely and without motivation, saying that the monk Gotama is a nihilist and preaches the annihilation, destruction and non-existence of a being. This I do not do, this I do not affirm. As I have done before, monks, so do I do today: I teach suffering and the cessation of suffering'[559].
It is obvious that after the Parinirvāṇa of the Buddha and the disappearance of his disciples such as Śāriputra, Kātyāyana, Ānanda, etc., the teaching of the Buddha, especially that on insubstantiality in relation to the problems of rebirth and liberation, were attacked by the brahminists. Naiyāyika Udyotakara even profited from the Bhārahārasutta in order to accuse the Buddhists of contradicting their master by their negation of the self (*ātman*)[560].

However, let us leave all these indirect data, erroneous interpretations and accusations concerning the *pudgala*. In order the better to understand the latter as it appears in their own explanations by the Pudgalavādins, it is advisable to examine the details of their theory of the *pudgala*, with its three designations.

PUDGALA-DESIGNATED-BY-THE-SUPPORTS (*āśrayaprajñaptapudgala*)

a. This is expressed by the Sns thus:

'What is the *pudgala*-designated-by-the-supports? — As the Buddha said to Pāpaka[561]: 'By relying on such-and-such compounded things (*saṃskāra*), we call (*pudgala*) that-which-is-designated-by-the-supports'. What is called (*pudgala*)-designated-by-the-supports is fire (in relation to fuel)[562]. The Buddha said to Śāriputra: Someone is named *Nāga* (because his shape is) brilliant, pure and beneficient. (Similarly), what is formed by the four great elements is called the person[563]. It is the same for everything. So take the example of milk[564]. Such is the explanation based on the sūtras. This is why that is called the (*pudgala*)-designated-by-the-supports.

For example, (with regard to) form and the person acquiring form[565], that person cannot be declared to be different from form, nor can form be declared to be different from the person. By relying on form, there is a designation of the person supported by form. If we say that it is form that is the person (or that the person) is accomplished by form, that is a belief in the self (*ātmadṛṣṭi*). If we say that form is the person, we are in error (by affirming) that the five aggregates (*skandha*)

---

559 MN I, 140: *Yathā vāhaṃ bhikkhave na, yathā cāhaṃ na vadāmi, tathā mam te bhonto samaṇa-brahmaṇā asatā tucchā musā abhūtena abbhācikkanti: venayikosamano Gotamo, sato sattassa ucchdedaṃ vināsaṃ vibhavaṃ paññāpetīti. pubbe cāham bhikkhave etarhi ca dukkhañ — c'eva paññāpeti dukkhassa ca nirodhaṃ.*

560 Nyāyavartika (Indian Library), p.342; La Vallée Poussin, 'Dogmatique bouddhique' I.A., 1902, II, p.266.

561 This name possibly refers to adherents of false views.

562 See below, 'The main thesis of the Pudgalavādins, Position of the *pudgala*' and n. 599.

563 The four elements underlying all material things, including the body of human beings. They are popularly called earth (*pṛthivī*), water (*ap*), fire (*tejas*) and wind (*vāyu*). Cf. DN I, 76.

564 See below, 'The main thesis of the Pudgalavādins, Position of the *pudgala*' and n. 600.

565 Sns, 446b 9:*Ch'e*r *tê chêrjên* 色得色人

constitute the person. Hence, what we said earlier on accomplishment is wrong. Moreover, if we say that the person acquiring form is different from form, this is a view maintaining that the person is different from the aggregates. If we say that the person is different (from the aggregates), we are in error (by affirming that) the *pudgala* is different from the five aggregates, which is wrong.

'Form and the person acquiring form inevitably depend on each other'; that is not the word of truth. If we say that form and the person acquiring form inevitably depend on each other, we are expressing a false view. If, (through) false view, we say that no person exists, then that is wrong, as was said earlier. That constitutes an error. This why those are the three errors (?).

Consequently, (a view upholding) the absolute difference (between form and the person acquiring form) is a false view (*mithyādṛṣṭi*). Not to follow (a view upholding) the absolute difference is not to fall into false view. It is possible to say that, based on form, there is a person acquiring form. That is why, in truth, it is possible to say that the person acquiring form and form (exist) together. Thus, at the instant that form comes to exist, the person acquiring form also comes to exist, and at the instant that form disappears, the person acquiring form also disappears. It cannot be said that it is not so. This is the case for the five aggregates (*skandha*), twelve domains (*āyatana*), five destinies (*gati*), which are seven destinies by adding the destiny of demons (*asura*) and the intermediate existence (*antarābhava*); (it is the case for) the domain of birth-existence (*upapattibhava*), (which includes) *kalala*, *arbuda*, *ghana*, the cellular mass (*peśi*), the embryo with its limbs (*praśakhā*)[566] ; the new-born child, infancy, adolescence, mature age and old-age; (it is the case for) determinate thoughts such as good or bad, virtuous or transgressing morality (*śīla*). It is thus for all the elements cited above, whether or not they agree or do not agree (with each other). Being supported on the preceding things (*dharma*), know that the *pudgala*-designated-by-the-supports is established' (Sns, 466*b* 3-26).

b. On the same subject, the *Ssū* expresses it thus: 'the designation of appropriation (*upādānaprajñapti*) is the designation of life (*jīva*) [the Sanskrit word for life (*jīva*) is synonymous with the word for living being (*sattva*)] (which is) internal appropriation (*upādāna*) in the present and is composed of the aggregates (*skandha*), elements (*dhātu*) and domains (*āyatana*) (?); that is to say that the phenomena of appropriation concerning the internal life in the present (?), which is formed by compounded things (*saṃskāra*) and the fetters (*saṃyojana*), is what is called the designation of appropriation (?); it does not pertain to the past or to the future'.

'(With regard to) the designation of appropriation relating to life (*jīva* = *sattva* = *pudgala*) that it is not the same as (the body; that) cannot be confirmed (?). If life and the body are the same, (life is) impermanent (*anitya*) and suffering (*duḥkha*). If it is different, it is eternal (*śāśvata*) and (not) suffering. If (life is) eternal, the pure life (*brahmacarya*) could not be practised. In eternity, a pure life is not necessary; the harvesting of the fruit, receiving and giving, have no meaning. (If life is) im-

566 These are the five stages of embryonic development, according to early Indian knowledge. Cf. *Traité* I, p.270, n.3.

permanent, that makes no sense. Since in either case, whether eternity (*śāśvata*) or annihilation (*uccheda*), neither suffering nor happiness exist' (*Ssū*, 10*a* 5-11).

c. The Tds speaks of the same designation as does the *Ssū*: 'The designation of appropriation (*upādānaprajñapti*) designates the being (*sattva*) which (in relation) to its appropriation (*upādāna*) of the aggregates (*skandha*), elements (*dhātu*) and domains (*āyatana*), is considered as (both) identical and different' (Tds, 24*b* 2-3).

Throughout the three preceding passages, we can see as we go along some notions of the first designation of the *pudgala* or *pudgala*-designated-by-the-supports. This designation indicates the *pudgala* itself. The *pudgala*-designated-by-the-supports (*āśrayaprajñaptapudgala* ?) of the Sns is none other than the designation of appropriation (*upādānaprajñapti*) of the *Ssū* and the Tds, and these two designations concern the relationship between the *pudgala* and the aggregates which are its support.

It is certain that the *pudgala* is not an absolute reality totally separated from compounded things in the past, present and future times. In fact, the designation of a conditioned person in relation to the elements is a special theory. The Vātsīputrīyas' affirmation of this thesis, presented by Vasubandhu in the Abhidharmakośa, is as follows:

'I say that the *pudgala* is; I do not say that it exists merely as a designation of the *skandhas*; for me, the designation *pudgala* occurs in relation to the present, internal, assumed *skandhas* (*skandhan upādāya*)'[567]

Hence the intepretations according to which the *pudgala* is an absolute reality or a single, substantial and permanent entity are not in conformity with Pudgalavādin doctrine. Among the erroneous interpretations of the *pudgala* in indirect or adverse sources, the following are models and well-known:

1 — The Vijñānakāyapādaśāstra II, T XVII, 1539, 527*b* 2-3, describes the *pudgala* as follows: 'In truth, the *pudgala* is acknowledged, is known, is, exists. Therefore, there is certainly a *pudgala*'.

2 — The Kathāvatthu and its Commentary define it thus: 'The *pudgala* is known in the sense of a reality and an ultimate fact'; — '*pudgala*' signifies soul, being, vital principle; 'is known': is approached and got at by the understanding, is cognized; 'is real': not taken as an effect of magic or mirage, actual; 'ultimate': highest sense, not taken from tradition or hearsay; '[it is] known' as one of the fifty-seven ultimates of our conscious experience[568].

3 — The refutation of the *pudgala* in the Tattvasaṅgraha by Śāntarakṣita is as follows: 'Some people who regard themselves as Buddhists describe the 'soul' (*ātman*) by the name of *pudgala* and declare it to be neither the same as, nor different from the aggregates'.

---

567 Kośa IX, p.233, n.2 (Pruden, p.1314): *pratyutpannādhyatmikopāttashandhān upādāya pudgalaḥ prajñapyate.*

568 Trans. by S.Z. Aung and C.A.F. Rhys Davids, *Points of Controversy*, p.8. According to n. 4, the 57 ultimates consist of the 5 aggregates, 12 sense–organs and objects, 18 elements, 22 controlling powers.

Kamalaśīla's Commentary has: 'some people' — the Vātsīputrīyas. Those people who regard themselves as *Saugatas* (sons of the Sugata, Buddha); yet, under the pretended name of *pudgala*, they postulate the 'soul' (*ātman*) which cannot be said to be either 'the same as', or 'different from' the aggregates. The question arises as to how persons who admit their being 'Sons' of the Blessed Buddha who has taught the doctrine of 'no-soul' (*anātmavāda*), have wedded themselves to a false view of 'soul', — the author answers it in a joking spirit, by the term '*who regard themselves as Buddhists*'.

'The character of the 'soul' is held [by them] to be as follows: (*a*) He who is the doer of the diverse good and bad deeds, (*b*) the enjoyer of the agreeable and disagreeable fruits of his deeds, and (*c*) who moves from the point of the abandonment of the preceding aggregates to the point of the assuming of other aggregates, and is also the experiencer, — is the 'soul'. — All this is held to be true (by the Vātsīputrīyas) of their *pudgala* also; the only difference [between the *ātman* and the *pudgala*] is in regard to the name'[569].

It is likely that the founder of the Pudgalavādin school had to base his establishment of the designation of the *pudgala* on the interpretation of the Buddha's teaching.

Although the Buddha had denounced the concept of an absolute self (*ātman*) as the internal or external entity or being, he never denied the empirical, functional self as a designation. In the Saṃyutta Nikāya (III, 189-90), the Buddha gave the definition of a being while answering a relevant question from the monk Rādha:

'A being! A being! — it is called. Why, Blessed One, is it called a being?'

'Because the desire, attachment, pleasure and craving which are attached to the body (. . . feeling, perception, mental factors and consciousness) and which intermingle with them, that is called a being'[570].

In the Poṭṭhapādasutta, although the Buddha refuted the blind attachment of Poṭṭhapāda to the concept of a self in relation to the three times, he did not oppose the designated self (*attapaṭilābha*). He approved the use of the word 'I' or 'self' as long as there was no attachment to it, as it is said: 'designated selves (*attapaṭilābha*) are expressions, figures of speech, designations of common worldly usage which the Tathāgata uses without avoiding them'[571].

Furthermore, the Pudgalavādins were probably not satisfied with the interprettion according to which a man is merely the result of a combination of psycho-physical factors. For a man is something different from a chariot; the latter is only an

---

569 *Ācārya Shāntarakṣita: Tattvasaṅgraha*, crit. and ed. Swami Dwarkikadas Shastri, vol.I, Bouddha Bharati, Varanasi 1968, *Ātmaparīkṣā*, p.159–6. *Vātsīputrīyaparikalpitātmaparikṣā*, v. 336: *Kecittu saugatammanyā apyātmāṃ pracakṣate, pudgalavyapadeśena tattvānyatvādivarjitam.* The Commentary by Kamalaśīla is taken from the English trans. by G. Jha, *The Tattvasaṅgraha of Shāntirakṣita with the Commentary by Kamalashīla* I, Baroda (G.O.S. LXXX) 1937, repr. Delhi 1986, p.217.

570 SN III, 190: *Satto satto ti vuccati. kittāvatā nu kho bhante satti ti vuccati. — Rūpe (vedanāya, saññāya, saṅkāresu, viññāṇe) kho Rādha yo chando yo rāgo yā nandi yā taṇhā tatra satto tatra visatto tasmā satto ti vuccati. Satto* is a synonym of *pudgala* in the sense of a designation of a person.

571 DN I, 202: *Itimā kho Citta loka-samaññā loka-niruttiyo loka-vohārā loka-paññatiyo yahi tathāgato voharati aparāmasan ti.*

assemblage of parts and separate pieces, whereas the former is essentially a being with its totality of which the psycho-physical parts develop after conception and birth. A new-born child is not an empty structure but contains a primordial programme through its attitude, such as emotional disposition, indispensible needs, physiology, sexuality, hatred, etc., as the Buddha said:

'Mālunkyāputta, if an innocent new-born child lying on its back has no lusts (*kāma*), why should desire (*kāmachanda*) in relation to sensual pleasures (*kāmesu*) arise in it? Truly, the tendency to attachment to sexual pleasures (*kāmarāgānusaya*) persists potentially in it'[572].

Thus it is that there exists, through essence, something that persists for the regularisation of all organic functions.

Moreover, in a positive sense, the discourse whose contents are similar to the Bhārahārasutta is one which is favourable to the Pudgalavādins' interpretation since it speaks of the burden as the basis of the bearer of the burden. Here is a significant excerpt from the Bhārahārasutta:

'I teach you, monks, the burden, the bearer of the burden, the taking up and laying down of the burden. Listen attentively.

— What is, monks, the burden?

— It is the five aggregates of grasping (*upādānaskandha*), is the reply.

— What are they?

— They are the five aggregates of grasping form, feeling, perception, mental factors, consciousness. This, monks is what is called the burden.

— What, monks, is the bearer of the burden?

— It is the person (*pudgala*), is the reply. For example, such-and-such a venerable one with such-and-such a name, such-and-such a clan. This, monks, is what is called the bearer of the burden.

— And what, monks, is the taking up of the burden?

— It is the craving that leads to rebirth, accompanied by delight in attachment which seeks pleasure sometimes here, sometimes there, namely: craving for sensuality (*kāmataṇhā*), craving for existence (*bhavataṇhā*) and craving for annihilation (*vibhavataṇhā*), That, monks, is what is called taking up the burden.

— And what, monks, is the laying down of the burden?

— It is the destruction of craving, the total cessation of attachment, abandoning, relinquishment, liberation, repugnance. That, monks, is what is called the laying down of the burden'[573].

---

572 MN I, 433: *Dahrassa hi Mālunkyāputta kumārassa mandassa uttānaseyyakassa kāmā ti pi na hoti, kuto pan'assa uppajjissati kāmesu kāmacchando anuseti ti-ev'assa kāmarāgānusayo.*

573 SN III, 25: *Bhāram ca vo bhikkhave desissāmi, bhārahāraṃ ca bhārādānaṃ ca bhāranikkhepanañca, tam sunātha. — katamo bhihhave bhāro. — pañcūpādānakkhandhā tissā vacanāyaṃ, katame pañca. seyyathidam rūpūpādānakkhandho vedanupādānakkhandho saññupādanakkhandho saṅkhāryapādānakkhandho viññāṇupādānakkhandho; ayaṃ vuccati bhikkhave bhāro. — katamo ca bhikkhave bhārahāro. puggalo tissa vacanīyam, yoyaṃ āyasmā evaṃnāmo evamgotto; ayaṃ vuccati bhikkhave bhārohāro. — katamam ca bhikkhave bhārādānaṃ. yāyam taṇhā ponobhavikā nandirāgasahagatā tatra tatrābhinandinī, seyyathīdam kāmataṇhā bhavataṇhā vibhavataṇhā; idaṃ vuccati bhikkhave bhārādānaṃ. — katamañca bhikkhave bhāranikkhe panaṃ, yo tassāyeva taṇhāya asesavirāganirodho cāgo paṭinissaggo mutti anālayo; idam*

On the other hand, the Buddha certainly used the terms consciousness (*vijñāna*) and mind (*citta*). They designate not only the conscious part but also the subconscious part of mentality. In fact, these two mental factors are nearly identical[574], at least in their function which produces the autonomy and continuity of beings. To a certain degree, consciousness (*vijñāna*) is more often designated for activities engaged in rebirth, while mind (*citta*) is more often designated for the realisation of Nirvāṇa. They rest on the other four aggregates (*skandha*) as if on a base[575].

According to the canonical texts, consciousness is one of the six great elements which constitute the universe and mankind. The material elements constitute the body, whilst the mental element, as much dichotomising intellect as consciousness, constitutes the mind:

'Monks, when it is said that this person possesses six elements, what conditions are being spoken of? The earth-element, the water-element, the fire-element, the wind-element, the space-element, the consciousness-element? Monks, it is because of those conditions that it is said: that person possesses six elements'[576]. Although consciousness is only an element like the other five, it is infinitely superior to the others through its basic and spiritual qualities, be it in the latent or virtual state:

> 'Consciousness is unmanifested, infinite and luminous everywhere.
> In it neither water, nor earth, nor fire, nor air can find a place.
> In it, length, shortness, subtelty, coarseness, beauty, ugliness and
> name and form cease completely.
> When consciousness ceases, all things vanish'[577].

Consciousness is also considered as the recorder of experiences, the accumulator

---

vuccati bhikkhave bhāranikkhepanan ti.

574 SN II, 95: Monks, that which is called thought is also called mind and consciousness (*yam ca kho bhikkhave vuccati cittam iti pi mano, iti pi viññanam*). Cf. Kośa II, 34. Vism, p.383.

575 SN III, 53: Monks, if someone were to declare, 'Outside the body, feeling, perception, mental factors, I demonstrate the coming, going, disappearance, appearance, growth, augmentation and abundance of consciousness', that is impossible (*yo bhikkhave evam vadeyya: aham aññatra rūpā aññatra vedanāya aññatra saññāya aññatra saṅkhārehi viññāṇassa āgatim vā gatim vā cutim vā upapattim vā vuddhim vā virūḷhim vā vepullam vā paññāpessamīti netam ṭhānam vijjati*).

576 MN III, 239: *Chadhāturo ayam, bhikkhu, puriso ti iti kho pan' etam vuttam. kin c'etam paṭicca vuttam? paṭhavīdhātu āpodhātu tejodhātu vāyodhātu ākāsadhātu viññāṇadhātu. chadhāturo ayam, bhikkhu puriso ti iti yan tam vuttam idam etam paṭicca vuttam.* Cf. AN III, 6, 61.

577 DN I, 223: *Viññāṇam anidassanam anantam sabbato pabham / ettha āpo ca paṭhavī ca tejo vāyo na gādhati / ettha dīghā ca rassan ca aṇum thūlam subhāsubham / ettha nāmañ ca rūpañ ca asesam uparujjhati / viññanassa nirodhena etth'etam uparujjhati.*

According to Buddhaghosa, the first of these consciousnesses (*vijñāna*) is a name for Nirvāṇa (*nibbānassa nāmam*), whilst the second is compounded consciousness (*abhisaṃkhāraviññāṇam*). Cf. MN-A II, p.413.

E. Conze, *Thirty Years of Buddhist Studies*, p.10: 'How otherwise could one account for the numerous references to a «person» (*pudgala*) or the assumption of an eternal «consciousness» in the *saddhātasūtra*, or the identification of the Absolute of Nirvāṇa, with an «invisible infinite consciousness, which shines everywhere» (*viññāṇam anidassanam anantam sabbato pabham*) in Dīghanikāya, XI, 85? Side by side with the oft-repeated negation of an *ātman* there are traces of a belief in the consciousness as the non-impermanent centre of the personality which constitutes an absolute element in this contingent world'.

of ripening actions (*karman*), whether meritorious or demeritorious, throughout successive existences:

'If a person, even an ignorant one, accomplishes a meritorious action, consciousness increases in merit'[578].

It is, furthermore, considered as an essential mental factor always associated with two other factors, vitality and heat, in order to have and maintain the functions of life[579]. However consciousness, under another aspect, is considered as a seed (*bīja*) which, associated with the power of action (*karman*) and thirst (*tṛṣṇā*), causes a new life to be born[580].

It is interesting to note that consciousness sometimes exists independently of corporeality. Consciousness, in the case of the conception of a new being, is a very clear example. It is consciousness which constitutes the point of association of the mental factors (*saṃskāra*) of previous lives and appears at the moment of the beginning of the formation of an embryo. It establishes the basis so that name-and-form (*nāmarūpa*) develop; without it, the life of a new being would not come about:

'Ānanda, if consciousness were not to descend into the mother's womb, would name-and-form form in the mother's womb?'

'No, Lord'[581].

Although the other aggregates, being compounded, disappear, consciousness stops only its functions but is never lost. Taking the positive sense of the last phrase of the following passage, it could be interpreted that consciousness is purified, transformed, and transcends or always remains in bliss:

---

578 SN II, p.82: *Avijjāgato yaṃ bhikkhave purisapuggalo puññaṃ ce saṅkkkāraṃ avhisaṃkaroti, puññāpagam hoti viññānam.*

Udāna, p.85: When one gives, merit will augment.
No hatred can accumulate in the control of the self.
Good conquers bad; Nirvāṇa is attained
Through the exhaustion of craving, hatred and delusion
(*Daḍato puññaṃ pavaddhati, saṃyamato veraṃ na cīyati,*
Kusalo ca jahāti pāpakaṃ rāgadosamohakkhayā parinibbuto).

579 DN II, 338: Friends, when the conch is associated with man, effort, breath, the sound of the conch is heard. . . Equally, Prince, when this body is associated with vitality, heat and consciousness, it can perform the action of walking, standing, sitting, lying down, seeing visibles with its eye, hearing sounds with its ear, smelling odours with its nose, tasting flavours with its tongue, touching tangibles with its body and knowing objects with its mind (*yadā kira bho ayaṃ saṅkho nāma purisa-sahagato ca hoti vāyāma-sahagato ca vayo-sahagato ca, tatāya saṅkho saddaṃ karoti . . . evam eva kho Rajañña yadāyaṃ kāyo āyu-sahagato ca hoti usmāsa-sahagato ca viññāna-sahagato ca, tadā abhikkamati pi paṭikkamati ti tiṭṭhati pi nisīdati pi seyyam pi kapetti, cakkhumā pi rūpaṃ passati, sotena pi saddaṃ suṇāti, ghānena pi gandhaṃ ghāyati, jivhāya pi rasaṃ sāyati, kāyena pi phoṭṭhabbam phussati, manasā pi dhammaṃ vijānāti*). Cf. also SN III, 142.

580 AN III, 76: That is why, Ānanda, action is the rice-field, consciousness the seed, and craving the moisture. The consciousnesses of beings hindered by ignorance and fettered by thirst are dulled in inferior spheres [the world of desire] (*Iti kho Ānanda kammaṃ khettaṃ viññāṇam bijam taṇhā sineho avijjānīvaraṇānaṃ sattānaṃ taṇhāsaṃyojanānaṃ hīnāya dhātuyā viññānam patiṭṭhitam*).

581 DN II, 63: *Viññāṇaṃ va hi Ānanda mātu kucchiṃ na okkamissattha, api nu kho nāma-rūpa mātu kucchismiṁ samucchissathāti? No h'etem bhante.*

'The body is burnt, perceptions cease, all feeling is frozen, the mental factors are stilled, consciousness goes to rest (or goes home)'[582]

With regard to the mind (*citta*), it is always luminous and purified, and only minor defilements blemish it. When the defilements are eliminated, the mind again becomes luminous and purified:

'That mind, monks, is luminous, but it becomes blemished by adventitious defilements. However, uneducated worldlings do not understand it for what it is. That is why I declare that uneducated worldlings do not cultivate the mind. That mind, monks, is luminous and it is purified of adventitious defilements. Learned disciples understand it for what it is. That is why I declare that, for learned disciples, there is cultivation of the mind'[583].

Consequently, the methods of purification taught by the Buddha have the sole aim of eliminating defilements, but no effect can be exercised on the nature of the mind, since:

'If the mind of a monk is detached from the elements of form, etc., he is freed from them for he is detached from defilements; and through his freedom he is stable; because of his stability, he is content; because of his contentment, he is unperturbed; being unperturbed, he himself attains Parinirvāṇa'[584].

Thus, consciousness and mind are the two key terms of Buddhist psychology which designate all the activities of the conscious in their aspects, from the dichotomising function at its fullest extent to a lasting and refined subconscious. Both terms gave the scholars of the Pudgalavādin school (as well as later Mayāhānist scholars) the idea of a psychological principle the function of which is similar to the notions covered by those two terms.

THE POSITION OF THE *PUDGALA*

We will attempt to clarify as far as possible the reasons for which the position of the *pudgala* in relation to the aggregates is established. It is probable that this very specific, and difficult to express, position was established after the Pudgalavādins had fully studied the attitude and findings of the Buddha and his disciples on false views concerning the world and the self.

It is certain that the Pudgalavādins wished to avoid the extremist ideas which the

---

582 Udāna, 93: *abhedi kāyo, nirodha saññā, vedanā pi 'tidahamsu sabbā, vūpasamiṃsu saṅkhārā, viññāṇan attham agamā.*

583 AN I, 10: *Pabhassaram idaṃ bhikkhave cittaṃ tañ ca kho āgantukehi upakkilesehi upakkiliṭṭham. taṃ assutavā puthujjano yathābhūtaṃ nappajānāti. tasmā assutavata puthujjanassa cittabhāvanā n'atthī ti vadāmī ti. pabhassaraṃ idaṃ bhikkhave cittaṃ tañ ca kho āgantukehi upakkilesehi ariyasāvakassa cittabhāvanā atthī ti vadāmī ti.*

584 SN III, 45: *Rūpadhātuyā ce bhikkhave bhikkhuno cittaṃ virattaṃ vimuttaṃ hoti anupādāya āsavehi . . . vimuttatā ṭhitaṃ, ṭhitattā santussitaṃ, santussitattā na paritassati, aparitassaṃ paccattaññeva parinibbāyati.*

Buddha denounced:

'The world, Kaccāyana, is generally based on these two notions: existence and non-existence. However, whoever correctly sees the appearance of the world as such does not admit the non-existence of the world, and whoever correctly sees the disappearance of things as such does not admit the existence of the world . . . Kaccāyana, «everything exists» is an extreme, and «nothing exists» is another extreme. By avoiding those two extremes, Kaccāyana, the Tathāgata teaches the doctrine of the middle . . .'[585].

These two opposing notions constitute, on the other hand, the origin of the extremist views (*antagrahādṛṣṭi*) which consist in the false view of eternity (*śāśvatadṛṣṭi*) and the false view of annihilation (*ucchedadṛṣṭi*)[586]. The former is a belief in a permanent substance or person which exists independently of the physical and mental elements which constitute life and which continue even after death. The latter, on the other hand, affirms the existence of an ego-entity or personality which is more or less identical to the physical and mental elements and which, consequently, is destroyed or dissolved after death. These points of view are false opinions since, not only do they not conform to reality, they are also sources of wrong aspirations and conduct and sometimes capable of leading beings 'to undesirable, displeasing and disagreeable states, unhappiness and suffering'[587].

Furthermore, before establishing the *pudgala* thesis, such as the ineffable (*avaktavya*), the founder of the Vātsīputrīya school was probably familiar with the conversation between the Buddha and the wandering recluse Vacchagotta:

' . . . the wandering ascetic Vacchagotta addressed the Blessed One:

— Venerable Gotama, does a self exist?

When he had spoken thus, the Blessed One remained silent.

— How then, Venerable Gotama, does a self not exist?

For the second time, the Blessed One remained silent.

Then the wandering ascetic Vacchagotta rose and went away. Shortly after the departure of the wandering ascetic Vacchagotta, Venerable Ānanda said to the Blessed One:

— Why did the Blessed One not answer the question of the wandering ascetic Vacchagotta?

— Ānanda, if, to the question of the wandering ascetic Vacchagotta 'Does a self exist?', I had answered that a self exists, then, Ānanda, that would have aligned me with the monks and brahmins who are eternalists.

---

585 SN II, 17: *Dvayanissito khvāyaṃ Kaccāyana loko yebhuyyena atthitañ ceva natthitañ ca. lokasamudayam kho Kaccāyana yathābhūtaṃ sammappaññāya passato yā loke natthitā sā na hoti, lokanirodham kho Kaccāyana yathābhūtaṃ sammappaññāya passato yāloke atthitā sā na hoti . . . sabbaṃ atthīti kho Kaccāyana ayam eko anto. sabbaṃ natthīti ayaṃ dutiyo anto. ete te Kaccāyana ubho ante anupagamma majjhena tathāgato dhammam desseti.*

586 On the two extreme views, see above, n.501

Kośa V, 7: Belief in the eternity, belief in the annihilation (*dhruva, uccheda*) of what one believes to be the self is *antagrāhadṛṣṭi*, belief in extremes, since it is to believe falsely in the extreme (*anta*) theories of eternity or of annihilation'.

587 AN I, 32: . . . *te dhammā aniṭṭhāya akantāya amanāpāya ahitāya dukkhāya saṃvattanti.*

If, to the question of the wandering ascetic Vacchagotta, 'does a self not exist?', I had answered that a self does not exist, then, Ānanda, that would have aligned me with the monks and brahmins who are nihilists.

Ānanda, if, to the question of the wandering ascetic Vacchagotta, 'does a self exist?', I had answered that a self exists, then, Ānanda, would my answer have been consistent with my knowledge that all things are insubstantial?

— Certainly not, Venerable Sir.

— Ānanda, if, to the question of the wandering ascetic Vacchagotta, 'Does a self not exist?', I had answered that a self does not exist, Ānanda, the wandering ascetic Vacchagotta, who was already confused, would have been even more so; he would have said to himself: 'Formerly, I really had a self, but now I no longer have one'[588].

The Buddha's silence over questions on the existence or non-existence of the self asked by Vacchagotta could constitute a significant basis for the *pudgala* thesis, the position of which is in the very middle between the two extreme notions — existentialism or non-existentialism — refuted by the Buddha.

With regard to the formulation of the very specific proposition of the *pudgala* in relation to the supports, it seems that the scholars of the Pudgalavādin school, on establishing this doctrinal point, had indeed adopted the Buddha's attitude towards the questions to be avoided (*avyākṛta*); just as the Buddha refused several times to answer the following question in front of the ascetics Mandissa and Jāliya:

'Venerable Gotama, is the life principle (*jīva*) the same thing as the body or is the life principle one thing and the body another?'

'I know thus and I see thus, friend, and yet I do not say «the life principle and the body are identical»; or «the life principle and the body are different»'[589].

The Buddha did not express himself in the same way when the ascetic Poṭṭhapāda asked him to explain things which had not been definitvely explained[590]. He also pointed out the danger of extremist opinions on the identification or differentiation of the life principle and the body, saying:

'Monk, if the view that the life principle is identical to the body is upheld, in such a case the pure life is inachievable; monk, if the view that the life principle is different from the body is upheld, in such a case the pure life is inachievable'[591].

In answer to questions which were often asked in order to know whether or not the Tathāgata exists after death, the Buddha said that even during life, the Tathāgata is not to be found, even less so after death and that none of the five aggregates should be considered to be the Tathāgata, or that the Tathāgata can be found outside

588 Cf. SN IV, 400–1 (Ānandasutta or Atthatasutta).

589 DN I, 157–8: *Kin nu kho āvuso bho Gotamo taṃ jīvam tam sarīraṃ udāhu aññaṃ ẹvaṃ aññaṃ sarīraṃ ti? . . . ahaṃ kho pan' etaṃ āvuso evaṃ janāmi evaṃ passāmi, attha ca panāhaṃ na vadāmi 'taṃ jīvaṃ taṃ sarīraṃ' ti vā 'aññam jīvaṃ aññam sarīram' ti vā.* Cf. also DN I, 159–60; SN IV, 392.

590 The things which have not been definitively explained are the questions to be avoided (*avyākṛta*) because they did not receive a response from the Buddha, whilst doctrinal points concerning the four Noble Truths, those which pertain to salvation or lead to Nirvāṇa, are things which have been definitively explained by the Buddha. Cf. DN I, 188–91; SN V, 418.

591 SN II, 61: *Taṃ jīvaṃ tam sarīranti vā bhikkhu diṭṭhiyā sati brahmacariyavāso na hoti; aññam jıvaṃ aññaṃ sarīranti vā bhikkhu diṭṭhiyā sati brahmacariyavāso na hoti.*

those psycho-physical phenomena. In other words, the Tathāgata or a liberated monk is not the same as the aggregates, nor different from them[592].

In this respect it is interesting to note the identification of the word Tathāgata with the word *sattva* (living being) by Buddhaghosa in his commentaries[593]. If it is certain that the word Tathāgata has the same sense as *sattva* as Buddhaghosa so precisely described it without confusing the meaning of the term[594], that would give a significant relationship between the notion and the proposition according to which the Tathāgata is neither identical to nor different from the aggregates. Furthermore, it is certain that, in the eyes of the Pudgalavādins, there is no total differentiation or rather discontinuity between the successive existences of a living being (*sattva* = *pudgala*) and the supreme person (= *uttamapuriso, paramapuriso*). Since in the Nikāyas, the words 'supreme person' (*uttamapuriso*), 'excellent person' (*paramapuriso*) are synonyms of the word Tathāgata[595]. This supposition could be confirmed by the establishment of the three Pudgalavādin designations, namely:

1) *pudgala* — designated-by-the-supports,
2) *pudgala* — designated-by-transmigration,
3) *pudgala* — designated-by-cessation.

These three designations are none other than the three aspects of a person designated

---

592 SN III, 118–19: How do you conceive this, Anurādha: do you think that form is the Tathāgata? — No, Blessed One. — Do you think that feeling, perception, the mental factors, consciousness are the Tathāgata? — No, Blessed One. — How do you conceive this, Anurādha: do you think that the Tathāgata is in form? — No, Blessed One. — Do you think that the Tathāgata is different from form? — No, Blessed One. — Do you think that the Tathāgata is in feeling, . . .different from feeling, . . .in perception, . . .different from perception, . . .in the mental factors, . . .different from the mental factors, . . .in consciousness, . . .different from consciousness? — No, Blessed One. — How do you conceive this, Anurādha do you think that the Tathāgata is form, feeling, perception, the mental factors and consciousness? — No, Blessed One. — How do you conceive of this, Anurādha: do you think that the Tathāgata does not possess form, feeling, perception, the mental factors and consciousness? — No, Blessed one. — Anurādha, if the Tathāgata, even in the present, should not be considered as existing in the present, can it in truth be said that the Tathāgata, supreme man, excellent being, he who obtains the highest fruit, should be designated in a manner other than those four ways: the Tathāgata exists after death, does not exist, both exists and does not exist, neither exists nor does not exist, after death? — No, Blessed One. — That is right, Anurādha! Formerly as today, Anurādha, I always teach suffering and the cessation of suffering.'

Cf. also SN III, 109–15, the dialogue between Sāriputta and Yamaka on the same subject.

593 Udāna-A, 340: The Tathāgata is the self (*tathāgato ti attā*). DN-A I, 118: in the statement *hoti tathāgato* etc., by *tathāgata* — is defined as being (*hoti tathāgato ti ādisu, satto tathāgato ti adhippeto.* We translate *attā* by self in the more or less conventional sense, as (*hoti hi attano nātho* — Dhp, 160; *attanā va kataṃ pāpaṃ* — Dhp, 161). Cf. also MN-A II, 117; K. Bhattacharya, *L'Ātman-Brahman dans le Bouddhisme ancien*, p.123 and n.5; K.N. Jayatilleke, *Early Buddhist Theory of Knowledge*, pp.244, 291–2.

594 We believe that Buddhaghosa, having explained the word Tathāgata by the word *sattva*, made no confusion in doctrine or language. Obviously, this is the fruit of his profound doctrinal reflection, whereas Jayatilleke, in *Early Buddhist Theory of Knowledge*, pp.291, 292, thinks that Buddhaghosa was wrong in identifying Tathāgata with *sattva*.

595 SN III, 118–19, gives the synonyms of the word Tathāgata by writing: '. . . the Tathāgata, supreme man, excellent being, he who has attained the highest fruit, . . .' (. . . *Tathāgato uttamapuriso paramappattipatto* . . .).

by itself.

Furthermore we find, in discussions between the Buddha and his disciples with respect to the concept of self, arguments concerning the two main notions (1) the identification and (2) differentiation of the self in relation to the aggregates. With regard to the concept saying that the self is identical to the aggregates, the criticism often states that if the self were identical to the aggregates, it would be like the identification of fire with fuel; in other words, the actor and the action would be one and the same thing. Moreover, if the self were identical to the aggregates, it would be subject to appearance and disappearance at the same time as the aggregates. This is unacceptable for the self as it has been designated.

With regard to the concept saying that the self is different from the aggregates, the criticism is that, if the self were different from the aggregates, it would be as if fire did not depend on fuel. If the fire were separated from fuel, there would be no need to make the effort to induce fire by burning fuel. Similarly, if the self were different from the aggregates, it would have nothing to do with the life of a being. That is why the concept saying that the self is different from the aggregates is an unfounded opinion[596].

The argument of the criticism, in fact, developed in parallel with the increase of 'semi-heretical' opinions of 'internal unbelievers', notably those of the Pudgalavādins, in the course of the history of Buddhist thought. Here is a significant extract on the preceding subject from the *Hsien yang shêng-chiao lun*顯揚聖教論, T XXXI, 1602, 553*c* 20-*554a* 16:

'Why should one know the unreality of the *pudgala* as a person? — Because, if the person exists, is it identical to the aggregates? Does it dwell in the aggregates? Does it dwell somewhere else? Is it different from the aggregates?' 'If you admit that the person is identical to the aggregates, (it) should be a hypothesis; that is contrary to your doctrine; that is why that is an error. The reason is because you presuppose a person by basing yourself on the aggregates themselves. If (the person) is separated from the aggregates and dwells elsewhere, it has no relation to the aggregates; that also is an error. The reason is because, in the aggregates, no person exists.'

'(In short), these three hypotheses do not conform to the truth. . .'. 'Moreover, if you admit that the real person dwells in the aggregates, that also is not correct! Why?' 'Because the real person dwelling in the aggregates which you admit, is it like the owner of a house dwelling in his house? Fire in relation to wood? Light depending on a lamp? Space sheltering things? If it is so, everything is incorrect! Why? Because there are five kinds of errors. Which are they?

1. 'If (the person) is like the owner of a house dwelling in his house, its shape should be different (from the aggregates), since the owner of the house and the form of the house are different'.
2. 'If (the person) is like fire in relation to wood, there is an error in the dependence on others (the person depends on the aggregates); since fire depends on the power

596 See below, n.599.

of the wood and has no freedom'.

3. 'If (the person) is like light depending on a lamp, there is a fault of impermanence; since, in depending on the existence or non-existence of the lamp, light appears or disappears'.

'Furthermore, the first two examples are equally an error in impermanence: the owner of a house who dwells permanently (in his house) does not exist; since, although the house exists for a long time, its owner either stays in another place or else disappears. Fire exists in relation to the power of wood, its existence and non-existence are undefinable since its nature is impermanent'.

4. 'If (the person) were like space, that would be an error of evident function. Space has a patent nature, which means that one can come and go in it unobstructed. The person is the same. That is why there is an error . . .' It is thus that the hypothesis according to which the person dwells in the aggregates does not conform to the truth'.

It is evident that, not neglecting such severe criticism, the Pudgalavādins had taken the position of the very middle for the thesis of the *pudgala* which is neither identical to the aggregates nor different from them. The Pudgalavādins, by supporting this position, wished that the *pudgala* thesis would not fall into this dilemma: if the *pudgala* is different from the aggregates, it must be a permanent substance and have no relation to life; if the *pudgala* is identical to the aggregates, it must be impermanent like the aggregates.

According to Kuei-chi, the Pudgalavādins, by attributing a specific nature to the *pudgala*, wished to avoid the two propositions admitted by the Yoga masters:

1. The first is that the person is identical to the aggregates; that is, a belief according to which the person is identical to form (*rūpa*), feeling (*vedanā*), perception (*saṃjñā*), the mental factors (*saṃskāra*) and consciousness (*vijñāna*);

2. the second is that the person is different from the aggregates; that is, that substance entirely escapes the elements. This proposition includes the other three contemporary beliefs:

a) the person is contained in the five aggregates;
b) the person is outside the five aggregates;
c) the person is neither inside nor outside (or the possessor of) the five aggregates[597].

It is thus that the preceding data enable us to conclude that the position of the *pudgala* in relation to the aggregates is well thought out and established, outside propositions concerning the twenty kinds of belief in individuality.

In order fully to understand the position of the *pudgala*, it is advisable to read the arguments on this subject, taken from works of the Pudgalavādin school:

The Tds writes: 'It is impossible to say that the being (*sattva* = *pudgala*) is different from the characteristics. If it were different from the characteristics, it would (in consequence) be eternal (*śāśvata*); and if it were identical to the characteristics, it

597 K'uei-chi, *Ch'êng-wei-shih lun shu-chi* 成唯識論述記, I. T XLIII, 1830, 246c sq.

would be non-eternal (*aśāśvata*). These two errors cannot be made' (Tds, 19*c* 3-5).

This idea is described in another way in the *Ssū*: '. . . is the *pudgala* different or is it not different from the characteristics (*lakṣaṇa*)? The *pudgala* is the ineffable (*avaktavya*); (that is why), if it is different, it is permanent (*nitya*); if it does not differ, it is impermanent (*anitya*). Both are errors in regard to the ineffable' (*Ssū*, 5*a* 28 sq.).

The same argument is treated in a more profound and detailed manner in the Sns. Before presenting the *pudgala* thesis, the Sns describes and refutes the seven adverse opinions concerning the person. These opinions are:

1. There is no person, but only aggregates;
2. It is impossible to say whether the person exists or does not exist;
3. The person really exists;
4. The person is identical to the aggregates;
5. The person is different from the aggregates;
6. The person is eternal;
7. The person is impermanent.

Among these seven opinions, the fourth and fifth are important, since they concern the two theories which oppose the Pudgalavādins' theory of the *pudgala* according to which the *pudgala* is neither identical to the aggregates nor different from them. The last two are opinions subordinate to the two preceding opinions. This is the refutation by the Sns of the thesis maintaining that the person is identical to the aggregates:

'(Certain people maintain that) the person exists by admitting that the aggregates are identical to the person or that the person is identical to the aggregates. If the aggregates were identical to the person, the aggregates would be ineffable, (since) the person is ineffable. If the person were identical to the aggregates, the person would be expressible, (since) the aggregates are expressible. (If) both were describable, the aggregates would cease to be identical to the person' (Sns, 465*b* 4-7).

'If the person were identical to the aggregates, when (the aggregates) disappear or appear, the person would also disappear or appear. When part of the body is cut off, a part of the person would also have to be cut off. Hence, one part would form several parts, one part and several parts would combine in a (single) part. Depending on the existence of the body, life (*jīva*) exists. When life exists, the body also exists. That is why the thesis according to which «the person is identical to the aggregates» should be refuted' (Sns, 645*b* 10-13).

As for the refutation of the opinion maintaining that the person is different from the aggregates, the Sns divides it into several arguments as follows:

1. To those who admit that the person is different from the aggregates by basing themselves on the example of the person who bears a heavy burden, it objects:

'Do the person, life and the self differ? That is not illustrated by the Sūtra since, by basing himself on the burden, (the Buddha) said that (the bearer of) the burden exists' (Sns, 465*b* 4 sq.).

2. 'To those who admit that the person is different from the aggregates because a

man acquires craving (*tṛṣṇā*) as his second (person), it objects that:

'If one possesses right view (*samyagdṛṣti*), one does not doubt that a man, bound by craving, transmigrates in the cycle of birth and death (*saṃsāra*). This is what the Buddha wished to make evident by saying that a man acquires craving as his second (person) and remains for a long time in birth and death. When craving is eliminated, there is no further transmigration. It is thus that the person is not different from the aggregates'.

3. To those who admit that the person and the aggregates are separate because the former collects the results (*vipāka*) of its actions (*karman*), it objects that:

'Being founded on impure birth and death, in this life or in a future life, one collects the results (of actions). That is why the person and the aggregates are not separate'.

4. To those who admit that the person and the aggregates are separate because (the Buddha) spoke of an 'I', it objects that:

'By being based on the theory of transmigration (of different existences), the Buddha said: «In the past, in the course of innumerable and incalculable cosmic eras (*asaṃkhyeyakalpa*), I was the supreme king of living beings». That is why the person and the aggregates are not separate'.

5. To those who admit that the person and the aggregates are separate because (the nature of the person) is classed among the questions to be avoided (*avyākṛta*), it objects that:

'It is impossible to affirm that the aggregates and the person are different or are not different. That is why the characteristic of things (*dharmalakṣaṇa*) cannot be described under the aspect of either permanence (*nityatā*) or impermanence (*anityatā*). It is the same with regard to the person. You presuppose a person different from the aggregates; however, the Buddha said:

«The person is different from the body (*kāya*) and the body is different from the person, this is not what is taught by the Buddha and illustrated by the Sūtra». If the person were different from the aggregates, it would either be found in the aggregates, or be spread everywhere. If it were to be found in the aggregates, when the body is cut or opened, the person would be visible, just like a mosquito found in an *udumbara* fruit[598]: when an *udumbara* fruit is opened, the mosquito is visible. It would be the same for the person differing from the body: should cold or heat reach the body, the person would not feel it. Moreover, should the ocular globe come out (of its socket), an object would be seen more clearly; even if the sense organs were destroyed, sound, odour, taste, the tangible, etc., would equally be known.

Furthermore, if the person were different from the body, (it) would go from this body to another one, then it would return to this body, just as one moves from one house to another, then returns to the first one. It would be thus for the person if it were different (from the aggregates) . . . That is why the thesis according to which the person is different from the body should be refuted' (Sns, 465*b* 3-*c* 17).

---

598 The *udumbara* is a fig tree, *ficus glomerata*, with edible fruit and very light wood.

In a condensed manner, the Sns affirms that the thesis of the *pudgala* is right view since it conforms to the Buddha's doctrine of the middle:

'If the *pudgala* could be described in terms of existence or non-existence, one would fall into nihilism (*ucchedadṛṣṭi*) or eternalism (*śāśvatadṛṣṭi*), but the Buddha does not allow us to uphold these two opinions. If one says that the *pudgala* does not exist, that is committing a fault in the order of the questions to be avoided. That expression is not justified. Why? If one affirms that no *pudgala* exists, that is a false view (*mithyādṛṣṭi*). If (on the contrary), one affirms that the *pudgala* exists (conditionally), that is a right view (*samyagdṛṣṭi*). That is why it is possible to say that the *pudgala* exists' (Sns, 464*c* 15-19).

It is certainly difficult to find a satisfactory and logical explanation of the position of the *pudgala*. The relationship of this ineffable with the supports is so vague that it cannot be described in a precise way. That is why the scholars of the Pudgalavādin school often illustrate it with the following popular examples:

a. The example of fire and fuel of which the Abhidharmakośa gives the following explanation: 'The world conceives fire in relation to fuel' (*indhanam upādāya*): it does not conceive fire independently of fuel; it believes that fire is neither identical to fuel, nor other than fuel. If fire were other than fuel, the fuel would not be hot; if fire were identical to fuel, the kindling (fuel) would be the kindled (fire). Equally, we do not conceive the *pudgala* as independent of the elements, we claim that the *pudgala* is neither identical to the elements, nor other than the elements, since it would be eternal (*śāśvata*) and therefore uncompounded (*asaṃskṛta*); if it were identical to the elements, it would be subject to annihilation (*uccheda*)[599].

b. The example of milk and the colour of milk, the explanation of which is also found in the Abhidharmakośa: '. . .It ensues from this very explanation that the *pudgala*, just like milk, exists only as a designation. When visual consciousness knows the colour of milk, it discerns, in the second place, milk; milk is therefore known by visual consciousness and it cannot be said that milk is the same thing as colour or different from colour'[600].

Because of the incomprehensibility of the nature of the *pudgala*, notably its position, there are many incorrect interpretations of the main thesis of the Pudgalavādin school to be found in several indirect or adverse sources. Even so, information of this subject can progressively be found on this subject in conformity with what is set out in the literature of the school. For example:

1. The Samayabhedoparacanacakra by Vasumitra, accompanied by K'uei-chi's commentary, describes the *pudgala* as follows: 'The general sense of the essential doctrine upheld by the Vātsīputrīyas is that «the *pudgala* is neither identical to the aggregates, nor separate from the aggregates». That is to say, a person really exists

---

599 Kośa IX, p.234.

600 *Ibid.*, p.239, n.1.

which pertains neither to compounded things (*saṃskṛta*) nor to the uncompounded (*asaṃskṛta*), but which, in relation to the aggregates, is neither identical nor separate. The Buddha advocated the absence of self; this implies that the self admitted by the heretics, identical to the aggregates or separate from the aggregates, does not exist; this does not imply that the ineffable (*avaktavya*), the person which is neither identical to the aggregates nor separate from the aggregates, categorically does not exist. Being ineffable, it cannot be described by shape, size, bigness, smallness, etc. Until the day of attaining perfect Enlightenment (Buddahood), that person permanently exists'.

'It is by relying on the aggregates, spheres and elements that the designation (*prajñapti*) is presupposed'.

'. . . it is the same meaning with the person which is neither identical to nor separate from the aggregates. Thus, when it is said that form (*rūpa*) is the self, and that the thing (*dharma*) is also the self, all that is nothing but the person as a designation based on the aggregates. That person is truly the person which does not pertain to the aggregates, etc.'[601].

2. In the *Pu chih i lun* 部執異論 by Paramārtha, T XLIX, 2033, 21*c* 22-23: 'The *pudgala* is that which is neither identical to the aggregates (*skandha*) nor different from the aggregates. It is because one bases oneself on the aggregates (*skandha*), elements (*dhātu*) and spheres (*āyatana*) that one establishes the designation of *pudgala*'.

3. The *Traité de la grande vertu de sagesse* (Mahāprajñāpāramitāśāstra), Vol.I, p.43, presents the *pudgala* as follows:

'In the Buddhist system also, there are *Tu tzŭ* (Vātsīputriya) bhikṣus who say: "Just as, through the reunion of the four great elements (*caturmahābhūtasaṃyoga*), there is a dharma «eye» (*cakṣus*), so, through the reunion of the five aggregates (*pañcaskandhasaṃyoga*), there is a dharma «individual» (*pudgala*)". In the *Tu-tzŭ a-pi-t'an* (Vātsīputrīyābhidharma), it is said: "The five aggregates (*skandha*) are not separate from the *pudgala* and the *pudgala* is not separate from the five aggregates. It cannot be said that the five aggregates are the *pudgala* or that, separate from the five aggregates, there is a *pudgala*. The *pudgala* is a fifth category, an ineffable (*avaktavya*) dharma, contained in the basket of texts (*piṭaka*)'.

4. Candrakīrti, in the Madhyamakavṛtti, also comments on the *pudgala*: '. . . they (the Vātsīputrīyas) maintain (that there is . . .) a *pudgala* which migrates (out of one existence into another). It escapes definition (*avācya*). It is neither eternal nor momentary (*anitya*). Its coming and going dependent every time on a changing substratum (*upādānam āśritya*). It then evolves obeying the law of causality. This very (principle) which evolves on the basis of changing elements, when the time comes for it to assume no new substratum, its evolution stops, it is said (to have entered) Nirvāṇa'[602].

---

601 K'uei-chi, Iptllsc, 230*a*.

602 From the translation by Th. Stcherbatsky in *The Conception of Buddhist Nirvāṇa*, p.197.

All the preceding arguments concerning the position of the *pudgala* explain why the *pudgala* does not pertain to either compounded things (*saṃskṛta*) or the uncompounded (*asaṃskṛta*). It constitutes one of the five things susceptible to being known (*pañcaidhaṃjñeyam*): 1-3. things of the three times: past, present, future; 4. the uncompounded (Nirvāṇa); and 5. the *pudgala*[603].

Saṃskṛta		*Asaṃskṛta*
1-3. Things of the three times	4. the *pudgala*	5. Nirvāṇa

This particular classification of the *pudgala* is denoted precisely in the Tds by the

603 Cf. Kośa IX, p.237; *Traité* I, p.43: Bareau, *L'Absolu*, p.253.

To understand fully this Pudgalavādin classification into five things, it is advisable to compare it with the following two classifications:

i. the Sarvāstivādin classification of the 75 elements:

compounded things (*saṃskṛta*)	the uncompounded (*asaṃskṛta*)
72 elements = *sāsrava* + *anāsravā*	3 elements of extinction: *anāsrava*

Cf. J. Takakusu, *The Essentials of Buddhist Philosophy*, p.66 sq.' Th. Stcherbatsky, *The Central Conception of Buddhism*, p.79 sq.; La Vallée Poussin, 'Les soixante quinze et les cent dharmas', ext. du *Muséon*, XXIV, 1905, p.17.

ii. the Theravādin classification of the four ultimate elements:

compounded things (*saṃskṛta*)	the uncompounded (*asaṃskṛta*)
Citta Cetasika Rūpa	*Nibbāna*

Abhidhammatthasaṅgaha, Chap. I, § 2: *Tattha vutt 'ābhidhammattha catudhā paramatthato. Cittam cetasikam rūpaṃ nibbānam "iti sabbathā".*

repetition of the sentence:

'Whether the *pudgala* is separated from the three times or not, it is impossible to say' (Tds, 19*a* 26).

In short, the *pudgala* is something more than the reunion of its constituent elements. It is the essential factor which unifies the process of the life of a person, the longest and most eventful. In other words, it is the *pudgala* which assumes and supports a body for a certain time and which constitutes the same person, from conception in the womb until death, and even spreads across other lives. The *pudgala* is certainly an autonomous person underlying phenomenal investments. The continuity of a person indicates the link between cause and effect which exist between the consecutive states of a life. The specific relationship between the *pudgala* and the supports is explained by the continuity of a single individual independent of others. There is continuity (*santāna*), there is therefore a possessor of continuity (*santānin*). According to the Pudgalavādins, to deny the possessor of continuity is to deny continuity.

It is the *pudgala* which constitutes a person that bears a certain name, lives a certain time, suffers and enjoys the consequences of its actions; this explains that a person has no link with the feelings and thoughts of others. The continual persistence of the person supplies the essence of memory and knowledge. If there were not this essence or centre, how could a thought, the disappearnce of which is instantaneous, recur, just like memory? It is explained that the appearance of memory results from impressions (*vāsanā*)[604] formed by the aggregate of mental factors (*saṃskāra*) and retained in the consciousness (*vijñāna*). This would be impossible if there were no continuity in a person, since the aggregate of mental factors and the aggregate of consciousness are instantaneous. Memory therefore can only occur if there is something that remembers.

With regard to knowledge, according to the Pudgalavādins, there must be a constant subject in cognitive actions which undergo and accumulate experiences. Similarly, there must be a Devadatta[605] for Devadatta to appropriate some money. If there were no *pudgala* to be the 'receiver' of experiences, how could knowledge even be formed?

Hence, the *pudgala* is not only the agent of memory — a part of the mental factors (*saṃskāra*) and consciousness (*vijñāna*) — but also the agent of feelings (*vedanā*) and perceptions (*saṃjñā*).

Thus it is that to deny the existence of the *pudgala* would be to deprive human

---

604 Sn, 1009 = *vāsanā*, or *pubbavāsanā*: the impression or impression of the past from a former life; *pubbavāsanāvāsita* = he who recalls (to mind) impressions of the past or of a former life. Sn–A, 583: *pubbavāsanāvāsitā: vāsanāya vāsitacitta.*

605 Devadatta, the son of Suppabuddha, was a first cousin and disciple of the Buddha. He was jealous of the Buddha and sought all means to harm him. In several discourses, the Buddha spoke of the offences committed by Devadatta, after the latter had left the Order. Cf. A II, 73; IV, 160; S I, 153; G.P. Malalasekera, *Dictionary of Pāli Proper Names*, p.1106 sq. The Kośa IX, pp.279–80, uses the name of Devadatta to illustrate the existence or non-existence of the self or *pudgala*. The same presentation is also found in the *Candrakīrti Prasannapadā Madhyamakavṛtti*, trans. by Jacques May, pp.158–9.

action of any meaning. In contrast, the designation of the *pudgala*, according to the Pudgalavādins, offers possibilities of resolving the problems of the person, of rebirth, of the fruition of actions and of liberation.

PUDGALA-DESIGNATED-BY-TRANSMIGRATION (*saṃkramaprajñaptapudgala* ?)

Different explanations are found in the Pudgalavādin works

a. The Sns writes thus on this subject:

'What is (*pudgala*)-designatd by transmigration?

— When, at a given moment, a being passes to another existence, then the Buddha called that «*pudgala*-in-transmigration».

Why is it called *pudgala*-designated-by-transmigration?

— Because of the designation of the past, future and present'.

'What does designation of the past (*atītaprajñapti* ?) mean?

— As in the discourse on 'The Messenger of the Gods' (*T'ien-shih ching* 天使經, Devadūtasūtra)[606] Yama declared loudly: «That person did not recognise his father, or his mother, or his brothers, etc.; he did not recognise merit, or good, or bad, etc. (I) wish that (Your Majesty) would teach him». As the Buddha said: «In a past life, I was the supreme king of living beings»[607]. That is what is called designation of the past'.

'What does designation of the future (*anāgataprajñapti* ?) mean?

— As the Buddha said: «When a Cakravartin is in the intermediate existence (*antarābhava*), he first enters the maternal womb as if he were entering a royal palace'[608]. Furthermore, as the Buddha said to Maitreya, «Ajita, later, when you become the Buddha, you will be named Maitreya»[609]. That is what is called designation of the future'.

'What does designation of the present (*pratyutpannaprajñapti* ?) mean?

— As the Buddha said: «The man of Aṅga (adorns himself) with earrings and puts numerous precious ornaments on his arms». (Furthermore), as the Buddha said: «The master of great wealth has an abundance of goods and great satisfactions at his disposal»[610]. That is what is called designation of the present.

'It should also be understood that the Buddha, basing himself on the compounded things (*saṃskāra*) of the three times, established these three designations. That is why the designation of the transmigration of compounded things (*saṃskāra*) is called

---

606 See above, Chapter Two, The Literature of the Pudgalavādins.

607 *(Fo shuo) Ting shêng wang ku shih ching* 佛說頂生王故事經 , T 1, 39, 822*b* 824*a* 2–5: Was the supreme king (*rājādhirāja* — Sn, 533) of that era another person? Do not suppose that. Why? Ānanda, it was myself (爾時頂生王者豈異人乎，莫作是觀何以故，爾時王者，阿難即我身是).

608 Sns, 466*c* 8–9: 初入母腹如入堂殿 .

609 See above, n.401.

610 Sns, 466*c* 14: 多有財寶大如意 This means that there is a designated person who possesses wealth in the present.

(*pudgala*)-designated-by-transmigration' (Sns, 466*b* 27-*c* 17).

b. The *Ssŭ* explains the same subject as follows:

'The designation of means (*upāyaprajñapti*) signifies the designation based on the past (*atīta*), future (*anāgata*) and present (*pratyutpanna*). It is associated with the three times. As (the Buddha said): «In the past I was the king Sunetra. In the future there will be (a man) named Ajita. In the present there is Gautama Siddhārtha, etc. . . . Through convention, this designation (is established) in order to (correct opinions) on annihiliation (*uccheda*) and eternity (*śāśvata*). If the king were annihilated, how could I exist (now)? If he had not been, how could I exist?» Based on conventional truth (*saṃvṛtisatya*), this designation of means (*upāyaprajñapti*) is spoken of' (*Ssŭ*, 10*a* 13-19).

c. Description of the same subject by the Tds:

'The designation of the past (*atītaprajñapti* ?) is information concerning the aggregates (*skandha*), elements (*dhātu*) and spheres (*āyatana*) of the past (*atīta*), such as when (the Buddha) said: «I existed in a certain era, with the name of *Chü-hsün-t'a*» (瞿句陀 Kuddāla or Kuddālaka?)'[611] (Tds, 25*b* 3-4).

A comparison of the three preceding passages leads us to think that the *pudgala*-designated-by-transmigration of the Sns and the designation of means (*upāyaprajñapti* ?) of the *Ssŭ* are wider in meaning than the designation-of-the-past of the Tds. Since the word transmigration (*saṃkrama* ?) indicates the whole cycle of birth and death (*saṃsāra*), the word means (*upāya*) indicates what serves to explain the continuity of life, whilst the word past (*atīta*) of the Tds only designates part of the time in which the aggregates (*skandha*), spheres (*āyatana*) and elements (*dhātu*) are found. Thus, the Tds insists on the past, whereas the Sns mentions what is designated-by-transmigration, the *Ssŭ*, designation-of-means; these two ideas place the emphasis on the passage from one life to another: from the past life to the present life, from the present life to the future life. This means that the Sns considers the *pudgala* in the light of the three times.

In fact, the existence of an individual consists of a series of lives of which births and deaths are merely phases of the same process, and consequently birth precedes death but, on the other hand, death precedes life. Birth and death correlate; one being abandoned, the other appears. Thus, a being is none other than a becoming (*bhava*), which at every moment, destroys and recreates itself. Death consists of birth. Birth in turn leads to old age and death. However, death itself is only a phase of becoming: the transition to another life, the state immediately preceding rebirth. It represents an

---

611 Tds 24*b* 3-4: 我於爾時名瞿句陀. The Sanskrit reconstruction of the Chinese characters *Chü-hsün-t'a* 瞿句陀 is difficult. One wonders whether *Chü-hsün-t'a* 瞿句陀 is a faulty transcription of Kuddāla or Kuddālaka, the proper name of a personality in a former life of the Buddha. Kuddālaka was one of 'six masters, who were ford-makers (*tītthaṅkara*), fully renounced (*vitarāga*), having several hundred disciples to whom they taught the doctrine of participation in the Brahmā-world (*brahmalokasahavyatā*). To criticise or insult them was a serious demerit (*bahuṃ apuññaṃ*)' (*Traité* I, p.520, note on Sunetra). Cf. also A III, 371-2; Jā I, 46, 312, 314, 315.

interruption in appearance which marks the end of a short human life but not the total cessation of the life-stream of a being. Since all these phenomena which end inevitably provoke the arising of new phenomena.

It is noteworthy that man, according to Buddhism, is merely one of manifold forms of being. Human beings, like certain beings superior or inferior to man, form a category of beings which differ from other categories through their body and mind. Other beings differ through their body, but not through their mind; yet others, through their mind, but not through their body; certain beings are identical both through their body and through their mind. Finally, there are four categories of formless beings[612]. In another classification, man is placed in one of the following categories: beings without feet, beings with two feet, beings with four feet, beings with many feet (possessing or not a material form), conscious beings, unconscious beings and superconscious beings[613]. The human worlds are always located half-way in the hierarchy of the universe. The life of man is a mixture of pleasure and suffering, good and bad.

After death, man, through the power of actions (*karman*), can be reborn in one or another of the various preceding categories by four means of birth, namely:

1) birth from an egg (*aṇḍaja*), such as that of birds;
2) birth from the mother's womb (*jarāyuja*), such as that of humankind;
3) Birth arising from moisture (*saṃsvedaja*), such as that of insects;
4) birth by metamorphoses (*upapāduka*)[614], such as that of heavenly beings and the hell-bound, etc.,

and in the five kinds of existence which are called destinies (*gati*)[615]:

1) (Beings in) the hells (*niraya, naraka*),
2) Hungry ghosts (*preta*),
3) Animals (*tiryak*),
4) Humankind (*manuṣya*), and
5) Heavenly beings (*deva*).

---

612 Cf. AN IV, 39–40; 410.

613 Cf. AN III, 35.

614 DN III, 230: *catasso yoniso, aṇḍaja, jalābujayoni, saṃsedjayoni, oppātikayoni*; cf. MN I, 73.

Kośa III, 8: There there are four 'wombs' of beings . . ..

i. Womb of beings born from an egg: beings which are born from an egg, goose, crane, peacock, parrot, thrush, etc.

ii. Womb of beings born from a chorion: beings which are born from a chorion, elephant, horse, ox, buffalo, ass, pig, etc.

iii. Womb of beings born from exudation: beings which are born from the exudation of the elements, earth, etc., worms, insects, butterflies, mosquitoes.

iv. Womb of apparitional beings: beings which are born instantly, not lacking or deficient in organs, with all limbs and minor limbs. They are called *upapāduka*, 'apparitional', because they are skilful in the act of appearing (*upādāna*), because they are born instantly (without an embryonic stage, without seed or blood); such as the gods, beings in the intermediate existence. Cf. the notes in *ibid.*, pp.27–8.

615 Cf. MN I, 73; below, 'The secondary theses of the Pudgalavādins: thesis No.11'.

It is thus that man is only a category of beings endowed with sensibility which inhabit the immensity of space. Man will never reach the limits of the universe even if he were to travel all his life at the speed of an arrow in the same direction[616]. That cosmic space shelters innumerable worlds which are not static or enduring, but constantly in the course of development or dissolution; this process occupies immensely long periods of time which are measured in aeons (*kalpa*)[617] until a cosmic catastrophe puts an end to them[618].

In such a large space and long time, a person whose origin is inconceivable appears and disappears sometimes in the form of a man, sometimes in the form of an animal or heavenly being. This cycle of life and death (*saṃsāra*) is never interrupted, unless complete appeasing (*parinirvāṇa*) or the attainment of Nirvāṇa without a remainder (*nirupadhiśeṣanirvāṇa*) intervenes. In the latter case, the person no longer pertains to compounded things (*saṃskṛta*) but to the uncompounded (*asaṃskṛta*). As long as a person is subject to the sphere of compounded things, it perpetually undergoes change like other things. Moreover, in reality, there is no frontier between the three times: past, present and future, since the existence of a person, as well as of a thing, are manifested and transformed continually in accordance with the law of cause and effect (*karmavipāka*). For the length of a being's life, whatever is past is not past and finished, whatever is present influences whatever will be in the future. A being is its very actions. Actions from a being's past follow it as closely as wheels follow the ox's feet or like a shadow which is never separated from what projects it[619]. We are what we have done. We will be what we construct. Our future life is an assemblage of combined effects incurred from causes which we have accumulated in the present life. This constant and beginningless succession of births and deaths, in correlation with the *pudgala*, flows forever as long as it is fed by craving (*tṛṣṇā*):

'At the moment, Vaccha, when a being abandons this body and reappears in

---

616 Cf. AN IV, 426.

617 An aeon or cosmic period (*kalpa*) is inconceivably long. It is divided into four sections: the destruction of the world, the continuation of chaos, the formation of the world and the continuation of the formed world. Of such things it cannot be said that they last 'so many years, or so many centuries, or millennia, or so many hundred million years'. Cf. AN II, 142. SN II, 181, contains a parable illustrating the inconceivable length of an aeon: 'Imagine, monks, a gigantic rock, a monolith a *yojana* in width, a *yojana* in height, without any crevice or fault, and a man comes to rub it with some Kāsi fabric once every hundred years. Well, that gigantic rock would be worn down and disappear more quickly than an aeon. So long, monks, is an aeon. Thus, monks, of such long aeons, several have already past, more than an hundred, a thousand, hundreds of thousands have passed'. Cf. Kośa III, 89–93, on a detailed explanation of the concept of various kinds of aeons: aeon of destruction (*saṃvartakalpa*), aeon of creation (*vivartakalpa*) and intermediate aeon (*antaḥkalpa*).

618 Cf. AN IV, 100–3.

619 Dhp, 1 and 2:

'. . . If one speaks or acts with an impure mind, suffering follows as wheels follow the ox's feet' (. . . *Manasā ce paduṭṭhena bhāsati vā karoti vā, tato naṃdukkhamanveti cakkaṃ va vahato padaṃ*)

'. . . If one speaks or acts with a pure mind, happiness follows like a shadow which is never separated (from what projects it)' (. . . *manasā ce pasannena bhāsati vā karoti vā, tato naṃ sukkhamanveti chāyā 'va anapāyinī*).

another body, for that I declare that craving is the fuel. Truly, Vaccha, in this case craving is the fuel'[620].

Whereas, the Skandhavādins[621] asserted that the continuity of existences is only that of the aggregates: the old ones are abandoned, the new are spontaneously acquired; in this process of perpetual transformation of the psycho-physical elements, there is no person that passes from one life to another, that is a sower, a reaper outside the five aggregates. In consequence, it is incorrect to speak of the suffering or happiness of 'a person', since it is not a matter of a person but of a psycho-physical process which is subjected to suffering or happiness:

> 'Suffering exists, but there is no sufferer.
> There is no agent, only action is found'[622].

Nevertheless, what constitutes an enigma for the Pudgalavādins is that, if there is no person, what is born and reborn? It is impossible for them to accept the doctrine of rebirth without an agent which wanders here and there. Craving (*tṛṣṇā*), not being an impersonal mental factor, cannot cause a being to be reborn. It is due to these reasons that the Pudgalavādins established the *pudgala*, of which the second designation or *pudgala*-designated-by-transmigration (*saṃkramaprajñaptapudgala* ?) is the corollary. Since *pudgala*-designated-by-transformation is classed in the same category as the *pudgala* (that is, it does not pertain to the eternal uncompounded, nor to impermanent compounded things), it is distinct from an eternal self (*ātman*) which is transmitted from life to life after death. Neither is it 'the subtle body which remains intact and establishes communication between two lives', as the Sankhyas maintain[623]. This ineffable (*avaktavya*), at the moment of death, is transformed into an intermediate being (*antarābhavika*) which appears immediately and which, at the same time, links the two consecutive lives. From the present existence it receives the intermediate existence, and from that intermediate existence (*antarābhava*) it receives the future existence. In other words, the *pudgala* never dies with the body, any more than do the consequences of actions (*karmavipāka*), as Th. Stcherbatsky wrote: 'This *pudgala* was also regarded as surviving, since it is maintained that it assumes new elements at birth and throws them off at death'[624].

Although the psycho-physical elements appear and disappear, the *pudgala*, because of its relationship with them, is not limited to one life but extends to other lives. It plays the part of an agent in rebirths and continues to wander from life to life. It is therefore possible to say that *pudgala*-designated-by-transmigration is a designation indicating the conscious of personified rebirth which appears in the mother's womb, in the case of a man with the conditions of actions (*karman*) comprised in the

---

620 SN IV, 400: *Yasmiñca kho Vaccha samaye imañ ca kāyaṃ nikkhipati satto ca aññataraṃ kāyaṃ anuppamano hoti, tam aham taṇhupādānam vadāmi, taṇhā hissa Vaccha tasmiṃ samaye upādānaṃ hotī ti.*

621 This term generally indicates the Buddhist schools or sub-schools which admit that the five aggregates 'transmigrate' (*saṃkramanti*) from this world to the other world.

622 Cf. Vism XVI, 90.

623 Cf. S. Radhakrishnan, *Indian Philosophy* II, London 1929, p.234.

624 Stcherbatsky, *The Central Conception of Buddhism*, p.71 and n.2.

preceding existence.

This doctrinal point in the Pudgalavādin works accords with what is expressed in the Saṃyuktāgama, T II, 99, 246-305*b*:

> 'It is thus that a person
> from this world arrives in another'[625].

As well as what is mentioned in the Samayabhedoparacanacakra by Vasumitra and its commentary by K'uei-chi:

'Phenomena (*dharma*), except for the *pudgala*, do not transmigrate (*saṃkranti*) from the previous life to the later life. Based on the *pudgala*, it could be said that there is transmigration' . . . 'That means that if phenomena do not transmigrate, it can be said that when the life faculty (*jīvitendriya*) has ceased, phenomena have also ceased. But, since the *pudgala* has not ceased, it can transmigrate from the former life to the later life. Phenomena not being separate from the *pudgala*, it can be said that there is transmigration'[626].

The explanations used by the Pudgalavādins to describe the autonomy and continuation of the *pudgala* are found in the canonical texts. Here are some examples:

— Description of the case of 'he who has no more than seven rebirths at the most' (*saptakṛdhbhavaparama*):

> 'After having abandoned the three fetters (*saṃyojana*)[627], he becomes one of those who will be reborn seven times at the most; it is only by wandering and transmigrating seven times, among mankind and heavenly beings, that he will put an end to suffering'[628].

or:

> 'This person, having transmigrated seven times at the most, becomes 'he who puts an end to suffering through the destruction of all the fetters'[629].

— Affirmation of the Buddha concerning the existence of a living being that wanders through the cycle of rebirth:

> 'The bones of a single person, monks, who continues to wander and transmigrate for an aeon would constitute a mountain, a heap, a pile, as high as Mount Vepulla, if there were a collector of those bones and the collection were not destroyed'[630].

---

625 SĀ, T II, 99, 246–305*b* (*Shou t'ien hua shêng ching* 受天化生經）：如是等士夫從此至他天

626 K'uei-chi, Iptllsc, 230*b*.

627 They are: i. belief in individuality (*satkāyadṛṣṭi*), ii. doubt (*vicikitsā*), iii. attachment to rules and rituals (*śīlavrataparāmarśa*). Çf. DN II, 107; AN I, 233; III, 87; Kośa V, 44; VI, p.117, n.3.

628 AN I, 233: *So tiṇṇaṃ saṃyojanānaṃ parikkhayā sattakkhattuparamo hoti sattakkhattuparamaṃ deve ca mānuse ca sandhāvitvā saṃsaritvā dukkhassa antaṃ karoti.*

629 Itivuttaka, § 24: *Sa sattakkhatuṃ paramaṃ sandhāvitvāna puggalo, dukkhassantakaro hoti sabbasaṃyojanakkhāyāti.*

630 SN II, 185: *Ekapuggalassa bhikkhave kappam sandhāvato saṃsarato siyā evam mahā aṭṭhikankalo aṭṭhipuñjo aṭṭhirāsi; yathāyam veppulo pabbato sace saṃharako assa sambhatañca na vinasseya.*

It is certain that the Buddha never taught that consciousness transmigrated as Sāti claimed. The Mahātaṇhākhayasutta (MN I, 258) tells how the monk Sāti maintained that, according to the teaching of the Buddha, it is consciousness itself that transmigrates, that wanders without losing its identity (*anañña*). The Buddha asked him to explain what he meant by 'consciousness'. The monk Sāti's answer is stereotyped:

'That consciousness wanders and transmigrates but is unchangeable' . . . 'It is that which expresses, feels, experiences the results of good and bad actions, here and there'.

The Buddha reproached him for his false opinion and explained:

'To whom, foolish man, have you heard me teach the Dhamma in such a fashion? Foolish man! Have I not, in many ways, explained consciousness as arising from conditions? There is no arising of consciousness without conditions'[631].

However, the Buddha clearly recognised a kind of consciousness, one of the six elements[632], as being the concrete seed of life, the principle of growth, the very condition of the development of a being:

> ' . . . Ānanda, action is the rice-field, consciousness the seed, and craving the moisture. Being hindered by ignorance and fettered by attachment, their consciousness takes up residence in the lower world[633]. Hence there will, in the future, be rebirth. And indeed, Ānanda, there is becoming[634].

Being changeable but continuous, consciousness is a means of rebirth, it provokes the formation of a new being after death and before conception, and it links two successive existences, as it is said:

'If consciousness, Ānanda, were not to descend into the mother's womb, would name-and-form (*nāmarūpa*) form in the mother's womb?'

— 'No, Lord'.

'If consciousness, Ānanda, after having descended into the mother's womb, were then to abandon its place, would name-and-form form this or that?'

— 'No, Lord'.

'And if consciousness, Ānanda, in a boy or girl while they are still small, again came to be lost, would name-and-form grow, develop, progress?'

— 'No, Lord'[635].

---

631 MN I, 258: . . . *idam viññāṇam sandhāvati saṃsarati, anaññan ti. . . . yvāyaṃ bhante vado vedeyyo tatra kalyānapāpakānam kammānam vipākam patisamvedetīti. . . . kassa nu kho nāma tvaṃ moghapurisa ·māya evaṃ dhammaṃ desitaṃ ājānāsi. nanu mayā mohapurisa anekapariyāyena paṭiccasamuppannaṃ viññāṇam vuttam aññatra paccayā natthi viññāṇassa sambhavo ti.*

632 The six elements are: i. earth element (*pṛthivīdhātu*), ii. water element (*abdhātu*), iii. fire element (*tejodhātu*), iv. wind element (*vāyudhātu*), v. space element (*ākāśadhātu*), and vi. consciousness element (*vijñānadhātu*). Cf. Kośa I, 27. The Dhātuvibhaṅgasutta (MN, No.140) givs a long explanation of the six elements. Cf. also the Chabbisodhanasutta (MN, No.112).

633 It is the same for the middle world (*majjhimāya dhātuyā*) and the higher world (*paṇitāya dhātuyā*).

634 AN I, 223–4: *Iti kho Ānanda kammaṃ khettaṃ viññāṇaṃ bījaṃ tanhā sineho avijjānīvaraṇānaṃ sattānaṃ taṇhāsamyojanānaṃ kī āya dhātuyā viññāṇaṃ patiṭṭhitaṃ. evaṃ āyatiṃ punbbhavābhinibbatti hoti. evaṃ kho Ānanda bhavo hotī ti.*

635 DN II, 63: *Viññāṇaṃ vā hi Ānanda mātu vokkamissatha, api nu kho nāmarūpaṃ mātu kucchismiṃ samucchissathāti? — No h'etaṃ bhante. — Viññāṇaṃ vā hi Ānanda mātu kucchim okkamitvā*

At the same time, consciousness is the conditioner of name-and-form. It is always an 'established consciousness', which means that it is established in name-and-form, and goes no further than name-and-form:

'If consciousness, Ānanda, were not established in name-and-form, in the future would birth, old age, death, suffering, the origin of suffering form?'

— 'No, Lord'.

'It is thus that, Ānanda, the cause, the circumstance, the origin, the condition of consciousness constitute name-and-form'[636].

Hence consciousness and name-and-form are interdependnent and form a vortex (consciousness) (name-and-form) for the conditions of existence:

'It is thus, Ānanda, that, conditioned by name-and-form, consciousness arises; conditioned by consciousness, name-and-form arises; conditioned by name-and-form, contact arises; conditioned by contact, feeling arises; conditioned by feeling, craving arises; conditioned by craving, attachment arises; conditioned by attachment becoming arises; conditioned by becoming, birth arises; conditioned by birth, old age and death arise; conditioned by old age and death, grief, lamentation, suffering, sorrow and despair arise. Such is the origin of this whole mass of suffering'[637].

It is interesting to note that this consciousness is considered, in the Sampasādanīyasutta of Dīgha Nikāya, as the uninterrupted 'stream of consciousness' (*viññāṇa-sota*) in successive lives[638]. In the Aṇañjasappāyasutta of Majjhima Nikāya, it is called 'evolved consciousness' (*saṃvattanikaviññāṇa*)[639].

This is a kind of consciousness, resulting from actions in the previous life, which appears at the moment of conception, that is, with the formation of a new life in the mother's womb. This consciousness, in fact, along with the other material elements, constitutes a new existence.

Furthermore, the Buddha demonstrated that the process of gestation or conception of an individual would be inconceivable without the presence of a third vital factor:

---

vokkamissatha, api nu kho nāmarūpaṃ itthattāya abhinibbattissathāti? — No h'etaṃ bhante. — Viññāṇaṃ vā hi Ānanda daharass'eva sato vocchijjissatha kumārassa vā kumārikāya vā, api nu kho nāmarūpaṃ vuddhiṃ virūḷhim vepullaṃ āpajjissathāti? — No h'etaṃ bhante.

636 *Ibid: . . . Viññāṇaṃ vā hi Ānanda nāmarūpe patiṭṭham nālabhissatha, api nu kho āyati jāti-jarā-maraṇa-dukkha-samudāya sambhavo paññāyethāti? — No h'etaṃ bhante — Tasmāt ih' Ānanda es'eva hetu etam nidānaṃ esa samudaya esa paccaya viññāṇassa, yadidaṃ nāmarūpaṃ.*

637 *Ibid*, 56: *Iti kho Ānanda nāmarūpa-paccayā viññāṇaṃ, viññāṇa-paccayā nāmarūpaṃ, nāmarūpa-paccayā phasso, phassa-paccayā vedanā, vedanā-paccayā taṇhā, taṇhā-paccayā upādānaṃ, upādāna-paccayā bhavo, bhava-paccayā jāti, jāti-paccayā jarā-maraṇaṃ, jarā-maraṇa-paccayā soka-parideva-dukkha-domanassupāyāsa sambhavanti. evam etassa kevalassa dukkhakkhandhassa samudayo hoti.*

On the interdependence of consciousness and name–and–form, cf. DN II, 62; SN II, 104–5.

638 DN III, 105: . . . it includes the stream of consciousness of a man who is established without interruption as much in this life as in the other (. . . *purisassa ca viññāṇa-sotaṃ pajānāti ubhayato abbochinnaṃ idha-loke patiṭṭhitañ ca para–loke patiṭṭhitaṁ ca*).

639 MN II, 262: After death, the dissolution of the body, this event occurs: the evolved consciousness, according to this condition, attains imperturbability (*Kāyassa bhedā paraṃ maraṇā thānaṃ etaṃ vijjati yaṃ taṃ saṃvattanikaṃ viññāṇaṃ assa āṇañjupagaṃ*).

the being-to-be-born (*gandharva*)[640]. 'This *gandharva*, the bearer of mentality, profits from the occasion of the union of a male and a female to incorporate itself in the embryo which results from that union. It is drawn by amorous desire to the male or female depending on whether it is itself female or male and it has a feeling of dislike for the other partner.'[641]. In other words, a foetus cannot be produced by the simple combination of spermatic and ovular cells. Unless the being-to--be-born survives and joins them, there is no formation of a being. As it is said:

Wherever, monks, the three elements are found together, a seed of life is planted. Thus, if the father and mother unite, but it is not the right time for the mother and the 'being-to-be-born' is absent, then no seed of life will be planted. Monks, if the father and mother unite, and it is the right time for the mother, but the 'being-to-be-born' is absent, then again no seed of life will be planted. But, if the father and mother unite, it is the right time for the mother and the 'being-to-be-born' is present, then, through the conjunction of those three elements, a seed of life will be planted'[642].

The Pudgalavādins' proposition on the relationship between the *pudgala* and the supports is also significant in the interpretation of the *pudgala*-designated-by-transmigration. Certainly, if the *pudgala* were identical to the supports, when the supports disappear at death, it would disappear; as the Sns explains: 'If the *pudgala* were identical to the aggregates, then when (the aggregates) disappear or appear, the *pudgala* would disappear or appear too' (Sns, 465*b* 10-11); if the *pudgala* is different from the supports, then the *pudgala* has no connection with life from which it is totally freed. If this were so, the problem of rebirth would make no sense. The Sns explains:

'. . . (if) the person were different from the aggregates, the person would not be reborn in the various destinies. If we consider rebirth in the various destinies, the person would be reborn in all the destinies at the same time. Hence it could not always reside in the body, and deliverance would then be difficult to achieve. If the person passed from destiny to destiny, it could not create action (*karman*). If there were no action or result, there would equally be no work, attachment, detachment and practice of meditation. That would indeed be deliverance!' (Sns, 465*c* 13-16).

Moreover, the Pudgalavādins, by maintaining that the *pudgala* is neither impermanent nor permanent, were free not to specify its nature; if the *pudgala* is neither impermanent nor permanent, the earlier existence is neither identical to nor different from the later existence. This doctrinal point accords with the words of the

---

640 Kośa III, 40*c*–41*a*: 'It is called ***gandharva*** because it eats odour'. Cf. Kośa III, 14*d*, 12*c*, and p.37, n.1. MN–A II, 310: the being that **penetrates** into the foetus (*tatrūpakasatta*). La Vallée Poussin explains *gandharva* as (tr.) 'a subtle being **that has** broken away from a human or animal body and is seeking to reincarnate' (*Nirvāṇa*, p.28, n.1.).

641 Tr. from *Inde classique* II, § 2287.

642 MN I, 265–6: *Tiṇṇaṃ kho pana bhikkhave sannipātā gabbassāvakkanti hoti: idha mātāpitaro ca sannipatītā honti, matā ca na utumī hoti, gandhabbo ca na paccupaṭṭhito hoti, n'eva tava gabbassāvakkanti hoti. idha mātāpitaro ca sannipatitā honti, mātā ca utumī hoti, gandhabbo ca na paccupaṭṭhito hoti, n'eva tāva gabbassāvakkanti hoti, yato ca kho bhikkhave mātāpitaro ca sannipatitā honti, mātā ca utumī hoti, gandhabbo ca pacupaṭṭhito hoti, evaṃ tiṇṇaṃ sannipātā gabbhassāvakkanti hoti.*

Buddha in this respect:

'He who has acted and he who undergoes the consequence are the same — that, brahmin, is an extreme' . . . 'He who acts and he who undergoes the consequences are not the same — that, brahmin, is another extreme. The Tathāgata, in not affirming either of those extremes, teaches you the doctrine of the middle'[643].

Further on, in order to simplify the aspects of the stream of life in the three times, the Pudgalavādins established three other categories under the designation of *pudgala*-designated-by-transmigration. These are the designation-of-the-past (*atītaprajñapti*), designation-of-the-future (*anāgataprajñapti*) and designation-of-the-present (*pratyutpannaprajñapti*).

It seems that the Pudgalavādins based these designations on the affirmation by the Buddha to Citta Hatthisāriputta, concerning the real empirical person in the past, present and future:

'I existed in the past, it is not (true) that I did not exist; I shall exist in the future, it is not (true) that I shall not exist; I exist in the present, it is not (true) that I do not exist'[644].

Existences in relation to the three times are only designations. They are similar to the designations of milk products: milk which is transformed into cream, yoghurt, curds and butter; when milk is transformed into one of those states, it cannot be called by any other name than the name which is appropriate to describe it. These designations can be used conventionally on condition that there is no attachment to them[645]. Furthermore, it is probable that the Pudgalavādins, in establishing the three designations, had the intention of appeasing worries engendered by the belief in a self and questions concerning existences in the three times, namely:

The designation-of-the-past (*atītaprajñapti*) is information concerning the existence of one or more previous lives. The best proof given by the Sns as well as the Tds in favour of this postulation are the words of the Buddha or holy ones who had acquired knowledge which permitted them to perceive past existences[646]. Whoever possesses that supernormal penetration (*abhijñā*) or higher knowledge (*vidyā*) can:

'. . . recall his manifold former existences, a particular birth, two, three, four, five births . . . or an hundred thousand such births; he recalls manifold formations and dissolutions of worlds: «I was there, I had such-and-such a name . . ., and, disappearing from there, I again reappeared here . . .». Thus, he recalls many former existences, always with their characteristic signs and particularities'[647].

---

643 SN II, 76: *So karoti so paṭisaṃvediyatīti kho brāhmaṇa ayaṃ eko anto . . .Añño karoti añño paṭisaṃvediyatīti kho brāhmaṇa ayaṃ dutiyo anto. ete te brahmāna ubho ante anupagamma majjhena tathāgato dhammaṃ deseti.*

644 DN I, 200: *Ahos' ahaṃ atītam addhānaṃ nāham nāhosiṃ, bhaviṣsam' ahaṃ anāgatam addhānam nāham na bhavissāmi, atthāhaṃ etarahi nāhaṃ n'atthīti.*

645 Cf. DN I, 201.

646 Cf. MN i, 8.

647 Cf. AN III, 18; MN I, 35.

In several discourses, the Buddha affirmed his former existences[648]. He also spoke of the former lives of others. It was at Nādika that the Buddha, having announced the rebirths of disciples in the higher worlds, taught Ānanda the mirror of the Dhamma (*dhammādāsa*) by means of which one can know one's future life[649]. Without the hypothesis of former existences, it is impossible to explain rebirth and the law of actions and their effects, particularly the accumulation of merit throughout successive lives.

The main point is that the Pudgalavādins speak of the *pudgala* but categorically refute the belief in an absolute origin of life (cf. Sns, 467*c* 15-469*a* 28). This means that the Pudgalavādins, like all Buddhists, never tackled the question of a Primal Cause of the cycle of rebirths. This is because, the incessant process of appearing and disappearing being considered in the complex sense of conditions relating one to the other — of the *pudgala* and its relationship with the aggregates, the aggregates themselves, the former aggregates and the later aggregates, etc. — a first cause is not necessary. In the logic of causality, no absolute beginning nor any single cause can be found.

The designation-of-the-future (*anāgataprajñapti*) is information concerning the existence of one or more former and later lives. This designation is based solely on the words of the Buddha and the holy ones:

'. . . All beings will become, will travel, after the relinquishment of the body . . .'[650].
and,

'The uneducated worldling creates and recreates his body'[651].
and,

'Even if his body is torn by crows, vultures, hawks, wolves, and gnawed by various insects, his mind (*citta*), having long and well practised trust (*saddhā*), morality (*sīla*), study (*suta*) and renunciation (*cāga*), rises up and attains excellence'[652].

According to the canonical texts, whoever obtains the divine eye (*divyacakṣus*) can perceive what will happen to beings in the cycle of existence:

'He who is pure, endowed with the divine eye (*dibbacakkhu*), sees beings disappearing and reappearing, the lowly and the noble, the lovely and the ugly, the happy and the wretched; he sees how beings reappear in accordance with their actions (*kamma*): «Those beings, in truth, have followed wrong ways in actions, words and thoughts, they have insulted nobles, held false views and they have acted in

---

648 In the previous lives of the Buddha, cf. Mahāsudassanasutta (MN, No.16); *The Jātaka or Stories of the Buddha's Former Births*, 6 vols, ed. P. Cowell, PTS, London 1969; *Choix de Jātaka*, tr. from the Pāli by Ginette Terral, 3rd ed., Paris 1958; A. Foucher, *Les vies antérieures du Bouddha*, Presses Universitaires de France, 1955.

649 Cf. DN II, 93–4; I, 82; AN I, 183.

650 Udāna, p.48: *ye keci bhūtā bhavissanti ye c'āpi sabbe gamissanti pahāya deham* . . .

651 SN III, 152: . . . *assutavā puthujjano rūpañneva. . . vedanañneva, saññaññeva, viññāṇaṃ yeva abhinibbattento abhininnatteti.*

652 SN V, 370: *tam (kāyo rūpi) idheva kāka vā khādanti gijjhā vā khādanti kulalā vā khādanti sunakhā vā khādanti sigālā vā khādanti vividhā vā pāṇakajātā khādanti. yañca khvassa cittaṃ dīgharattaṃ saddhāparibhāvitaṃ sīla-suta-cāga-paribhāvitaṃ taṃ uddhagāmi hoti visesagāmi.*

accordance with their false views. On the dissolution of their body after death, they will reappear in the lower destinies, in painful states of existence, in the world of suffering, in hell. Whereas the others endowed with good actions . . . will appear in a happy state of existence, in a heavenly world . . .»'[653].

The Buddha also predicted events which were to happen in the future lives of others. For example:

'The worldly (people), infatuated with their youth, health, life, follow a wrong course of actions, words and thoughts; because of that, on the dissolution of the body after death, they pass to a lower world, to a painful course of existence, to a state of suffering and to hell'[654].

With regard to the designation-of-the-present (*pratyutpannaprajñapti*), the Pudgalavādins illustrate this with the words of the Buddha affirming the existence of a man and his self nature. In practice, there is no divergence between Buddhists on the existence of a designated person. The difference is the doctrinal point accepted by the Pudgalavādins beyond the designated person. For man and his activities in the present are only, according to the Pudgalavādins, the manifestation of *pudgala*. As and when required, this designation is identical to the *pudgala*. Consequently, everything that is written under the heading of *pudgala*-designated-by-the-supports (*āśrayaprajñaptapudgala*) also implies the designation. It is probable that the establishment of these three designations in the Sns merely has the aim of clarifying the continuity of the *pudgala* in the three times. For that, simply the designation-of-the-past (*atītaprajñapti*) suffices in the Tds.

Furthermore, it should be noted that the establishment of the *pudgala*-designated-by-transmigration, with its three designations, is directed towards responsibility for actions (*karman*) since, if there were no *pudgala*, who would be the actor and enjoyer? If there were no-one to create meritorious and demeritorious actions and to enjoy their good and bad fruit, there would be no more good and bad (Sns, 465*a* 17-*b* 1); whereas the law of action (*karman*) incurring reaction (*vipāka*) is a basic doctrine aimed at establishing the ideal life for Buddhists.

This point of views conforms to the thesis attributed by the author of the Vijñānakāyapādaśāstra. According to this treatise, it is the *pudgala* which is the subject in the creation of actions and the reception of pleasant or unpleasant fruition[655].

On the doctrine of actions, the Buddha declared:

'Deeds are the assets of beings, deeds are their inheritance, deeds are the womb that bears them. Deeds are their kin, deeds are their resort'[656].

---

653 Cf. AN III, 19; MN I, 35.

654 Cf. AN I, 146.

655 Cf. Vijñānakāyapādaśāstra II, T XXVI, 1539b, or the translation by La Vallée Poussin, 'Notes Bouddhiques' (*Bulletin de la classe des Lettres et des Sciences morales et politiques de l'Académie Royale de Belgique*, 6 Nov. 1922, pp.515–26), pp.519–20.

656 MN III, 203: *Kammassakā, mānava, sattā kammadāyādā kammayoni kammabandhu kammapaṭisaraṇā*. Cf. AN III, 186; VI, 87–8.

The law of action and reaction is continually manifested in the process of the cycle of births throughout the three times:

'In truth, actions of a person are never lost; they return to him and their master rediscovers them.'

'The foolish man who does wrong knows the suffering by himself in the other world'[657].

or,

'He who sees in accordance with the Dhamma enjoys happiness
In this world and the future world'[658].

or,

'Monks, an action done through greed, born of greed, produced by greed, arising from greed, such an action will ripen when one's own existence appears and when the action is ripe; there will be a person who will experience the fruit of that action, either in the present life, or in the future life, or in some other life'[659].

It is with this meaning that the Sns declares that, without the *pudgala*, there is no responsibility for actions: 'The Buddha said:

'The *pudgala* exists as a designation (*prajñapti*). This is why that is opposed to (the opinion on) the non-existence of the person. If it is true that a person does not exist, then there is nothing-that-kills, nor anything-that-is-killed. It is the same for theft, illicit sensuality, falsehood and the absorption of intoxicants. This is (a lacuna in the opinion on) the non-existence of a person. If a person were not to exist, neither would there be the five major misdeeds; (if) the sense faculties were not to arouse good and bad actions, there would be no bonds; if there were nothing that detaches the bonds, there would be nothing that is attached; equally, there would be no actor, no action, no result (of action). If there were no action, there would be no result' (Sns, 465*a* 17-22).

Briefly, the establishment of the *pudgala*-designated-by-transmigration, for the Pudgalavādins, is necessary in order to explain:

1. The continuity of a person which is like a flux interrupted by psycho-physical phenomena, flowing not only in the present, but having its source in the past and ever continuing to flow in the future;

2. The responsibility for actions (*karman*), in order to answer the accusation according to which Buddhism is a nihilistic and immoral doctrine, since the existence of the *pudgala*, the bearer of a force which travels through the flux of existences, and which acts and gathers its fruition, responds to an ideal of justice in the universe and to the justification of good actions.

---

657 Cf. Dhp, 127, Sn, 666.

658 Dhp, 168–9: *Dhammacārī sukhaṃ seti / asmin loke paramhi ca //*

659 AN I, 134: *Yaṃ bhikkhave lobhapakataṃ kammaṃ lobhajaṃ lobhanidānaṃ lobhasamudāyaṃ yatth'assa attabhāvo nibbattati tattha taṃ kammaṃ vipaccati, yattha tam kammaṃ vipaccati tattha tassa kammassa vipākaṃ paṭisaṃvedeti diṭṭh'eva dhamme uppajje vā apare vā pariyāye.*

PUDGALA-DESIGNATED-BY-CESSATION (*nirodhaprajñaptapudgala*)

1. On this subject, the Sns explains:

'What does (*pudgala*)-designated-by-cessation (*nirodhaprajñaptapudgala*) mean? — After *pudgala*-designated-by-the-supports and *pudgala*-designated-by-transmigration, the Buddha speaks of *pudgala*-designated-by-cessation. When the body from the past is destroyed, that is what is called the designation of cessation. As the Buddha said:

The ceasing of the five impermanent aggregates of monks whose defilements (*āśrava*) are exhausted is called the designation of cessation (*nirodhaprajñapti*). (Furthermore,) as the Buddha said in this stanza:

«The sage cannot be measured
as he has attained unshakeable joy».

That is what is called (*pudgala*)-designated-by-cessation' (Sns, 466*c* 19-24).

2. The *Ssū* explains the same ideas clearly:

'What does the designation of cessation (*nirodhaprajñapti*) mean? — It is the designation of cessation in which appropriation is exhausted, and where one no longer appropriates anything' (Sūtra).

'Appropriation is as it has been explained above. That appropriation is exhausted; one no longer appropriates anything, one no longer takes hold of another (life). Individuality having ceased because nothing remains, one reaches the other shore. It is through the designation of cessation that the views of annihilation and eternity are remedied. Thus, it is certainly merely a synonym of the designation of Parinirvāṇa (?) which is equally ineffable (*avaktavya*). If (the ineffable) is different (from the body), there is no Parinirvāṇa. If it is not different, there is (equally) no Parinirvāṇa. If this, the ineffable, is understood in this way, it is inevitably understood that Parinirvāṇa is like a lamp that goes out . . . The designation of cessation (*nirodhaprajñapti*) means, in the first place, the cessation of appropriation (*upādāna*) (as when it is said): «The Blessed One (has attained) Parinirvāṇa»' (*Ssū*, 10*a* 19-28).

3. On the same subject, the Tds briefly explains:

'The designation of cessation (*nirodhaprajñapti*) is information concerning appropriation (*upādāna*) which has ceased, as when it is said that the Buddha (attains) Parinirvāṇa' (Tds, 24*b* 45).

The *pudgala*-designated-by-cessation of the Sns is no different from the designation of cessation (*nirodhaprajñapti*) of the *Ssū* and Tds, because all three designate the ceasing of the five aggregates, or the Parinirvāṇa of the Arhat or Tathāgata.

In order to grasp fully this designation, it is useful to recall the notion of Nirvāṇa, according to the Pudgalavādins' interpretation: Nirvāṇa is absolute truth (*paramārtha*) (Tds, 25*a* 5), unique (Tds 25*a* 12), consisting of two aspects: Nirvāṇa with a remainder (*sopadhiśeṣanirvāṇa*) and Nirvāṇa without a remainder (*nirupadhiśeṣanirvāṇa*).

With regard to Nirvāṇa and its two aspects, the Pudgalavādins wisely retained the oldest interpretation, since they admitted that Nirvāṇa was an ultimate and unique reality and did not divide it into several types as did other schools. This means that they held to the notion of Nirvāṇa as the uncompounded (*asaṃskṛta*), the transcendental reality in contrast to compounded things (*saṃskṛta*). Thus the Buddha said:

'What is the uncompounded thing? — The definitive exhaustion of craving, hatred and delusion, the definitive exhaustion of all the passion, such is the uncompounded thing' . . . 'What has been said is valid for the difficult to see, the unshakeable, the unbowed, the immortal, the pure, the refuge, the ford, the support, the protection, the omnipresent, the most pure, the subtle, the peaceful, the unafflicted, the not-come to existence, Nirvāṇa'[660].

As for the two aspects of Nirvāṇa, they constitute two stages of liberation: that which consists of the total destruction of impurities, that is, that of the Arhat or Tathāgata who, having obtained this, continues to live in the world with his old psycho-physical elements, and that which is acquired later, when those holy ones reach the end of their life with the definitive cessation of the elements of existence. This was explained by the Buddha as follows:

'There are, O monks, two elements of Nibbāna. Which are those two elements? The element of Nibbāna with a remainder of conditioning and the element of Nibbāna without a remainder of conditioning. What, O monks, is the element of Nibbāna with a remainder of conditioning? Here, O monks, the monk who becomes an Arahant, having destroyed his impurities, practised the ascetic life, accomplished his task, laid down his burden, attained the supreme goal, completely destroyed the fetters of existence, acquired right knowledge and so is delivered; five faculties remain to him and, due to the fact that they are not destroyed, he experiences the agreeable and the disagreeable, he feels pleasure and pain; that which is the exhaustion of craving in him, the exhaustion of his hatred, the exhaustion of his delusion, is called, O monks, the element of Nibbāna with a remainder of conditioning. What, O monks, is the element of Nibbāna without a remainder of conditioning? Here, O monks, the monk who becomes an Arahant . . . (as above) . . . is delivered; in him, O monks, here, all feelings which will not have been experienced with pleasure will cool; that is what is called, O monks, the element of Nibbāna without a remainder of conditioning. Such are, O monks, the two elements of Nibbāna'[661].

Hence, the Pudgalavādin doctrinal point on Nirvāṇa in relation to the characteristics, by comparing it with the ideas expressed in the preceding passage, is a special interpretation. Since, with regard to Nirvāṇa, the Pudgalavādins held the same view as on the position of the *pudgala* in relation to the supports; that is, the Pudgalavādins admitted that the *pudgala* and Nirvāṇa were not identical to the characteristics (*lakṣaṇa*) nor different from the characteristics. It is said in the Tds:

'With respect to the living being (*sattva* = *pudgala*) and Nirvāṇa, we have a doubt: do the living being and Nirvāṇa also possess those characteristics (*lakṣaṇa*)? If

---

660 SĀ, T II, 99, 224*a* (Sūtra No.890). Translation after A. Bareau in *Le Bouddha*, p.141.

661 Itivuttaka II, 7. Translation in part after A. Bareau in *Le Bouddha*, p.141. On the two kinds of Nirvāṇa, cf. also Itivuttaka, pp.38–9.

they possess them, there is a serious error, since they are impermanent (*anitya*). If that is not the case, then it must be admitted that this book contains faults (or then) it should be said that arising (*utpāda*), enduring (*sthiti*) and degeneration (*vyaya*) are characteristics of the compounded (*saṃskṛtalakṣaṇa*). It is impossible to say that the living being is other than the characteristics (since), if it were different from the characteristics, it would (in consequence) be eternal (*śāśvata*); if it were identical to the characteristics, it would be non-eternal (*aśāśvata*). Those two errors cannot be uttered. It is the same for Nirvāṇa. That is why it must be said that the characteristics (*lakṣaṇa*) are exclusively characteristics of the compounded (*saṃskṛtalakṣaṇa*)' (Tds, 19*b* 29-*c* 6).

This doctrinal point conforms to what was said in thesis No.6 in Bhavya's treatise on the schools:

'It should not be said that Extinction (*Nirvāṇa*) is truly identical to all things (*dharma*), nor that it is truly distinct'[662].

One might wonder whether there exists any connection between this thesis and the notion according to which the Tathāgata is not identical to the aggregates nor separate from them[663]. This question would be reasonable if the identification of the word Tathāgata with the word *sattva* (living being) by Buddhaghosa were understood as based on profound doctrinal reflection. In fact, if it were certain that the word Tathāgata has the same meaning as the word *sattva*, as Buddhaghosa indeed said, that would give a positive meaning to the pre-eminent person, that is, the Tathāgata, after the Parinirvāṇa which the Pudgalavādins designated by the expression '*pudgala*-designated-by-cessation' (*nirodhaprajñaptapudgala*)[664]. If one reasons with logic based on the doctrine of insubstantiality (*anātmavāda*), there is no person who attains Nirvāṇa or Parinirvāṇa:

'Nibbāna exists, but no-one attains it'[665]. Apart from the Pudgalavādins, nearly all the Buddhist schools or sub-schools are faithful to this doctrinal point. Furthermore, Parinirvāṇa or Nirvāṇa without a remainder (*nirupadhiśeṣanirvāṇa*) is defined as the total cessation of becoming: 'Cessation of becoming is Nibbāna'[666].

For the continuity of a being only appears when there is a vital process animated by thirst (*tṛṣṇā*). With the exinction of thirst, the process stops; equally, when the kernels are removed, empty seeds no longer germinate; when the oil and wick are exhausted, the flame goes out:

'The old arising is exhausted without a new one appearing.
The thought of becoming is destroyed, it is like empty seeds which no longer germinate.

---

662 Trans. after Bareau, *Sectes*, p.117.
663 See above, n. 592.
664 See above, nn. 593, 594, 595.
665 Vism XVI, 90 : *Atthi nibbuti, na nibbuto pumā.*
666 SN II, 117: *Bhavanirodho nibbānam ti.*

The wise who attain Nibbāna are like a lamp that goes out'[667].

or,

'To him who attains the liberation of the exhaustion of thirst, through the cessation of consciousness,

deliverance of mind is like the going out of a lamp'[668].

The Buddha refused all discussions on the nature of Nirvāṇa or Parinirvāṇa which, in reality, is a real although ineffable thing (*dharma*). In several texts, the Buddha demonstrated that Nirvāṇa or Parinirvāṇa as the supreme goal can be attained by practice according to the path but not intellectuallly by speculation. On being questioned by Rādha:

— 'But, Blessed One, to what does Nibbāna lead?'

The Buddha said:

— 'That question goes too far and oversteps the bounds of a question. The aim of the pure life, Rādha, is to plunge into Nibbāna, to attain Nibbāna, to end in Nibbāna'[669].

It is obvious that questions concerning the problem of what happens after the death of an Arhat or Tathāgata are always considered as questions to be rejected by the Buddha. These questions, in fact, spring from a false view in relation to the five aggıegates. It is incomprehension of the insubstantiality and impermanence of the supports of life which gives rise to a mistaken concept of the Tathāgata after death. In other words, the false view maintaining that a substantial and permanent self exists leads to other false views on the Tathāgata after death which are expressed in four ways:

> 'Friend, by not knowing, not seeing form (and the other four aggregates) as such, the origin, cessation and the path leading to the cessation of form as such, one provokes the questions: the Tathāgata exists after death, the Tathāgata does not exist after death, the Tathāgata both exists and does not exist after death, the Tathāgata neither exists not does not exist after death'[670].

Equally, it is incomprehension of the reality of the Tathāgata, who is neither identical to the five aggregates nor different from them, that gives rise to mistaken opinions on the Tathāgata after death. For example, the opinion maintaining that the Tathāgata is identical to the five aggregates probably gives rise to aberrations on the

---

667 Sn, 235: *Khīṇaṃ purānaṃ, navaṃ n'atthi sambhavaṃ, virattacittā āyatike bhavasmiṃ te khīṇabījā avirūḷhicchandā-, nibbanti dhīrā yathāyam padīpo . . .*

668 AN I, 236: *Viññāṇassa nirodhena taṇhakkhaya-vimuttino / pajjotass'eva nibbānaṃ vimokkho hoti cetaso ti //* Cf. DN II, 157.

669 SN III, 189: *Nibbānam pana bhante kimatthiyanti. assa Rādha pañhaṃ na sakkhi pañhassa pariyantaṃ gahetuṃ. nibbānogadham hi Rādha brahmacariyaṃ vussati nibbānaparāyanaṃ nibbānapariyosānan ti.* Cf. SN V, 217.

670 SN IV, 386: *Rūpaṃ kho āvuso ajānato apassato yathābhūtaṃ, rūpasamudāyaṃ ajānato apassato yatyhābhūtaṃ, rūpanirodhaṃ ajānato apassato yathābhūtaṃ, rūpanirodhagāmaniṃ paṭipadam ajānato apassato yathābhūtaṃ. hoti tathāgato paraṃ maraṇā ti pissa hoti. na hoti tathāgato paraṃ maraṇā ti pissa hoti. hoti ca na hoti tathāgato paraṃ maraṇā ti pissa hoti. neva hoti na na hoti tathāgato paraṃ maraṇā ti pissa hoti.*

Tathāgata after death. As it is said:

'Friend, the view that the Tathāgata exists after death (and the other three possibilities) is engendered by the view that the Tathāgata is identical to form (and the other four aggregates)'[671].

The passages of the preceding text enable us to understand why the Buddha attempted to dissuade his disciples from forming any precise idea on the Parinirvāṇa of an Arhat and the Tathāgata; in particular, he refused categorically to answer the following four, most characteristic questions:

'Does the Tathāgata exist after death? Not exist after death? Both exist and not exist after death? Neither exist nor not exist after death?'[672].

This is the Buddha's opinion of badly worded questions from the wandering ascetic Vacchagotta:

'. . . The Tathāgata exists after death' . . . 'The Tathāgata does not exist after death' . . . 'The Tathāgata both exists and does not exist after death' . . . 'The Tathāgata neither exists nor does not exist after death' . . . O Vaccha, this is a false view, a thicket of views, a jungle of views, a conflict of view, a battle of views, a bondage of views; it is linked to suffering, distress, torment, feverishness; it does not lead to disgust, detachment, cessation, appeasing, supernormal knowledge, complete enlightenment, Nibbāna. Such is, O Vaccha, the danger which I see and because of which I completely avoid those views'[673].

After having also rejected questions of the same nature but differently expressed, such as: 'Is he reborn?' 'Is he not reborn?' 'Is he both reborn and not reborn?' 'Is he neither reborn nor not reborn?', the Buddha, knowing that Vaccha, with his different philosophical and religious training, could not understand his teaching, illustrated the depth and subtlety of the total disappearance of all the existences of a liberated monk with this example: It is just as inexpressible as the extinction of a fire resulting from the exhaustion of fuel. The Buddha then specified what he had said by explaining it as follows: the cessation of the five aggregates of the Tathāgata and the ineffability of Parinirvāṇa.

' — Similarly, in truth, O Vaccha, the form by which the Tathāgata can be recognised, that form of the Tathāgata is abandoned, its roots severed, it is uprooted, deprived of existence [This obviously only means existence in this world of suffering, in the form of a man, god, animal, ghost or hell-bound being], subject to the law of non-arising in the future. He is freed from the denomination 'form', in truth, O Vaccha, the Tathāgata is deep, immense, unfathomable as the ocean, and it cannot be said: «he is reborn», or «he is not reborn», or «he is both reborn and not reborn», or «he is neither reborn nor not reborn». Feeling . . . Perception . . . Mental factors . . .

---

671 SN V, 385: *Hoti tathāgato paraṃ maraṇā ti kho āvuso rūpagataṃ etaṃ*. For the other three ways, the same expression is used in relation to the other four aggregates.

672 Cf. AN IV, 68.

673 MN I, 484–5. Trans. after A. Bareau, *Le Bouddha*, p.147.

Consciousness by which the Tathāgata can be recognised is abandoned, its roots are severed, it is uprooted, deprived of existence, subject to the law of non-arising in the future. He is freed from the denomination 'consciousness', in truth, O Vaccha, the Tathāgata is deep, immense, unfathomable as the ocean, and it cannot be said: «he is reborn», or «he is not reborn», or «he is both reborn and not reborn», or «he is neither reborn nor not reborn»'[674].

The Buddha's own words concerning the Tathāgata after death with respect to the four unexplained questions in the preceding dialogue enable us to specify that the Tathāgata after death is a pre-eminent person who is deep, immense and unfathomable as the ocean. In consequence, all the characteristics pertaining to compounded things, and attributed to the Buddha after death, are not in conformity with reality.

THE BEING OF THE BEYOND

It is certain that the scholars of the Pudgalavādin school were monks well versed in the teaching of the Buddha, particularly the doctrine of the insubstantiality of the self (*anātmavāda*). All the same, they were troubled by questions concerning the Tathāgata after death or Parinirvāṇa. Is there a person who attains Nirvāṇa without a remainder (*nirupadhiśeṣanirvāṇa*) after the total disappearance of the aggregates? After death, does the Tathāgata accede to eternity without happiness or does he enjoy the bliss of Parinirvāṇa?

In admitting the *pudgala*-designated-by-cessation, they tried to explain the continuity of the person, even after the Parinirvāṇa of an Arhat or the Tathāgata. In other words, the Pudgalavādins, by establishing the designation of cessation (*nirodhaprajñapti*), wished to denounce the wrong interpretation of the Buddha's teaching on the problem of what happens after the death of an Arhat or the Tathāgata. The heretical view of the annihilation of the liberated person who attains Nirvāṇa without a remainder existed in the community of monks even at the time of the Buddha. For example, Yamaka declared:

'As I understand the doctrine taught by the Blessed One, as a monk whose impurities are exhausted, on the dissolution of the body, he becomes annihilated, destroyed and no longer exists after death'[675].

According to the Pudgalavādins, the holy one who attains Parinirvāṇa is the pre-eminent person, having achieved the destruction of the fetters (*saṃyojana*) in his lifetime. However, the total disappearance of the impure aggregates does not imply the extinction of the life of a being or of the liberated person.

This interpretation of the Pudgalavādins is not entirely without basis since, if the

674 Cf. MN I, 488. Trans. after Bareau, *Le Bouddha*, pp.149–50.

675 SN III, 109: *Tathāham bhagavatā dhammaṃ desitaṃ ājānāmi: yathā khīṇāsavo bhikkhu kāyassa bhedā ucchijjati vinassati na hoti paraṃ maraṇā ti.*

Buddha certainly did not use the expression *pudgala*-designated by cessation which the Pudgalavādins attributed to him, he nonetheless used similar terms, such as: unmanifested consciousness (*anidassanaviññāṇa*)[676], unestablished consciousness (*appatiṭṭhaviññāṇa*)[677], mind come to the state of dissolution (*visankhāragataṃ cittaṃ*)[678], luminous mind (*pabhassaramidacitta*)[679], etc. It is possible to say that the Arhat or Tathāgata attains Nirvāṇa or Parinirvāṇa with his consciousness or mind freed from any connection with past supports:

'Monks, if the mind of a monk is not attached to the elements of form (feeling, perception, mental factors, consciousness) and is freed from impurities by the absence of supports then, as a consequence of freedom from impurities, he is immovable; as a consequence of immobility, he is satisfied; as a consequence of satisfaction, he is not perturbed; not being perturbed, he himself attains Nibbāna'[680].

The story of Godhika equally authorises us to draw the same conclusion, that is to say, the continuity of consciousness, the identity and responsibility of a person. Having been weakened by illness, Godhika was unable to remain in a state of meditation. In order not to fall into a wretched existence, this holy one decided to put an end to his life by cutting his throat. On achieving this suicide, he obtained the Arhat fruit, and Māra was unable to find Godhika's consciousness. He came in disguise to ask the Buddha where Godhika's consciousness had gone. The Buddha answered him that the place of birth of that consciousness could not be found since it had not established itself anywhere.[681].

Similarly, the story of Vakkali is another illustration of this idea. Suffering from an incurable illness, Vakkali killed himself. The Buddha, having seen Māra searching for Vakkali's consciousness, said: 'Monks, with an unestablished consciousness Vakkali, the son of good family, has attained Parinibbāna'[682].

Monks such as Godhika and Vakkali, who achieved deliverance, as well as the Tathāgata are among those who have attained transcendental liberation. Their old supports totally cease funtioning, but their consciousnesses become unestablished and ineffable. They leave the triple world and no longer pertain to any category of worldly beings. That is why they are undiscoverable by beings still imprisoned in the cycle of birth and death:

'Monks, when the mind of a monk is thus delivered, the gods — those with Indra, those with Brahma, those with Pajāpati — do not succeed in their search, if they think thus: «This is the support of the Tathāgata's consciousness». Why is that? Monks,

---

676 DN I, 223: *Viññāṇam anidassanaṃ anantaṃ sabbato pahaṃ . . .*

677 SN III, 119: *Appatiṭṭhena ca bhikkhave viññāṇena vakkali kulaputto parinibbuto ti.*

678 Dhp. 154: *Visankhāragataṃ cittaṃ tanhānaṃ khayam ajjhagā.*

679 AN I, 10: *Pabhassaram idaṃ bhikkhave cittaṃ tañ ca kho āgantukehi upakkilesehi upakkiliṭṭham ti / pabhassaraṃ idaṃ bhikkhave cittaṃ tañ ca kho āgantukehi upakkilesehi vippamuttan ti.*

680 SN III, 45: *Rūpadhātuyā (vedanā, saññā, sankhārā, viññāṇa-dhātuyā) ce bhikkhave bhikkhuno cittaṃ virataṃ vimuttaṃ hoti anupādāya āsavehi vimuttatā ṭhitam, ṭhitattā santussitaṃ, santussitattā na paritassati, aparitassaṃ paccattaññeva parinibbāyati.*

681 Cf. SN I, 120.

682 SN III, 124: *Apatiṭṭhena ca bhikkhave viññāṇena vakkali kulaputo parinibbuto ti.*

I declare that the Tathāgata, even at present, is undiscoverable'[683]. They are undiscoverable and ineffable because no criterion exists which can measure them and no word exists which can make them known:

'For him who has attained the goal, there is no measure.
Of words with which one might speak
Of him, there are none either.
When all things are removed,
Removed also are all means of expression'[684].

In fact, the Arhat and the Tathāgata, in life and after death, are undiscoverable only by worldlings.

However, among themselves they can always recognise each other, since they still possess their minds (*citta*) as personal identity. For example, Mahāmoggallāna, accompanied by five hundred Arhats, could perceive that they were true Arhats; as it is said:

'Venerable Mahāmoggallāna then noted intuitively that their minds were delivered, unconditioned by rebirth'[685].

Moreover, the Buddha, on proclaiming that he was not a nihilist (*venayika*), declared that his teaching was aimed at eliminating suffering but not the existence of a being. In this sense, he presented a significant simile:

— 'In this Jeta grove, if a man were to take away grasses, twigs, branches and leaves and burn them or deal with them in some other way, do you then think: It is us that that man carries away, or burns, or deals with in some other way?

— No, Lord. Why? Because that, Lord, is not our self or what pertains to our self.

— Equally, monks, you renounce what does not belong to you. That renunciation leads you to prolonged welfare and happiness'[686].

The extracts from the canonical collections which follow also illustrate the significance of the preceding simile:

'I (the Buddha) become cool and attain Nibbāna'[687].

'He who attains Nibbāna is as cool as water in the lake'[688].

---

683 MN I, 140: *Evaṃ vimuttacittaṃ kho bhikkhave bhikkhum sa — Indā devā sa-Brahmakā sa-Pajāpatikā avesam nādhigacchanti; idaṃ nissitaṃ tathāgatassa viññāṇan-ti, tan kissa hetu? diṭṭhe vāhaṃ bhikkhave dhamme tathāgataṃ ananuvejjo to vadāmi.* Cf. SN III, 118; IV, 384.

684 Sn, 1076: *Atthaṅ gatassa na pamāṇam atthi, upasīva ti bhagavā yena naṃ vajju, taṃ tassa n'atthi, sabbesu dhammesu samūhatesu samūhatā vādapathā pi sabbe ti.*

685 SN I, 194: *Tesaṃ sudaṃ āyasmā Mahāmoggallāna cetasā cittaṃ samannesati vippamuttaṃ nirupadhiṃ.*

686 MN I, 141: . . . *Yaṃ imasmin jetavane tiṇakaṭṭha-sākhā-palāsaṃ taṃ jano hareyya vā ḍaheyya vā yathāpaccayaṃ vā kareyya; api nu tumhākaṃ evam-assa: amhe jano harati vā dahati vā yathāpaccayam vā karoti — no h 'etam bhante, tam kissa hetu: na hi no tam bhante attā vā attaniyaṃ vā ti. — evam-eva kho bhikkhave yaṃ na tumhākaṃ taṃ pajahatha, taṃ vo pahīnam dīgharattaṃ hitāya sukhāya bhavissati.*

687 MN I, 171: . . . *Sītibhūto 'smi nibbuto.*

688 Sn, 467: *Parinibbuto udakarahado va sīto.*

'The holy one, having crossed (the stream), reaches the other shore and stands on firm ground'[689].

'Having crossed, he does not retrace his steps'[690].

'He does not reach the other shore twice'[691].

'Bliss, friend, is Nibbāna, bliss, friend, is Nibbāna. How can there be bliss, friend Sāriputta, where there is no feeling? — That there is no feeling, friend, is precisely bliss'[692].

It is in this way that the Buddha did not categorically reject the 'existence' of a liberated person who, having elminated suffering and its origin, enjoys the bliss of Nirvāṇa or Parinirvāṇa.

Furthermore, in several discourses the Buddha affirmed that the Tathāgata was a superior person, an excellent being, he who obtains the supreme fruit. During his lifetime, he transcends what is in the world, and consequently he cannot be known by the forms of existence. After death, he is beyond all categories of beings and has no equal, consequently the four means of common expression cannot be applied to him[693].

Thus, the Tathāgata, whether during his lifetime or after his death, is a person freed from the world. He has left the cycle of birth and death. That is why the dissolution of the psycho-physical process and the remainder of old actions do not affect the Tathāgata whose knowledge is perfect and whose bliss is constant:

'The destruction of the body is considered as happiness by the holy ones,
In contrast to how it is seen by all the world'[694].

With regard to this subject, A. Bareau wrote: 'Only the Pudgalavādin schools could claim that the person, because it is not truly identical to the elements that compose it, subsists in Nirvāṇa. Also, the state in which it dwelt would, after the definitive cessation of all its mental and biological functions, seem like deep and dreamless sleep, complete unconsciousness'[695].

Going even further, Th. Stcherbatsky affirmed that the invention of the *pudgala* has the most positive significance from the point of view of the Absolute. This is what he said on the existence of an Arhat or Tathāgata after Parinirvāṇa:

'It is also clear that the Vatsīputriyas (*Vajjiputtakas*) established their *pudgala-vāda* with no other aim than that of supporting the doctrine of a supernatural, surviving Buddha from the philosophical side'[696], and :

---

689 SN IV, 175: . . . *tiṇṇo pāraṃgato thale tiṭṭhati brahmaṇo.*

690 Sn, 803: . . . *pāraṃgato na pacceti tādi.*

691 Sn, 714: . . . *na pāraṃ digunam yanti.*

692 . . . *sukhaṃ idaṃ āvuso nibbānaṃ, sukhaṃ idaṃ āvuso nibbānan ti . . . kiṃ pan 'ettha āvuso Sāriputta sukhaṃ, yad ettha natthi vedayitan ti? — etad eva khv' ettha āvuso sukhaṃ, yad ettha natthi vedayitaṃ.*

693 Cf. SN III, 116–19; IV, 380–4, and above, n. 671.

694 Sn, 761: *Sukhan' ti diṭṭham ariyahi sakkāyass' uparodhanaṃ / paccanīkaṃ idaṃ hoti sabbalokena passataṃ.*

695 Tr. from A. Bareau, 'La notion de la personne dans le bouddhisme indien', *op. cit.*, p.94.

696 Th. Stcherbatsky, *The Conception of Buddhist Nirvāṇa*, p.31, n. 1.

'The *pudgala* of a Buddha seems to be an Omniscient Eternal Spirit'[697].

To summarise, the preceding interpretation, in fact, is not in conformity with Buddhist orthodoxy, but it has a meaning for the Pudgalavādins who had admitted the *pudgala*-designated-by-cessation in order to denounce a nihilistic view of the liberated person after Parinirvāṇa.

EXISTENCE IN THE BEYOND

If the pre-eminent person enjoys the bliss of Nirvāṇa, Nirvāṇa is certainly the abode of supreme bliss[698]. Under its two aspects — Nirvāṇa with a remainder and Nirvāṇa without a remainder — Nirvāṇa constitutes the sole uncompounded (*asaṃskṛta*) domain, beyond all contingency and without any connection to anything whatever other than itself. In consequence, the speech and thought of a man pertaining to the compounded domain cannot speak or have any idea of it.

From the philosophical and mental point of view, the Buddha and his disciples often defined Nirvāṇa in negative terms. For example, Nirvāṇa means the destruction of thirst[699], of bad roots[700], the cessation of suffering[701], the end of birth and death[702] etc.

This is easy to understand, since any positive definition of Nirvāṇa can lead to philosophical speculation and sensory attachment. That does not mean that the Buddha never spoke of Nirvāṇa in its positive aspects. He declared that a domain exists in the beyond, far from this terrestrial world full of suffering:

'There where there is nothing, where no attachment subsists, the island, the only; it is that which I call Nibbāna, the end of old age and death'[703]

or,

'There is, monks, a domain where there is no earth, or water, or fire, or air, or infinity of space, or infinity of perception, or non-perception. It is not of this world, or of the other world, neither of one nor the other, not of the sun, or of the moon. That state, monks, I call neither coming nor going, neither appearing nor disappearing. It has no origin, no evolution, no stopping: this, in truth, is the end of suffering'.

'Difficult to see is the infinite, difficult to see is the truth. Attachment is severed by him who knows. For him who sees, nothing remains.

---

697 Th. Stcherbatsky, *The Central Conception of Buddhism*, p.58.

698 Dhp, 203: . . . *nibbānaṃ paramaṃ sukhaṃ*.

699 SN III, 190: *Taṇhakkhayo hi Rādha nibbānan ti*; SN I, 39: . . . *taṇhāya vippahānena, nibbānaṃ iti vuccati*.

700 SN IV, 251: *Yo kho āvuso rāgakkhayo dosakkhayo mohakkhato idaṃ vuccati nibbānaṃ*. Cf. AN V, 332; Sn, 1093–4.

701 Udāna, 80: . . . *es' ev' anto dukkhassā 'ti*.

702 Sn, 467: He who abandons pleasures, as the vanquisher enjoys the end of birth and of death (*Yo kāme hitvā abhibhuyyacarı / yo vedi jātimaraṇassa antaṃ*).

703 Sn, 1094: *Akiñcanaṃ anādānaṃ etaṃ dīpaṃ anāparaṃ / nibbānaṃ iti naṃ brūmi, jarāmaccu-parikkhayaṃ*.

'There is, monks, an unborn, unarisen, uncreated, unformed. If, monks, an unborn, unarisen, uncreated, unformed, were not to exist, there would be no deliverance for what is born, arisen, created, formed. But, monks, since there is an unborn, unarisen, uncreated, unformed, so what is born, arisen, created, formed, can be liberated'[704].

Noteworthy is the affirmitive expression 'there is' through which Nirvāṇa cannot be conceived as pure extinction, nor as camouflaging an absolute zero. In another discourse, the Buddha compared Nirvāṇa to a gain or an asset which the wise man should win through a vigorous fight. Therefore, Nirvāṇa is described not only as a negative state but also a a positive recompense of the efforts of a person on the Path:

'Penetrating in meditation,
being valiant in perseverance,
the wise attain
supreme security'[705].

In the Saṃyutta Nikāya IV, 368-72, there is a description of the nature of Nirvāṇa by various synonyms. The following synonyms are the most significant in the positive meaning of Nirvāṇa: purity, peace, happiness, security, kindness, excellence, freedom, well-being, etc.[706].

Despite everything, we should consider that the 'existence of Nirvāṇa' is outside two notions: existence and non-existence of the world. That is why Nirvāṇa is invisible to people who do not have the noble eye[707]. Conversely, Nirvāṇa is only perceived by the clear-sighted[708], and comprehensible to the wise[709]. Thus, Nirvāṇa is a transcendental domain[710], the island where there is no other existence[711]. In other words, Nirvāṇa is existence in the beyond.

It is probable that it is with the same meaning that the Pudgalavādins wished to demonstrate that the *pudgala*-designated-by-cessation was the pre-eminent person who, having reached the end of his last existence, attains Nirvāṇa without a remainder or Parinirvāṇa and abides there in bliss.

Obviously, what is admitted by the Pudgalavādins with regard to the problem of

---

704 Udāna, 80. Cf. also Itivuttaka II, 6, and the translation by A. Bareau in *Le Bouddha*, pp.139–40.

705 Dhp, 23: *Te jhāyino sātatikā niccam dalhaparakkamā / phusanti dhīrā nibbānaṃ, yogakkhemaṃ anuttaraṃ.*

706 SN IV, 370–2: *suddhi, santaṃ, sivam, khemaṃ, avyāpajjho, vimutti*; MN I, 511: *Idan taṃ ārogyaṃ, idan nibbānan ti.* Cf. SN I, 421; MN I, 49, 299; III, 251; Vin. I, 10.

707 MN I, 510: Equally, Māgandiya, the monks of other religions being blind, having no eye, not knowing well-being, do not see Nibbāna . . . (*Evam-eva kho Māgandiya aññatitthiyā paribbājakā andhā acakkhukā, ajānantā ārogyaṃ apassantā nibbānaṃ* . . .). MN II, 202: the same expression, *andho acakkhuko*, addressed to Pokkharasāti.

708 Itivuttaka, p.38: These two kinds of (Nibbāna) are declared by the Clear-sighted One. . . (*Duve ime cakkhumatā pakāsita, nibbānadhātu* . . .).

709 AN I, 159: Thus, brahmin, Nibbāna is visible in this life, immediate, engaging, attractive and comprehensible to the wise man (*Evaṃ kho brāhmaṇa sandiṭṭhikam nibbānam hoti akālikaṃ ehipassikaṃ opanayikaṃ paccattaṃ veditabbaṃ viññūhī ti*).

710 Cf. Udāna, p.80.

711 Sn, 1092: . . . *me dīpam akkhāhi, yathā-y-idam nāparaṃ siyā.*

existence after the death of an Arhat or Tathāgata, despite the designation (*prajñapti*), constitutes a new and remarkable doctrinal notion with regard to the unexplained domain in the teaching of the Buddha.

In connection with the establishment of the three designations, the Tds, 24*a* 29-*b* 8, explains that the threee designations have the aim of remedying false views:

The first designation is twofold: the designation of the underlying conditioning (*upādānaprajñapti*) and the designation of the absence of underlying conditioning (*anupādānaprajñapti*). The former remedies nihilism (*nāstidṛṣṭi*), which maintains that 'nothing exists', since, if the existence of a person is understood in relation to the underlying conditioning, nihilism is not admitted. The latter remedies realism (*astidṛṣṭi*) which claims that 'everything exists', since, if it is understood that nothing exists, that there is no underlying conditioning, realism is not admitted.

The second designation is the designation of the past (*atītaprajñapti*). This remedies annihilation (after death) (*ucchedadṛṣṭi*) which denies rebirth and the ripening of actions, since, if it is understood that former lives exist, it is also believed that later lives exist. Therefore the doctrine of rebirth is admitted.

The third designation is the designation of cessation (*nirodhaprajñapti*). It remedies eternalism (*śāśvatadṛṣṭi*) which considers that nothing has changed after death, since, if it is understood that a pre-eminent person exists after Parinirvāṇa, there is no attachment to eternalism.

On the other hand, according to the Sns, the Sāṃmitīyas consolidated the thesis of the *pudgala* with vigorous arguments relating to all the important doctrinal ideas of Buddhism, with strong refutations and even unreserved condemnations with regard to people who denied the theory of the *pudgala*, as this text testifies:

'The Buddha said: 'The *pudgala* exists as a designation (*prajñapti*). This is why that is opposed to (the opinion on) the existence of the person. If it is true that a person does not exist, then there is nothing-that-kills, nor anything-that-is-killed. It is the same for theft, illicit sensuality, falsehood and the absorption of intoxicants. This is (a lacuna in the opinion on) the non-existence of a person.

'If the person were not to exist, neither would the five major misdeeds; (if) the sense faculties were not to arouse good and bad actions, there would be no bonds, there would be nothing that is attached; equally, there would be no actor, or action, or result (of action). If there were no action, there would be no result. (If) there were no action or result, there would be no birth or death. However, living beings, because of actions and their results, transmigrate in the cycle of birth and death (*saṃsāra*). If there were no birth or death, there would be no cause (*hetu*) of birth and death. If there were no cause, there would be no cessation of the cause. If there were no cessation of the cause, there would be no directing towards the Path (*mārga*). Hence, there would be no four Noble Truths (*āryasatya*). If there were no four Noble Truths, there would be no Buddha teaching the four Noble Truths. If there were no Buddha teaching the four Noble Truths, there would be no Community (*saṃgha*) of monks. Thus the refutation of the *pudgala* incurs the refutation of the Three Jewels (*triratna*) and four Noble Truths. Such is the refutation of all those opinions. That is why the refutation of the *pudgala* gives rise to the errors mentioned above, and other errors would also occur.

'If it is admitted that a person (*pudgala*), a self, exists, the above-mentioned errors would not occur. As the Buddha said in the Sūtra, it is necessary to know exactly. That is why the person truly exists' (Sns, 465*a* 17-*b* 1).

In conclusion the *pudgala*, according to the Pudgalavādins, is a designation (*prajñapti*) but not an absolute reality. Its nature is totally different, on the one hand, from the concept of a metaphysical self (*ātman*) in the brahmanical philosophical system, and on the other, from the concept of a conventional self according to the majority of Buddhist schools.

It is thus that the *pudgala*, with its three designations, is an effable (*avaktavya*) which, through its unlimited perpetuity, constitutes the agent of knowledge, memory, the processes of rebirth, the ripening of actions (*karman*) and which, after having passed through the multiplicity of different lives, plunges into bliss.

In other words, by establishing the *pudgala*, the Pudgalavādins wished to make known the real existence of a being and, at the same time, respond to fundamental problems, namely, knowledge, memory, rebirth, the fruition of actions and liberation.

The diagram given below summmarises the preceding ideas[712].

P u d g a l a	the life of a being	a man + intermediate existence + a heavenly being	a holy one in Nirvāṇa or Parinirvāṇa
	knowledge and memory	+++++++++++++++++++++++++++++++++++	omniscience of the Buddha
	actions and results	+++++++++++++++++++++++++++++++++++	the bliss of Nirvāṇa or Parinirvāṇa

*

* *

712 See also E. Conze, *Buddhist Thought in India*, p.125.

II — *The secondary theses of the Pudgalavādins*

Alongside the main thesis are also found fifteen secondary theses in the four works[713] These theses, which are connected with the Pudgalavādins, are as follows:

> 1 — Existence of an imperishable thing (*avipraṇāśadharma*) which plays an important rôle in the process of action and fruition.

This thesis, established a little later by the Sāṃmitīyas, completes that of the *pudgala*, in the sense of transmigration which links two successive existences. Since rebirth, according to Buddhism, means the continuity of existences as well as the fruition of actions (*karmavipāka*). Although good or bad actions perish as soon as they arise,

---

713 Account is taken here only of secondary theses found in the extant Pudgalavādin works. For the complete lists of the theses of the Pudgalavādin school, cf. A. Bareau, *Sectes*, pp.114–30; Kathāvatthu (*Points of Controversy*), p.XVIII.

The Samayabhedoparacanacakra of Vasumitra gives us a summary of the theses of the Vātsīputrīya school and the stanza, different interpretations of which created schisms in the school. This is a translation from the Samayabhedocanacakra, T XLIX, 2031, 16c 14–16: 'The general idea of the main doctrine upheld by the school of the Vātsīputrīyas: the *pudgala* is neither identical (*sama*) to the aggregates (*skandha*) nor different (*sisama*) from them. Based on the aggregates, elements (*dhātu*) and domains (*āyatana*), this name is a designation (*prajñapti*)'.

(Among) compounded things (*saṃskṛta*), some endure for a while, others disappear instantaneously (*kṣaṇika*).

If things (dharma) are different from the *pudgala*, they cannot transmigrate (*saṃkrānti*) from this world to a future world. It is possible to speak of transmigration by basing oneself on the *pudgala*.

Even heretics (*tīrthika*) can acquire the five superknowledges (*abhijñā*).

The five kinds of consciousness (*vijñāna*) are neither supplied with passions (*sarāga*) nor without passions (*virāga*).

The abandoning of the fetters (*saṃyojana*) of the world of desire (*kāmadhātu*) which should be abandoned through cultivation (*bhāvanāprahātavya*) is what is called dispassion (*virāga*). This is not the abandoning (of the fetters) which should be abandoned through vision (*darśanaprahātavya*).

Patience (*kṣānti*), the name (*nāma*), the characteristic (*lakṣaṇa*) and the supreme worldly dharma (*laukikāgradharma*) are called the entry into the predestination to the Good (*chêng-hsing-li-shêng* 正性離生 . *samyaktvaniyāma* ?).

If one has already acquired entry into the predestination to the Good, at the moment of twelve thoughts, one is called 'orientated' (*pratipannaka*). At the thirteenth thought, one is called 'dweller in the fruit' (*phalāvastha*).

Thus there are different notions. Due to differing opinions in the interpretation of a stanza, this school is divided into four sub-schools:

1) the Dharmottarīya sub-school,
2) the Bhadrayānīya sub-school,
3) the Sāṃmitīya sub-school, and
4) the Ṣaṇṇāgārika sub-school.

the stanza in question being:

Being delivered, one falls back again,
Falling back comes from covetousness, where one can return,
The acquisition of security and joy is happiness.
Pursuing the practices of happiness, one reaches happiness.

their impressions or seeds should be deposited and accumulated in an imperishable thing, dissociated from the mind, neutral from the moral point of view, and affecting all living beings including the holy ones. This imperishable thing, continuing to exist through the flux of existences, is the essential basis for the mechanism of the fruition of actions. This point of view is described in several propositions in the Sns:

'What is acting in oneself? It is 'the reception (of the fruits of action)'. What is the action (*karman*) of oneself? It is the differentiation of one's own action and those of others. Why? Because the results of the action do not go to another. This is the accumulation (*Shêng* 生, *upacaya*) (of the fruit of action). What? It is the means. It is the domain of compounded things (*hsing* 行, *saṃskṛta*). Why? Because they are conditioned by others. It is an imperishable thing (*pu-mie* 不滅, *avipraṇāśadharma*). Why? It is receptivity. That thing is a manifestation: actions (*karman*) accomplished in this life are not perishable' (Sns, 462*a* 13-16).

This doctrinal point is clearly expressed in Bareau, *Sectes*: [tr.] 'There is an imperishable (*avipraṇāśa*) thing which is dissociated from the mind (*cittaviprayukta*)'[714]. According to Bareau, this thing is identical to that which is defined by Candrakīrti: 'When action arises, there also arises in the series a thing dissociated from the mind, undefined (*avyākṛta*), destroyed by cultivation (*bhāvanā*), which is called imperishable, which yields the fruit of action'[715].

In fact, we can further grasp the meaning of this imperishable thing from the definition by Vasubandhu:

'It should be admitted that the two actions of body and speech, good or bad, deposit in the psycho-physical series (*skandhasaṃtāna*) a separate dharma, existing in itself (*dravyasat*) and classed among things dissociated from the mind (*cittavipraykutasaṃskāra*). For some, this dharma is called accumulation (*upacaya*); for others, 'without perishing' (*avipraṇāśa*). By reason of this dharma, one realises (*abhinirvṛt*) the future agreeable or disagreeable fruit. As for mental action (*manaḥkarman*) also, the existence of this dharma should be admitted. Otherwise (*anyatra*), when a thought arises and mental action disappears (*nivṛtta*), if this particular dharma had not been deposited in the mental series (*cittasaṃtāna*), how would one realise the future fruit? Therefore, the existence of such a dharma must necessarily (*niyataṃ*) be admitted'[716].

2 — There are twelve knowledges in the path of vision (*darśanamārga*)

This thesis is set out in the Tds as follows:

'It is necessary to have an extensive understanding of twelve knowledges in the

714 A. Bareau, *Sectes*, p.126.

715 *Ibid.*; cf. Kośa IX, p.295, n.4.

716 Vasubandhu, *Le Traité de l'acte* (Karmasiddhiprakaraṇa), trans. É. Lamotte, p.123 [Pruden trans, p.55]. Cf. Lamotte, *History*, p.609 and n. 133.

path of vision (*darśanamārga*)' (Tds, 19*b* 26-27).

According to that treatise, from the status of a worlding (*pṛthagjana*) to that of an Arhat, the practitioner must traverse three stages:

a) the stage of vision (*darśanabhūmi*);
b) the stage of cultivation (*bhāvanābhūmi*); and
c) the stage of him who has no more to train in (*aśaikṣabhūmi*).

It is at the stage of vision that the practitioner begins to see what was not seen before, that is, he acquires twelve knowledges concerning the four Truths in relation to the three worlds. Hence, the Tds writes:

'The stage of vision (*darśanabhūmi*) consists of the knowledge of things (*dharmajñāna*), the knowledge of deliberation (*vicārajñāna ?*) and the knowledge of what-is-not-yet-known (*ajñātajñāna ?*). These three knowledges constitute the knowledges of the stage of vision (*darśanabhūmi*). Among those three, the knowledge of things has the meaning of direct comprehension of the truth (*abhisamaya*). For example, a good surgeon who, having seen an abscess, (decides to) open it with a cutting lancet. Then he presses it with his fingers in order to empty (the humour) without harming the vessels. It is only after that that he really opens the abscess. It is the same for the practitioner who, with correct reflection (*yoniśomanaskāra*), by examining suffering (*duḥkha*) in relation to the world of desire (*kāmadhātu*), eliminates (the category of) passions to be destroyed by the vision of suffering (*duḥkhadṛgheyakleśa*); it is after that that the second knowledges arises. Since the world of desire is subject to suffering and impermanence (*anityatā*), it is the same for the world of form (*rūpadhātu*) and the formless world (*ārūpyadhātu*): through that knowledge, the passions (*kleśa*) of the world of form and the formless world are abandoned. That is what is called the three knowledges relating to suffering (*duḥkhajñāna*). 'Understanding thirst (*tṛṣṇā*) to be the cause of suffering (*duḥkhasamudaya*) is the knowledge of things; it is also the knowledge of deliberation. It is the same for the knowledge of what-is-not-yet-known of the world of form and the formless world. These are what are known as the three knowledges relating to the path (*mārgajñāna*)' (Tds, 19*b* 14-27).

This doctrinal point is wholly identical to that which is mentioned in the Samayabhedoparacanacakra of Vasumitra: 'Having entered the predestination to the Good (*samyaktvaniyāma*) and in the moment of the twelve thoughts, one is called 'orientated' (*pratipannaka*). At the thirteenth thought, one is called 'dwelling in the fruit' (*phalastha*)'[717].

The Pudgalavādins discovered this experience of meditation and they also indicated for themselves the results obtained. According to the Pudgalavādins, when the practitioner enters the truth of suffering relating to the world of desire, he acquires the first knowledge which is called the knowledge of things (*dharmajñāna*). The perfection of clear comprehension of each Truth requires very profound de-

717 Cf. Samayabhed., T XLIX, 2031, 16*c* 21–22.

liberation, the result of which is called the knowledge of deliberation (*vicārajñāna* ?). After having attained those two knowledges, the practitioner acquires the third knowledge of the Truth of suffering in relation to the two other worlds, namely, the world of form and the formless world. This knowledge is called knowledge of what-is-not-yet-known (*ajñātajñāna* ?). The same process is applied to the other three Truths. Thus, in total, there are twelve knowledges. The diagram below can summarise the preceding passage.

I. *Duḥkhe*	1. *Dharmajñāna* 2. *Vicārajñāna* ?	*Kāmadhātu*
	3. *Ajñātajñāna* ?	*Rūpadhātu* and *Arūpyadhātu*
II. *Samudaye*	1. *Dharmajñāna* 2. *Vicārajñāna* ?	*Kāmadhātu*
	3. *Ajñātajñāna* ?	*Rūpadhātu* and *Arūpyadhātu*
III. *Nirodhe*	1. *Dharmajñāna* 2. *Vicārajñāna* ?	*Kāmadhātu*
	3. *Ajñātajñāna* ?	*Rūpadhātu* and *Arūpyadhātu*
IV. *Mārge*	1. *Dharmajñāna* 2. *Vicārajñāna* ?	*Kāmadhātu*
	3. *Ajñātajñāna* ?	*Rūpadhātu* and *Arūpyadhātu*

According to the opinion of the Vātsīputrīyas, meditation should be practised twice in reference to the world of desire. The first time, correct reflection (*yoniśomanaskāra*) examines suffering. The second time, there takes place the elimination of the passions to be destroyed by the vision of suffering (*duḥkhadṛgheyakleśa*). The third time, one refers to the two higher worlds (*rūpadhātu* and *ārūpyadhātu*) in order to abandon the passions relating to those two worlds. These are the three knowledges concerning the first Truth (*duḥkhasatya*).

It is the same for the other nine knowledges concerning the other three Truths, namely: the cause of suffering (*duḥkhasamudaya*), the cessation of suffering (*duḥkhanirodha*) and the Path (*mārga*).

A passage extracted from Bareau's *Sectes* can illustrate this process although the names of the thoughts or knowledges are slightly different.

'Three thoughts are devoted to each Truth (*satya*). Thus, with regard to the Truth of suffering (*duḥkhasatya*):

1 — Knowledge of painful things (*duḥkhadharmajñāna*), by means of which one examines the suffering of the world of desire (*kāmadhātu*);

2 — Patience with regard to painful things (*duḥkhadharmakṣānti*): after having examined the Truth of suffering in the *kāmadhātu*, one abandons (*prajahāti*) delusion (*moha*) which was as yet not yet abandoned (*aprahīṇa*) [in the *kāmadhātu*] (since there is still delusion in the higher worlds (*dhātu*)), by means of repeated examination;

3 — Knowledge of the different kinds of suffering (*duḥkhānvayajñāna*), by examining together the suffering of the world of form (*rūpadhātu*) and the formless world (*arūpyadhātu*), one thus exhausts the Truth of suffering in the three worlds. The third thought is either a thought in contiguity (*santati*) with general knowledge of the Path (*mārgānvayajñāna*) or a thought of clear comprehension of the four Truths together. After having successively gone beyond [the first twelve thoughts], one obtains the first fruit (*phala*), then, also successively, the second and third fruits'[718].

---

718 Trans. from A. Bareau, *Sectes*, p.117. It is advisable to make a comparison between this stage of vision and the gradual order of the comprehension of the Truth consisting of sixteen thoughts (*evaṃ ṣoḍasacitto 'yam satyābhisamayaḥ* — Kośa VI, p.185, n.1.) the essential of which can be summarised in the following diagram (cf. Kośa VI, 27):

I. *Duḥkhe*	*dharmajñānakṣānti*	*Kāmadhātu*
	dharmajñāna	
	anvayajñānakṣānti	*Rupadhātu* and *Arūpyadhātu*
	anvayajñāna	
II. *Samudaye*	*dharmajñānakṣānti*	*Kāmadhātu*
	dharmajñāna	
	anvayajñānakṣānti	*Rūpadhātu* and *Arūpyadhātu*
	anvayajñāna	
III. *Nirodhe*	*dharmajñānakṣānti*	*Kāmadhātu*
	dharmajñāna	
	anvayajñānakṣānti	*Rūpadhātu* and *Arūpyadhātu*
	anvayajñāna	
IV. *Mārge*	*dharmajñānakṣānti*	*Kāmadhātu*
	dharmajñana	
	anvayadharmakṣānti	*Rūpadhātu* and *Arūpyadhātu*
	anvayajñāna	

Kośa VI, 28: 'Fifteen moments, from the *duḥkhe dharmajñānakṣānti* to the *marge 'nvayajñānakṣānti*, constitute the *darśanamārga* — Why? — Because the vision of what was not seen continues'.

A. Bareau, *Sectes*, p.139 (tr.): When one enters the predestination to the Good (*samyaktvaniyāma*), at the moment of the first fiteen arousals of thought (*cittotpāda*), one is called 'orientated' (*pratipanna*), at the sixteenth one is called 'fruit of dwelling' (*sthitiphala*).

On the sixteen thoughts of the Sarvāstivādins, cf. also J. Masuda, *Origin and Doctrines of the Early Buddhist Schools*, p.41, n.1.

According to the Sarvāstivādins, meditation is practised four times for each of the four Truths: twice with reference to the world of desire (*kāmadhātu*) and twice with reference to the two higher worlds (*rūpadhātu* and *arūpyadhātu*).

By comparing the two preceding processes of the stage of vision (*darśanabhūmi*), we find that that of the Vātsīputrīyas is different from that of the Sarvāstivādins with regard not only to the number, but also the names of the thoughts or knowledges. By comparing the process of the twelve knowledges with that of the sixteen thoughts, some people have concluded that the course of vision of the Vātsīputrīyas is weaker than that of the Sarvāstivādins. (Cf. Masuda, *op. cit.* p.56, n.2). With regard to the difference of names in the two processes, this is illustrated in brief by the following diagram:

3 — The adjoining concentration includes four stages; patience (*kṣānti*), name (*nāma*), perception (*saṃjñā*) and the supreme worldly dharma (*laukikāgradharma*)

With regard to this thesis, the Tds writes:

'The adjoining concentration (*chin hsing ch'an* 近行禪, *upacārasamādhi ?*) includes patience (*kṣānti*), name (*nāma*), and perception (*saṃjñā ?*). Adjacency to reflection (*manaskāra*) is what is named adjoining concentration' (Tds 18*b* 7-8).

'. . . it is adjacency to the Supreme Good' (Tds, 18*b* 8).

'. . . In the examination of the aggregates (*skandha*), elements (*dhātu*) and domains (*āyatana*) which are impermanent (*anitya*), painful (*duḥkha*), empty (*śūnya*) and devoid of a self (*anātman*), if one is keen, one finds pleasure. That is what is called patience (*kṣānti*). In correct reflection (*yoniśomanaskāra*), if the mind is unshakeable (*āniñjya*), that is what is called name (*nāma*). Perception (*hsiang* , *saṃjñā ?*) in the examination of suffering is as clear as (that of) a beloved being in a dream (*svapna*) and an image in a mirror; that is the supreme worldly dharma (*laukikāgradharma*), since (it is like) the perception of the Blessed One (*bhagavat*)' (Tds, 18*b* 14-18).

Whilst the Tds includes the stage of supreme worldly dharma at the stage of perception (*hsiang* 想, *saṃjñā ?*), the *Lü ming-liao lun* places the supreme worldly dharma at the fourth stage (*Lü ming-liao lun*, 665*c* 13).

According to the Tds, the adjoining concentration (*upacārasamādhi ?*), the preparatory practice just preceding penetration into the stage of vision (*darśanabhūmi*), is divided into three stages:

1) Patience (*kṣānti*): the stage where the practitioner deeply penetrates the reality of compounded things;
2) Name (*nāma*): the stage where the mind of the practitioner becomes imperturbable in correct reflection (*yoniśomanaskāra*);
3) Perception (*hsiang* 想, *saṃjñā ?*): the stage where comprehension becomes clear;

The sixteen thoughts of the Sarvāstivādins	The twelve thoughts of the Vātsīputrīyas
1. *Duḥkhe dharmajñānakṣānti*	1. *Duḥkhe dharmajñāna*
2. *Duḥkhe dharmajñāna*	2. *Duḥkhe vicārajñāna ?*
3. *Duḥkhe anvayajñānakṣānti*	3. *Ajñātajñana ?*
5–8. Four thoughts concerning the second Truth (*samudaya*)	4–6. Three knowledges concerning the second Truth (*samudaya*)
9–12. Four thoughts concerning the third Truth (*nirodha*)	7–9. Three knowledges concerning the third Truth (*nirodha*)
12–16. Four thoughts concerning the fourth Truth (*mārga*)	10–12. Three knowledges concerning the fourth Truth (*mārga*)

The Theravādins do not speak of knowledges or thoughts in the path of the streamwinner (*sotāpannamagga*) equivalent to the eighth (*aṣṭamaka*). Aṭṭhasālinī, p.43: 'The path of the Sotāpanna is called *dassana* because it is vision of Nibbāna for the first time . . .'. Cf. Kośa VI, p.191, n.3 — cited and trans. by La Vallée Poussin). *Dassana* = *dukkha-, samudayanirodha-, maggadassana.*

it includes the stage of the supreme worldly dharma (*laukikāgradharma*) since it is like the perception of the Buddha.

Like the *Lü ming-liao lun*, the Samayabhedoparacanacakra of Vasumitra also lists all four stages or the four good roots (*kuśalamūla*): patience (*kṣānti*), name (*nāma*), characteristic *(hsiang* 相 , *lakṣaṇa ?)* and the supreme worldly dharma (*laukikāgra-dharma*) are called 'entry into the predestination to the Good' (*samyaktvaniyāma*).

What follows defines the four good roots: 'The stage of patience is that where, at the beginning of clear comprehension, (*abhisamaya*) of the four Truths (*satya*), the latter are only examined together. The stage of the name is that where one can examine things (*dharma*) in the teaching (*śāsana*). The stage of the aspects is that where, in the clear comprehension of the Truths, one examines the essence of their principles. In the stage of the supreme worldly dharmas, which succeeds without interruption the stage of appearance, one attains the path of vision (*darśanamārga*)'[719].

According to the Tds, 18*b* 15, the levels of the three stages are not the same. Except for the first stage — *kṣānti* —, the second and third stages — *nāma* and *saṃjñā* + *laukikāgradharma* — are imperturbable[720]:

---

719 Trans from A. Bareau, *Sectes*, p.117. In comparing what is described in the Tds with the above passage, it is noticeable that there are several differences in the terms as well as in their definition; for example, the stage of 'perception' (*hsiang* 想 , *saṃjñā*) of the Tds, 18*b* 7, is none other than the stage of 'aspects' in *Sectes*, p.117, and the Tds, 18*b* 17 presents it thus: 'since it is (nearly) the perception of the Blessed One', like the definition of the stage of the supreme worldly dharma (*laukikāgradharma*) which is included in the stage of perception. Tds, 18*b* 16–17: 是世間第一法由世尊想 , whilst the *Sectes*, p.117, defines it thus: 'In the stage of the supreme worldly dharmas, which succeeds without interruption the stage of appearance, one attains the path of vision (*darśanamārga*)'.

As for the number of stages, it is probable that the author of the Tds reduced the four good roots (*kuśalamūla*) to three, which is the number fixed by the title of the treatise. Furthermore, the word 'name' which the author of the Tds defines as the stage in which correct reflection (*yoniśomanaskāra*) becomes imperturbable, does not contradict the definition 'stage where one can examine the things of the teaching', since it is after the general examination, without discriminating between what are things and what is taught, that one attains the second phase of the examination: only things in the teaching, such as suffering (*duḥkha*), the origin of suffering (*duḥkhasamudaya*), etc, are considered in a more advanced stage than the first. And the third is the stage of clear perception which can be compared to him who examines the essence of their principles, since clear perception is not totally different from profound examination of the principles of the truth.

Moreover, the three or four stages of the adjoining concentration of the Tds, 18*b* 7, are equivalent to the four stages preceding penetration of the Path (*nirvedhabhāgīya*) of the Kośa VI, 17–20, i.e.: heat (*usmagata*), summits (*mūrdha*), patience (*kṣānti*) and supreme dharmas (*agradharma*), since both lead to the Srotaāpanna fruit.

Furthermore, the third stage — *saṃjñā?* — can be compared to the stage of the appearance of the double/similar image (*paṭibhāganimitta*), the perfectly clear and immobile mental image which appears at a higher degree of meditation (Vism, p.125); the stage of the supreme worldly dharma (*laukikāgradharma*) corresponds to the *gotrabhū*, the stage of him who has attained ripeness, immediately preceding entry into the Noble Path (*ariyamagga*), which is found in Pug, p.12, n. 2, or what is called the ninth noble person (*ariyapuggala*) in AN V, 23 (cf. AN IV, 373) and the Aṭṭhasālinī III, 508.

720 According to the Kośa IV, 17–20, among the four stages only the last two are fixed stages, that is, from which one cannot fall back again. Thus the differences in the levels of the stages between the Tds and the Kośa are not the same:

Upacārasamādhi ?		
1. *Kṣānti*		
2. *Nāma*		imperturbable
3. *Saṃjñā*	+ 4. *Laukikāgradharma*	

4. Clear comprehension (*abhisamaya*) is progressive (*anupūrva*)

This thesis is described in the Tds as follows:

'In that concentration (adjoining concentration), one examines the truth (*satya*) progressively. For example, a man who has just crossed the desert discovers wonderful flowers (*puṣpa*), magnificent pools (*hrada*), streams of pure and abundant water and marvellously well-ordered flowering tress. Having seen that, he says to himself:

'The desert cannot make such lovely things grow. They have to be near an agglomeration.

'Similarly, the practitioner who, in the desert of life and death, is tormented by craving (*kāma*), anger (*krodha*) and delusion (*moha*), encounters a virtuous friend (*kalyāṇamitra*), due to whom he obtains correct reflection (*yoniśomanaskāra*) . . .' (Tds, 18*b* 10-14).

This doctrinal point is identified with the thesis of the Andhakas:

'Clear comprehension of the fruits and Truths is gradual'[721].

The following extract and translation of texts made by A. Bareau clarify this thesis very well; it is said in the Suttas: 'All the same. O monks, the great Ocean (*mahāsamudra*) is progressively deeper (*anubbaninna*), progressively sloping (*anupubbapabbhāra*), *and does not fall (papāta)* in an abrupt manner (*āyatakena*), all the same, O monks, with regard to the Dhamma and discipline (*dhammavinaya*), there

Nirvedhabhāgīya (Sarvāstivādins)		*Upacārasamādhi ?* (Pugdalavādins)	
1. *Usmagata*		1. *Kṣānti*	
2. *Mūrdha*		2. *Nāma*	
3. *Kṣānti*	imperturbable	3. *Lakṣaṇa* or *Saṃjñā*	imperturbable
4. *Laukikāgradharma*		4. *Laukikāgradharma*	

721 A. Bareau, *Sectes*, p.90; cf. Kathāvatthu II, 7.

is progressive study (*anupubbapaṭipadā*), and not a sudden penetration of supreme knowledge (*āyatakeneva annāpativedha*)', and again: 'The intelligent (*medhāvi*) goldsmith (*kammāra*) removes (*niddhamme*) impurity (*mala*) from gold (*rajata*) progressively (*anuppubena*), little by little (*thokaṃ thokaṃ*), from instant to instant (*khaṇe khaṇe*)'; and again: 'He, O monks, who sees suffering (*dukkha*) sees the origin itself of suffering (*dukkhasamudayampi*), sees the cessation itself of suffering (*dukkhanirodhampi*), sees the path itself leading to the cessation of suffering (*dukkhanirodhagāminīpaṭipadāyampi*). He who sees the origin of suffering sees suffering itself, sees the cessation itself of suffering, sees the path itself leading to the cessation of suffering. He who sees the cessation of suffering sees suffering itself, sees the origin itself of suffering, sees the path itself leading to the cessation of suffering. He who sees the path leading to the cessation of suffering sees suffering itself, sees the origin itself of suffering, sees the cessation itself of suffering'[722].

5 — The five superknowledges (*abhijñā*) can be acquired by worldlings (*pṛthagjana*) or heretics (*tīrthika*)

This thesis is set out in the Tds, 20*a* 18. The treatise also devotes lengthy passages to explaining the five superknowledges (*abhijñā*). The main points follow:

1. Supernormal power (*ṛddhi*) is sovereignity (*aiśvārya*): of

a — movement (*gamana*) in space (*ākāśa*), which is the power of walking on water, walking in the air, entering the earth, passing through rocks and walls, touching the sun and moon;

b — transformation (*nirmāṇa*), which is the power of causing the appearance of a man, elephant, horse, chariot, mountain, forest, citadel, ramparts;

c — holiness (*āryātva*), which is the power of making life longer, transforming water into butter, earth into stone and gold into silver (Tds, 20*a* 13-16).

2. The divine ear (*divyaśrotra*) is hearing, engendered by the power of concentration (*samādhi*) which is fixed on a single object and develops the four pure elements (*dhātu*), by means of which one hears the voice of the gods (*deva*), mankind (*manuṣya*) and beings in the bad destinies (*durgati*), depending on the level [of hearing] (Tds, 20*a* 5-7).

3. Knowledge of the minds of others (*paracittābhijñāna*) is knowledge of such-and-such thoughts of living beings; this resembles knowledge when one sees their form and hears their voice.

4. (Knowledge of the) recollection of former lives (*pūrvanivāsānusmṛtijñāna*) is recollection (*anusmṛti*) of actions one performed in the past (Tds, 19*c* 21).

---

722 A. Bareau, *Sectes*, p.90. The Dharmaguptakas, Mahāsāṃghikas, Mahīśāsakas, etc., admit the opposite thesis: 'There is clear comprehension (*abhisamaya*) of the four Noble Truths (*āryasatya*) at one time. When the Truth of suffering (*duḥkhasatya*) is seen, all the Truths can be seen' (*Id.*, *ibid.*, p.183). The Theravādins are of the same opinion: 'Clear comprehension (*abhisamaya*) of the four Paths (*magga*) and four Truths (*sacca*) is not progressive (*anupubba*)' (*Id.*, *ibid.*, p.216). Cf. Kathāvatthu II, 7.

5. Knowledge of births and deaths (*upapādacyutijñāna*), which corresponds to the divine eye (*divyacakṣus*), is knowledge of action and fruition (*karmavipāka*) (Tds, 19*c* 21-22).

These five superknowledges constitute the five superknowledges of worldlings (*pṛthagjanapañcābhijñā*) (Tds, 20*a* 18).

This doctrinal point conforms with thesis No.4 of the Vātsīputrīya school in the Samayabhédoparacanacakra of Vasumitra[723] which A. Bareau translates thus: 'There are also heretics (*tīrthika*) who possess the five superknowledges (*abhijñā*)'[724].

6 — Morality (*śīla*) designates (actions) of body (*kāyakarman*) and speech (*vacīkarman*)

The Tds presents this thesis with the following definitions and examples:

'Morality (*śīla*) designates (action of) body (*kāya*) and (action of) speech (*vāc*), accomplished to lead others, not to harm others and to increase welfare. Morality (*śīla*) consists of three characteristics (*lakṣaṇa*) which are aroused by the body (*kāya*) and speech (*vāc*). What do you mean? — Among those three characteristics, leading others means pardoning and not harming (*ahiṃsā*) living beings who cherish life (*jīva*) (particularly) in times of famine and drought; equally, not stealing their goods, (abstaining from relations with) their wife, this is leading others. Avoiding slander (*paiśunyavāda*), harsh speech (*pāruṣyavāda*), falsehood (*mṛṣāvāda*) and frivolous talk (*saṃbhinnapralāpa*), is not harming others. Moreover, the seven factors (of the body and speech) which do not oppress others constitute the deed of not harming others. When living beings are overwhelmed by suffering and do not know where to seek refuge, if they are given help, that is leading beings' (Tds, 16*b*, 3-9).

This conforms to the thesis attributed to the Vātsīputrīyas by the Kathāvatthu: 'Intimation (*viññatti*) is virtue'[725]. A. Bareau explains thus: 'Intimation by the body (*kāyaviññatti*) is bodily action (*kāyakamma*) and intimation by the voice (*vacīviññatti*) is vocal action (*vacīkamma*). In fact, virtue is bodily action and vocal action. Therefore, intimation by the body and intimation by speech are virtue. Furthermore, it cannot truly be said (*nahevam vattabe*) that intimation is immoral (*dussīlya*)'[726].

The explanation of morality (*śīla*), given by the Buddha himself, is more precise due to the qualifying adjectives, bad (*akuśala*) or good (*kuśala*), given before the terms morality (*śīla*), bodily action (*kāyakamma*), etc. He said: 'Now, carpenter, what does good morality mean? It is good bodily action, good vocal action and also the

---

723 Samayabhed., 16*c* 18.

724 Trans. from Bareau, *Sectes*, p.116. This thesis is also supported by the Haimavatas and Sarvāstivādins. The Theravādins are of the same opinion as the Pudgalavādins (cf. Jā I, 29, vv. 210, 213). In contrast, the Mahīśāsakas and Dharmaguptakas maintained that non-Buddhists did not possess the superknowledges (*abhijñā*) (Kośa VII, p.97, n.4).

725 Kathāvatthu X, 9.

726 Trans. from A. Bareau, *Sectes*, p.125.

perfect purity of means of livelihood that I call morality'[727].

It should thus be understood that morality (*śīla*) is merely a method of mind and will (*cetanā*) which is manifested in either bodily action or words. In this sense, the definition of morality (*śīla*) given by the Tds is quite precise and correlates to bodily and vocal actions. In other words, according to the Pudgalavādins, abstaining from three wrong bodily actions, avoiding four wrong kinds of speech with the aim of leading beings and not harming others, constitutes morality (*śīla*)[728].

7 — Merit (*puṇya*) accumulates continually even during sleep

With an explanation and example, the Tds presents this thesis as follows:

'If, by receiving and practising these two (kinds of morality)[729], merit (*puṇya*) accumulates continuously; it is the accumulation of the good. 'Henceforth, I shall abstain from killing living beings'. That resolve is then augmented by an accumulation of the good, just as capital accumulates and (yields) interest each day. When the resolve to observe morality (*śīla*) is taken, the good (*kuśala*) develops continually, just as in a rotten fruit, a seed begins to germinate in the kernel and grow. If the good is not abandoned and if it is continually preserved, merit (*puṇya*) will become greater, even during sleep; that is the accmulation of the good. Such is morality (*śīla*)' (Tds, 16*b* 9-13).

This doctrinal point conforms to what is mentioned in refutation of it in the Kathāvatthu: 'Merit (*puñña*) consisting of enjoyment in use (*paribhogamaya*) accumulates (*vaddhati*)'[730]. Clearly the following quotations by A. Bareau illustrate this thesis: 'The Buddha said: 'For those who give (*dadanti*) drink (*papa*), fruit (*adapāna*) or shelter (*upassaya*), merit increases (*pavaddhati*) by day (*divā*) and by night (*ratti*), always (*sadā*)'. In another *Sutta*, the Buddha said: 'For him thanks to whom a monk (*bhikkhu*) enjoys the use of (*paribhuñjamāna*) a garment (*cīvara*), alms-food (*piṇḍapāta*), etc., there is an acquisition of merit (*puññābhisanda*), a good consequence (*kuśalābhisanda*), food of happiness (*sukhasāhāra*), a happy fruition (*sukhavipāka*), celestial (*sovaggika*), leading to heaven (*saggassasamvattanika*) . . .' Such gifts consisting of enjoyment in use are gifts through moral obligation (*deyyadhamma*)'[731].

---

727 MN II, 27: *Katame ca, thapati, kusalasīla? kusalaṃ kāyakammaṃ, kusalaṃ vacīkammaṃ ājivaparisuddhiṃ pi kho ahaṃ, thapati, sīlasmiṃ vadāmi.*

728 The Mahīśāsakas supported the same thesis (Kathāvatthu VIII, 9). The Theravādins refuted this thesis by denying that: 'Intimation (*viññatti*) is not exclusively virtue (*sīla*)' (Kathāvatthu VIII, 9; Bareau *Sectes*, p.226).

729 These are the two kinds of morality: natural morality (*shou-shêng chieh* 受生戒, *prakṛtiśīla?* — see above, n.202) and morality of release (*ch'u-yao chieh* 出要戒, *niḥsaraṇaśīla* — see above, n.203). Cf Tds, 16*b* 2–4; 18*b* 22–28.

730 Kathāvatthu VII, 5; Bareau, *Sectes*, p.124.

731 Bareau, *Sectes*, p.124. This Pudgalavādin thesis is also supported by the Rājagirikas and Siddhattikas (*Id.*, *ibid.*, p.269). The Theravādins, in contrast, do not agree with the Pudgalavādins: 'Virtue (*sīla*) caused by commitment (*samādānahetuka*) does not increase (*vaddhati*)' (*Ib.*, *ibid.*, p.226; cf. Kathāvatthu X, 9).

8 — It is imposssible to say whether the characteristic of things (*dharmalakṣaṇa*) is permanent or impermanent

In the Sns, this thesis is treated with the rejection of the differentiation of the person and the aggregates: 'It is impossible to say that the person is identical to or different from the aggregates. That is why it is impossible to say, in the first place, that the characteristic of things (*dharmalakṣaṇa*) is permanent or impermanent. It is the same for the person' (Sns, 465*b* 29 - *c* 11).

This doctrinal expression is also found in the Samayabhedoparacanacakra of Vasumitra as the second thesis of the Vātsīputrīyas: 'Compounded things (*saṃskṛta*) either endure temporarily or disappear in a single instant (*ekakṣaṇika*). Bhavya tells us the same thing, as the third thesis of the Vātsīputrīyas[732].

According to the *I pu chung lun lun shü-chi* of K'uei-chi[733], the Sāṃmitīyas divided compounded things into two categories, the characteristics of which differ: the mind (*manas*) endures only for a single instant (*ekakṣaṇika*), as the commentary says: 'the mind (*citta*) and mental functions (*caitasika*) are instantaneous like a lamp and the vibrations of a bell; form (*rūpa*) can endure for a time'; as the commentary also says: 'among material things, for example, the earth endures for an aeon (*kalpa*) and the life faculty (*jīvitendriya*) has a duration which depends on the longevity (of living beings)'[734].

This is the way the commentary by K'uei-chi describes it. Since no Pudgalavādin commentaries are extant, it is difficult to understand this thesis exactly. Nevertheless, to a certain degree the following words of the Buddha led the Pudgalavādins to establish this thesis with the aim of modifying the dogmatic interpretation of the doctrine of impermanence:

'It would be better, monks, if an illiterate worldling were to take as the self the body formed of the four great elements rather than if he were to take the mind. Why? This is because, monks, the body, formed of the four great elements, seems to persist for one or two years . . . or it seems to persist for an hundred years or more. But that which, monks, is called the mind or thought or consciousness, that arises and disappears in a perpetual changing of day and night'[735].

---

732 Cf. Bareau, *Sectes*, p.116.

733 K'uei-chi, Iptllsc, p.230 *a-b*.

734 These ideas are similar to those in a passage from the *Chü-shê lun chi* 俱舍論記 (Abhidharmakośaśāstra), XIII, T XLI, 182*b*, 202*a*: 'The Sāṃmitīya school says: material things like the great earth, wood, etc., and things dissociated (from the mind) (*citta-*) (*viprayuktadharma*), such as the life faculty, etc., are those which endure for a certain time. Nonetheless, (they) admit that a lamp, the sound of a bell, etc., and mental functions are things which cease after a single instant (of duration)'.
（正量部說：大地薪等色法及命根等的不相應法亦是一期暫住，而主張燈焰鈴聲等及心法是刹那滅）.

735 SN II, 94–5: *Varaṃ bhikkhave assutavā puthujjano imaṃ cātumahābhūtikaṃ kāyaṃ attato upagaccheyya na tveva cittaṃ. taṃ kissa hetu? Dissatāyaṃ bhikkhave cātumahābhūtiko kāyo ekaṃ pi vassaṃ tiṭṭhamāno, dve pi vassāni tiṭṭhamāno . . . vassasatam pi tiṭṭhamāno, bhiyyo pi tiṭṭhamāno. Yaṃ ca kho etaṃ bhikkhave vuccati cittaṃ iti pi mano iti pi viññāṇaṃ iti pi, taṃ rattiyā ca divasassa ca*

In any case, the preceding thesis is a more or less direct interpretation of original Buddhism, since the Buddha frequently affirmed: 'All things engendered by causes are the nature of cessation'[736].

9 — There is an intermediate absorption (*dhyānāntara*)
between the first and second absorptions

This thesis is set out in the Tds, 28*b* 29 - *c* 1-2. According to that treatise, the world of form (*rūpadhātu*) includes the sphere of joy (*prīti*), the sphere of joylessness (*aprīti*) and the sphere of equanimity (*upekṣā*). The sphere of joy (*prīti*) consists of:

a) the stage with reasoning (*savitarka*);
b) the stage without reasoning (*avitarka*);
c) the stage with only deliberation (*savicāra*) (Tds, 28*b* 27-28).

Of the latter, the stage with reasoning is the first absorption (*prathamadhyāna*), the stage without reasoning is the second absorption (*dvitīyadhyāna*), and the stage with only deliberation (*savicāramātra*) comes in the middle, between the first and second meditation (*dhyānāntara*).

On this intermediate absorption, A. Bareau gives this explanation: 'In the fivefold method (*pañcakanaya*), there are five distinct (*vibhatta*) absorptions, and three concentrations (*samādhi*) only (*kevelaṃ*) are manifested (*uddiṭṭha*). The appearance (*okāsa*) of the concentration without reasoning but with only deliberation (*avitakkavicāramatta*), which is located between (*antare*) the first and second meditations, is called intermediate stage of absorption'[737].

It is interesting to note this remark in the Vyākhyā concerning the intermediate absorption (*dhyānāntara*): ' . . . in the *dhyānāntara*, there would be no fruition in the form of feeling, from no matter what action different from action in the *dhyānāntara*, since it cannot be said that fruition experienced in the *dhyānāntara* is the fruit of an action to be felt agreeably in the sphere of the first *dhyāna*, or that it is the fruit of an action to be felt disagreeably in the sphere of the *kāmadhātu*, or that it is the fruit of an action from the sphere of the fourth *dhyāna*'[738].

The Kathāvatthu confirms that the Sāmmitīyas supported this thesis: 'There are intermediate (*antarika*) stages between the absorptions (*jhāna*)'[739].

---

aññad eva uppajjati aññaṃ nirujjhati.

736 MN I, 380: *yaṃ kiñci samudayadhammaṃ sabban-tam nirodhadhamman-ti.* Cf. DN III, 237; SN III, 195; IV, 211; AN I, 152.

737 Trans. after Bareau, *Sectes*, p.126.

738 Kośa IV, p.111, n.1.

739 Bareau, *Sectes*, p.126; Kathāvatthu XVIII, 7. The Sarvāstivādins have the same thesis as the Kośa VIII, 22, which writes: 'The *dhyānāntara* is without *vitarka* . . . Only the *dhyānāntara* is endowed with *vicāra*, without being endowed with *vitarka*; consequently, it prevails over the first *dhyāna* and is inferior to the second. That is why it is called *dhyānāntara*'. Cf. also Kośa VIII, p.181, n.1. Like the Mahīśāsakas and Andhakas, the Theravādins opposed this thesis. They recognised that 'between the first and second (absorptions) there is a concentration (*samādhi*) devoid of reasoning (*avitakka*) but with only deliberation (*vicāramatta*), and which should not be counted as an intermediate stage of absorption'. Cf. Bareau, *Sectes*,

10 — Only one absolute truth exists: Nirvāṇa

This is the description of this thesis in the Tds: 'Only one truth exists, not two' (Tds, 25*a* 6). According to that treatise, there are three truths, namely: conventional truth (*saṃvṛtisatya*), characteristic truth (*lakṣaṇasatya* ?) and absolute truth (*paramārtha-satya*). The first designates traditional manners, customs of society and rules of training (*śikṣā*). The second designates the three Noble Truths (*āryasatya*) which are: suffering (*duḥkha*), the origin of suffering (*samudaya*), and the Path (*mārga*). The third is absolute truth which is identical to Nirvāṇa. Absolute truth is what is contrasted to conventional truth and it is higher than characteristic truth. It constitutes the supreme goal of Buddhists, which should be understood as 'the negation, absence, cessation of all that constitutes the world in which we live, act and suffer'[740].

Hence, the Tds describes: 'Absolute truth is the definitive cessation of all activities, of speech (*vāc*) and of all thoughts (*citta*). Activity is bodily action (*kāya-karman*); speech (*vāc*) is that of the voice (*vākkarman*); thought is that of the mind (*manaskarman*). If these three (actions) cease definitively, that is absolute truth which is Nirvāṇa (Tds, 25*a* 2-5).

Nirvāṇa is absolute truth since it pertains to the uncompounded (*asaṃskṛta*) domain, the characteristics of which are totally different from those of the domain of

---

p.235; Kathāvatthu XVIII, 7. The Nikāyas mention only four absorptions; cf. *Points of Controversy*, p.329, n.1.

Later, perhaps to facilitate the counting of the factors of the meditations, the Abhidhamma masters classed the intermediate concentration in the second absorption. The absorptions were thus raised to five in number and correspond to the order of the abandoning of their factors (cf. Dhammasaṅgaṇi, p.160; Aṭṭhasālinī, p.179; Abhidhammasaṅgaha I, § 21):

Five absorptions	Essential factors
1st absorption	*vitakka* — *vicāra* — *pīti* — *sukha* — *ekaggatā*
2nd absorption	*vicāra* — *pīti* — *sukha* — *ekaggatā*
3rd absorption	*pīti* — *sukha* — *ekaggatā*
4th absorption	*sukha* — *ekaggatā*
5th absorption	*upekkhā* — *ekaggatā*

Thus, in the system of five absorptions, reasoning (*vitarka*) and deliberation (*vicāra*) are successively eliminated in two different absorptions, whilst in the system of four absorptions, the second absorption is attained through the elimination of reasoning (*vitarka*) as well as deliberation (*vicāra*) and only retains three factors: joy (*prīti*), happiness (*sukha*) and singlemindedness (*cittaikāgratā*):

Four absorptions	Essential factors
1st absorption	*vitarka* — *vicāra* — *prīti* — *sukha* — *cittaikāgratā*
2nd absorption	*prīti* — *sukha* — *cittaikāgratā*
3rd absorption	*sukha* — *cittaikāgratā*
4th absorption	*upekṣā* — *cittaikāgratā*

740 After Bareau, *L'Absolu*, p.252.

compounded things (*saṃskṛta*) which are arising, disappearing and changeability:

'Neither arising, nor disappearing, nor changeability are known. That, monks, constitutes the three characteristics of uncompounded things'[741].

Thus it is that Nirvāṇa transcends all activities based on the three modalities, namely: body, speech and mind. In consequence, Nirvāṇa, the Ultimate Truth or Reality, is beyond reasoning and expression by a being. In other words, it is the domain where no compounded things exist[742]. On this subject, A. Bareau writes [tr.]: 'It [Nirvāṇa] transcends the world, with which it has no connection, of which it is pure negation. In contrast to the world, it is permanent, it undergoes no birth, nor change, nor cessation'[743].

Furthermore, the Pudgalavādins, like the Sinhalese Theravādins, remained strictly faithful to the letter of the sūtras and never recognised but one *asaṃskṛta*: Nirvāṇa[744].

The Pudgalavādins went even further by accusing other schools which recognised several uncompounded things (*asaṃskṛta*)[745] and they cited, in the Tds, this stanza by the Buddha:

'There exists only one truth, not two.
From one life to another, he who is deluded
In believing to see several truths,
Then, Ānanda, he cannot be called Śramaṇa' (Tds, 25*a* 6-7).

A. Bareau explains thus the faithfulness of the Pudgalavādins to the singleness of Nirvāṇa [tr]: 'Their exodus towards western India, where they established their main residence, as is attested both by inscriptions and the testimonies of Hsüan-tsang and I-ching, enabled them, like the Theravādins, to preserve intact the thesis of singleness[746]

---

741 AN I, 152: *Na uppādo paññāyati na vayo paññāyati na ṭhitassa aññathattaṃ paññāyati. imāni kho bhikkhave tīni asaṅkhatassa asaṅkhatalakkhaṇānīti.*

742 Cf. DN I, 223.

743 Bareau, 'L'Absolu dans le Bouddhisme', Entretiens, 1955.

744 Bareau, *L'Absolu*, p.263.

745 Apart from the Pudgalavādins and Theravādins of the Vimuktimārgaśāstra school, nearly all the other schools admit a multiplicity of *asaṃskṛtas*. Bareau, in *L'Absolu*, pp.260–1, gives various lists of the *asaṃskṛtas* of the schools and works of early Buddhism:

A — a single term: *Nirvāṇa* — a) Theravādins, Vātsīputrīyas, Sāṃmitīyas; b) Vimuktimārgaśāstra.

B — Three terms: two *nirodhas* and *ākāśa* — a) Sarvāstivādins, Sautrāntikas; b) Satyasiddhiśāstra.

C — Four terms: two *nirodhas*, *niyāma* and *nirodhasamāpatti* — Andhakas.

D — Five terms:

1) two *nirodhas*, *ākāśa*, *tathatā* and *pratītyasamutpāda* — Southern Mahīśāsakas;
2) two *nirodhas*, *tathatā*, *pratītyasamutpāda* and *niyāma* — Pubbaseliyas.

E — Nine terms:

1) two *nirodhas*, *ākāśa*, three *tathatās*, *pratītyasamutpādatathatā*, *mārgatathāta* and *āñenjya* — Northern Mahīśāsakas;
2) two *nirodhas*, *tathatā*, *pratītyasamutpāda*, *mārga* and four *ārūpyas* — Northern Mahāsāṃghikas;
3) two *nirodhas*, *dharmasthitatā*, *pratītyasamutpāda*, *niyāma* and four *ārūpyas* — a) Pubbaseliyas; b) Śāriputrābhidharmaśāstra.

Cf. also the explanation in *L'Absolu*, p.262 sq.

746 Bareau, *L'Absolu*, p.263.

The doctrinal points cited above fully confirm what was said by La Vallée Poussin [tr.]: 'Certain philosophers, the Vātsīputrīyas, say that there is a single *asaṃskṛta*, namely, Nirvāṇa'[747].

11 — There are five, six and seven destinies (*gati*)

The Pudgalavādin literature does not give us the number of destinies (*gati*) in the three worlds (*dhātu*).

1 — The five destinies found in the Tds: 'The world of desire (*kāmadhātu*) includes mankind (*manuṣya*), the gods (*deva*) and the bad destinies (*durgati*)' (Tds, 26*b* 29). . . 'The bad destinies (*durgati*) are the hells (*niraya, naraka*), the animal kingdom (*tiryagyoni*) and hungry ghosts (*preta*)' (Tds, 27*a* 14-15).

It is remarkable that, in the whole treatise, no trace is found of the idea according to which the Asuras formed a separate destiny. Even within the framework of the hungry ghosts (*preta*), there are found only three categories of hungry ghosts which are the wretched, the poor and the rich, but not Asuras[748]. Hence, the Vātsīputrīyas, at least in the early centuries, admit only five destinies[749].

2 — The six and seven destinies found in several passages of the Sns. The latter cites the arguments of various schools (cf. Sns, 469*b* 15 sq. and 670*a* 1 sq.). The Sns, in establishing its thesis of an intermediate existence (*antarābhava*), deals intentionally with:

a) six destinies: 'A man, by accumulating actions (*karman*), receives birth in the six destinies' (Sns, 470*a* 12),

b) seven destinies, by counting the intermediate existence as a seventh destiny: 'Thus (through) the five aggregates (*skandha*), twelve domains (*āyatana*), there (exists) a person (*pudgala*) who may have seven destinies (*gati*): the five destinies, the destiny of the Asuras, the destiny of the intermediate being' (Sns, 466*b* 22-23).

It is therefore evident that the Sāṃmitīyas admit six destinies. Consequently, the attribution by the Vibhāṣā to the Vātsīputrīyas of six destinies may be understood as an attribution to the Vātsīputrīya-Sāṃmitīyas; since, some time later, the Sāṃmitīya school eclipsed that of the Vātsīputrīyas. This notion may be reinforced by the following sentence from the Mahāprajñāpāramitāśāstra which cites the words of the Pudgalavādins: 'Formerly, five destinies were spoken of, today, the *gati* of the Asuras should be added'[750].

As for adherence to seven destinies, this is a particular doctrinal point in the Sns stressing the intermediate existence.

---

747 Kośa I, p.7, n.2.

748 Cf. Tds, 28*a* 27 - *b* 22.

749 The Sarvāstivādins (cf. Kośa III, p.11, nn. 2 and 3; *Traité* I, p.613, n.1) and early Theravādins (cf. Bareau, *Sectes*, p.223; Kathāvatthu VIII, 1) also maintained that there are only five destinies. The later Theravādins added the destiny of the Asuras (cf. Abhidhammatthasaṅgaha, chapter V, § 2).

750 *Traité* I, p.614, n.1.

12 — Knowledge (*jñāna*) is also called the Path (*mārga*)

This thesis is explained clearly by the Tds:

'Knowledge (*jñāna*) consists of feeling (*vedanā*), perception (*saṃjñā*) and consciousness (*vijñāna*). These three (elements) constitute knowledge (*jñāna*) which are also called the factors of the Path (*mārgāṅga*), since the Path (*mārga*) does not separate them' (Tds, 25*b* 27-28).

This means that feeling, perception and consciousness are the three aggregates (*skandha*), among the five, which constitute knowledge (*jñāna*), associated with wisdom (*prajñā*)[751]. which pertains to the aggregates of the mental factors (*saṃskāra*).

It is impossible to track down the frontier between the aggregates, particularly the three mental groups, namely, feeling, perception and consciousness, since they are associated with each other:

'Friend, feeling, perception and consciousness are associated and dissociated things; and it is impossible to demonstrate the difference of those things after having analysed them several times'[752].

Also, wisdom (*prajñā*) cannot be separated from consciousness (*vijñāna*) because they are interdependent:

'What is understood (by wisdom), friend, is known (by consciousness); what is known, is understood; that is why things are associated or dissociated; and it is impossible to show the difference in those things after having analysed them several times'[753].

It was probably because of the association of consciousness (*vijñāna*) and wisdom (*prajñā*) or knowledge (*jñāna*) that the Pudgalavādins admitted knowledge, the right view of the four Noble Truths, particularly the thirty-seven auxiliaries of enlightenment (*bodhipākṣika*), and which they also call the Path (*mārga*). Thus it is that the first — knowledge — and the second — the Path — are not separable. In other words, knowledge in conformity to reality forms part of the Path.

This doctrinal point of the Tds confirms thesis No.16 in the Vibhāṣā indicated by A. Bareau: 'Knowledge (*jñāna*) is only a limb of the Path (*mārgāṅga*) and consciousness (*vijñāna*) is only a limb of existence (*bhavāṅga*)'[754]. The explanation, also given by the Vibhāṣā, is based on the following sentence: 'The *Sūtra* says in fact that

---

751 Genjun H. Sasaki, 'Jñāna, Prajñā, Prajñāpāramitā' (*Journal of the Oriental Institute* XV, No.3–4, March–June 1966), pp.258–9: '*Ñāṇa* and *Paññā* are not distinctively differentiated from each other' . . . 'The distinction is not really found in the *Nikāya*' . . . 'In early Buddhism, however, this distinction was not so clear, as sometimes both terms were used as synonyms'. On the appearance and relationship of the perceptions (*saññā*), wisdom (*paññā*) and consciousness (*ñāṇa*), cf. DN I, 185.

752 MN I, 293: *Yā c'āvuso vedanā yā saññā yañ ca viññāṇam ime dhammā saṃsaṭṭhā no visaṃsaṭṭhā, na ca labbhā imesam dhammānam vinibbhujitvā nānākaranaṃ paññāpetum-ti.*

753 MN I, 292–3: *Yaṃ h'āvuso pajānāti tam vijānāti, yaṃ vijānāti taṃ pajānāti, tasma ime dhammā saṃsaṭṭhā no visaṃsaṭṭhā, na ca labbhā imesa, dhammānaṃ vinibbhujitvā nānākaranaṃ paññāpetun-ti.*

754 Bareau, *Sectes*, p.118.

right view (*saṃyagdṛṣṭi*) is a limb of the Path, whilst the object of consciousness is compounded things (*saṃskāra*).'[755].

13 — The Arhat is susceptible to regression

It is clearly affirmed that the Pudgalavādins maintained the thesis: the Arhat is susceptible to regression; as the Tds, 21*a* 15, deals with the three faculties of the Arhat: the sharp (*tīkṣṇendriya*), the middling (*madhyendriya*) and the weak (*mṛdvindriya*). Each faculty consists of three categories. He-who-regresses (*parihāṇadharman*) belongs to that of the weak faculty; he who regresses falls either into inferior states, (but) not from (comprehension of) the Noble Truths, or to the stage of cultivation (*bhāvanābhūmi*) (cf. Tds, 21*a* 25-26). Regression does not mean falling into the worldly state of living beings (cf. *Ssū*, 6*c* 14)[756].

---

755 *Ibid.*; cf. Vibhāṣā, T XXVII, 1545, 8*b*.

756 Since the texts are not clear, it is necessary to cite here, in context, the passages concerning the regression of an Arhat so that readers can check for themselves:

Tds, 21*a* 25–29: 退法者，或差降退非聖諦故曰退法，或於修地退，修者
修習，說以（已）不修習是名退，如學經已不數習忘，如是不修
習修地退，是病業誦和諍遠行觀故退，以是故名修地

Ssū, 6*c* 14–16: 滅法不眾生滅，分別地滅分別行行，是說如（一）所說
章不誦失，彼不行分別地失，彼滅病事誦長行觀
（遊觀）是五事滅，是亦分別地滅

It is evident that the two sentences: (1)或差降退 非聖諦故曰退法 (i.e., falling to an inferior state, (but) not from (comprehension of) the Noble Truths, that is why he is called he–who–regresses ?) of the Tds, and 2) 滅法不眾生滅 (regression does not mean falling among living beings ?) of the *Ssū*, are not clear. With no commentary, we cannot be sure of their meaning. Nonetheless, the confirmation of the regression of the Arhat in the stage of cultivation is found in two works (Tds, 21*a* 27–28: 如是不修習地退 : 'Hence, not being trained, he (the Arhat) falls into the stage of cultivation'; *Ssū*, 6*c* 15: 彼不行分別地失 : As he (the Arhat) does not practise, he falls into the stage of cultivation', leads us to conclude that the Pudgalavādins admitted that the Arhat falls only to the stage of cultivation. He goes no further in his regression. for 'the holy one cannot fall from the Srotaāpanna fruit, established by the abandoning of the passions to be abandoned through the vision of the Noble Truths' (cf. Kośa VI, 58, p.257 and n.1; above, n.392). This also means that the Arhat never again becomes a worldly being (cf. above, n.391).

The Sarvāstivādins had the same opinion as the Pudgalavādins on the regression of the Arhat. Kośa VI, 56, admits that among the six kinds of Arhat able to exist in the three worlds (*dhātu*), the first five (except he who is immovable — *akopyadharman*, since he is not susceptible to falling, cf. Kośa VI, 57) are all susceptible to regression: four (except he–who–regresses — *parihāṇadharmin*) fall from the family (*gotra*), five fall from the fruit (cf. Kośa VI, 58). Nonetheless, they do not fall from the first family or the first fruit (cf. *ibid.*).

The Theravādins always considered that to admit the regression of the Arhat is a false view (cf. Kathāvatthu, pp.69, 398; *Points of Controversy*, pp.34, 228). In Pug, pp.5, 11, 12, 14, the term *parihāṇadhamma* is applied only to practitioners who acquire the absorptions (*jhāna*) of the world of form (*rūpadhātu*) and the attainments (*samāpatti*) of the formless world (*ārūpyadhātu*), but not in relation to the Path (*magga*). Furthermore, the words *sekkhassa parihāni* in AN III, 116, only designate the regression of those who have not as yet obtained the Arhat fruit. The Peṭakopadesa II, p.32, counts he–who–regresses (*parihānadhamma*) [one of the texts in Burmese characters contains *aparihāṇadhammo*

The causes of regression are sickness, business, quarrels, arbitrations, long journeys (cf. Tds, 21*a* 28, and *Ssŭ*, 6*c* 15-16). A. Bareau affirmed that the Vātsīputrīyas 'maintain that the mind of the Arhat is pure and endowed with omniscience, but recognise that he can regress and remain subject to the mechanism of the fruition of actions'[757]. This affirmation conforms to what was said by Buddhaghosa in the Kathāvatthu[758].

Although the Buddha did not say that the Arhat is susceptible to regression, he stated the dangers to which the Arhat is exposed:

> 'Monks, even for a monk who is an Arahant whose impurities are destroyed, I say that gains, honours and renown are dangers'[759].

Equally, in AN III, 173, the Buddha spoke of five causes of regression for an occasionally delivered (*samayavimukta*) monk who, according to the Abhidharmakośa, is an Arhat[760] or one of two categories of him-who-is-doubly-delivered (*ubhayato-*

---

instead of *parihānadhammo*] or he who-attains-both-aims-simultaneously (the destruction of impurities and the end of life (*samisīsī*)) as one of the nine categories of Arhat (cf. Pug, p.13; Nettipakaraṇa, p.190). In other words, according to the Peṭakopadesa, he-who-regresses (*parihānadhamma*) is effectively defined in relation to the path (*magga*). This doctrinal point is a peculiarity of the Pāli texts. However, the Peṭakopadesa II, 32, classes he-who-regresses (*parihānadhamma*) in the category of guidable persons (*neyyo puggalo*); that is, he who is not devoted to the pursuit of the development of cultivation (*bhāvanā*) and is different from other people: he-who-obtains-knowledge-through-the-condensed-teaching, and he-who-obtains-knowledge-through-the-developed-teaching (cf. Peṭakopadesa II, 31-2).

The agreement and disagreement of the different schools over the regression of the Arhat can be summarised in the following diagram:

Regression of the Arhat	
Agreement	Disagreement
Pudgalavādins Sarvāstivādins Pūrvaśailas A section of the Mahāsāṃghikas	Theravādins Sautrāntikas Mahāsāṃghikas Mahīśāsakas Vibhajyavādins

Cf. A. Bareau, *Sectes*, p.261; Kośa VI, 58 (p.255, n.4; p.264, n.2); Kathāvatthu I, 2; II, 2; J. Masuda, *Origin and Doctrines of the Early Indian Buddhist Schools*, p.27; Akanuma Shizen, 赤沼智善 , *Indo Bukkyō Koyū Meishi Jiten* 佛教固有名詞辭典 , Kyoto 1967, p.186.

757 A. Bareau 'Les controverses relatives à la nature de l'Arhant dans le Bouddhisme ancien', *Indo-Iranian Journal* I, 1957, No.3, p.250. Cf. Bareau, *Sectes*, p.118.

758 Kathāvatthu I, 2; *Points of Controversy*, p.64.

759 SN II, 239: *Yo bhikkhave bhikkhu arahaṃ khīnāsavo tassa pāhaṃ lābhasakkārasilokaṃ antārāyāya vadāmīti.*

Kośa VI, 58, cites thus: Undoubtedly the Bhagavat said: 'Ānanda, I declare that, even for an Arhat, property and honours are causes of an obstacle'. Furthermore, an interesting case is mentioned at SN I, 120 sq., which relates the regression of an Arahant: Godhika attains the mental deliverance achieved by concentration (*samādhicetovimutti*) six times and falls from that state each time; finally, he 'commits suicide' in order not to regress again. Cf. also Kośa VI, 58 (p.262).

760 Kośa VI, 56: 'Mental deliverance (*cetovimukti*) of those five Arhats should be understood as being occasional (*sāmiyikī*) and cherished (*kānta*), since it should be constantly guarded. Consequently, those

bhāgavimukta)[761], or, according to the Tds, one of nine categories of Arhat, he-who-has-attained-complete-deliverance[762]:

'O monks, five things (*dharma*) lead (*saṃvattanti*) to the regression (*parihāṇa*) of the occasionally delivered (*samayavimutta*) monk. Which are those five things? — The fact of delighting in action (*kammārāmatā*), the fact of delighting in speech (*bhāsārāmatā*), the fact of delighting in sleep (*niddārāmatā*), the fact of delighting in society (*sanganikārāmatā*), the fact that, having obtained the delivered (*vimutta*) mind (*citta*), one does not observe (*paccavekkhati*) them. In truth, O monks, these five things lead to the regression of the occasionally delivered monk'[763].

14 — There is an intermediate existence (*antarābhava*) in the world of desire (*kāmadhātu*) and the world of form (*rūpadhātu*)

The Tds and Sns admit that there is a intermediate existence (*antarābhava*). Whilst the Tds demonstrates indirectly and in a general way the existence of this thesis:

'Being delivered from the world of desire (*kāmadhātu*) and the world of form (*rūpadhātu*), the intermediate existence is completely abandoned; there is no intermediate existence in the formless world (*ārūpyadhātu*)' (Tds, 20*c* 10-12).

The Sns devotes numerous passages to the explanation of this thesis. This is the most important passage concerning the relationship between the intermediate existence and the three aspects of *pudgala*:

'At the moment when a man is very near death (and) the moment when the intermediate existence is about to begin, (the *pudgala*) depends on the five (aggregates) of the intermediate existence. It is therefore possible to call *pudgala* that which is constituted by (the five aggregates of) the intermediate existence. Based on the designation of the past (*atītaprajñapti*) and the designation of transmigration (*saṃkramaprajñapti ?*), it can be given the name *pudgala*. In consequence, the intermediate existence does not depend on the *pudgala*; that is why the intermediate existence does not depend on reality (*artha*). It is possible to say that it is not the *pudgala*. Hence, things (*dharma*) are seen with their instantaneous disappearance. Instantaneous disappearance is not a (total) extinction of compounded things; such is the teaching of the Buddha. That should be understood. So, abandoning the body of the five aggregates once it is entirely destroyed, the *pudgala* passes from this life to another one. That is why it is said that a *pudgala* exists which abandons the five aggregates of the birth existence (*upapattibhava*) and receives the five aggregates of the intermediate existence' (Sns, 467*b* 20-26).

Arhats are called *samayavimukta*'.

761 Kośa VI, 65: 'The *ubhayatobhāgavimukta* who is *samayavimukta* is complete from the point of view of the faculties and attainments'.

762 See below, 'The Pudgalavādin lists of Śrāvakas'.

763 Trans. after Bareau, *Sectes*, p.118. Cf. Kośa VI, 57 (p.254, n.1).

It is interesting to note another passage concerning the birth existence and the intermediate existence:

'When a man has come near to death, while the last thought moment (*cyuticitta*) has just appeared, the thought of the intermediate existence (*antarābhavacitta*) has not yet appeared; when the last thought moment disappears, then the thought of the intermediate existence appears. At the moment of the thought of the intermediate existence, the *pudgala* (constituted of) the five (aggregates) of the intermediate existence is formed. That is why it is called abandoning the human aggregates and receiving (those of) the intermediate existence. But why? — The moment of the accomplishment of the appearance of the intermediate thought (is also) the moment of the formation (of the abandoning) of the human existence and death in the intermediate existence. When the thought (*citta*) remains in that state, that is what is called (the state of) death and birth. Therefore it should be understood that the time is the same. It is everything that concerns a man who abandons the five aggregates of the birth existence and who receives the five aggregates of the intermediate existence' (Sns, 467*c* 8-14)[764].

It is evident that the doctrine of the intermediate existence influenced the Pudgalavādins' interpretation of the category called 'he-who-attains-Parinirvāṇa-in-the-intermediate-existence' (*antarāparinirvāyin*) in the fruit named 'he-who-is-endowed-with-vision' (*dṛṣṭiprāpta*) pertaining to the stage of the abandoning of desire (*vītarāgabhūmi*). According to the Tds, he-who-attains-Parinirvāṇa-in-the-intermediate-existence' is 'he who, his life having ended and whose rebirth in the other (world) has not yet occurred, obtains the Path (*mārga*) and attains Parinirvāṇa in the intermediate existence; this can be compared to a spark which goes out before touching the ground' (Tds, 20*c* 5-6).

This doctrinal point is firmly reinforced by the following Sāṃmitīya arguments: 'They (the Buddhas and śrāvakas) receive the intermediate existence from the intermediate existence[765] ; that is not the case for worldlings (*pṛthagjana*). How is that so? The srotaāpanna, still having seven more births and seven more deaths in this world, receives the heavenly intermediate existence (*devāntarābhava*); dwelling in that state he attains the fruit of the once-returner (*sakṛdāgāmin*). This is in the human intermediate existence (*manuṣyāntarābhava*); dwelling in that state, he attains (the fruit of) disgust for the world of desire (*kāmadhātunirvedita*). It is in the human intermediate existence that he receives the intermediate existence of the world of form. It is when he dwells in that intermediate existence that he aims towards the stage of Parinirvāṇa (*parinirvāṇabhūmi*); from there, he enters a special intermediate existence; it is in that place that he attains Parinirvāṇa. Hence, the śrāvaka passes through four intermediate existences' (Sns, 462*a* 24 - *b* 1).

---

764 The Sarvāstivādins. Pūrvaśailas, later Mahīśāsakas and Dārstāntikas also upheld this thesis (cf. Bareau, *Sectes*, p.291). Like the Mahāsāṃghikas, Ekavyāvahārikas, Lokottaravādins, Kukkuṭikas and (early) Mahīśāsakas (cf. Kośa III, p.32, n.1), the Theravādins (cf. Bareau, *op. cit.*, p.223, Kathāvatthu VIII, 2) rejected the intermediate existence.

765 Sns, 462a 24–25: 從中間有受中間有

In fact, the Pudgalavādins also admitted that a bodhisattva could become a Buddha in the intermediate existence, as is said in thesis No.11 of Vasumitra: 'The bodhisattva, when he is reborn in an intermediate existence, if he had formerly engendered the knowledge of destruction (*kṣayajñāna*) and the knowledge of non-arising (*anutpādajñāna*), can acquire the title of Buddha'[766].

15 — There are seventeen categories of heavenly beings in the world of form (*rūpadhātu*)

The Tds divides the world of form into four absorptions diffused over seven categories of heavenly beings according to the five factors of absorption. They are classed into three main groups according to their present psychological states on the following levels:

A - The level of joy (*prīti*) consists of :

1. The first absorption (*prathamadhyāna*), comprising:
   1. The ministers of Brahma (*brahmapurohita*),
   2. the beings of Brahma (*brahmakāyika*),
   3. the retinue of Brahma (*brahmapāriṣadya*);
2. The intermediate absorption (*dhyānāntara*), comprising:
   4. the great Brahmas (*mahābrahma*);
3. The second absorption (*dvitīyadhyāna*), comprising:
   5. those whose light is small (*parīttābha*),
   6. those whose light is immense (*apramāṇābha*),
   7. those whose light is pure and infinite (*ābhāsvara*);

B — The level of joylessness (*aprīti*) consists of:

1. The third absorption (*tṛtīyadhyāna*) comprising:
   8. those whose beauty is inferior (*parittaśubha*),
   9. those whose beauty is immense (*apramāṇaśubha*),
   10. those whose beauty is assured (*śubhakṛtsna*);

C — The level of equanimity (*upekṣā*) consists of:

1. The stage with perception (*saṃjñā*), which designates:

---

766 Bareau, *Sectes*, p.119. The Sarvāstivādins have the same interpretation: 'he-who-attains-Parinirvāṇa-in-the-interval' (*antarāparinirvāyin*), one of the five fruits of the anāgāmin, 'is he who attains Nirvāṇa (*parinirvati*) in the intermediate existence (by entering the *rūpadhātu*)' (Kośa VI, 37), whilst the Theravādins gave it a different interpretation: '*Antarāparinibbāyī*: he who attains Nibbāna within the limits of the first half of life, that is, immediately after having appeared there, or without having passed beyond the middle of his life term, attains the path of realisation by abandoning the higher fetters' (cf. Pug, p.42).

11. those whose fruit is true (*bṛhatphala*);

2. the stage without perception (*asaṃjñā*), which designates:
   12. the non-perceptive (*asaṃjñin*);

3. the stage associated with the awakened mind, which designates the three of five pure abodes (*śuddhāvāsika*), comprising:
   13. the magnificent (*sudṛśa*),
   14. the keen-sighted (*sudarśana*) and the pure (*śuddha*) which include:
   15. the unshakeable (*avṛha*),
   16. the serene (*atapa*),
   17. the superior (*akaniṣṭha*).

The diagram below summarises the preceding expressions:

RŪPADHĀTU	A. The level of joy	I. *Prathamadhyāna*	1. *Brahmapurohitas* 2. *Brahmakāyikas* 3. *Brahmapāriṣadyas*
		II. *Dhyānāntara*	4. *Mahābrahmas*
		III. *Dvitīyadhyāna*	5. *Parīttābhas* 6. *Apramaṇābhas* 7. *Ābhāsvaras*
	B. The level of joy-lessness	IV. *Tṛtīyadhyāna*	8. *Parīttraśubhas* 9. *Apramāṇaśubhas* 10. *Śubhakṛtsnas*
	C. The level of equa-nimity	V. *Caturthadhyāna*	11. *Bṛhatphalas*
		VI. *Asaṃjñika*	12. *Asaṃjñins*
		VII. *Śuddhāvāsika*	13. *Sudṛśas* 14. *Sudarśanas* *Suddhas*: 15. *Avṛhas*, 16. *Atapas*, 17. *Akaniṣṭhas*

It is interesting to note that, according to the Tds, only those whose fruit is true (*bṛhatphala*) constitute the realm in which will be reborn all those who have practised the fourth absorption (*caturthadhyāna*) in a weak, middling or complete manner. The other two, those who are non-perceptive (*asaṃjñin*) and from the three pure abodes (*śuddhāvāsika*), are categories linked to the essential factors of the fourth absorption, namely, equanimity (*upekṣā*) and one-pointedness of mind (*cittaikāgratā*)[767].

---

767 Kośa III, 2, also admits the existence of 'the seventeen places of the Rūpadhātu'. However, it classes them in another way: '*Dhyānas* each of whish have three levels. But the fourth has eight levels':

RŪPADHĀTU	I. *Prathamadhyāna*	1. *Brahmakāyikas*
		2. *Brahmapurohitas*
		3. *Mahābrahmas*
	II. *Dvitīyadhyāna*	4. *Parīttābhas*
		5. *Apramāṇābhas*
		6. *Ābhāsvaras*
	III. *Tṛtiyadhyāna*	7. *Parīttaśubhas*
		8. *Apramāṇaśubhas*
		9. *Śubhakṛtsnas*
	IV. *Caturthadhyāna*	10. *Anabhrakas*
		11. *Puṇyaprasavas*
		12. *Bṛhatphalas*
	V. *Śuddhāvāsikas*	13. *Avṛhas*
		14. *Atapas*
		15. *Sudṛśas*
		16. *Sudarśanas*
		17. *Akaniṣṭhas*

If this is compared with the Tds, the Kośa omits:

1 — the retinue of Brahma (*brahmapāriṣadya*) in the first absorption at the level of joy;

2 — non-perceptive beings (*asaṃjñin*) at the level of equanimity; and adds two other categories, i.e.: the cloudless (*anabhraka*) realm; the realm where one is born through merit (*puṇyaprasava*) in the fourth absorption (*caturthadhyāna*) and classes the Brahma beings in the lowest category of the first absorption (*prathamadhyāna*). (Cf. Kośa III, p.2, n.5 sq.).

In their turn, the Pāli sources admit the existence of sixteen categories only in the world of form (*rūpadhātu*): three categories for each of the first three absorptions (*jhāna*).

Beings of the great fruit (*vehapphala*) and non-perceptive beings (*asaññasatta*) are in the fourth absorption and, in the five pure abodes (*suddhāvāsa*), only the non-returner (*anāgāmi*) will be reborn:

RŪPADHĀ...	I. *Pathamajjhāna*	1. *Brahmaparisajjas*
		2. *Brahmapurohitas*
		3. *Mahābrahmas*
	II. *Dutīyajjhāna*	4. *Parittābhās*
		5. *Appamāṇābhās*
		6. *Abhassaras*
	III. *Tatīyajjhāna*	7. *Parittasubhās*
		8. *Appamāṇas*
		9. *Subhakiṇhakas*
	IV. *Catutthajjhāna*	10. *Vehapphalas*
		11. *Asañña-sattas*

C – *THE PUDGALAVĀDIN LISTS OF ŚRĀVAKAS*

There are two complete lists of śrāvakas which we find in the Pudgalavādin literature:

I — The list in the Tds consists of twenty-nine categories corresponding to three stages:

A. The stage of still unabandoned desires (*avītarāgabhūmi*) includes three fruits or nine categories:

a) the first fruit is the Eighth (*aṣṭamaka*) who acquires the twelve knowledges[768] and consists of three categories, namely:

1 — the pursuer of the truth through faith (*śraddhānusārin*),
2 — the pursuer of the truth through wisdom (*prajñānusārin*),
3 — the pursuer of the truth through faith and wisdom (*śraddhāprajñānusārin*).

These three categories appear as soon as the practitioner is at the stage of maturity

---

T U	V. *Suddhāvāsas*	12. *Avihās* 13. *Atappās* 14. *Sudassās* 15. *Sudassīs* 16. *Akaniṭṭhākas*

A comparison of the categories of the world of form in the Pāli texts with those of the Tds show us that there is a considerable concordance between the two lists, apart from a few differences in the first absorption. Because the majority of the Pāli canonical texts do not admit the intermediate absorption (*dhyānāntara*) (DN I, 73; MN I, 276; SN V, 307–8), the category of the great Brahmas (*mahābrahmā*) is classed in the first absorption (*pathamajjhāna*). Moreover, the category of Brahma beings is missing in the list in the Pāli texts since it seems that the term 'Brahmakāyikas' is the generic name of all the gods of the first *dhyāna*, of all the gods of the Brahma world (cf. Kośa III, p.2, n.5 sq.), and the Pāli texts consider Brahma's retinue (*brahmapārisajja*) as the lowest category and Brahma's ministers as the second, whilst the Tds classes them in another way: the first is that of Brahma's ministers (*brahmapurohita*), the second that of Brahma's beings (*brahmakāyika*) and third, that of Brahma's retinue (*brahmapāriṣadya*). The idea underlying this particular classification remains obscure since there is no commentary. Furthermore, there are other, different lists, for example that of the sixteen categories of the Kaśmīrians which is like the list of seventeen above, but the realm of the great Brahmas (*mahābrahma*) is not an intermediate stage (*bhūmi*) but a higher abode in the realm of Brahma's ministers (*brahmapurohita*) (Kośa III, 2, the list of eighteen categories by granting three categories to the first absorption, a special category for the great Brahmas and a special category for non-perceptive beings (*asaṃjñisattva*); cf. Kośa III, p.3, n.1, the list of twenty-two categories has the following peculiarities:

I — The existence of four categories of Brahmas:

1. Brahma's beings (*brahmakāyikas*),
2. Brahma's ministers (*brahmapurohita*),
3. Brahma's retinue (*brahmapāriṣadya*),
4. great Brahmas (*mahābrahmas*).

Categories 5 - 12 do not differ from those of the other lists.

II — The fourth absorption consists of ten categories:

13. majesties; 14. lesser majesties; 15. unlimited majesties; 16. majesties of great fruit; 17. the non-perceptive (*asaṃjñin*); 18. non-creative beings; 19. the serene (*atapa*); 20. the keen-sighted (*sudarśana*); 21. the great keen-sighted (*mahāsudarśana*); 22. the superior (*akaniṣṭha*) (DĀ, T I, 1, 136*a* sq.).

768 See above, 'The secondary theses of the Pudgalavādins: Thesis No.2'.

(*gotrabhūmi*), in which the knowledge of things (*dharmajñāna*) arises. In other words, these three faculties receive different names depending on the dominant faculty. The first category, in which faith prevails, is that of the weak faculty (*mṛdvindriya*), the second, in which wisdom prevails, is the medium faculty (*madhyendriya*) and the third, in which both faculties are equally potent, is that of the sharp faculty (*tīkṣṇendriya*)[769].

b) the second fruit is the stream-winner (*srotaāpanna*). This is the fruit which one obtains after rising in the Path (*mārga*). Depending on which faculty dominates, when the practitioner is at the stage of vision (*darśanabhūmi*), this fruit is divided into three categories:

1 — he who is reborn seven times at the most (*saptakṛdbhavaparama*)[770],
2 — he who is reborn in several families (*kulaṃkula*),
3 — he who is middling (*madhyama ?*).

The first category exhausts the three fetters, that is:

1) belief in individuality (*satkāyadṛṣṭi*),
2) attachment to useless rules and rituals (*śīlavratapārāmarśa*), and
3) doubt (*vicikitsā*)[771] ;

he is of weak faculty (*mṛdvindriya*) because faith prevails. The second, having exhausted the three fetters, lessens the passions to be destroyed by cultivation (*bhāvanāheyakleśa*)[772] ; he is of medium faculty (*madhyendriya*) because wisdom prevails. The third, in which both faculties — faith and wisdom — are equally potent, is of sharp faculty (*tīkṣṇendriya*); he does not necessarily pass from one noble family to another, nor is he reborn seven times at the most[773].

---

769 Kośa VI, 29, only knows of two categories and the second is called *dharmānusārin*, not *prajñānusārin*, with the meaning of 'pursuit by means of dharmas', i.e. by means of the twelve-fold texts. 'In those moments (fifteen moments on the path of vision), the ascetics with weak or sharp faculties are respectively *śraddhānusārin* and *dharmānusārin* (*mṛdutīkṣṇendriya teṣu śraddhādharmānusāriṇau* — Kośa VI, p.193, n.1). The Pāli texts also admit two kinds of candidates to the *sotāpanna*: *saddhānusārin* and *dhammānusārin* (cf. MN I, 479; AN I, 74).

770 There is disagreement among the schools over the number of existences. For details of the subject, see Kośa VI, 34 (pp.200-2).

771 These three fetters eliminated by the *saptakṛdbhavaparama*, according to the Tds, are not cited in the same order in the canonical texts; see above, n.627.

772 Here the tenuity of *rāga* and *dveṣa* pertaining to the Kāmadhātu is indicated.

773 Kośa VI, 34, admits two categories only: (1) *saptakṛdbhavaparama*, who has not yet destroyed what should be abandoned by meditation; (2) *kulaṃkula*, who has abandoned three or four categories of the passions of the Kāmadhātu, and which is divided into two types: *devakulaṃkula* and *manuṣyakulaṃkula*.

According to the Pāli texts (AN I, 233; III, 87; IV, 380-1; SN V, 205; Peṭakopadesa II, 30; Pug, pp.16, 39), *sotāpanna* is divided into three categories: (1) *saptakkhattuparama*, (2) *kolankola*, (3) *ekabījī* (the one-seeder, the person who acquires knowledge through the condensed teaching, whose faculty is either weak or sharp; being at the stage of vision (*dassana*) he is reborn once again as a man, after which he will reach the end of suffering — cf. AN I, 233). The first two categories are identical to what is described in the Tds. By comparing the three lists of *srotaāpannas*, we can conclude that he-who-is-middling (*madhyama ?*) in the Tds list is an intermediate category between the first two, but which is not recognised in the canonical texts.

c) The third fruit is the stage of attenuation (*tanūbhūmi*). It is the stage of him who, having possessed all the qualities of a stream-winner (*srotaāpanna*), has attenuated the passions of the world of desire (*kāmadhātu*). It consists of three categories:

1 — the once returner (*sakṛdāgāmin*),
2 — the one seeder: he who will be reborn once only (*ekabījīn*),
3 — he who is middling (*madhyama ?*).

The first category, in which faith prevails, is that of the weak faculty (*mṛdvindriya*); it is he who, having died here, is reborn among the gods, then returns once again among mankind before attaining Parinirvāṇa. The second category in which both faculties, faith and wisdom, are equally potent, is that of the sharp faculty (*tīkṣṇendriya*); it is he who will receive no more than one rebirth, before attaining Parinirvāṇa, in order to increase his merits. The third category, in which wisdom prevails, is that of the middling faculty (*madhyendriya*); it is he who is in one or other of the first two[774].

To summarise, the stage of still unabandoned desires (*avītarāgabhūmi*) includes nine categories in all. The main categories are six in number, namely:

1 — the pursuer of the truth through faith (*śraddhānusārin*),
2 — the pursuer of the truth through wisdom (*prajñānusārin*),
3 — he who will be reborn seven times at the most (*saptakṛdbhavaparama*),
4 — he who is reborn in several families (*kulaṃkula*),
5 — the once returner (*sakṛdāgāmin*),
6 — the one seeder (*ekabījīn*).

The three other categories, namely:

1 — the pursuer of the truth through faith and wisdom (*śraddhāprajñānusārin*),
2 and 3 — he who is middling (*madhyama ?*), belonging to the category of the fruit of stream winner (*srotaāpanna*) and that of the stage of attenuation (*tanūbhūmi*), are only auxiliary categories. It seems that these categories were added by the author of the Tds in order to make up the number three[775].

---

774 Kośa VI, 35–6, maintains that there are only two categories: (1) *sakṛdāgāmin* and (2) *ekavīcika*. The difference between the two is that the former is destined to two births (going to the gods, returning to mankind) and the latter is destined to only one birth, and is also a candidate to the second fruit.

The Pāli tradition does not divide the category of *sakadāgāmin* (cf. Peṭakopadesa II, 31). It classes the *ekabijin* in the *sotāpanna* category, which is lower than the *sakadāgāmin*.

By comparing the lists of the stage of the attentuation of desire (*tanūbhūmi*), we find there is a similarity between the list of two in the Kośa and that of three in the Tds, since he-who-is-middling (*madhyama ?*) is in an intermediate category in the Tds. The Pāli texts consider the *sakadāgāmin* as a single category which is equivalent to the stage of attentuation (*tanūbhūmi*) in the Tds.

775 The following table enables us to summarise the stage of still unabandoned desires (*avītarāgabhūmi*) of the Tds and to compare it with the other two lists in the Kośa and the Pāli texts:

(see next page)

B. The stage of the abandoning of desire (*vītarāgabhūmi*) consists of three fruits or nine categories:

a) the first fruit is he who is delivered through faith (*śraddhādhimukta*). He is so named bcause faith (*śraddhā*) is the dominant factor of his deliverance. This fruit includes three categories, namely:

1 — the stream winner (*ūrdhvasrotā*),

2 — the attainer of Parinirvāṇa through compounded things (*sābhisaṃskāra-parinirvāyin*),

3 — the attainer of Parinirvāṇa through the uncompounded (*anabhisaṃskāra-parinirvāyin*).

The first is the practitioner who is on the point of attaining the higher stages. The second is he who attains Parinirvāṇa by means of compounded things (*saṃskṛta*). The third is he who attains Parinirvāṇa by means of the uncompounded (*asaṃskṛta*) such as the knowledge of cessation (*nirodha*)[776].

b) the second fruit is he who is endowed with vision (*dṛṣṭiprāpta*). This is the pursuer of the truth through wisdom (*prajñānusārin*) who rises to the stage

A V Ī T A R Ā G A B H Ū M I		
TRIDHARMAKAŚĀSTRA	ABHIDHARMAKOŚA	PĀLI TEXTS
I. AṢṬAMAKA		
1. *Śraddhānusārin*	*Śraddhānusārin*	*Saddhānusārī*
2. *Prajñānusārin*	*Dharmānusārin*	*Dhammānusārī*
3. *Śraddhā-prajñānusārin*		
II. SROTAĀPANNA		
4. *Saptakṛdbhavaparama*	*Saptakṛdbhavaparama*	*Sattakkhuparama*
5. *Kulaṃkula*	*Kulaṃkula*	*Kolankola*
6. *Madhyama ?*		*Ekabījī*
III. TANŪBHŪMI		
7. *Sakṛdāgāmin*	*Sakṛdāgamin*	
8. *Ekabījin*	*Ekavīcika*	*Sakadāgāmin*
9. *Madhyama ?*		

776 Kośa VI, 37, also admits three categories the definitions of which, attributed to the Vaibhāṣikas, are identical to those in the Tds. However, Kośa VI, 37, treats them as three of five categories of *anāgāmins*, and not of *śraddhādhimuktas* as does the Tds, whilst in the Pāli texts, these three categories, found together in the group of five *anāgāmins* (cf. Pug, 16–17, Peṭakopadesa, 31), are defined differently. According to Pug, 17, *sasankāraparinibbāyī* and *asaṅkhāraparinibbāyī* are interpreted respectively as the attainer of Parinibbāna with effort (. . . with little pain and after having made great efforts: *appad-dukkhena dhimattaṃ akatvā* — PugA, 119) and the attainer of Parinibbāna without effort (. . . with pain, difficulty and after having made great efforts: *dukkhena kasirena dhimattaṃ payogaṃ katvā* — PugA, 119). Cf. also AN II, 155–6; Kośa VI, 37 — p.212).

By comparing the three lists, it is noticed that there is an identification between the Tds list and that of the Kośa (Vaibhāṣikas' opinion) on the definition of the last two categories, and that there is a difference between the Tds list and that of the Pāli texts on the same subject.

of the abandoning of desires (*vītarāgabhūmi*) and who is called he who is endowed with vision (*dṛṣṭiprāpta*). Wisdom is the dominant element in his deliverance. The second fruit includes three categories:

1 — the attainer of Parinirvāṇa in the intermediate existence (*antarāparinirvāyin*),
2 — the attainer of Parinirvāṇa in rebirth (*upapadyaparinirvāyin*),
3 — the stream winner (*ūrdhvasrota*).

These three categories are those which are also found in the group of five corresponding to the non-returner (*anāgāmin*) and belonging to categories which reach the world of form (*rūpadhātūpaga*)[777].

c) The third fruit is the bodily witness (*kāyasākṣin*). This is the supreme fruit among the fruits of the stage of the abandoning of desires (*vītarāgabhūmi*) and, due to it, one obtains deliverance (*vimokṣa*) during one's lifetime[778]. This fruit includes:

1 — the attainer of Nirvāṇa through compounded things (*sābhisaṃskāraparinirvāyin*),
2 — the attainer of Parinirvāṇa through the uncompounded (*anabhisaṃskāraparinirvāyin*),
3 — the attainer of Parinirvāṇa in rebirth (*upapadyaparinirvāyin*).

According to the Tds, there is no tautology in repeating the categories of the preceding fruits since these first three categories of the third fruit (*kāyasākṣin*) pertain to the formless world (*ārūpyadhātu*)[779].

---

777 Kośa VI, 38: These five are *anāgāmins* because they go to the Rūpadhātu (except to transcend it): the *rūpadhātūpaga* is of five kinds: antarāparinirvāyin, upapadyaparinirvāyin, sābhisaṃskāraparinirvāyin, anabhisaṃskāraparinirvāyin, ūrdhvasrotas. These categories are also found in the Pāli texts with different definitions since there is no intermediate existence in the Theravādin doctrine. Pug, 42–6, defines them thus: the *antarāparinibbāyin* is he who attains Parinibbāna in the first half of his life term; the *upahaccaparinibbāyin* is he who attains Parinibbāna after reaching the second half of his life term, the *uddhamsota-(akaniṭṭhā-gāmi)* is he who wins the stream up to the higher gods. Cf. Peṭakopadesa, 31.

778 Kośa VI, 43. The anāgāmin who has acquired *nirodha* is considered as a kāyasākṣin.

779 Cf. AN IV, 51; Pug, 14. These three categories are identical to three of the four categories of *anāgāmins* who go to the formless world (*ārūpyadhātu*). Kośa VI, 38: Another, who goes to the Ārūpya, is of four kinds. (There is no intermediate existence in the Ārūpya births, that is why the *antarāparinirvāyin* is separate from the group of five *anāgāmins*.) The Pāli texts consider that the bodily witness (*kāyasakkhī*) is he of the seven noble disciples who has achieved deliverance by practising the eight liberations (*vimokkhā*) (Pug, 32; AN IV, 451). The *kāyasakkhī* is not mentioned in the Peṭakopadesa. Is he considered an arahant? A comparison of the three sources shows that the Tds attributes the bodily witness (*kāyasākṣin*) to the formless world (*ārūpyadhātu*) by dividing it into three categories. The Kośa maintains that the bodily witness (*kāyasākṣin*) is the attainer of Nirvāṇa in his lifetime, and deals separately with another category, consisting of four kinds who reach the formless world (*ārūpyapaga*). The Pāli texts do not attribute the *kāyasakkhī* to any world and consider him simply as a noble disciple who has achieved deliverance from the lowest degree to the highest.

Among the three lists concerning the fruits of the stage of the abandoning of desires (*vītarāgabhūmi*), the list of three fruits and nine categories in the Tds is a very complete list, which includes all the

C. The Arhat.

The Pudgalavādins maintain that the Arhat is subject to regressing and on this subject deal with three faculties or nine categories:

a) the sharp faculty (*tīkṣnendriya*):
1 — he who is stable (*sthitākampya*),
2 — he who progresses (*prativedhanādharman*),
3 — he who is immovable (*akopyadharman*),

b) the weak faculty (*mṛdhvindriya*):
4 — he who regresses (*parihāṇadharman*),
5 — he who wills (*cetanādharman*),
6 — he who preserves (*anurakṣanādharman*),

c) the middling faculty (*madhendriya*):
7 — he who is delivered through wisdom (*prajñāvimukta*),
8 — he who attains complete deliverance,
9 — he who attains incomplete deliverance.

These last two categories are also together called the doubly delivered (*ubhayato-*

---

various categories of *anāgāmin*, whilst the Kośa list contains seven categories including the *kāyasākṣin*. The list in the Pāli texts consists of five categories. The *kāyasakkhī* is an independent category. The diagram below summarises the differences:

VĪTARĀGABHŪMI		
TRIDHARMAKAŚĀSTRA	ABHIDHARMAKOŚA (Cf. Kośa VI, 215, 223, 226)	PĀLI TEXTS
I — Śraddhādhimukta: *1. Ūrdhvasrota* *2. Sābhisaṃskāraparinirvāyin* *3. Anabhisaṃskāraparinirvāyin* II — Dṛṣṭiprapta: *4. Antarāparinirvāyin* *5. Upapadyaparinirvāyin* *6. Ūrdhvasrota* III — Kāyasākṣin: *7. Sābhisaṃkāraparinirvāyin* *8. Anabhisaṃskāraparinirvāyin* *9. Upapadyaparinirvāyin*	I — Rūpyapaga: *1. Antarāparinirvāyin* *2. Upapadyaparinirvāyin* *3. Sābhisaṃskāraparinirvāyin* *4. Anabhisaṃskāraparinirvāyin* *5. Ūrdhvasrota* II — *6.* Ārūpyopaga: *a. Upapadyaparinirvāyin* *b. Sābhisaṃskāraparinirvāyin* *c. Anabhisaṃskāraparinirvāyin* *d. Ūrdhvasrota* III — 7. Kāyasākṣin: (The attainer of Nirvāṇa in this life)	Anāgāmi: *1. Antarāparinibbāyī* *2. Upahaccaparinibbāyī* *3. Sasaṅkhāraparinibbāyī* *4. Asaṅkhāraparinibbāyī* *5. Uddhaṃsota-akaniṭṭhā-gāmi.* *(Kāyasakkhī)*

bhāgavimukta)[780].

---

780 It is likely that there is a relationship between the Tds and the Dakṣiṇīyasūtra of the Madhyamāgama (T 1 26, 616*a* 5–25) for the nine categories of Arhat since, despite the minimal differences in the terms constituting the classification, the two texts — Tds and Dakṣiṇīyasūtra — admit nine categories of Arhat.

These are the nine kinds of Arhat in the Dakṣiṇīyasūtra:

1) he who wills (*cetanādharman*),

2) he who progresses (*prativedhanādharman*),

3) he who is immovable (*akopyadharman*),

4) he who regresses (*parihāṇadharman*),

5) he who does not regress (*aparihāṇadharman*),

6) he who preserves (*anurakṣanādharman*),

7) he who is stable (*sthitākampya*),

8) he who attains deliverance through wisdom (*prajñāvimukta*),

9) he who is doubly delivered (*ubhayatobhāgavimukta*).

In comparison to the list of nine categories of Arhat in the Tds, this list additionally contains the *aparihāṇadharman*, whilst the *ubhayatobhāgavimukta* in it is a single category and is not divided into two categories — he who attains complete deliverance and he who attains incomplete deliverance, as the Tds has.

Considering that the Arhat is perfected and that the affirmation of regression of the Arhat is an heretical opinion, the canonical texts in Pāli rarely distinguish several categories of Arhat. Exceptionally, the Peṭakopadesa, 31–2, admits there are nine categories of Arhat:

1) he who is doubly delivered (*ubhayatobhāgavimutta*),

2) he who attains deliverance through wisdom (*paññāvimutta*),

3) he who remains for a cosmic period (*ṭhitakappi*),

4) he who progresses (*paṭivedhanābhava*),

5) he who wills (*cetanābhabba*),

6) he who preserves (*nakkhaṇābhabba*),

7) he who does not attain Parinibbāna if he does not preserve (*sace anurakkhati na parinibbāyī*),

8) he who attains Parinibbāna if he preserves (*no ce anurakkhatiparinibbāyī*),

9) he who regresses (*parihāṇadhamma*) or he who is level-headed (*samasīsī*).

Of these nine categories of Arhat, the first two derive from the sharp faculty which obtains knowledge through the condensed teaching; the third and fourth, from the weak faculty which obtains knowledge through the condensed teaching; the fifth and sixth, from the sharp faculty which obtains knowledge through the developed teaching; the seventh and eighth, from the weak faculty which obtains knowledge through the developed teaching; the ninth (including the level-headed) is the guidable person who is not devoted to the pursuit of development. Cf. Peṭakopadesa, 31–2.

Compared to the list of the nine Arhat categories in the Tds, the Peṭakopadesa list contains four categories — namely: *ṭhitakappi* (3), *sace anurakkhati na parinibbāyī* (7), *no ce anurakkhati parinibbāyī* (8), *samasīsī (= parihāṇadhamma)* — which are lacking in the Tds; whilst the others (1, 2, 4, 5, 6, and *parihāṇadhamma* (9) are identical to the Tds list.

According to Kośa VI, 56 (p.251, n.2), Pug. p.12, contains a definition of *samayavimutta, asamayavimutta, kuppadhamma, akuppadhamma, parihāṇadhamma, aparihāṇadhamma, cetanābhabba* and *anurakkhanābhabba*.

In turn, Kośa VI, 56: 'six kinds of Arhat are recognised' (*arhantaḥ ṣaṇ mataḥ* — p.251, n.1):

1) he who regresses (*parihāṇadharman*),

2) he who wills (*cetanādharman*),

3) he who preserves (*anurakṣanādharman*),

4) he who is stable (*sthitākampya*),

5) he who progresses (*prativedhanādharman*),

6) he who is immovable (*akopyadharman*).

In brief, the list of śrāvakas in the Tds consists of three divisions and each division contains three fruits:

1. Avītarāgabhūmi:

I. AṢṬAMAKA
1. Śraddhānusārin
2. Prajñānusārin
3. Śraddhāprajñānusārin

II. SROTAĀPANNA
4. Saptakṛdhbhavaparama
5. Kulaṃkula
6. Madhyama

III. TANUBHŪMI
7. Sakṛdāgāmin
8. Ekabījin
9. Madhyama

2. Vītarāgabhūmi:

I. ŚRADDHĀBHIMUKTA
1. Ūrdhvasrota
2. Sābhisaṃskāraparinirvāyin
3. Anabhisaṃskāraparinirvāyin

II. DṚṢṬIPRĀPTA
4. Antarāparinirvāyin
5. Upapadyaparinirvāyin

Compared to the Tds list, the Kośa omits: the *prajñāvimukta*, he who attains complete deliverance and he who attains incomplete deliverance (*ubhayatobhāgavimukta*). Nonetheless, the Kośa, in fact, takes these three categories into account, without classing them together with the preceding six categories. According to the Kośa, he who attains deliverance through wisdom (*prajñāvimukta*) is 'he who is delivered by *prajñā*' or 'by the power of *prajñā*, he is delivered from the *kleśāvaraṇa*' (Kośa VI, 64), 'he is delivered not occasionally (*asamayavimukta*) and he is complete from the point of view of the faculties' (*ibid.*, 65). This category is lower than that of him who is doubly delivered (*ubhayatobhāgavimukta*) because it obtains the fruit of wisdom (*prajñā*) only. As for the doubly delivered (*ubhayatobhāgavimukta*), this is 'he who possesses destruction (*ibid.*, 64) through the power of wisdom (*prajñā*) and concentration (*samādhi*), he is delivered from the *kleśāvaraṇa* and *vimokṣāvaraṇa*'. He is he who is delivered occasionally (*samayavimukta*) and is complete from the point of view of concentration; he is both he who is delivered not occasionally (*asamayavimukta*) and he who is complete from the point of view of the faculties and concentration (*ibid.*, 65). We do not find the second category of the doubly-delivered (*ubhayatobhāgavimukta*) of the Tds (he who attains incomplete deliverance) in the Kośa.

An examination of the three main lists of Arhats leads us to the following conclusion: the Tds list is very complete as much for the faculties as for the categories; it is unique in its discovery or its classification if it is compared to the Kośa list, which is nothing other than the list found in the sūtras. The Peṭakopadesa list appears a peculiarity if it is compared to the totality of the Pāli texts. The table below shows, in summary, the differences between these three lists:

6. *Ūrdhvasrota*

III. KĀYASĀKṢIN
7. *Sābhisaṃskāraparinirvāyin*
8. *Anabhisaṃskāraparinirvāyin*
9. *Upapadyaparinirvāyin*

3. Arhat:

I. TIKṢṆENDRIYA:
1. *Sthitākampyadharman*
2. *Prativedhanādharman*
3. *Akopyadharman*

II. MṚDVINDRIYA
4. *Parihāṇadharman*
5. *Cetanādharman*
6. *Anurakṣaṇādharman*

III. MADHYENDRIYA:
7. *Prajñāvimukta*
Ubhayatobhāgavimukta: 8. complete
9. incomplete.

II — The Sns list consists of ten or twelve categories[781], in which that of the Arhat is not divided:

THE CATEGORIES OF ARHAT		
TRIDHARMAKAŚĀSTRA	ABHIDHARMAKOŚA	PEṬAKOPADESA
I. Tikṣṇendriya:		
1. *Sthitākampyadharman*	1. *Parihāṇadharman*	1. *Ubhayatobhāgavimukta*
2. *Prativedhanadharman*	2. *Cetanādharman*	2. *Paññāvimutta*
3. *Akopyadharman*	3. *Anurakṣaṇādharman*	3. *Ṭhitakappi*
II. Mṛdvindriya:		
4. *Parihāṇadharman*	4. *Sthitākampya*	4. *Paṭivedhanābhāva*
5. *Cetanādharman*	5. *Prativedhanādharman*	5. *Cetanābhabba*
6. *Anurakṣaṇādharman*	6. *Akopyadharman*	6. *Rakkhaṇābhabba*
III. Madhyendriya:		
7. *Prajñāvimukta*		7. *Sace anurakkhatiparinibbāyī*
Ubhayatobhāgavimukta		8. *Noce anurakkhatiparinibbāyi*
8. Complete		9. *Parihāṇadharma* or
9. Incomplete.		*Samasīsī.*

781 In reality the Sns lists contains thirteen or sixteen categories. As the first three categories: — (1) he who is not yet disgusted by the world of desire, (2) he who is disgusted by the world of desire, and (3) he who is disgusted by the world of form — are outside the list of holy ones (*ārya*), that is why they are set aside. It is for this reason that the list of śrāvakas given by the Sāṃmitīyas contains ten or twelve categories.

1 — he who has seven more deaths and seven more births (*saptakṛd-bhavaparama*),
2 — the once returner (*sakṛdāgāmin*),
3 — the once returner (who attains ParinirVāṇa by being born in several families) (*kulaṃkulasakṛdāgāmin*)[782],
4 — the once returner (who is separated from Parinirvāṇa by the interval of one birth) (*ekavīcikasakṛdāgāmin*)[783],
5 — the once returner (who attains Parinirvāṇa) through disgust for the world of desire and through rebirth in the higher stages (*kāmadhātunirvedha ūrdhvasrotasakṛdāgāmin*),
6 — This category is divided into three:
   a. he who attains Parinirvāṇa in rebirth (*upapadyaparinirvāyin*)
   b. he who attains Parinirvāṇa through compounded things (*sābhi-saṃskāraparinirvāyin*)[784],
   c. he who attains Parinirvāṇa through the uncompounded (*anabhi-saṃskāraparinirvāyin*)[785],
7 — he who attains Parinirvāṇa in the intermediate existence (*antarā-parinirvāyin*),
8 — he who is disgusted by the world of form and who is reborn in the higher stages (*rūpadhātunirvedha ūrdhvasrota*),
9 — he who attains Parinirvāṇa through the compounded things of rebirth (*upapadyasaṃskāraparinirvāyin*)[786],
10 — the Arhat (cf. Sns, 472*a* 15-21).

The existence of the two preceding lists of śrāvakas progressively confirms the opinion according to which the separation between the Vātsīputrīyas and Sāṃmitīyas was caused by different interpretations of the stanza common to the Pudgalavādins[787]. It is clear that the fruits, according to the order of the list of twelve categories given by the Sns, are practically identical to the fruits of that of six categories indicated in the stanza common to the Pudgalavādins (according to the Sāṃmitīya interpretation). The difference between the two lists is that the first considers the *kulaṃkula* as a category associated with the *sakṛdāgāmin*, whilst the second classes the *kulaṃkula* in

782 Sns, 472*a* 16: *chieh-chieh-shê-t'a-han* 家家斯陀含 . Without a commentary it is difficult to explain why he who is reborn in several families (*kulaṃkula*) is classed in the fruit of the once returner (*sakṛdāgāmin*). It is possible that the *kulaṃkulasakṛdāgāmin* is a category specific to the Sāṃmitīyas.

783 Sns, 472*a* 17: *i-chien-shê-t'a-han* 一間斯陀含. It should be noted that the Chinese translation here is *i-chien* 一間 , whilst that of the Tds is *i-chung* 一種 (Tds, 21*a* 13).

784 Without a commentary, and as the Sns admits that there is an intermediate existence (*antarābhava*), the names of this and the following categories can be translated in this way.

785 See previous note.

786 Sns, 472*a* 20: *shêng-hsing-ju-nieh-pan* 生行入涅槃 . The translation is based on an examination of the three preceding categories, namely: *shêng-i ju-nieh-pan* 生已入涅槃 (he who attains Parinirvāṇa in rebirth — *upapadyaparinirvāyin*), *hsing-ju-nieh-pan* 行入涅槃 (he who attains Parinirvāṇa through compounded things — *sābhisaṃskāraparinirvāyin*) and *pu-hsing-ju-nieh-pan* 不行入涅槃 (he who attains Parinirvāṇa through the uncompounded — *anabhisaṃskāraparinirvāyin*) (Sns, 472*a* 18–19).

787 Cf. É. Lamotte, *History*, pp.608–9.

the *srotaāpanna* fruit.

The table below allows a comparison of these two lists:

The Categories of Śrāvakas	
According to the Sāṃmitīya interpretation of the stanza common to the Pudgalavādins	According to the Sāṃmitīyanikāyaśāstra
1 — *Srotaāpanna* 2 — *Kulaṃkula*	1. *Saptakṛdbhavaparama*
3 — *Sakṛdāgāmin*	2. *Sakṛdāgāmin* 3. *Kulaṃkulasakṛdāgāmin*
4 — *Ekavīcika*	4. *Ekavīcikasakṛdāgāmin* 5. *Kāmadhātunirvedha ūrdhvasrotasakṛdāgāmin*
5 — *Anāgāmin*	(*Anāgāmin* includes 6 categories): 6. *Upapadyaparinirvāyin* 7. *Sābhisaṃskāraparinirvāyin* 8. *Anabhisaṃskāraparinirvāyin* 9. *Antarāparinirvāyin* 10. *Rūpadhātunirvedha ūrdhvasrota* 11. *Upapattibhavasaṃskāraparinirvāyin*
6 — *Arhat*	12. *Arhat*

It is interesting to compare the Vātsīputrīya list of śrāvakas in the Tds with that of the Sāṃmitīyas in the Sns. Although the list of twenty-seven categories in the Tds is more developed than that of the twelve categories in the Sns, the main categories of both lists are similar with regard to the four fruits of the śrāvakas, namely: *srotaāpanna, sakṛdāgāmin, anāgāmin* and *arhat*.

The differences which separate the two lists are the following:

1. The Sns list only counts the *saptakṛdbhavaparama* as a single category of *srotaāpanna*, whilst the Tds list admits that the *srotaāpanna* is divided into three: *saptakṛdbhavaparama, kulaṃkula* and *madhyama*;
2. The Sns list counts four categories of *sakṛdāgāmin*, namely: *sakṛdāgāmin, kulaṃkulasakṛdāgāmin, ekavīcikasakṛdāgāmin* and *kāmadhātunirvedha ūrdhvasrotasakṛdāgāmin*, whilst the Tds list only accepts three categories: *sakṛdāgāmin, ekabījin* and *madhyama*;

3. The Sns list counts six categories of *anāgāmin*, namely: *upapadyaparinirvāyin*, *sābhisaṃskāraparinirvāyin*, *anabhisaṃskāraparinirvāyin*, *antarāparinirvāyin*, *rūpadhātunirvedha ūrdhvasrota* and *upapattibhavasaṃskāraparinirvāyin* (of these six categories, the first five are essential catgories found in the canonical texts, the sixth is an auxiliary category, invented by the Sāṃmitīyas by combining the following three categories: *upapadyaparinirvāyin*, *sābhisaṃskāraparinirvāyin* and *anabhisaṃskāraparinirvāyin*), whilst the Tds list admits that there are only nine categories, of which the five categories of *anāgāmin*, in conformity to the canonical texts, are always essential.
4. The Sns list does not divide the *arhat* fruit, whilst the Tds list admits that there are nine categories of *arhat*.

It is noteworthy that the Sns classes the *kulaṃkula* in the *sakṛdāgāmin* fruit, whilst the Tds list considers *kulaṃkula* as a category of *srotaāpanna*; both lists agree on this point: the *ekavīcika* (Sns) or *ekabījīn* (Tds) pertains to the *sakṛdāgāmin* fruit. In brief, the Vātsīputrīyas and Sāṃmitīyas each have their own list of śrāvaka fruits. By comparing the two lists, we find that that of the Vātsīputrīyas given by the Tds is richer, as much for the faculties as for the categories, than that of the Sāṃmitīyas supplied by the Sns.

CONCLUSION

The study of the personalist schools of early Buddhism has enabled us to understand the doctrinal problems of the Pudgalavādins.

Although the literary documents left by the Pudgalavādins are few in number in comparison to those of other schools, Theravādin, Sarvāstivādin, etc., we have attempted to reconstruct the main thesis concerning the *pudgala*, the fifteen secondary theses and the two lists of śrāvakas, by basing ourselves on the four treatises which have been preserved.

The establishment of the *pudgala* thesis is certainly a significant, unique and courageous creation in the history of Buddhist thought. If we set aside all the exaggerations and condemnations concerning this thesis and if we understand it clearly as it was explained by the author or his disciples, we can appreciate its true value.

It answers two questions at the same time, by affirming on the one hand the existence of the individual and by refuting on the other the condemnation of nihilism and eternalism brought by Buddhism.

It is, indeed, difficult to explain the existence of a successive chain of former and later lives without designating a person defined as being something more than the sum of its constituent parts (*skandha*) which, for its continuing subsistence, supplies a continuing support for action (*karman*), memory and knowledge, and which attains deliverance through destruction of the fetters (*saṃyojana*), but not through that of an individual life.

Although the *pudgala* was treated by the Pudgalavādins as a designation (*prajñapti*) aimed at clarifying the existence of living beings (*sattva*), they did not fail to declare that this principle of individuality is neither identical to the aggregates nor different from them by explaining that it can exist in bliss after total stilling (*parinirvāṇa*).

Thus, the thesis of the *pudgala*, according to the Pudgalavādins, remains in conformity with the doctrine of the middle way (*madhyamāpratipad*) and does not fall into the two extremes: nihilism (*ucchedadṛṣṭi*) and eternalism (*śāśvatadṛṣṭi*). The Pudgalavādins were careful to show that their doctrine was not contrary to the doctrine of insubstantiality which is the essence of the teaching of the Buddha. They also insisted on the fact that adherence to the *pudgala* does not prevent the treading of the Path and the attaining of the result, by presenting the list of twelve knowledges (*jñāna*) and that of the fruits (*phala*) proper to their school.

In order to complete the *pudgala* thesis, the creation by the Vātsīputrīyas and, later, the Sāṃmitīyas, consisted of admitting the existence of an imperishable thing (*avipraṇāśadharma*), destined to explain the mechanism of the fruition of actions (*karmavipāka*). This thing is dissociated from the mind: neutral from the point of view of morality, it can affect the ordinary as well as the liberated man. The Sāṃmitīyas upheld, with the richest and most convincing arguments, the thesis of intermediate existence (*antarābhava*) illustrating the fact that, at the moment of death, the individual changes into an intermediate being who is reborn spontaneously and who, at the same time, links the two consecutive lives.

On the other hand, with the help of the *Lü ming-liao lun*, we have shown that the Pudgalavādins also possessed an important Vinayapiṭaka.

In this respect, the question of the value of these various inventions or contributions arises: is it due to them that the Pudgalavādins subsisted for more than ten centuries with a great number of monasteries and monks, doctrinally influencing other schools, whether early or Mahāyānist? To a certain degree the answer is positive, since it is certain that Buddhism, after the Parinirvāṇa of the Buddha, developed in a climate of effervescence, and that Buddhist scholars researched all the possibilities of interpreting the doctrinal problems that might arise.

Furthermore, the doctrine of insubstantiality (*anātmavāda*), together with the concept of rebirth and deliverance of the Buddha, was a difficult idea to understand, even for Buddhists, and was the subject of many criticisms on the part of their adversaries.

This is the reason why the 'semi-heretical' concepts of the Pudgalavādins, the *pudgala*, the imperishable thing (*avipraṇāśadharma*) and the intermediate existence (*antarābhava*), became important notions in early Buddhism.

ESSENTIAL BIBLIOGRAPHY

I — *WORKS FROM THE JAPANESE EDITION OF THE CHINESE CANON, Taishō shinshū daizōkyō*, Tokyo 1924-35:

Abhidharmakośaśāstra (*A p'i t'an hsin lun* 阿毘曇心論), T XXVIII, 1550.

Ch'êng wei-shih-lun shi-chi 成唯識論述記 , T XLIII, 1830.

Chiu-mo-lo-shih fa shih ta-i 鳩摩羅什法師大義 , T XLV, 1856.

Ch'u san-tsang chi chi 出三藏記集 , T LV, 2145.

Dvādaśadhutasūtra (*Shih-êrh t'ou t'o ching* 十二頭陀經), T XVII, 783.

Kao-sêng chuan 高僧傳 , T L, 2059.

K'ai-yüan shih-chiao lu 開元釋教錄 , T LV, 2155.

Laṅkāvatārasūtra (*Ta ch'eng ju lêng ch'ieh ching* 大乘入楞伽經), T XVI, 672.

Lü êrh-shih-êrh ming-liao lun 律二十二明了論 T XXIV, 1461.

Mahāvibhāṣāśāstra (*A p'i ta mo ta p'i p'o sha lun* 阿毘達磨大毘婆沙論), T XXVII, 1545.

Pu chih i lun 部執異論 , T XLIX, 2033.

Samayabhedoparacanacakra (*I pu tsung lun lun* 異部宗輪論), T XLIX 2031.

San fc tu lun 三法度論), T XXV, 1506.

San-mi-ti pu lun (三彌底部論), T XXXII, 1649.

San lun hsüan-i 三論玄義 , T XLV, 1852.

Satyasiddhiśāstra (*Ch'êng shih lun* 成實論), T XXXII, 1646.

Ssŭ a-han-mu ch'ao-chieh 四阿鋡暮抄解 , T XXV, 1505.

Ta chih tu lun 大智度論 (Mahāprajñāpāramitopadésa), T XXV, 1509.

Ta-ch'êng-ch'êng-yeh lun 大乘成業論 (Karmasiddhiprakaraṇa), T XXXI, 1609.

Vijñānakāyapādaśāstra (*A p'i ta mo shih shên tsu lun* 阿毘達磨識身足論), T XXVI, 1539.

Vimuktimārgaśāstra (*Chieh-t'uo tao lun* 解脫道論), T XXXII, 1648.

II — *TRANSLATIONS OF SANSKRIT, TIBETAN AND CHINESE TEXTS*

L'Abhidharmakośa de Vasubandhu, tr. Louis de La Vallée Poussin, 6 vols, Paris 1923-31, repr. Brussels, 1971; English version tr. Leo M. Pruden, *Abhidharmakośabhāṣyam*, 4 vols, Berkeley 1988-90.

Biographies des Moines Eminents (Kao seng tchouan) de Houei-Kiao I, tr. R. Shih, Louvain 1968.

Bu-ston, *History of Buddhism*, 2 vols, tr. E. Obermiller, Heidelberg 1931-2; repr. *The Teaching of Bu-ston*, Delhi 1987, and *The History of Buddhism in India and Tibet*, Delhi 1986.

Candrakīrti Prasannapadā Madhyamakavṛtti, [French] tr. Jacques May, Paris 1959.

Le Compendium de la Super-doctrine (philosophie) (Abhidharmasamuccaya) d'Asaṅga, tr. Walpola Rāhula, Paris 1971.

La Concentration de la marche héroïque Śūraṃgamasamādhisūtra), tr. É. Lamotte, Brussels 1965, repr. 1975.

L'Enseignement de Vimalakīrti (Vimalakīrtinirdeśa), tr. É. Lamotte, Louvain 1962, repr. 1987; English version tr. Sara Boin, *The Teaching of Vimalakīrti*, London 1976.

Harṣacarita, English tr. E.B. Cowell and F.W. Thomas, London 1897; repr. Delhi 19-.

Hsüan-tsang, *Si yu ki [Hsi yü chi] (Buddhist Records of the Western World)*, tr. S. Beal, 2 vols, London 1884, Boston 1962; repr. in 1 vol. Delhi 1981.

I-ching (I-tsing), *A Record of the Buddhist Religion as Practised in India and the Malay Archipelago (AD 671-695)*, tr. J. Takakusu, Oxford 1896; repr. New Delhi 1966.

Mahāvastu, The, tr. J.J. Jones, 3 vols, London 1949; repr. 19?.

Sāṃmitīyanikāyaśāstra, English tr. K. Venkataramanan, Santiniketan 1953.

Das Saṅgītisūtra und sein Kommentar Saṅgītiparyāya, ed. and tr. K. Mittal and V. Stache-Rosen, Berlin 1968.

Tāranātha's History of Buddhism in India, tr. Lama Chimpa and Alaka Chattopadyaya, Simla 1970, repr. Delhi 1990.

Tattvasaṅgraha of Ācarya Shāntarakṣita, crit. ed. Swami Dwarikadas Shastri, Vol.I, Varanasi 1968.

The Tattvasaṅgraha of Shāntarakṣita, with the Commentary by Kamalashīla, tr. by Ganganatha Jha, 2 vols, Baroda 1937, repr. Delhi 1986.

Le Traité de l'acte de Vasubandhu (Karmasiddhiprakaraṇa), tr. É. Lamotte, Bruges 1936; English version tr. Leo M. Pruden, *Karmasiddhiprakaraṇa, The Treatise on Action by Vasubandhu*, Berkeley 1988.

Le Traité de la grande vertu de sagesse (Mahāprajñāpāramitāśāstra) de Nāgārjuna, tr. by É. Lamotte, 5 vols, Louvain and Louvain-la-Neuve, 1944-1980 [English version in the press].

Vijñaptimātratāsiddhi, French tr. and ann. Louis de La Vallée Poussin, Paris 1928, Index, Paris 1948; English tr., *Vasubandhu's Vijñapti-Mātratā-Siddhi*, with Sthiramati's Commentary, by K.N. Chatterjee, Varanasi 1980.

III — *PĀLI TEXTS AND TRANSLATIONS*

Abhidhammatthasaṅgaha *(The Abhidhamma Philosophy)* I, tr. and comm. Bhikkhu J. Kashyap, Patna 1954; repr Delhi 1993.

Abhidhammatthasaṅgaha *(Compendium of Philosophy)*, tr. S.Z. Aung, (PTS) London 1910; repr. 1979.

Aṅguttara Nikāya, ed. R. Morris and E. Hardy, 5 vols, (PTS) London 1885-1900, repr. 1960-89; tr. F.L. Woodward, *The Book of Gradual Sayings*, 5 vols, (PTS) London 1932-36; repr. 1972-88.

Aṭṭhasālinī, ed. E. Muller, (PTS) London 1897, rev. ed. 1979.

Dhammapada, ed. S. Sumangala, (PTS) London 1914.

Dhammapada aṭṭhakathā, ed. K. Ratnasara, Simon Hewavitarne Bequest Series, Part 1 (Vol V), Colombo 1919, Part 2 (Vol. XIII) Colombo 1922.

Dhammasaṅgaṇī, ed. L. Muller, (PTS) London 1885, repr. 1978; tr. C.A.F. Rhys Davids, *A Buddhist Manual of Psychological Ethics*, (PTS) London 1900, 3rd ed. 1974, repr. 1993.

Dhammasaṅgaṇī, French tr. and ann. André Bareau, Paris 1951.

Dīgha Nikāya, ed. T.W. Rhys Davids and J.E. Carpenter, 3 vols, new ed. (PTS) London

1960, repr. 1975-92; tr. by T.W. and C.A.F. Rhys Davids, *Dialogues of the Buddha*, 3 vols, (PTS) London 1899-1921; repr. 1989-92.

Itivuttaka, ed. E. Windisch, (PTS) London 1890, repr. 1975.

Jātaka, ed. V. Fausbøll, 6 vols, (PTS) London 1877-96, repr. 1990-1.

Kathāvatthu, ed. A.C. Taylor, 2 vols. (PTS) London 1894-7, repr. in 1 vol, 1979; tr. S.Z. Aung and C.A.F. Rhys Davids, *Points of Controversy*, (PTS) London 1915; repr, 1993.

Majjhima Nikāya, ed. V. Trenckner and R. Chalmers, 3 vols, new ed. (PTS) London 1954-59, repr 1977-93; tr. by I.B. Horner, *Middle Length Sayings*, 3 vols, (PTS) London 1954-59, repr. 1989-93.

Milindapañha, ed. V. Trenckner, new ed. (PTS) London 1963 repr. (with ṭīkā) 1986; tr. I.B. Horner, *Milinda's Questions*, 2 vols, (PTS) London 1963-64; repr. 1990-1.

Nettippakaraṇa, ed. E. Hardy, new ed., (PTS) London 1961; tr. Bhikkhu Ñāṇamoli, *The Guide*, (PTS) London 1962, repr. 1977.

Peṭakopadesa, ed. A. Barua, (PTS) London 1949, rev. ed. 1982; tr. Bhikkhu Ñāṇamoli, *Piṭaka Disclosure*, (PTS) London 1964; repr. 1979.

Puggalapaññatti, ed. R. Morris (PTS) London 1883; repr. (with aṭṭhakathā) 1972; tr. B.C. Law, *A Designation of Human Types*, (PTS) London 1922; repr. 1992.

Puggalapaññatti aṭṭhakathā, ed. G. Landsberg and C.A.F. Rhys Davids, *Journal of the Pali Text Society*, London 1914, rev. ed. (with Puggalapaññatti) 1972.

Saṃyutta Nikāya, ed. L. Feer, 6 vols, (PTS) London 1884-1904, repr. 1975-91; tr. C.A.F. Rhys Davids and F.L. Woodward, *The Book of the Kindred Sayings*, 5 vols, (PTS) London 1917-30 repr. 1980-92.

Suttanipāta, ed. Dines Andersen and Helmer Smith, (PTS) London 1913, repr. 1990.

Udāna, ed. P. Steinthal, (PTS) London 1885, repr. 1982.

Udāna aṭṭhakathā, ed. F.L. Woodward, (PTS) London 1926, repr. 1977.

Vinaya, ed. H. Oldenberg, 5 vols, London 1879-83, repr. 1969-84; tr. I.B. Horner, *The Book of the Discipline*, 6 vols, Oxford 1938-66; repr. (PTS) London 1982-92.

Visuddhimagga, ed. C.A.F. Rhys Davids, 2 vols, (PTS) London 1920-21, repr. in 1 vol 1975; tr. Bhikkhu Ñāṇamoli, *The Path of Purification*, Colombo 1956; repr. in 2 vols, Berkeley 1976, combined vol, Kandy 1992.

IV — *MODERN WORKS*

Akanuma, Chizen 赤沼智善, *The Comparative Catalogue of Chinese Āgamas and Pāli Nikāyas*, Nagoya 1929, repr. Tokyo 1958.

Akanuma Chizen, *Indo Bukkyō Koyū Meishi Jiten* 印度佛教固有名詞辭典, new ed., Kyoto 1967.

Bagchi, P.C. *Le Canon bouddhique en Chine*, 2 vols (Sino-Indica No.1, IV) Paris 1927-38.

Bagchi, P.C., 'On the Original Buddhism, Its Canon and Language', *Sino-Indian Studies* II.

Bareau, André, 'Les origines du Śāriputrābhidharmaśāstra, *Le Muséon* LXIII, 1-2 (Louvain 1950), pp.69-95.

Bareau, André, *L'Absolu en philosophie bouddhique (Evolution de la notion d'Asaṃskṛta)* (Centre de Docum. Universitaire) Paris 1951.

Bareau, André, *Les Religions de l'Inde (Bouddhisme)*, Paris 1951.

Bareau, André, *Les sectes bouddhiques du Petit Véhicule* (Publ.EFEO XXXVIII) Saigon 1955.

Bareau, André, *Les premiers conciles bouddhiques* (Annales du Musée Guimet LX) Paris 1955.

Bareau, André, 'L'absolu dans le Bouddhisme', Entretien [Interview] 1955, Inst. Fr. d'Indologie, Pondichery 1956.

Bareau, André, 'Les controverses relatives à la nature de l'Arhant dans le Bouddhisme ancien', *Indo-Iranian Journal* I, 3, 1957.

Bareau, André, 'Richesse de la pensée bouddhique ancienne', *Presence du Bouddhisme, France-Asie* 153-7, Saigon 1959.

Bareau, André, *Bouddha* (Coll. Philosophes de tous les temps), Paris 1962.

Bareau, André, 'La notion de la personne dans le bouddhisme indien', *Problèmes de la personne*, ed. Ignac Meyerson, Paris 1973.

Beal, Samuel, *Si-yu-ki* 西域記 *(Buddhist Records of the Western World)*, 2 vols, London 1884, Boston 1962; repr. in 1 vol. Delhi 1981.

Beal, Samuel, *The Romantic Legend of Śākya Buddha* (佛本行集經), London 1875, repr. Delhi 1985.

Bechert, Heinz, ed. *The Dating of the Historical Buddha*, 2 parts, Göttingen 1991-2.

Bhattacharya, Kamaleswar, *l'Ātman-Brahman dans le Bouddhisme ancien* (Publ. EFEO XXX) Paris 1973.

Chavannes, E., 'Voyage de Song-Yun dans l'Udyāna and le Gandhāra (518-522 p.C.)', BEFEO III, 1903, pp.379-441.

Ch'en, Kenneth, *Buddhism in China*, Princeton 1964.

Ch'en-yüan 陳垣 *Shih shih i nien lu*, Peking 1964.

Chih Hsü 智旭 *Yueh tsang chih chin* 閱藏知津 ('The Guide to the Buddhist Tripiṭaka'), Shanghai 1930.

Conze, Edward, *Buddhist Thought in India*, London 1962, rev. ed. 1983.

Conze, Edward, *Thirty Years of Buddhist Studies*, London 1967.

Couvreur, S., *Ho-Kien-fou, Dictionnaire chinois-français*, Imprimerie de la Mission Catholique, 1890.

Dasgupta, S., *A History of Indian Philosophy*, 5 vols, Cambridge University Press, 1963.

Demiéville, Paul, *Choix d'études bouddhiques* (collected articles), Leiden 1973.

Demiéville, Paul, 'L'état actuel des études bouddhiques', *Revue de théologie et de philosophie* XV, 62 (Lausanne 1927), pp.43-65.

Demiéville, Paul, 'Sur l'authenticité du *Ta tch'eng k'i sin louen*', *Bull. de la Maison Franco-Japonaise* II, 1929, pp.1-79; repr. in *Choix*, pp.1-79.

Demiéville, Paul, 'L'origine des sectes bouddhiques d'après Paramārtha', *Mélanges chinois et bouddhiques* I, Brussels 1931-32, pp.15-64; repr. in *Choix*, pp.80-130.

Demiéville, Paul, 'La pénétration du bouddhisme dans la tradition philosophique chinoise', *Cahiers d'histoire mondiale* III, 1956, pp.19-38; repr. in *Choix*, pp.241-60.

Dharmasiri, Gunapala, *A Buddhist Critique of the Christian Concept of God*, Colombo 1974.

Dutt, Nalinaksha, *Buddhist Sects in India*, Calcutta 1970; repr. Delhi 1978.

Dutt, Nalinaksha, *Mahāyāna Buddhism*, London 1978.

Dutt, Sukumar, *Buddhist Monks and Monasteries of India*, London 1962; repr. Delhi

1988.

Edgerton, Franklin, *Buddhist Hybrid Sanskrit Dictionary*, New Haven 1953; repr. Delhi 1993.

Filliozat, Jean and Paul Demiéville, *L'Inde classique* II, with the collab. of L. Renou, O. Lacombe, P. Meille, Publ.EFEO, Paris and Hanoi 1953, repr. Paris 1985.

Filliozat, Jean, *Les philosophies de l'Inde*, Paris 1970.

Foucher, A., *La vie du Bouddha d'après les textes et monuments de l'Inde*, Paris 1949.

Ghosh, N.N., *Early History of Kauśāmbi*, Allahabad 1935.

Giles, H.A., *The Travels of Fa-hien*, London 1877, rev. ed. 1923, rep. 19-.

Glasenapp, Helmuth von, *Buddhism — A Non-Theistic Religion*, tr. by Irmgard Schloegel, London 1970.

Gonda, J., *Védisme et Hindouisme ancien*, Paris 1962.

Hōbōgirin, Dictionnaire encyclopédique du bouddhisme d'après les sources chinoises et japonaise, ed. Paul Demiéville, Jacques May, Jean Gernet, Anna Seidel and Hubert Durt, 1928 -

Hurvitz, Leon, 'The Road to Buddhist Salvation as Described by Vasubhadra', JAOS 87, No.4, Oct.-Dec. 1967.

Jayatilleke, K.N., *Early Buddhist Theory of Knowledge*, London 1963, repr. Delhi 1988.

Joshi, L.M., *Studies in the Buddhistic Culture of India*, 2nd ed., Delhi 1977.

Keith, J. Berriedale, *Buddhist Philosophy of India and Ceylon*, Oxford 1923, repr. New Delhi 1993.

Kern, H., *Histoire du Bouddhisme dans l'Inde*, Paris 1901; tr. from *Manual of Indian Buddhism*, Strasbourg 1898, repr. Delhi 1989.

Kimura, Taiken木村泰賢*Kimura Taiken Zenshi* 木 村 泰 賢 全 集 (*Shojō Bukkyō Shisō Ron* 小 乗 佛 教 思 想 論), new ed., Tokyo 1972.

Kloppenborg, Ria, *The Paccekabuddha, A Buddhist Ascetic*, Leiden 1974.

La Vallée Poussin, Louis de, 'Les soixante quinze et les cent Dharma', *Ext. du Muséon* XXIV, 1905.

La Vallée Poussin, Louis de, *The Way to Nirvāṇa*, Cambridge University Press, 1917, repr. Delhi 1982.

La Vallée Poussin, Louis de, *Nirvāṇa*, Paris 1925.

La Vallée Poussin, Louis de, 'La controverse du temps et du *pudgala* dans le *Vijñānakāya*', EA (*Etudes Asiatiques publ. à l'occasion du 25e anniv. de l'EFEO*), Paris 1925, pp.358-76.

La Vallée Poussin, Louis de, 'Les Buddha et les abhijñā', *Le Muséon*, 1931, pp.335-42.

Lamotte, É. (tr. S. Boin-Webb), 'A composite sūtra from the Ekottarāgama', *Buddhist Studies Review* 12, 1 (1995), pp.27-46.

Lamotte, É, *Histoire du Bouddhisme indien, des origines à l'ère Śaka*, Louvain 1958, repr. 1976; English version, referred to here, by Sara Boin-Webb, *History of Indian Buddhism, from the origins to the Śaka era*, Louvain-la-Neuve 1988.

Law, Bimala Churn, *Geography of Early Buddhism*, London 1932.

Law, Bimala Churn, *Kauśāmbi in Ancient Literature*, Delhi 1939.

Liebenthal, W., 'Shih Hui-yuan's Buddhism', JAOS 70, 1950.

Lin Li-kouang, *L'aide-mémoire de la Vraie Loi (Saddharmasmṛtyupasthāna-sūtra)*, Paris 1949.

Lüders, H., *A List of Brahmī Inscriptions from the Earliest times to about A.D.400* (EI X, 1912).

Malalasekera, G.P., *Dictionary of Pāli Proper Names*, 2 vols, new ed. London 1960, repr. 1975.

Malalasekera, G.P., *The Truth of Anattā*, Buddhist Publication Society, Kandy 1966.

Masson, Joseph, *La religion populaire dans le canon bouddhique pāli*, Louvain 1942.

Masuda, J., *Origin and Doctrines of Early Indian Buddhist Schools. A translation of the Hsüan-Chwang version of Vasumitra's Treatise (Ibushūrin-ron)*, Leipzig 1925.

Minh Chau, Thích, *Hsuan-tsang: The Pilgrim and Scholar*, Nhatrang-Vietnam 1963.

Minh Chau, Thích, *The Chinese Madhyama Āgama and the Pāli Majjhima Nikāya (A comparative study)*, Saigon 1964, repr. Delhi 1991.

Mochizuki, Shinkō 望月信享, *Bukkyō Daijiten* 佛教大辭典, 10 vols, Tokyo 1957-63.

Murti, T.R.V., *The Central Philosophy of Buddhism: A Study of the Mādhyamika System*, London 1955, repr. 1980.

Mus, Paul, *La lumière sur les six voies*, Travaux et mémoires de l'Inst. d'Ethnologie XXXV, Paris 1939.

Ñāṇananda, *Concept and Reality in Early Buddhist Thought*, Kandy 1971.

Nanjio, Bunyu, *A Catalogue of the Chinese Translation of the Buddhist Tripiṭaka*, Oxford 1883; repr. Delhi 1989.

Nilakanta Sastri, K.A. *Fa-hien, the Chinese Pilgrim*, ??

Nyanatiloka, *Buddhist Dictionary*, 3rd ed., Colombo 1972, repr. Kandy 1988.

Nyanatiloka, *Vocabulaire bouddhique des termes et doctrines du canon Pāli*, tr. S. Karpelès, Paris 1961.

Nyanatiloka, *Guide through the Abhidhamma-Piṭaka*, 1st ed., Colombo 1938; 2nd ed. Kandy 1957, 3rd ed. 1971.

Oda, Tokunō 織田得能, *Bukkyō Daijiten* 佛教大辭典, Tokyo 1928.

Przyluski, Jean, *Le Concile de Rājagṛha, Introduction de l'histoire des canons et des sectes bouddhiques*, Paris 1926-29.

Radhakrishnan, S., *Indian Philosophy* II, London 1929; repr. Delhi 1989.

Rahula, Walpola, *L'enseignement du Buddha*, Paris 1961.

Rahula, Walpola, *What the Buddha Taught*, London 1959, repr. 1990.

Renou, Louis, *Les littératures de l'Inde*, Paris 1966.

Robinson, R.H., *Early Mādhyamika in India and China*, Madison 1967, repr. Delhi 1978.

Sasaki, H. Genjun, 'Hīnayāna Schools in China and Japan' (*Présence du Bouddhisme*), *France-Asie* 153-7, Saigon 1959.

Seyfort Ruegg, David, *La théorie du Tathāgatagarbha et du Gotra*, (Publ.EFEO) Paris 1969.

Shastri, Ajay Mitra, *An Outline of Early Buddhism*, Varanasi 1965.

Silburn, Lilian, *Instant et Cause, Le discontinu dans la pensée philosophique de l'Inde*, Paris 1955.

Stcherbatsky, Th., *The Conception of Buddhist Nirvāṇa*, Leningrad 1927, repr. Delhi 1989.

Stcherbatsky, Th., *The Soul Theory of the Buddhists*, St. Petersburg, 1919, repr.

Varanasi 1970.

Stcherbatsky, Th., *The Central Conception of Buddhism and the Meaning of the Word Dharma*, new ed., Calcutta 1956, repr. Delhi 1988.

Takakusu, Junjirō, 'The Abhidharma Literature of the Sarvāstivādins', *Journal of the Pali Text Society*, 1905 (repr. 1978), pp.67-146

Takakusu, Junjirō, *The Essentials of Buddhist Philosophy*, ed. W.-T. Chan and C. Moore, Honolulu 1947; repr. Delhi 1975.

Thien Chau, Thích, 'Le Tridharmakaśāstra, Etudes philologiques et doctrinale', unpublished thesis.

Thomas, Edward J., *The History of Buddhist Thought*, London 1933, repr 1971.

Ui, Hakuju , *Shaku Dōan kenkyū* , Tokyo 1956.

Upasak, C.S., *Dictionary of Early Buddhist Monastic Terms*, Varanasi 1975.

Watters, T., *On Yuan Chwang's Travels in India*, 2 vols, London 1904-5; repr. New York 1971 and Delhi 1974.

Wogihara, Unrai 荻原雲來 , *The Sanskrit-Chinese Dictionary of Buddhist Technical Terms* 梵漢對譯佛教辭典 *(Mahāvyutpatti)*, Tokyo 1959.

Wright, Arthur P., *Buddhism in Chinese History*, London 1959; repr. New York 1965.

Zürcher, E., *The Buddhist Conquest of China*, 2 vols, Leiden 1959, repr. 1972.

INDEX OF PLACE NAMES

- A-fan t'u (14)
- Ahicchatra (14)
- Ànandapura (14)
- Aviddhakarna (14)
- Ayumukha (14)
- Badkshan (14)
- Bombay (16)
- Ch'ang-an (40, 42)
- Ceylon (4)
- China (1, 38, 41, 42, 87)
- Chi-chou (37)
- Ching-chou (42)
- Chien-K'ang (38)
- Hsiang-yang (38)
- India (1, 5, 15, 32, 95)
- Iranaparvata (14)
- Junnar (16)
- Kanheri (16, 17)
- Kapilavastu (14)
- Kapitha (14)
- Karnasuvarna (14)
- Kashmir (32, 37, 38)
- Kosala (18)
- Kausámbi (6)
- Lo-yang (38, 39, 40)
- Lu-shan (38, 39)
- Magadha (15, 18)
- Màlava (14)
- Mrgadàva (14)
- Nàsik (16, 17)
- Pàtaliputra (6)
- Sàrnàth (9, 12, 14)
- Sindh (13, 14)
- Sràvasti (14)
- Sri Lanka (1)
- Tibet (1)
- Vaisali (1, 3, 10, 15)
- Valabhì (14)
- Visska (8, 14)

INDEX OF AUTHORS' NAMES

- A. Bareau (VII, IX, 1, 2, 3, 4, 5, 6, 8, 9, 10, 11, 12, 13, 15, 16, 17, 18, 26, 27, 30, 31, 34, 50, 51, 54, 58, 71, 77, 84, 126, 131, 137, 138, 139, 145, 176, 177, 179, 180, 183, 185, 188, 189, 194, 195, 196, 197, 198, 199, 200, 201, 202)
- A. Berriedale Keith (138)
- A. M. Shastri (17)
- Arthur P. Wright (41)
- Bagchi, P.C. (31, 33, 36, 37, 42, 88, 92)
- Bareau, André (*see* A. Bareau)
- Beal, Samuel (9)
- Bhattacharya, K. (132, 141)
- B. M. Law (114)
- Buddhaghosa (153)
- Bunjù Nanjio (33, 34)
- Buston (31)
- Ch'en, Kenneth K. (44)
- Conze, Edward (1, 141, 148, 156, 187, 196)
- Dasgupta, S. (132, 133, 141, 159, 166, 183, 184)
- Demiéville, Paul (2, 4, 5, 6, 7, 8, 10, 12, 17, 18, 27, 28, 29, 34, 39, 40, 117, 123)
- Dharmasiri, Gunapola (81)
- Dutt, Nalinaksha (2, 5, 10, 13, 14)
- Dutt, Sukumar (9, 10)
- Edgerton, Franklin (131)
- È. Lamotte (1, 2, 3, 5, 6, 9, 10, 11, 14, 15, 16, 17, 20, 21, 25, 26, 27, 28, 29, 32, 38, 64, 66, 189, 221)
- E. Zùrcher (20, 38, 40, 85, 87)
- F. Edgerton (*see* Edgerton Franklin)
- Filliozat, Jean (134)
- Ghosh, N.N. (6)
- G. H. Sasaki (41, 204)
- Glasenapp, Helmuth von (81)
- Gonda, J. (82, 87, 131, 132, 138, 139)
- Gottingen (1, 9, 10)
- G. P. Malalasekera (134, 137)
- Gunapàla Dharmasiri *see* Dharmasiri, Gunapola
- H. Kern (131)
- Helmuth von Glasenapp (*see* Glasenapp, Helmuth von)
- Hòbògirin (33, 34, 37, 39, 140)
- Hurvitz, Leon (21)

- Jayatilleke, K.N. (81, 82, 86, 153, 161)
- J. Filliozat (*see* Filliozet, Jean)
- J. Gonda (*see* Gonda, J.)
- J. Masson (79)
- J. Masuda (134, 140, 146, 192, 202, 216)
- J. Przyluski (6, 7, 9, 138, 145)
- K. Bhattacharya (*see* Bhattacharya, K.)
- K. Ch'en (*see* Ch'en Kenneth, K.)
- K. N. Jayatilleke (*see* Jayatilleke, K. N.)
- Keith, A. Berriedale (138)
- Kern, H. (*see* H. Kern)
- Kloppenborg, Ria (54)
- L. Renou (*see* Renou, L.)
- La Vallée Poussin, L. de (5, 7, 9, 20, 25, 27, 52, 131, 140, 143, 173, 192, 202)
- Lamotte, Étienne (*see* É. Lamotte)
- Law, B. M. (*see* B. M. Law)
- Leon Hurvitz (*see* Hurvitz, Leon)
- Malalasekera, G.P. (*see* G.P. Malalasekera)
- Masson, J. (*see* J. Masson)
- Masuda, J. (*see* J. Masuda)
- Minh Chau, Thích (9, 20, 36, 38)
- Murti, T. R. V. (128, 137)
- Ñāṇananda (135)
- Nanjio, Bunyū (*see* Bunyū Nanjio)
- N. Dutt (*see* Dutt, Nalinaksha)
- N. N. Ghosh (*see* Ghosh, N.N.)
- Nyanatiloka (26, 48, 146)
- P. C. Bagchi (*see* Bagchi P. C.)
- P. Demiéville (*see* Demiéville, Paul)
- Pruden, Leo M. (56, 59, 60, 63, 64, 77, 78, 83, 114, 119, 153, 189)
- Przyluski, Jean (*see* Jean Przyluski)
- Radhakrishnan, S. (132, 139, 166, 174)
- Rahula, Walpola (54, 60, 66, 71)
- Renou, L. (*see* L. Renou)
- Robinson, R. H. (*see* R. H. Robinson)
- R. H. Robinson (39)
- Rhys Davids (*see* Rhys Davids, C.A.F.)
- Rhys Davids, C.A.F. (5, 74, 78)
- Ria Kloppenborg (*see* Kloppenborg, Ria)
- Samuel Beal (*see* Beal Samuel)
- Sasaki, G.H. (*see* G.H. Sasaki)
- Shastri, A.M. (*see* A.M. Shastri)

- S. Dasgupta (*see* Dasgupta, S.)
- S. Radhakrishnana (*see* Radhakrishnana, S.)
- Stcherbatsky, Th. (17)
- Sukumar Dutt (*see* Dutt, Sukmar)
- Takakusu, J. (13, 18, 28, 30, 168)
- Th. Stcherbatsky (*see* Stcherbatsky, Th.)
- T. R. V. Murti (*see* Murti, T. R. V.)
- T. Watters (9, 13, 18, 20)
- Thich Minh Chau (*see* Minh Chau Thích)
- Watters, T. (*see* T. Watters)
- W. Rahula (*see* Rahula, W.)
- Wright, Arthur P. (*see* Arthur P. Wright)
- Zürcher, E. (*see* E. Zùrcher)

INDEX CHINESE AND SANSKRIT NOUNS MENTIONED IN THE BOOK

			page
San fa tu lun	三法度論	Tridharmakaśāstra	IX
Ssū a-han-mu ch'ao chieh	四阿鋡暮抄解		IX
San-mi-ti pu lun	三彌底部論	Sāṃmitīyanikāyaśāstra	IX
Lü êrh-shih-êrh ming-liao lun	律二十二明了論	Vinayadvāviṃśatividyāśāstra	IX
K'ê-chu	可住	vatsya, vāsī	7
T'an-wu-tê	曇無德		10
San fa tu lun	三法度論	Tridharmakaśāstra	19
Ssū a-han-mu ch'ao chieh	四阿鋡暮抄解		-
San fa tu	三法度	Tridharmaka	-
San-mi-ti pu lun	三彌底部論	Sāṃmitīyanikāyaśāstra	-
Lü êrh-shih-êrh ming-liao lun	律二十二明了論	Vinayadvāviṃśatividyāśāstra	-
Chung-a-han	中阿鋡		20
Ch'ang-a-han	長阿鋡		-
Tsêng-i-a-han	增一阿鋡		-
Tsa-a-han	雜阿鋡		-
Pieh-i-tsa-a-han	別譯雜阿鋡		-
Tao-an	道安		-
Shêng fa yin ching	聖法印經	Āryadharmamudrāsūtra	21
Shuo ch'u ching	說處經	Deśanasthānasūtra	-
Tsui-shang-nü-jên hsiu-to-lo	最上女人修多羅	Uttamāstrīsūtra	-
Pa-ch'a-yeh-na hsiu-to-lo	跋蹉耶那修多羅	Vātsyāyanasūtra	-
T'ien-shih hsiu-to-lo	天使修多羅	Devadūtasūtra	22
T'ien-shih ching	天使經	Devadūtasūtra	23
Chung-tan ching	重擔經		24
Wu-chih ching	無使經		25
Shê-li-fu-a-p'i-t'an	舍利弗阿毘曇	Sāriputrābhidharma	26
Ch'ang-an	長安		27
P'o-shu-tou lü	婆籔斗律	Vinayavastu	28
Tu-pa-t'i-shih lü	優波提舍律	Upadeśavinaya	-
Pi-ch'iu-ni lü	比丘尼律	Bhikṣuṇīvinaya	-
Po-lo-t'i-mu ch'a lun	波羅提木叉論	Prātimokṣaśāstra	-
Po-lo-i	波羅夷	Pārājikas	29
Sêng-ch'ieh-ti	僧伽胝施沙	Saṅghādisesas	-
Po-lo-i-ni-ka	波羅逸尼柯	Pārāsarnikas	-
Po-ti-t'i-sha-ni	波胝提舍尼	Pratideśanīyas	-
Tu-k'a-to	獨柯多	duṣkṛtas	-
P'o-shu-tou lü	婆籔斗律	Vinayavastu	-
T'ou-lan-chih-yeh	偷蘭遮耶	Sthūlātyayas	-
Ni-sa-ch'i-po-lo-i-ni-k'a	尼薩耆波羅逸尼柯	Niḥsargikapārāsarnikas	-
Hsiu tui	學對	Śaikṣadharmas	30
San fa tu lun	三法度論	Tridharmakaśāstra	34
Ssū a-han-mu ch'ao chieh	四阿鋡暮抄解		-
San-mi-ti pu lun	三彌底部論	Sāṃmitīyanikāyaśāstra	-
Lü êrh-shih-êrh ming-liao lun	律二十二明了論	Vinayadvāviṃśatividyāśāstra	-
San fa tu lun	三法度論	Tridharmakaśāstra	-
Taishō Shinshū Daizōkyō	大正新修大藏經		
Yüan, Ming	元明		34
Shan-hsien	山賢		-
Hui-yüan	慧遠		-
Fa-hsien	法賢	Dharmabhadra	-
Kung-tê-hsien	功德賢	Guṇabhadra	-
Chih-hsien	智賢	Jñānabhadra	-
Chung-hsien	眾賢	Saṅghabhadra	-
Hsien	賢		-
Shih-ch'in	世親	Vasu	-

INDEX CHINESE AND SANSKRIT NOUNS MENTIONED IN THE BOOK

			page
Shih	世		-
Shan	山		-
P'o-su-pa-t'o	婆素跋陀		-
Shan-hsien	山賢		34
Shan-hsien	山賢		35
P'o-su-pa-t'o	婆素跋陀		-
P'o-su-pa-t'o	婆蘇跋陀		-
P'o-su-pa-tu	婆素跋度		-
Chin-hsien	今賢		-
Shan-hsien	山賢		-
Ts'ai-wu	財物		-
Chin	金		-
Chin-hsien	山賢		-
Chin	金		-
Chin	今		-
Chin	金		-
Chin	金		-
Chin	今		-
Chin-hsien	今 賢		-
Ming	明		-
Yüan	元		-
Shan-hsien	山賢		-
Sêng-ch'ieh-hsien	僧伽先	Sanghasena	-
San fa tu ching chi	三 法 度 經 記		-
San fa tu lun hsü	三 法 度 論 序		-
Shan-hsien	山 賢		-
Ming	明		-
Yüan	元		36
Wei-yüan	爲 遠		-
Chung-t'ien	眾 天	Sanghadeva	-
Ch'ü-t'an	瞿 曇	Gautama	-
Chi-pin	罽 賓	Kashmir	-
Chien-yüan	建 元		-
Sêng-ch'ieh-po-ch'êng	僧 伽 跋 澄	Shaṅghabhūti	-
Tsun-p'o-hsü-mi-p'u-sa-so-chi lun	尊 婆 須 密 菩 薩 所 集 論	Āryavasumitra saṅgītiśāstra	-
Tan-mo-nan-t'i	曇 摩 難 提	Dharmanandīn	-
Kuang-shuo	廣 說	Abhidharma vibhāṣa	37
San fa tu	三 法 度	Tridharmakaśāstra	-
Fa-ho	法 和	śramaṇa	-
Chichou	冀 州		-
Lo-yang	洛 陽		-
A-p'i-t'an	阿 毘 曇		-
Kuang shuo chung ching	廣 說 眾 經		-
T'ai-yüan	太 元		-
Yang-tzū	江 子		-
Yao-hsing	盧 山		-
Lu-shan	姚 興		-
A-p'i-t'an hsin lun	阿 毘 曇 心 論	Abhidharmahṛdayaśāstra	-
San fa tu lun	三 法 度 論	Tridharmakaśāstra	-
Pan-jo	般 若	prajñā	-
Lung-an	隆 安		-
Chien-K'ang	建 康		-
Nanking	南 京		-
Chin	晉		-

INDEX CHINESE AND SANSKRIT NOUNS MENTIONED IN THE BOOK

			page
Wang-Hsün	王旬		-
Shih Hui-ch'i	釋慧持	śramaṇa	-
T ung T'ing	東亭		-
Tsêng-i a-han ching	增一阿含經		-
Chung a-han ching	中阿含經	Madhyamāgama	-
Sêng-chieh-lo-ch'a	僧伽羅刹	Saṅgharakṣa	-
Tao-tsu	道慈		38
Yü-chou	豫州		-
Li-pao	李寶		-
T'ang-hua	唐化		-
Ch'ien Chin	前晉		-
A-p'i-t'an pa chien tu	阿毘曇八犍度	Abhidharmāṣṭaskandhśāstra	-
A-p'i-t'an hsin lun	阿毘曇心論	Abhidharmahṛdayaśāstra	-
Pi-po-sha-a-p'i-t'an	鞞婆沙阿毘曇	Abhidharmavibhāṣā	-
Kuang shuo chung ching	廣説衆經		-
Hsi Chin	西晉		-
Chung a-han ching	中阿含經	Madhyamāgama	-
Chung i a-han ching	增一阿含經	Ekottarāgama	-
A-p'i-t'an hsin lun	阿毘曇心論	Abhidharmahṛdayaśāstra	-
San fa tu lun	三法度論	Tridharmakaśāstra	-
Chiao-shou pi-ch'ü-ni fa	教授比丘尼法		-
Hui-yüan	慧遠		-
Chia	賈		-
Yen-men	鴈門		-
Hsü-ch'ang	許昌		-
Hsiang-yang	襄陽		-
A-p'i-t'an hsin lun	阿毘曇心論	Abhidharmahṛdayaśāstra	39
San fa tu lun	三法度論	Tridharmakaśāstra	-
Fa-lin	法琳		-
Po-lien-shê	白蓮社		-
Ching-t'u tsung	淨土宗		-
San fa tu lun	三法度論	Tridharmakaśāstra	-
A-p'i-t'an hsin lun	阿毘曇心論	Abhidharmahṛdayaśāstra	-
Chiu-mo-lo-shih fa-shih ta-i	鳩摩羅什法師大義		-
Po-su-pa-t'o	婆素跋陀		-
Chin	晉		40
T'ai-yüan	太元		41
Si Chin	西晉		-
Sui	隋		-
T'ang	唐		-
Chin	晉		-
Chin	晉		-
Fa-hsien	法顯		42
Han	漢		-
Chin	晉		-
Chin	晉		-
Chieh	覺	jñāna	43
Tê	德	kuśala	-
Ê	惡	akuśala	-
I	依	niśraya	-
Hsiang	想	saṃjñā	48
Shou-shêng chieh	受生戒	prakṛtiśīla	-
Ch'u-yao chieh	出要戒	niḥsāraṇaśīla	-
Nu	怒	krodha	49

INDEX CHINESE AND SANSKRIT NOUNS MENTIONED IN THE BOOK

			page
Wu-hsiang	無想	asaṃjñāsamādhi	50
Fei wo	非我	anātamaka	51
Shêng shê chih	生死智	upapādacyutijñāna	52
Hui	恚	pratigha	65
Hui	恚	pratigha	66
Wu-hsiang	無想	asaṃjñāsamādhi	71
Yü shêng t'ien	欲生天	apsarā	77
Li yü t'ien	離欲天	vitarāgadeva	-
Shuo yü shêng t'ien	説欲生天	Nirmanāṇaratis	-
Ch'in yü shêng t'ien	親欲生天	Paranirmitavaśavartins	-
Shi hua yü shêng t'ien	細滑欲生天		-
Hsi hua ju	細滑入	spraṣṭavyāyatana	80
Tu ju	度入	tarkāyatana	-
Chieh-t'uo ju	解脱入	vimokṣāyatana	-
Hsi hua ju	細滑入	spraṣṭsvyāyatana	-
Ching chieh	境界	viṣaya	-
Chin ching chieh	近境界	saṃnikṛṣṭaviṣaya	-
Pu chin ching chieh	不近境界	viprakṛṣṭiviṣaya	81
Wu ching-chieh	無境界	aṇṣayātana	-
Tu ju	度入	tarkāyatana	-
I ch'u yin shuo	一處因説	ekahetudṛṣṭi	-
Pu chêng yin shuo	不正因説	visamahetudṛṣṭi	-
Pu-mie	不滅	avipraṇāśa	85
Ssū a-han-mu ch'ao chieh	四阿鋡慕抄解		-
San fo chieh t'uo tu	三法解脱度		-
P'a-su-pa-t'o	婆蘇跋陀		-
P'a-su-pa-t'o	婆素跋陀		-
P'a-su-pa-t'o	婆素跋度		-
Chin-hsien	今賢		-
Shan-hsien	山賢		-
Ch'ao chieh	抄解		90
Chien-yüan	建元		-
Yeh	鄴		-
Chang-tê	漳德		-
Honan	河南		-
Fo-nien	佛念		-
Fo-hu	佛護		-
Sêng tao	僧導		87
T'an-chiu	曇究		-
Sêng-jui	僧叡		-
Fan	梵		-
Ch'in	秦		-
Fo-hu	佛護		88
Chien-yüan	建元		-
Yüeh tsang chih chin	閱藏知津		-
Chih-hsü	智旭		-
Shou	受		89
Chieh	覺		90
Chin ch'an	近禪	upacārasamādhi	-
Hsiang	想	samjña	-
Nu	怒	Krodha	-
Shuo-chu hsiu-tu-lu	説處修妒路	Deśanasthānasūtra	91
Kuo-ch'ü hsiu-tu-lu	過去修妒路	Atītasūtra	-
Chi shen	己身		-

INDEX CHINESE AND SANSKRIT NOUNS MENTIONED IN THE BOOK

			page
Wo	我		92
Fa shih	法 智	dharmajñāna	-
Kuan shih	觀 智	vicārajñāna	-
Wei chih chih	未 知 智	ajñatajñāna	-
Yin shing	婬 行		93
Chêng sê-wei	正 思 惟		-
Chung shêng	眾 生	sattva	94
Chung shêng	眾 生	sattva	95
Shou chieh-shou	受 教 授	upādānaprajñapti	-
Fang-pien chieh-shou	方 便 教 授	upāyaprajñapti	-
Mieh chieh-shou	滅 教 授	nirodhaprajñapti	-
Chih nien	及 念		99
Yu hsi	有 喜	prīti	-
Lo	樂		-
San-mi-ti pu lun	三 彌 底 部 論	Sāṃmitīyanikāyaśāstra	-
I-shuo-lun	依 説 論		-
Hsi chin	西 晉		-
Kai yüan shih-chieh lu	開 元 釋 教 錄		-
Chin	秦		-
yin	陰	skandha	-
Túng	痛	vedanā	-
Shêng yin	盛 陰	upādanaskandha	-
Chih-hsü	智 旭		101
Shêng	生	upacaya	-
Pu-mieh	不 滅	avipraṇāśa	-
I-shuo-jên	依 説 人	āśrayaprajñaptipudgala	108
Ti-shuo-jên	度 説 人	saṅkramprajñaptipudgala	-
Mieh-shuo-jên	滅 説 人	nirodhaprajñaptipudgala	109
Lü êrh-shih-êrh ming-liao lun	律 二 十 二 明 了 論	Vinayadvāviṃśatividyāśāstra	117
Fu-t'o-to-lo-to	弗 陀 多 羅 多		-
Fo-t'o-to-lo-to	佛 陀 多 羅 多		-
Fa-shih	法 師		-
Chen-ti	真 諦	Paramārtha	-
Kou-lo-na-t'o	拘 羅 那 陀	Kulanātha	-
Nanking	南 京		-
Wu	武		118
Ta-ch'êng mei-shih lun	大 乘 唯 識 論		-
Shê ta-ch'êng lun	攝 大 乘 論	Mahāyānasaṃgraha	-
Chuan-shih lun	轉 識 論		-
Hsien-shih lun	顯 識 論		-
San wu-hsing lun	三 無 性 論		-
Shih pa pu lun	十 八 部 論	Samayabhedoparacanacakra	-
I pu tsung lun lun	異 部 宗 輪 論	Samayabhedasparacanacakra	-
Ch'en	陳 光 大		119
Mou tsê, Fa-t'ai	戊 子 、 法 泰		-
Ting-lin, Nankai	定 林 、 南 海		-
Kuang-chu	廣 州		-
Chü-na-lo-to	俱 那 羅 陀		-
T'a	他		-
Hui-K'ai	慧 愷		-
Jên, Ming	忍 名	kṣānti; nāma	122
Hsiang	想	lakṣana	-
Shih chieh ti i	世 界 第 一	Laukikāgradharma	-
I pu tsung lun lun	異 部 宗 輪 論		130
Shih-pa pu lun	十 八 部 論		-

INDEX CHINESE AND SANSKRIT NOUNS MENTIONED IN THE BOOK

			page
Ta-p'i'p'o-sha lun	大毗婆沙論	Mahāvibhāṣā	-
Chiao-hsao	假號	prajñapti	135
Ching-ch'ieh	境界	viṣaya	136
Shêng fa yin ching	聖法印經	Āryadharmamudrāsūtra	-
Hsiang	相	lakṣaṇa	-
Hsien yang shêng-chiao lun	顯揚聖教論		154
Pu chih i lun	部執異論		-
T'ien shih ching	天使經	Devadūtāsūtra	162
Chü-hsün-t'a	瞿id陀	Kuddāla; Kuddālaka	163
Shêng	生	upacaya	189
Hsing	行	saṃskṛta	-
Pu-mieh	不滅	avipraṇā	-
Ching hsing ch'an	近行禪	Upacārasamādhi	193
Hsiang	想	saṃjñā	-
Hsiang	想	saṃjñā	194
Hsiang	想	saṃjñā	-
Hsiang	想	lakṣaṇa	-
A p'i t'an hsin lun	阿毘曇心論	Abhidharmakośaśāstra	226
Shih-êrh t'ou t'o ching	十二頭陀經	Dvādaśadhutasūtra	
Kao-sêng chuan	高僧傳		-
K'ai-yüan shih-chiao lu	開元釋教錄		-
Chiu-mo-lo-shih fa shih ta-i	鳩摩羅什法師大義		-
Ta ch'eng ju lêng ch'ieh ching	大乘入楞伽經	Laṅkāvatārasūtra	-
Lü êrh-shih-êrh ming-liao lun	律二十二明了論	Vinayadvāviṃśatividyāśāstra	-
A p'i ta mo ta p'i p'o sha lun	阿毘達磨大毗婆沙論	Mahāvibhāṣāśāstra	-
Pu chih i lun	部執異論		-
I pu tsung lun lun	異部宗輪論	Samayabhedasparacanacakra	-
San fa tu lun	三法度論		-
San-mi-ti pu lun	三彌底部論		-
San lun hsüan-i	三論玄義		-
Ch'êng shih lun	成實論	Satyasidhiśāstra	-
Ssū a-han-mu cháo chieh	四阿鋡暮抄解		-
Ta chih tu lun	大智度論	Mahāprajñaparamitatopadeśa	-
Ta-ch'êng-ch'êng-yeh lun	大乘成業論	Karmasiddhiprakaraṇa	-
Ch'êng wei-shih-lun shi-chi	成唯識論述記		-
Ch'u san-tsang chi chi	出三藏記集		-
A p'i ta mo shih shên tsu lun	阿毘達磨識身足論	Vijñānakāyapādaśāstra	-
Chieh-t'o tao lun	解脫道論	Vimuktimārgaśāstra	-
Si-yu-ki	西遊記		-
	佛本行集經		229
Chih Hsü; yueh tsang chih chin	智旭 閱藏知津		-
Ch'en-yüan: shih shih i nien lu	陳垣 釋氏疑年錄		-